Adventure Motorcycling

HANDBOOK

A ROUTE & PLANNING GUIDE – ASIA, AFRICA, LATIN AMERICA

CHRIS SCOTT

TRAILBLAZER PUBLICATIONS

The Adventure Motorcycling Zone
Selected highlights

ARCTIC

Greenland

Iceland

Alaska

Canada

NORTH ATLANTIC OCEAN

Norway

Denmark

Ireland UK

France Swit

USA

Portugal Spain

Across the Darien Gap
You can fly from Panama to Bogota or spend a few days cruising on a sailboat to Cartagena via the San Blas Islands. *Page 278*

Morocco and the Atlantic Route
Morocco is a great destination in itself, or you could set off across the Sahara to West Africa.
Page 239

Morocco

Algeria

Western Sahara

Mauritania

Mexico

Cuba

Haiti Dom. Rep.

Belize
Guatemala Honduras
El Salvador Nicaragua
Costa Rica
Panama

Venezuela & the Guianas
Get off the PanAm tramrails.
Pages 299-303

Mali

Senegal
Gambia
Guinea Bissau Guinea
Sierra Leone

Burkina Faso
Ivory Coast

Nig

Ghana
Togo
Benin

Venezuela
Colombia

Suriname
French Guiana

Liberia

Galapagos Islands

Ecuador

Guyana

Equatorial Guinea

Brazil

Trans-Amazon
La Paz to Caracas or Quito to Rio. It's a jungle out there.
Pages 291 and 305

Peru

Bolivia

The West Coast Route
There's no easy finish: either a race across Angola or the gruelling '2400-km fortnight' to Lubumbashi and Zambia.
Pages 244–252

Paraguay

Argentina

Uruguay

SOUTH PACIFIC OCEAN

Chile

Atlantic Cruise
Take a few weeks to sail with your bike between Montevideo and Hamburg
Page 299

Carretera Austral & Ruta 40
Chile's Heavenly Highway will blow you away while Argentina's Ruta 40 will probably blow you over.
Pages 293-298

Falkland Islands

SOUTH ATLANTIC OCEAN

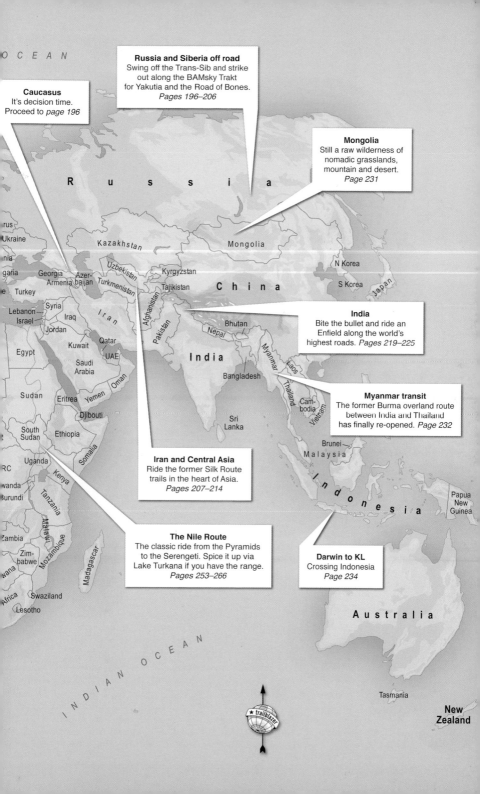

Caucasus
It's decision time.
Proceed to *page 196*

Russia and Siberia off road
Swing off the Trans-Sib and strike
out along the BAMsky Trakt
for Yakutia and the Road of Bones.
Pages 196–206

Mongolia
Still a raw wilderness of
nomadic grasslands,
mountain and desert.
Page 231

India
Bite the bullet and ride an
Enfield along the world's
highest roads. *Pages 219–225*

Myanmar transit
The former Burma overland route
between India and Thailand
has finally re-opened. *Page 232*

Iran and Central Asia
Ride the former Silk Route
trails in the heart of Asia.
Pages 207–214

The Nile Route
The classic ride from the Pyramids
to the Serengeti. Spice it up via
Lake Turkana if you have the range.
Pages 253–266

Darwin to KL
Crossing Indonesia
Page 234

CHRIS SCOTT's first motorcycle adventure got him half-way to North Wales on a moped. A long affair with bikes ensued, including a dozen years as a despatch rider in London, riding anything from IT250s to a 900SS (with one especially productive week on a nitrox XS650). Most winters were spent exploring the Sahara on trail bikes. Two self-published memoirs recall this period: *Desert Travels* (1996) and *Adventures in Motorcycling: Despatching in 80s London* (2015) which was *Ride* magazine's 'Book of the Year'.

In the early 90s he went on to write *Desert Biking, A Guide to Independent Motorcycling in the Sahara* which evolved into *AMH* (see p6). At this time he also worked for Rough Guides, specifically their Australia title, and a phase producing DVDS saw his films from the Sahara and the Yukon featured on National Geographic Channel. His other books for Trailblazer include *Sahara Overland*, *Overlanders' Handbook* and *Morocco Overland*.

Adventure Motorcycling
HANDBOOK

A ROUTE & PLANNING GUIDE

CHRIS SCOTT

WITH

**Mark Harfenist, Steph Jeavons, Lois Pryce,
Dr Paul Rowe and Lisa Thomas**

AND

**Jussi Hyttinen, Guarav Jani, Grant Johnson,
Sam Manicom, Ted Simon, David Smith, Nick Taylor,
Simon Thomas and Austin Vince**

ADDITIONAL MATERIAL BY

**Hugh Bergin, Cristian Boboc, Kelston Chorley, Jamie Duncan,
Bill Eakins, Jacqui Furneaux, Karim Hussein, Chris Lockwood,
Pat McCarthy, James Morrison, Andy Pag, David Radford,
Peter Scheltens and Leonie Sinnige, Margus Sootla,
Mikhail Sorokin, Ken Thomas, Richard Virr,
Dan Ward and Dave King, Robin Webb and Richard Wolters**

ILLUSTRATIONS BY
Simon Roberts

TRAILBLAZER PUBLICATIONS

Adventure Motorcycling Handbook

Seventh edition: 2016

Publisher
Trailblazer Publications – The Old Manse, Tower Rd, Hindhead, Surrey, GU26 6SU, UK
info@trailblazer-guides.com   www.trailblazer-guides.com

British Library Cataloguing in Publication Data
A catalogue record for this book is available from the British Library

ISBN 978-1-905864-73-7

Editors: Clare Weldon & Bryn Thomas
Series Editor: Bryn Thomas
Layout: Chris Scott
Proofreading: Jane Thomas & Bryn Thomas
Cartography: Nick Hill
Graphics: Simon Roberts (www.sr-illustration.com)
Index: Patrick D. Hummingbird

Acknowledgements

Contributions from riders all around the world help make the *AMH* what it is, a collection of guidelines for adventurous travel by motorcycle, in Asia, Africa and Latin America. Without them *AMH-7* would have been a pretty thin book, so a big thank you to the three dozen contributors listed on the previous page as well as to credited photographers who supplied material for free or for negligible fees. Some of their biogs appear on pp332-3. Thanks also to the team at Trailblazer.

A request

The author and the publisher have tried to ensure that the information in this book is as up to date as possible. Nevertheless, things are certain to change; even before the ink is dry. If you notice any changes or omissions that you think should be included in the next edition or have any other feedback, please email the author at the website below or via Trailblazer (address above).

Warning

Overseas travel by motorcycle is unpredictable and can be dangerous.
Efforts have been made by the author, contributors and the publisher to ensure that the information contained herein is as accurate as possible. However, they are unable to accept responsibility for any inconvenience, loss or injury sustained by anyone as a result of the advice and information given in this book – so be careful and check the latest news.

Updates and a whole lot more at:
www.adventure-motorcycling.com

Photos: Front cover: Kyzylart Pass (4280m), Tajikistan © Simon Thomas
Frontispiece: Doorway, Morocco © Karim Hussain **Back cover:** Argentina © Mathieu Bernage
Page 7: Ted Simon's 1970s pannier © Andrew Harbron

Printed in China; print production by D'Print (☎ +65-6581 3832), Singapore

CONTENTS

PART 3: LIFE ON THE ROAD (*cont'd*)

LIST OF BOXED TEXT

PART 4: ASIA ROUTE OUTLINES

PART 5: AFRICA ROUTE OUTLINES

PART 6: LATIN AMERICA ROUTE OUTLINES

PART 7: TALES FROM THE SADDLE

APPENDIX

INDEX

25 YEARS OF THE *ADVENTURE MOTORCYCLING HANDBOOK*

In the summer of 1991 I was dishwashing in a Mexican restaurant, recovering from a broken leg and another costly Saharan fiasco. The job was not too intellectually taxing so I thought I'd get into writing, having enjoyed describing my travels for bike magazines in the 1980s.

I decided to compose a short report on what I'd learned the hard way in the previous decade's biking in the Sahara. Many riders, myself included, had trouble-strewn first trips, partly on account of a lack of hard information on all aspects of what's now become known as 'adventure motorcycling'.

I bought myself an Amstrad, worked out how to turn it on and after a lot of wasted paper, dropped off a 30-page report entitled *Desert Biking: A Guide to Independent Motorcycling in the Sahara* at the Royal Geographical Society in London. For all I know the original is still tucked away in the Map Room's archives today.

Rather pleased with the end result, I figured the report might have some faint commercial value and proposed this idea to what was then the Travellers Bookshop off London's Charing Cross Road. It was good timing as they were considering publishing niche travel guides and an expanded version of *DB* fitted the bill.

I spent a couple of months padding out the RGS report into the 100-page first edition of *Desert Biking* which was eventually published in late 1993. It didn't exactly hit the bookshops. Instead, as word got around and demand trickled in, batches were Xeroxed and stapled in a copy shop in Notting Hill and then sent out.

Following the moderate success of this hand-made version, a revised and suitably expanded paperback edition (right) was published in September 1995. The updated format included the addition of 'travellers' tales' in the back.

With nothing similar around in English and seeing promise in the concept, Compass Star picked up the idea and took it a big step further with the publication of the retitled *The Adventure Motorbiking Handbook* (*AMH*) in November 1997. It featured the practicalities and yarns of *Desert Biking* but brought in a network of two-wheeling contributors from around the globe to add expertise and help fill the gaps. It's a collaborative formula which helps make the *AMH* what it is today.

I created 🖳 **adventure-motorcycling.com** around the same time, which featured over a thousand of your trip reports as well as whatever else was going on.

Compass Star in turn passed the rights on to Trailblazer Guides which, 25 years down the line, brings us to the seventh edition of the *AMH*. In recent years the range of gear, bikes, know-how and tours are now greater than ever, but the fundamentals of trip planning and bike preparation remain much as they did in the original *Desert Biking* report.

Enjoy the ride.

INTRODUCTION

Welcome to edition seven of the *AMH*, a handbook for planning, preparing and riding in the developing countries in Asia, Africa and Latin America. Out there you're beyond the safety net of conventional motorcycle touring closer to home and so the word 'adventure', with its associations of risk and uncertainty, is appropriate.

The adventure-motorcycling scene continues to flourish, with new bikes, tours and magazines as well as a greater range of gear and services. Social media is packed with riders' updates of their epic journeys. But prices have also climbed so the option to adapt your own gear remains, while political instability continues to undermine routes across parts of Africa and Asia.

We're in a golden age of global motorcycle travel, if for no other reason than it's become a less eccentric activity and many people have shown how easy – and yet how fulfilling – it can be. You don't need a huge bike or an array of sponsors, you just need the curiosity to ride out into the real world to see it for yourself.

A map, a bike and a track. What the picture doesn't show is the months of planning and bike preparation to get to that stage.

PLANNING & PREPARATION

*P*repare. That's still the first word of the first chapter of this edition. The motorcycle adventure you're about to take on is going to be expensive, demanding and maybe even dangerous. Preparation doesn't mean running the most expensive bike adorned with all the latest adventure motorcycling accessories; it means having as good an understanding as possible of what you're taking on and being appropriately equipped to deal with it.

The decision to set off on a long motorcycle journey can germinate from a moment's inspiration, a decision to take on the 'Big Trip' after a succession of easier rides, or just the plain old desire to cut loose from the rat race and have a big adventure.

You may not think so yet, but within a few pages you'll appreciate the mushroom effect of taking on such a venture. Choosing and preparing your bike might take up the lion's share of your time and the budget, but realigning your initial itinerary with the reality of visa acquisition, open borders and a realistic and safe route also takes a huge amount of research. The situation will have changed since this was written and that won't end once you're on the road, so the planning is never really over until you stop.

The more you learn the more there is to consider, until you get to a magical point where, however briefly, you're ahead of the game. If you're very lucky, that moment of overlanding nirvana will coincide with your departure.

The extent of preparation varies greatly between individuals. Some will want booked accommodation linked by a string of GPS waypoints. Others will be satisfied with a good map and a loose schedule for any visa applications that must be made en route. You want to try reach a level of preparation that gives *you* enough confidence in a venture that'll always be largely unpredictable.

Acquiring the correct **paperwork and visas** and sorting out your **money** arrangements is tedious but essential. It's common to worry about carrying half a year's cash with you, acquiring visas on the road and motor insurance at each new border, as well as trying

If you're very lucky, that moment of overlanding nirvana will coincide with your departure

to get by without a carnet (see p23). Without just one of the several documents listed in this section, your trip could grind to a halt, but the two key items are and always will be: a **passport** and the **vehicle ownership document**.

Spontaneity is a wonderful thing but it's best saved for short-range route deviations once on the road. There'll be enough unexpected dramas to handle without adding to them with inadequate planning. Do yourself a favour and set off knowing that, whatever happens, you've done all the preparation you intended to do. The more effort you put into planning, the smoother your trip is likely to be. But don't worry, it'll still be an adventure – you can count on that. No one's ever set off to ride around the world but given up because it just got too darn boring.

A plan

Before the preparation comes **a plan**, an outline of the regions and destinations you'd like to visit. It's not uncommon to initially come up with a certain romantic flow or theme: following the Silk Road to Beijing or following the Mediterranean coast counterclockwise from Casablanca to Istanbul. Or setting off on an old AJS like your parents did before you came along. Then you discover there's no single 'Silk Road', that North Africa is having a bad time at the moment, and that these days an old AJS is better pampered than ridden for months on end.

This is just the start. If you make it past p25 your expertise in the whole business will have multiplied exponentially. A few edges may have been knocked off your starry-eyed dream too, but you'll be in much better shape to take on what lies ahead.

Once you've got over that possible disappointment there comes another shock that can be paraphrased from the Prussian military strategist Helmuth von Moltke's famous quote: 'no plan survives contact with the road'. It's hard to imagine not having some sort of outline before you leave, if only to avoid undesirable interruptions and expenses. But soon enough that **schedule** becomes derailed, in some cases before you even leave. Your big adventure is like a major civil engineering project: it will be late and over budget. It's rare to leave on your original departure date, so don't set this or what follows in stone. Without necessarily adorning yourself with a headband and sandals like Peter Fonda in *Easy Rider*, once on the road be ready to be adaptable and 'go with the flow'. Compared to the life you've probably been leading up to now, life on the road will be unpredictable and requires flexibility.

> **Without necessarily adorning yourself with a headband and sandals, once on the road be ready to 'go with the flow'.**

Be wary of **over-ambitious goals**, especially something like trying to get to a certain border thousands of miles away in a fortnight. Even in the right season (see p12) most first-time overland riders greatly **underestimate** the time it takes to cover ground in parts of Asia and Africa, let alone the desirability of simply slowing down.

To want to try and **see it all** is understandable when you consider the cost and effort you're investing in the project, but once you're inching out of a Far Eastern container depot into the chaos of the city, or rolling off the end of a sealed highway onto a remote desert track, reality bites. The good thing is: you're there and there's nowhere to go but forward.

WHICH CONTINENT?

Assuming that most of us come from the rich nations of the developed West – North America, Europe, Southern Africa and Australasia – certain **classic overland routes** present themselves. They're illustrated and described in more detail in each of the Route Outline maps for **Africa** (pp246-7 & p259), **Asia** (pp192-3, p204, p221 & p233) and **Latin America** (pp272-3 & p281), with an overview map at the front of the book (pages ii-iii).

It's worth comparing these three big continents in terms of difficulty. Assuming you live there, **European departures** offer the most overland options, with both Asia and Africa accessible without getting bogged down in shipping and air freight (Africa only by the Straits of Gibraltar at the moment). From Europe, the northern route across **Asia** goes as far as Far Eastern Russia. The southern route runs via India and now continues overland via Myanmar (with escorts) to Southeast Asia. China remains a special case – see p229. The southern route to India can be comfortably done on a road bike with as few as four visas.

Alternatively, departing from Europe you can head down the length of **Africa**, typically ending at the Cape of Good Hope. With the situations in Libya and Syria blocking overland access to Egypt, Africa still represents a challenge, a real adventure both in terms of riding conditions, visa acquisition, security and even expense.

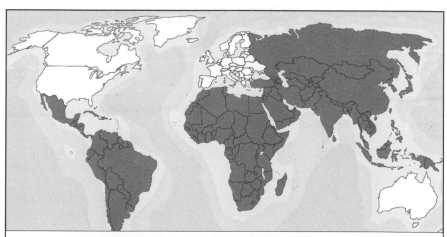

The Adventure Motorcycling Zone
NOT ALL COUNTRIES SHOWN ARE ACCESSIBLE OR SAFE TO VISIT

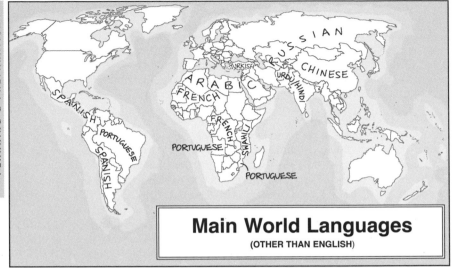

Main World Languages
(OTHER THAN ENGLISH)

Many riders not from North America choose to start their transit of **Latin America** above the Arctic Circle in Alaska to end it some 25,000km (15,000 miles) later in Tierra del Fuego, just 1000km (600 miles) from the Antarctic mainland. Assuming you follow the line of least resistance, Latin America is the least challenging of the three big continental routes in terms of paperwork, riding conditions and language, while offering as impressive scenic and cultural attractions as anywhere, particularly in the Andean countries.

If you're intent on **ringing the globe**, shipping across the oceans that separate these continents is easily done from certain key ports described on p188.

SEASONS AND CLIMATE

The season and expected weather at certain key stages of your route must be factored in. Seasons and the climate can be anticipated (worldclimate.com); the actual weather on a given day cannot. In regions where the road infrastructure cannot deal with extremities, progress may be slow or briefly impossible. At other times, even if the riding is straightforward, extreme temperatures can make simple survival a challenge. The Sahara is a good example; it's no hotter than the interior of Australia, Pakistan or Arizona in **summer**, but riding alone on anything other than the main trans-desert highways reduces your safety margin to the amount of water carried per person per day.

To head blithely across northern Asia or into the Andes in **winter**, or the equatorial regions of the Amazon or Congo basin in the **wet season**, is also asking for trouble. Ironically, in Far Eastern Russia (as in northern Canada), some ice roads only exist in winter, following the courses of deeply frozen rivers able to support 20-ton trucks. Whether your heated clothing can support you is another matter.

By and large Himalayan passes over 4000m (13,100') close at the end of October until late spring, while in the Congo Basin transportation takes to the rivers at the height of the **rains** and can be a fun interlude on a bike.

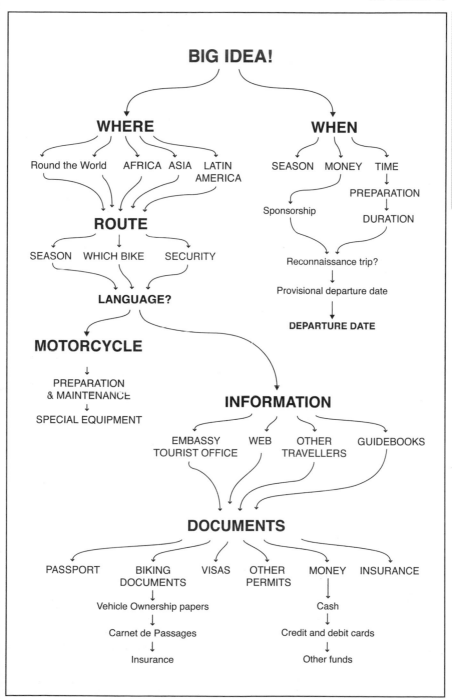

BIG IDEA!

WHERE

Round the World   AFRICA ASIA LATIN
AMERICA

ROUTE

SEASON   WHICH BIKE   SECURITY

LANGUAGE?

MOTORCYCLE

↓
PREPARATION
& MAINTENANCE
↓
SPECIAL EQUIPMENT

WHEN

SEASON MONEY TIME
↓
PREPARATION
↓
Sponsorship   DURATION

Reconnaissance trip?
↓
Provisional departure date
↓
DEPARTURE DATE

INFORMATION

EMBASSY   WEB   OTHER   GUIDEBOOKS
TOURIST OFFICE   TRAVELLERS

DOCUMENTS

PASSPORT   BIKING   VISAS OTHER   MONEY   INSURANCE
DOCUMENTS   PERMITS
↓   ↓
Vehicle Ownership papers   Cash
↓   ↓
Carnet de Passages   Credit and debit cards
↓   ↓
Insurance   Other funds

TIME AND BUDGET

Once the spark has been lit, assuming that you're beginning preparations while in full-time employment, organising a trans-continental journey for the first time requires about **a year**. If you're just taking an exploratory nibble into one continent, six months will do. Preparing to explore a wilderness region within your own country may only require a few weeks of planning and, as you'll soon learn, doing so as a test-trip prior to the Big Day is a good idea.

Are you ready to throw the dice and take an entirely new direction in your life for several months or even years?

Ask yourself how much of a commitment you want to make to your overland adventure. Do you have an urge to see some distant part of the planet, but still like the idea of returning to a job, house and family? Or are you able to throw the dice and take an entirely new direction in your life for several months or even years? When heading into an unknown future, having enough money to deal with the predictably unpredictable will of course help. If you're organised you ought to be able to **calculate an average daily expenditure** fairly closely. How precisely you need to plan your budget will depend on whether you've cut loose from life back home, whether you'll still have (or can generate) some sort of income while on the road – like rent or a pension for example – or if you've given yourself a set amount of money or time to undertake a journey.

Assess carefully if you have the will and opportunity to put the money together in the time you've given yourself – let alone to be on the road for months. To cross Africa expect to **budget** on at least £3500 or US$5600, in addition to the cost of your machine. The expense of the carnet and some visas apart (see p23 and p18), Asia can be cheaper. You could probably ride from Europe to India for around £2500 or $4000. To cross the length of the Americas costs at least as much as Africa, and a genuine round-the-world (RTW) trip is going to set you back around £10,000 or $15,000, mostly in fuel and getting your motorcycle from one continent to the next. Some people will achieve the above for less, most will spend more, but these estimates account for at least some of the unplanned expenses that most trips encounter.

FUEL PRICES AROUND THE WORLD

Fuel prices vary staggeringly around the world, from a few cents a litre in Venezuela and Iran (a fraction of the price of the crude oil from which it is actually refined), to at least double the fuel's true value. Extreme subsidisation in a dozen or so countries and heavy taxation in many more is what explains this dramatic discrepancy.

With the global price drop in early 2015, at currently around $0.70 a litre, the **price of fuel in the US** can be considered comfortably below the international average of $1.06: neither amazingly cheap nor ridiculously expensive. Compared with the US, many countries in Africa with low GDPs tax fuel extremely highly, as does the UK, Ireland, Holland, Turkey and Norway. This can have a big impact when the size of a country is taken into consideration. The **cost of fuel in a neighbouring country** has an impact too, especially where fuel is as much as ten times more expensive across the border, as it is in Venezuela rather than Brazil and in Iran rather than Turkey.

Continent by continent

Things will change of course but excepting Venezuela, Bolivia and Ecuador, the US has among the cheapest fuel in the **Americas**, and Peru and Brazil the priciest. In Central America fuel costs in Mexico are cheaper than the US but in Costa Rica they're nearly double US prices. South of the Darien Gap petrol is much more expensive in Brazil, Chile, Uruguay and French Guiana.

In **Africa**, South African prices fall about midway between the most expensive countries immediately to its northeast and the heavily subsidised fuel across North Africa in Algeria, Libya and Egypt. Although among the cheapest in the world, these three examples show how the price of fuel doesn't necessarily make them the cheapest places to visit. Egypt and Libya demand a carnet (see p23) and Algeria and probably Libya (by the time tourism resumes) require escorts when riding in the Sahara, which cost around €100 (£82) a day. So what you save on fuel you pay in other ways.

Riders setting off from Australia into **Asia** won't find petrol noticeably less expensive (mostly 20–30% pricier than in the US), with only a couple of Central Asian countries plus Jordan, Malaysia, Indonesia and of course Iran being cheaper. Turkey, a large and key gateway country, is somewhere you'd also want to spend more time exploring if it didn't have just about the priciest petrol in the world.

As you'll read on p213, Iran imposes certain caveats on buying fuel that's otherwise cheaper than water. Taking the high route across Asia (see p194), Mongolia is another worthwhile but large country on the overlander's map where not only is fuel expensive but it's of a notoriously low quality. Fuel in any **remote location** is often very pricey. To help you budget on fuel costs see the Wikipedia page titled 'Gasoline and diesel usage and pricing'.

© LANDON ODA

Getting information

You may well have a lot to learn, but particularly regarding information about routes and border regulations, this book was probably out of date long before the ink was dry. Here are the most likely sources of up-to-date information.

ONLINE
Everything you need to know (including the contents of this book rearranged and repeated to near infinity) is online. The trouble is it's spread all over cyberspace like the Milky Way; the task is to track down what you need to know sometime before the Milky Way implodes.

The Horizons Unlimited Bulletin Board, aka the **HUBB** (💻 www.horizonsunlimited.com/hubb) is a good place to start. Its dozen **regional forums** (North Asia, South America, sub-Saharan Africa, etc) cover topics that relate to all wheeled travellers and a day or two browsing the HUBB will answer many questions as well as raise a few you'd not thought of. Nothing else in English comes close to its truly global reach.

Lonely Planet's **Thorn Tree** (💻 www.thorntree.lonelyplanet.com) isn't vehicle-oriented, but has border and route details, and for a North American perspective the **Advrider** (💻 advrider.com/forums) is especially good on trip reports with hits on popular ones running into the millions.

GOVERNMENT OVERSEAS DEPARTMENTS
More useful to you than a country's tourist office is the opinion of your country's foreign ministry. In the UK it's the Foreign & Commonwealth Office (FCO) Travel Advice Unit; in the US it's the Department of State; and the French Ministère des Affaires Étrangères is better than most for the Francophone countries of Africa. In Britain at least, the lazier end of the travel media has a habit of taking the FCO's *advice* as gospel. The FCO has got much better at acknowledging that distant or outdated threats need not write off a whole country, but like all these agencies they're primarily concerned with avoiding international incidents involving their nationals, if not discouraging casual visits to countries with whom political relations may be strained. Take everything these advisories say with a pinch of salt and be aware that politics and convenience inevitably colours their advice. At the same time be warned that many **travel insurance** providers (see p20) won't offer cover for countries deemed unsafe by the FCO or its equivalent. There's more on this subject in 'When Things Go Wrong' on p170.

NATIONAL MOTORING ORGANISATIONS
Again not a lot of help for the aspiring motorcycle adventurer, but sometimes useful on documentation and essential when it comes to coughing up for a Carnet de Passage. In the UK this, along with an International Driving Permit, is all the **RAC and AA** can do for you.

TRAVEL GUIDEBOOKS

Although users often grumble about their inaccuracies or opinions, for what it costs, a guidebook will repay you in advice and recommendations many, many times over. Lonely Planet and Rough Guides are the two best-known series in English; the former covers just about every country on the planet, but both have their origins in the backpacker or independent traveller market, not motorcyclists. Because of this you'll find only the most general advice on riding, and accommodation offering secure parking is an example of a commonly overlooked detail.

In the place of guidebooks, be they used paper copies for a penny on amazon, or e-book versions more practical for a motorcycle traveller, **Trip Advisor** (🖥 tripadvisor.com/forums) has become the world's most visited travel website. For a biker it will be most useful in the users' accommodation recommendations when faced with too great a choice in a foreign city. Very often knowledgable ex-pats also contribute to the website's forum.

ONCOMING TRAVELLERS

Don't dismiss the likelihood and usefulness of running into other overland travellers coming from where you're going. You couldn't ask for a more up-to-date source of information unless you're bitten by the horse's mouth itself. They'll be able to calm your anxieties about fuel prices, road conditions and the friendliness or otherwise of border officials, and, likely as not, will be as keen to hear your news too.

Travel documents

For any journey covering half a dozen countries or more, visas are something you'll need to address early on because some can take weeks and occasionally even months to arrange. With some visas starting from the date they're issued or only available in your home country, this sort of planning ahead is easier said than done.

PASSPORT

If you don't yet own a passport, get onto it straight away. If you already own one, make sure it's **valid for at least six months after** your anticipated journey's end, better still a year. Many countries won't issue visas for passports that have less than six months left to run. As ever, by ensuring that your passport has plenty of use left in it (as well as pages), you're one step ahead of some awkward border official. Once you get your passport, check all the details. Discrepancies between it and your other vital documents, even just the misspelling of one word or date, can be all the excuse someone needs to bring your day to a premature stop.

Many countries issue so-called **'diplomatic' passports** with up to double the number of pages for frequent overseas travellers. Visas acquired in advance tend to fill a whole page and anyone who's travelled in Africa will know how officials love to 'mark their territory' by slapping a blurred triangular stamp bang in the middle of a blank page. Count on each country that requires **a visa taking up two pages** in your passport. At this rate the 23 usable pages of a standard (non-diplomatic) British passport won't go so far on a round-the-world trip.

Although they don't exactly shout it from the rooftops, in Britain at least, it's possible to get a **second passport**. The Passport Office will want a good reason; the most convincing is to explain you need to make protracted visa applications en route during which time you'll also need your other passport to cross borders. Better still is to somehow tie it in with your work. If your request is sound and you have documentary evidence, ideally from an employer, a second passport may be issued without a fuss. Dual nationality – passports in your name from two countries – is not the same thing but can be as useful. It's better never to declare to an immigration official that you're travelling with two passports or under two nationalities, chances are it's not legal but as you'll soon learn, what is considered legal in one territory and what is actually useful or permitted don't always overlap.

VISAS

A visa is a temporary immigration permit allowing nationals of one country to visit another. Some countries (very often neighbouring) don't require a visa at all, others will issue one at the border allowing a stay up to a certain period, usually a month or 90 days. Some countries require visas to be secured **in advance** or even in your home country and it's these that'll make up the bulk of your bureaucratic headaches and can govern the pace and direction of your travels. Brits and Americans will have few visa hassles in Latin America, but across Africa or Central Asia anyone might end up paying hundreds in **visa fees**. Very often the onerous demands and associated delays are down to similar regulations imposed on that country by your country, or an antipathy towards your country which has its origins in colonial times; it's something that Brits and Americans experience more than, say, Canadians or Irish.

Applying for a visa

Some visas **start** from the day of issue, others require you to specify the exact date and place that you expect to arrive at a border – something hard to pinpoint when there's 1500 miles of desert, jungle and yeti-infested mountains between you and that place. Still others have no set entry date, just a certain amount of time before their validity expires. You need to understand the difference between this **validity** – say three months before you must begin using the visa by entering the county– and the **duration** of a visa, typically 30 days as mentioned. On some borders where a visa in advance is considered essential, just turning up may get you one issued right there or, if that border is remote, a pass to get one in the nearest city.

Don't expect to get all your visas nicely sorted out before you go. Instead, work out as closely as you can where you'll pass a consulate for your next country. (Very often the websites of previous overlanders will spell out the routine.) On a trans-continental trek this need to **apply for visas as you go** will be a game of careful timing and anticipated arrival dates that'll mould your itinerary. You may find yourself racing across a country or taking a thousand-mile detour just to be sure you can gain entry to your next destination. Crossing Africa down the west side, for example, once out of Nigeria (and depending on your nationality), the need to acquire a succession of visas across the western Congo basin will dominate the journey and, for some, will culminate in what can be just a few days to get across Angola.

When applying back home, consider using a **visa agency**. Though pricey, these agencies earn their money by providing a speedy postal service as well as doing the queuing and applying for you. They can make getting visas from consulates not represented in your country much easier and they may also be clued up on tricks or procedures that can help facilitate a successful application. Even for relatively straightforward applications, an agency can save you valuable time if you're busy working or live far away from the capital, where consulates are usually located.

As a rule, avoid **business visas**: they're more expensive and risk awkward questions on arrival. Russia is known as an exception. Stick to simple, innocuous **tourist visas**.

Before applying for any visa find out:
• What other documentation apart from your passport must you present on application? Besides a handful of passport photos, this might also include bank statements or other evidence of funds, letters of introduction or onward travel tickets.
• How to pay? Many consulates are very specific about the currency.
• How long do you have before you need to use the visa (typically from one month to a year)?
• Is the visa easily renewable or extendable, and if so for how long?
• Can you easily get a **multiple-entry visa** (which often have longer validities), enabling you to make excursions to neighbouring countries?

Visa problems
All you can do is give yourself plenty of time do deal with **problems**, expect those problems to crop up and have a Plan B to Z. Without experience it's hard to know this in advance, but don't underestimate your ability to deal with problems en route; it's one of the key lessons learned from this sort of travelling. Remember that countless others have succeeded in traversing the same route; they've all worked it out by using their wits, being flexible and, as a last resort, offering an 'incentive'. So can you.

It must be remembered that having a visa will not guarantee you entry into that country; if they don't like you for whatever reason, the rules have changed or something is wrong with your paperwork, you'll be turned away. And being sent back to a country that's just officially wished you *bon voyage* can be tricky.

Although what appears above might seem like a rigid set of **rules** created to discourage international travel, these rules can get usefully mushy once on the road: expired visas need not mean a firing squad at dawn (but could mean a big fine). Not keeping WFO on the aforementioned transit of Angola from DRC down to Namibia can cost you $70 or just a scowl, while overstaying in Russia will put you in the doghouse for sure.

Take visas seriously but recognise that once on the road, the further you are off the beaten track anything goes; this is where the fluid interpretation of laws and regulations in the Adventure Motorcycling Zone (AMZ) can work in your favour. If you happen to stumble into a country via an **unmanned border**, present yourself at the nearest police station unless you're leaving soon in the same clandestine manner.

A word of warning: most of the countries in the AMZ are paranoid about their security and very often have tense relationships with their neighbours. Accusations of being 'a spy' might seem absurd, but might well be taken very seriously, especially if you happen to turn up in a country without proper documentation.

LOCAL PERMITS

Once you're on the road, **additional documentation** will be gleefully issued by local officials for any number of reasons (mainly to get more money out of you, or 'fine' you for not having it). Typical examples include registering with the police within so many days of arrival, photography and filming permits (although your tiny modern video recording devices are often immune to these), 'tourist registration cards', currency declaration forms (see p130), and permits to cross 'forbidden' areas such as China, Egypt's Western Desert or tribal homelands/reserves. As these are the sorts of places where police road-blocks are frequent, not getting one of the required permits may cost you more in the long run.

As much as following correct procedure, paperwork is a game of wits as well as an opportunity for corrupt officials to create difficulties that can only be solved with a **bribe**. By at least starting your journey with proper docu-mentation you'll have a good chance of getting well underway without unnec-essary hassles until you learn the ropes and find out what you can and can't get away with.

TRAVEL AND MEDICAL INSURANCE

For what it costs, travel insurance covering you to an adequate level can set your mind at ease. Ordinary travel insurance that can come free with your credit card may offer 'package holiday' cover but is unlikely to cover a frac-tion of the cost of an evacuation from a Cambodian village. Getting travel insurance for anything involving motorcycling has become easier in recent years but it's still best to approach insurance companies who specialise in adventurous activities. A recent online quote from a UK specialist for a three-month world ride cost from £165 to £200, depending on the level of cover. Including North America, the Caribbean cost another £10-20.

Whoever you end up with, make sure they're in no doubt about the nature of your intended trip and where you'll be going. As well as covering you for all the mundane events like robbery, cancellation and lost baggage, travel insurance also includes **medical cover and repatriation** – realistically the most vital component. The worst-case scenario is getting yourself evacuated by air from some remote spot while requiring intensive medical care.

Along with admitting to any previous **medical history**, which the insur-ers may dig up anyway, it's vital to obtain travel insurance that's compatible with your motorcycling and the regions you'll visit. In the UK, many insurers won't offer cover for countries that are on the FCO 'black list' – countries where your government advises against all travel – or if they do it won't be valid. Right now on the FCO website that's a short list of countries that you can guess from watching the news. There follows, however, a very long list advising against all travel *to parts of* nearly half the countries in the world, all but a few of which are covered in this book.

If you're a European in Africa, most medical emergencies involve **repatriation**, which is where the greater expense can lie. As a European or US national in Central or South America, the US might end up as your ultimate destination if you need urgent medical treatment. Anything involving repatriation to the US, even from neighbouring Mexico, could run into six figures so it's vital that you have sufficient medical cover: £500,000 may sound like an astronomical sum but is just a starting point, £1m ($1.5m) is better. Make sure this figure covers *everything* to do with an accident, including medivac, ambulances, hospitalisation and possible surgery.

Remember too that to get an insurance claim underway you must first make that all-important phone call to the country where the policy was issued. When you receive your policy, find this **telephone number**, highlight it and write it clearly somewhere obvious and easy to get to; in your wallet or passport and somewhere on the bike. This way you can direct someone to ring the number it you can't do so yourself. For more on what to do in a dire emergency see p170.

Vehicle documents

Riding overland might seem a fairly innocuous activity but unfortunately, just as with visas, a bureaucracy of **paperwork** developed early on in the history of motoring and these days in some places it's easier to import a gun. The explanation might be that in many developing countries a large-capacity motorcycle is a highly prized commodity the ownership of which is restricted by swingeing import taxes.

Of all the documentation required, the **carnet** presents the biggest financial burden, while getting **third-party insurance** is not always possible and so not something to worry about unduly – until you have an accident, that is.

You'll accumulate a whole lot of **additional paperwork** at various borders, mostly to do with temporary vehicle importation. Keep it all until you're in the next country, even if you don't know what it's about. Now's the time to invest in a wallet that expands like a French accordion.

With all the documentation listed below you need to establish early on:
• Which papers you already have.
• What additional items are needed before departure.
• Which others you can get on the road.

You also need to know:
• How long it'll take to get what you don't have.
• How much it will all cost.

VEHICLE OWNERSHIP DOCUMENT

Your **vehicle ownership document** is much more important than a driver's licence and will be inspected so many times you may want to get it laminated. In the UK it's still called a 'logbook' or, officially, a vehicle registration document (VRD); the US has a state registration document as well as a 'title' or ownership document. In French it's a *carte grise*, in Hispanic Latin America it's a *titular* and in Russian it's your *svidelstvo* or *registratsja motocyklova*. The lingua franca is of course, 'Papers!', with or without a 'Halt!' beforehand.

Having a vehicle ownership document that's **not in your name** is not always a problem. All you need is a good story and official-looking letter from the owner in the local language(s) – official-looking stamps help too.

At many borders you'll need to present your passport and vehicle documents simultaneously. It's crucial that the details on the ownership/registration document, particularly **the chassis and engine numbers** (aka 'VIN') match those on your vehicle and carnet, if applicable. Outside Latin America, photocopies may not be good enough, but a duplicate is always handy. If your bike has had a replacement frame or engine, check those numbers or risk losing all to some nit-picking official down the track.

The reason for these elaborate checks is to ensure you've not committed the cardinal crime against humanity of selling your motorcycle in the country concerned. Even slightly damaged engine or chassis numerals may be grounds for raising complications. To you the very idea of selling your dream machine is absurd, but because of punitive import taxes, rich locals will go to extreme lengths to acquire a desirable foreign-registered model using the right local papers. It explains why you see so many clapped-out bikes in some developing countries.

I also find that it helps to **highlight your Vehicle Identification Number** (VIN; usually the same as the chassis number) on your vehicle ownership document. This is what the customs guy will be looking for amongst all the other details, so it helps speed things up. It also doesn't hurt to sign your ownership document somewhere, even if you don't need to.

DRIVING LICENCE, IDP AND ICMV

Like your passport, your **driving licence** ought to show correct (or, at least, consistent) information with other documentation and be valid long after your trip expires. In the UK your driving licence lasts till you're 70, elsewhere in the world they're valid for as little as a year. If you expect to be on the road for longer than that and renewing it is not possible by post, making a good facsimile is a way round it.

If your licence doesn't show the bearer's **photograph**, it should be supplemented with an **International Driving Permit** (IDP) that does. These multilingual translations of your domestic driving licence can be picked up over the counter by presenting your driving licence plus a photo or two at your local motoring organisation's office. In the UK it costs just £5.50 and is issued at the post office.

Although IDPs are not mandatory, in Asia they're especially useful and in Latin America officials will often ask to see your driving licence, something that's rarely demanded in Africa. You may never have to show your IDP, but be on the safe side and get one. With their official-looking stamps they can double-up as another important document with which to dazzle a semi-literate official.

There are two different IDPs. The '1949' version covers most of the world, except **Brazil, Burundi, Iraq, Nigeria and Somalia**; the '1926' version covers those five countries only. If you're including Brazil or Nigeria in your itinerary you'll need both versions; otherwise, unless you're a mercenary or have a terrible sense of direction, just the 1949 should do you.

An **International Certificate for Motor Vehicles** (ICMV) is to your vehicle registration document what an IDP is to your driving licence; a multilingual translation issued by motoring organisations (in the UK it's the RAC) for countries that don't recognise or can't read the original. It's especially useful in Russia and Mongolia.

CARNET DE PASSAGES EN DOUANE (CDP)

Many an overlander panics when they discover the need to **finance a carnet** (or 'CdP' as it's commonly abbreviated), something that could cost several thousand pounds. To summarise, a carnet is bit like a duty-dodging visa for your bike, being an internationally recognised temporary importation document that allows you to bring your bike into countries which require it. In exchange for you having insured yourself against any indemnity, your carnet provides accredited security for the payment of any local duties or import taxes should the vehicle not be re-exported.

Not all countries require a CdP; a few issue their own while also accepting a worldwide version, while others, such as Egypt, offer their own version but may also require a large deposit. Most other countries will just be content to stamp your passport as having entered with a vehicle and may also issue a **temporary vehicle importation permit** (TVIP), which adds up to the same thing but without the financial burden of a CdP. You can ride across the Americas, much of Africa and northern Asia just buying TVIPs as you go.

Carnets are issued by certain **national motoring organisations** accredited by the FIA (Federation Internationale de l'Automobile) based in Switzerland. These national organisations will list which countries require CdPs, although this list is not always borne out by experience. In the UK it used to be the RAC (🖳 www.rac.co.uk); for Canadian *and* US-registered vehicles the Canadian Automobile Association (🖳 www.caa.ca) used to do the job, but at the time of writing the FIA is seeking a new agency for North America and the UK. In South Africa it's the AA of SA (🖳 www.aa.co.za); and in Australia it's the AAA (🖳 www.aaa.asn.au). Look up the latest on the HUBB's carnet thread.

Carnets essentially guarantee your ability to cover the cost of the highest level of duty on your bike in the countries you expect to visit. For somewhere like Iran, Pakistan, India and Nepal it is **five times** your bike's estimated value, in Egypt it's 800%. This is bearable for a crummy 125, but with a £15,000 BMW you'll need to pay out over £4500 and have only half of that refunded! Of course the **valuation** of your bike is open to interpretation and is something that, in Britain at least, the RAC used to treat with some flexibility.

In 2013 the rules to **cover the bond** changed with the RAC: the bank guarantee (using say, property as collateral) was dropped, so was cash in the bank.

PLANNING & PREPARATION

BACK-UP DOCUMENTS

With all these documents, keeping photocopies, duplicates, a list or even just photos of the vital details, makes replacement easier if they go missing. Stash paper **copies** somewhere secure or better still scan or photograph them and put the information onto an SD card or a USB stick plus a private web page or the cloud. You may also want to add travel insurance details, consular offices en route, your bike's main dealers in the countries you pass through – in fact your whole overlanding dossier. This way even if your bike and luggage are burned to a crisp or sink on the high seas, you'll be able to retrieve the details online.

Another good idea is to carry **duplicates** or 'spare' originals: ownership documents can be duplicated, either officially or by 'losing' the original and requesting a replacement (sometimes for a small fee).

Up to 2015 a nominated insurance company underwrote your carnet. The latest in the UK is that with a letter of no objection from the RAC, you get your CdP from the German ADAC (and for a much smaller cost, too).

A carnet **lasts one year** and might be renewable from the motoring organisation in the country where it's about to expire. (Make sure this extension is noted on every page and not just the front cover). There's a list (see p192 for Asia, p246 for Africa) of **which countries require a carnet**, but to cut a long story short they include: central, east and southern Africa plus Egypt, the Middle East, west Asia and the subcontinent; and it'll help in Australia.

How a carnet is used

Carnets come in a number of pages from five to twenty-five, each page is used for a country where this document is mandatory. A page is divided into three perforated sections, or **vouchers**: an entry voucher (*volet d'entrée*), an exit voucher (*volet de sortie*), and a counterfoil (*souche*) which remains as a stub.

When you enter a country that requires a carnet, the customs official will stamp your counterfoil and exit voucher and tear off and keep the entry voucher. When you leave that country, the counterfoil will be stamped again and then the exit voucher will be retained. When your travels are complete you return the carnet to the issuing organisation for discharging. What they'll want to see is a bunch of double-stamped counterfoils and probably a few unused but intact pages.

Should you **sell your bike** and slip out of the country, your carnet will not be discharged and you'll eventually be liable for the duty in that country – remember, they have your money. Should you have **missed a stamp** for whatever reason, all is not lost. On arrival back home get the customs in the port to inspect your bike's VIN and issue some sort of official notification that the vehicle as described in the carnet has returned. This is important if you want to get your money back.

THIRD-PARTY MOTOR INSURANCE

If you're boldly going where no one has gone before, don't expect to be able to get motor insurance from your domestic broker. In the UK you can get cover as far east as Turkey as well as Morocco and Tunisia, although travellers on the Continent have long been able to get both motor insurance as well as vehicle recovery insurance to cover the Mediterranean rim, which potentially includes countries like Algeria and Egypt.

Instead, **buy motor insurance as you go** but, again, don't expect to be able to buy it everywhere. You can often buy insurance at the border; if not, border officials may be able to advise where to get it. In the economic confederation of Francophone West Africa, around £3/$4.50 a day covers several adjacent countries; in Uzbekistan you pay a few pounds for two weeks' cover; in Colombia even less (see p282).

The dubious validity of motor insurance in the developing world or the impossibility of getting it at all underlines the fact that should you **cause an accident** such as killing someone's child or, worse still, a breadwinner, the complications may take years and large amounts of money to resolve. You may find yourself getting nailed for compensation even if you were not at fault.

Motor insurance is an unravellable quandary; rigorously enforced in western countries, out in the world it may be unattainable or of little actual value but a necessary part of your papers to present at checkpoints. Make an effort to buy it and if you can't then ride carefully and avoid doing so at night when the risks are far greater (more on p125).

Money

Along with insurance, money and how to carry it is another thing that many riders worry about unnecessarily as year by year it gets easier to get hold of cash, the most useful form of money, in faraway places. Any major trip is likely to cost you a few thousand on the road and carrying that sort of money through the insecure parts of Asia, Africa and Latin America is enough to make anyone nervous. For advice on changing money, bargaining and dealing with the black market, see p130.

Best currencies
The **US dollar** is well known in the remote corners of the world where other hard currencies might cause incomprehension. Certainly, throughout South America and some parts of Asia this is the most readily convertible hard currency to carry. In Africa, especially the north, they're now more used to the **Euro**, though in East Africa it's still the US dollar. These two currencies are by far the best to carry; nothing else comes close any more. Avoid collecting too many US$100 or €100, far less a €500. They may save space but are rarely seen abroad and are often thought to be fakes. Avoid street deals for $100 bills anywhere around Nigeria where they're printed by the roll.

CREDIT AND DEBIT CARDS
Plastic cards are the most useful way of avoiding the need to carry rolls of cash. Although it may be a while before we see ATMs along the Ho Chi Minh Trail, a compact selection of debit and credit cards are essential items on a long overland journey. **Take a few** because, despite reassuringly familiar logos, there's a good chance one won't work with a certain bank's ATM somewhere, although it's hard to ascertain this for sure until you actually get there.

PLANNING & PREPARATION

SPONSORSHIP

Thank you for your enquiry. We regret to inform you that as we have already allocated our annual marketing budget we are unable to consider your request at this time but do wish you the best with your exciting venture. (Marketing Department)

For some travellers getting sponsorship is part of the challenge of their overlanding adventure. Some go out of their way to secure it, often in the name of a good cause or charity. It's an idea many overlanders toy with, ostensibly for the very tangible appeal of getting free stuff, but just as often as a means of validating or – when it involves charitable causes – even justifying the journey.

Forty years ago in western countries it was fairly easy to get gear on a pretty thin premise. These days the field is much more competitive and while it's still possible to get free stuff for stickers, it takes a lot of work, luck or good connections to get **actual financial support**, unless you're some kind of celebrity or take on an outlandish stunt.

Unless you're doing something truly extraordinary and original, there's a certain vanity in assuming your adventure deserves sponsorship. Applicants often get resentful when they receive replies like the one quoted above, or when replies aren't forthcoming or appear patronising. You must remember that the most obvious targets are constantly hit by these sorts of requests.

The big question that must be addressed is: **what's in it for them?** What does Touratech have to gain by supplying you with the fruits of their catalogue so you can ride to Cape Town, as thousands have done before you? Even if a spirit of outdoor adventure helps sell Touratech products, they'd rather lavish their equipment on someone who's likely to get on TV on Sunday night.

Getting some

Sponsorship can broadly be divided into four categories:

- Being funded in return for some form of promotion.
- Receiving products or services for promotion.
- Doing it for charity, involving both the above as well as donations.
- Crowdfunding or simply asking for donations. You are the 'good cause'.

If your trip captures readers' imaginations it can work, but setting out with this plan is presumptuous.

The minimum you should offer a conventional sponsor is exposure of their product or service in the form of prominently positioned branding, just like on racing cars. If you can also promise to feature photos online, in magazines or on TV, a local business may be thrilled to support your big trip. An honest review of a product, warts and all, is what the public deserve but rarely get. That's the nature of what might be called selling out. I once read a report by a well-sponsored rider who threw in rather clumsy approbations to his sponsors' gear, as if he'd nearly forgotten to mention them.

Sponsors are often eagerly offered all this, but it's not uncommon for the sponsored to lose interest and fail to deliver. Oddly enough I've also found supporters lose interest in acknowledging the publicity put their way. Nevertheless, whether they appreciate it or not, it's good form to notify sponsors of any publicity you secure. Invite them to any events you may give or attend, and try to make them feel as if their contribution was valued rather than exploited.

My experience is that having a genuinely great proposal or an appropriate background is not enough. Rewards are far more likely if you have a certain self-promotional acumen allied with thick-skinned persistence – or of course are happy to accept trivial, low-value items in exchange for stickerage and hotlinked website banners.

I know of a few genuinely noteworthy expeditions that put themselves hugely in debt, partly due to a lack of self-marketing nous but also a stubborn and refreshing resistance to capitalising on their marketability, while other comparatively ordinary trips get better results. It's who you know of course, but also your ability to sell yourself – something that's all too commonly confused with persistence.

Overlanders typically overestimate the importance of their venture, but if approached in the right way or with good connections, sponsors can still be won over. I suspect it's something much more easily done in small, non-Anglo countries where it's easier to attract the attention both of local sponsors and the media, who like to trumpet a plucky local hero.

One day, somewhere, you're going to bless one of those little plastic rectangles for getting you out of a fix, most probably to cover shipping to the next place or just paying for a restful night in a plush hotel when you're out of cash. And across North America, Europe, Australasia and South Africa you need hardly ever use cash at all.

Contrary to the reasonable assumption that credit card companies hit you hard for overseas purchases, they actually offer the best rates of exchange for the day of your purchase (at least with Visa in Europe). Drawbacks include **service charges** when withdrawing from ATMs or banks abroad, and the possibility of **fraud** when paying for a service or goods like a night in a hotel.

There are many stories of credit card accounts getting hung out to dry – in fact it's surprising it doesn't happen more often. For this reason it's best to **withdraw cash from ATMs only and pay for everything in cash**. Resist using your card as liberally as you might at home, even if it's possible. By doing so you greatly reduce the chance of someone cloning your card details to make fraudulent withdrawals or purchases. Although there's a good chance any suspicious purchases will be refunded, before that's cleared up your card may get blocked until you contact the issuer and prove it hasn't been lost or stolen. Use cards to get cash, use cash to pay for things and check your online statements once in a while.

> **Use cards to get cash from ATMs, use cash to pay for things and check your online statements once in a while**

Keep tabs on how much you're spending on the card, and at the very least, get your **minimum monthly payment** sorted out (arrange a direct debit with your bank before you go, assuming you have an income or adequate funds in the bank to pay it off). Or simply load up your card before you leave.

With the prevalence of credit card fraud, it's not uncommon to find your **account frozen** when you try and withdraw cash in places like Khabarovsk or Kampala. Some companies do this automatically, others might try and call you at home to confirm a purchase. If your contact number is a mobile that happens to be on, you're in the clear but the way round this is to call your credit card company before you leave and explain where you may be using your card. It may be worth confirming it in writing as some travellers still get their accounts blocked. As with insurance, have the magic phone number and any passwords or other security information handy so you can call them and set about unlocking your card.

A good travel guidebook should tell you which of the three main brands (Visa, American Express or MasterCard) are widely used in your destination, but with the negative connotation 'America' has in some countries or to some individuals, the more anonymous Visa or MasterCard are more reliable.

Travelling companions

Most of us instinctively know whether we want to set off alone, with a partner sitting snugly behind them, their mate in the mirror, or in a group, perhaps as part of an organised tour. Nevertheless, below are some considerations to mull over when considering travelling companions.

Alone in the desert. Was it something I said?

Alone

The perils and rewards of **going solo** are clear cut. On the debit side there's no one to help you in times of difficulty and no friendly face with whom to share your experiences. There's no one to help fix the bike or guard it while you nip into a store in a dodgy neighbourhood. All this will make your trip harder and inevitably introspective. This may be because you don't know anyone who's got the nerve or commitment to set off on a trip such as yours, or you're independent-minded and like the idea of doing it alone.

It all sounds miserable until you consider the rewards of solitary travel. Riding solo, your social exposure can be more acute; unless you're a real hardcore loner you're forced to commune with strangers who'll often make up the richest (and sometimes the most frustrating!) aspect of your trip; you have to look *out* at the world instead of being protected by the bubble of companionship. And unless you're going somewhere really outlandish, you're bound to meet up with other riders and in most cases be very glad to ride with them.

Tough overland stages like the Sahara, Far Eastern Russia and Patagonia, or intimidating regions in Africa, Central Asia and Central America are where overland riders often bind together, irrespective of their origins or mode of travel. Alone you can choose to join in the safety of a convoy, and when you feel like going your own way, you can split with no awkwardness. This **freedom** to be your own boss is the biggest attraction of riding solo. A romantic location to rest up for a while, or who knows, maybe even a promising romance, can be explored with no pressure that your companion wants to press on; it's this **disparity in pace** that often causes tensions in groups.

Overall, you'll get more of a raw experience alone while at times may have the option of companionship – this is the ideal scenario for most adventure riders. Be under no illusions that at times it will be utter misery and frustration, but this is all part of the adventure and typically your fortunes will swing the other way before long.

ADVENTURE MOTORCYCLING MINDSET

As the plan takes shape trust your instincts and resist the pressure to be seen as a brave individual or get swept up as a reluctant member of a team. Do what feels right for you which can be a lot easier if you don't make a big issue of it. You need some level of stability to face the countless trials that will be thrown at you daily. Without an optimistically fatalistic attitude your trip could develop into a litany of miseries.

My first trip (pictured left) was like this. Blundering into the void it was amazing I got as far as I did before events turned on me halfway across the Sahara (see *Desert Travels*). Turning back then was the right thing to do. Returning just five weeks later but a lot older, it wasn't an enjoyable trip but a depressing baptism of fire.

Many motorcyclists are attracted to the idea and romance of an overland journey without truly facing up to the gruelling practicalities of the commitment required. Your own trip is likely to be one of the major events of your life, give it your best chance. Don't bite off more than you can chew – a tour or rental (see p30) could be much more fun as well as an educational test for the realities of undertaking your own trip.

Two's company

The advantage of travelling with a friend is that, psychologically and literally, the huge load of your undertaking is halved. Two people also tend to be **braver**; checking out a crowded market café or following a remote short-cut become shared adventures instead of missed opportunities if you're alone – even if behind it all is a mild competitiveness of 'sure, I'm n-not scared...'. There's no doubt about it, you can have a lot more fun if there are two of you and you get on.

One drawback to travelling in company is that you tend to remain rather exclusive to social interaction. There's no need to be outgoing because there's always someone to talk to, whine at or help you out. You can miss out on a lot that travel has to offer by hiding in the security of your **companionship**, because there's no need to meet others.

Another problem which won't surprise anybody is **getting on**. Alone you can indulge your moods which will swing from one extreme to another as days go by. In company you have to put on a brave or polite face when you might not feel like it; your partner thinks they're the problem, becomes resentful and the whole day becomes edgy as you wish the road would open up and swallow your buddy.

Having a united goal doesn't help, once the rot sets in your whole trip can become shrouded in tension. If it gets bad, there is only one solution: **split up**. It may well be that they want to take the high road and you the low road, but whatever it is, it's far better to accommodate differing personal wishes, even if they mean temporarily breaking up.

It's well known that such conflicts occur in the stress of expeditions which is effectively what you're undertaking; try and anticipate how you might deal with these sorts of problems and don't feel that separation down the road turns the trip into a failure. **Discuss** the possibility of this eventuality during the planning stage and always prepare yourself and your bike for **autonomy**.

With a group of two or more, one thing that may be obvious but ought to be mentioned is **choose the same bike**. Doing this has countless advantages in fault diagnosis, quantity of spares and shared know-how.

Two up and all's well. © Ken & Carol Duval

Two-up on one bike? Well as long as the machine is spacious and stable enough it can of course **reduce costs**. It can also make life easier and more fun, especially with an intercom. The stoicism or long-range **comfort** of the pillion really needs to be addressed. Don't set off on an unfamiliar machine and hope that just because it has an extra set of footrests it'll be fine. It helps of course if both parties can confidently ride the bike, though usually this isn't the case. And of course the weight of a passenger will for most rule out difficult off-road stages.

Big groups

Outside of tours, big groups are much less common than solo or twinned riders, if for no other reason than forming a group of like-minded individuals and keeping them together is a tricky proposition. Numbers will fluctuate during the planning stage and even on the road the chances of a bunch of riders staying together for the whole trip are slim. As in any group, the dynamics evolve as the trip moves on, although inevitably a leader will dominate from the start, alternately respected or despised by the others. Expect never to want to talk to certain members of your merry gang by the time you return!

With a large group there's usually a shared or even officially-established goal which itself can cause pressures. It may help with sponsorship, and the mutual support is enviable but, as you'll find on the road, most people are more comfortable alone or with one or two companions.

Road-based **tour groups** need not be as bad as they sound as you don't ride in convoy, day after day. Most riders set off at their own pace with a road book to meet up in the evening.

RENTALS AND ORGANISED TOURS

The opportunities for joining a tour or renting bikes all over the world are greater now than ever before. Don't be put off by the idea of joining a tour to a remote location or renting a bike abroad and doing your own thing. Both these options allow you to dip your toe into the adventure motorcycling pool with only a financial commitment.

For many it's a worthwhile endeavour. Without taking on a big trip from a standing start they can discover that this foreign travel malarkey is not so hard after all. I would say 20% of the people that have come on my Sahara tours (in 4WDs and on bikes) have gone on to pursue their own adventures, including packing it all in and setting off round the world.

You can even see a tour as a **reconnaissance trip** (something that's recommended, on p122, as a practical shakedown anyway). Only on this occasion you'll be testing yourself rather than your machine.

Some trips were never meant to happen but when you have the momentum that months of preparation engenders, your pride can be too great to call it off because you don't have enough confidence or even just money, so you decide to go ahead, despite the uncertainties. If it's a few weeks' overseas rental or a tour that's not turned out as expected, the commitment has been smaller, the disappointment is less galling and you'll have learned a lot about how to do it right next time.

BIKE CHOICE & PREPARATION

2

Big trips have been done on everything from step-thru scooters to full-dress 2.3-litre cruisers, covering vast distances in a fortnight or up to a lifetime. Any machine that starts, turns and stops will do the job, but ask yourself would you like to chug across the Bolivian altiplano flat out on a moped while llamas trot past, struggle over the Grand Erg on a tourer weighing half a ton, or ride a bike they stopped making before you were born? Probably not because most of us narrow it down to a bike that will be versatile, trouble-free and enjoyable to ride.

From R1 to C90 it takes all sorts of course, but being undaunted by the prospect of the Kazakh or Patagonian steppe, and especially taking a spontaneous gravel road excursion, is just about the biggest guarantee of having an actual adventure in terms of the places you'll see and the people you'll encounter. In the end a **do-it-all mid-weight bike** with

some off-road ability ticks most of the boxes. The alternative is a road-bound tour on the world's sealed highways from one border to the next – actually not as bad as it sounds – or riding an unconventional or inappropriate machine with a fixed grin just to prove a point or attract attention.

Is that a beak in your pocket?

MOTORCYCLES FOR ADVENTURE

What is an adventure motorcycle or, as I prefer to call it now, a 'travel bike'? According to manufacturers capitalising on the trend, it's a big trail bike with wide 'bars and a beak – a 'Sports Utility Bike' – and the bike most associate with 'adventure motorcycling' is BMW's flat-twin GS1200, In well over a decade of dominance the GS has developed a refinement and intangible poise that none can match. As a result all BMW's competitors can do is to try to out-power or out-gadget the all-conquering GS. This competition at the top end of the adventure bike market means we're spoiled with a

A BMW GS owners rally? No, just a rally.

stunning range of quarter-ton tourers like Triumph's Explorer, Honda's Crosstourer 1200, the Super Ténéré, Multistrada and Caponord, KTM V-twins from 1050 to 1290, the one-litre V-Strom and Versys, and now the S1000XR and, by the time you read this, the new CRF1000L Africa Twin.

There's no doubt these are all brilliant machines but the chances of seeing a Crosstourer passing a Multistrada on the Kolyma Highway are slim because what sells in the name of adventure to affluent middle-aged road riders with a dodgy back, and what's actually used out in the world are in most cases different things.

Most riders accept that part of a real adventure will mean dealing with inadequate infrastructure which will include riding on imperfect highways, unsealed roads and gravel tracks. By the nature of their layout, weight and not least, tyres, some bikes handle such conditions better than others. In fact tyres have a whole lot to do with it (see p82), but the improved visibility and comfort of upright seating and wide bars plus sump protection and long-travel suspension all help on truck-mashed back roads at appropriate speeds, while on regular highways you'll have a smooth, comfortable and fast machine.

For those who value a lighter and potentially more agile motorcycle for off-highway riding that will cruise well enough on the open road in the Adventure Motorcycling Zone (AMZ), the big singles currently made by Yamaha, BMW and KTM – or the low-cost, air-cooled versions still sold in North America like Honda's XR650L, the KLR650 and Suzuki's DR650SE, will fit the bill for most adventure riders, even as we wait patiently for those 650 dinosaurs' DNA to be transferred into something more modern.

But as the as-yet unpublished *Zen and the Art of Adventure Motorcycle Selection* advises, once in the teeth of the AMZ, adopting the **middle way** to

Consider the Middle Way.

avoid the 'extremes of sensual pleasure' (160hp) and also 'self-mortification' (big-single vibes and snatchiness) will provide righteousness and harmony. Bikes which fit this category include Triumph's brilliant 800cc triples, BMW's well-established 800cc GS twins, Yamaha's more recent MT-09 Tracer triple (and probably an MT-07 twin Tracer by the time this book's out), Honda's dinky CB500X and the two NC700s and NC750X, and Suzuki's erstwhile DL650 'Wee Strom'. Any one of them will deliver enough power to haul you securely past a soot-belching bus up a mountain pass, the potential fuel economy to cross deserts and, at best, possess a **lack of weight and sheer bulk** to make the aforementioned spontaneous excursions less daunting.

WHICH BIKE: FACTORS TO CONSIDER

Here, in no particular order, are some factors to mull over. They're then discussed in more detail on the following pages:
- What's available in your area at your budget
- Your itinerary
- Your marque and image preferences
- Weight
- Comfort
- Mechanical and electronic simplicity
- Build quality and reputation for reliability
- Fuel economy
- Parts availability and service know-how en route

And here's another thing: the bike you'll eventually choose is going to be accessorised and loaded to gain up to 40kg (88lbs), more if you're riding two-up. This weight will erase your bike's agility as well as accelerate wear on all components, especially tyres, brakes and drive chains. So whatever bike you settle on, consider the worst-case scenario: riding it fully-loaded up a muddy track in a downpour, falling over and then trying to pick it up.

If you're not concerned about making an outlandish statement on two wheels and just want a machine to ride get a **single or twin cylinder machine from 400 to 650cc**. A 50hp engine in this capacity will produce enough power to carry you and your gear through the worst conditions while not over-stressing the motor. These days a bike like this ought to return an average fuel economy of up to 70mpg (25kpl, 4l/100km or 58.3 miles per US gallon). Multi-cylinder engines may be smoother but are unnecessary and, in case you hadn't guessed, **four strokes** are far superior to two strokes on a long trip, despite the latter engine type's power-to-weight advantage.

Budget and availability

How much should you spend on an overlanding bike? Or better to ask: why do riders spend so much? Around £2500 (or a bit more in dollars in the US) for a mid-weight machine is a good figure to start with. Twice that could get you a well-equipped motorcycle that's a year or two old. Otherwise, don't forget you can easily spend another £1000/$1600 equipping the machine.

Once you decide, don't make life too hard on yourself by coveting a machine that's not available in your home market. As a rule the range of bikes in North America is a little different – and for some marques much reduced – to those found in Europe, South Africa and Australasia, and the latter two will also sell a bigger range of farm bikes too (see p46 and p70). In 2011 the US finally got their hands on the Yamaha's Super Ténéré when in fact what many riders wanted was the 660Z single which now may be coming to the end of its lifespan in the UK.

XR650L imported from the other side of the world, but no regrets.

BIKE CHOICE & PREPARATION

That's ironic as comparatively slack emission regulations have seen bikes like DRZ400s, DR650s, XR650Ls and KLRs – bikes that haven't been sold in the UK or Europe for years – survive in the US (though sometimes not in California). The US also missed out on nearly all previous Ténérés and the Transalp and original Africa Twin. Having said that, in 2002 we didn't regret importing 'exotic' XR650Ls from Australia as in some ways it was genuinely better than what we could've bought locally at the time. Many years later I can see other European riders being attracted to importing 'old school' XRL/DRs/KLRs from the US.

Although it worked out fine for Kelston Chorley and his CCM GP450 (p39), think twice before taking a **brand new and untested model** on a big trip. Because of cost cutting in R&D it's not unusual for new models to have all sorts of teething problems, even – or perhaps more so – from the big manufactures like BMW. Within a year or two they're usually ironed out – or the bike is withdrawn or repackaged. It's one reason to stick with the well-known models whose faults and solutions have become common lore, or stay close to dealer services in the early miles. An 'ECU upgrade' is a typically discreet improvement that may not even get mentioned.

Your itinerary

It gets easier year by year but some continents are less effort to cross or explore than others, while some riders actively seek out unmade back roads or the 'wrong' season as part of their overland adventure because, as mentioned earlier, taking the road less travelled is one sure way of getting one. While what have become known as 'adventure motorcycles' claim to offer off-tarmac utility, you can actually see enough of this planet from a road bike. All you have to do is appreciate its limits when it comes to dirt-road diversions. You could potentially ride all the way from London to Bangkok or Cape Town, or down the length of the Americas on tarmac, and in South America at least, not feel like you've missed out much. But if your target includes the jungles of Indochina, South America and equatorial Africa, the deserts of Africa or sodden tracts of Far Eastern Russia, anything over a 650 will be a handful. Here is where a sub-150 kilo trail bike will be in its element, if not necessarily in the overland journey getting there.

Image preferences

For many, especially first timers, the motorcycle they choose is central to the whole endeavour. Our perceived self image has as much to do with what we ride as whether the gearbox has five or six speeds. A purposeful-looking KTM, an alloy-clad GS or a matt-black Bonneville all send out signals about how you'd like to be seen by others, even if to a Samburu goatherd, the V-Strom with ABS and adjustable screen was the obvious choice.

... Whatever bike you decide on, remember it's your adventure and you'll probably only do it once ...

You want to **feel inspired** by your adventure and what you choose to ride for the months ahead is a big part of that. Some choose to make an ostentatious statement, be it goofy or over the top (possibly to assist with self promotion), while others, many experienced travellers among them, recognise that it's not about the bike anymore, and adopt a lower profile astride what might be considered a drab machine.

Whatever you decide on, remember it's your adventure and you'll probably only do it once, so choose with the heart and, if it comes to it, beat yourself up over it later. You may never fully use your trail bike's off-road ability, but until you found that out for yourself it was nice to know it was there. Acknowledge all the other sensible factors listed here, but don't forget the value of a machine that, even after weeks on the road, still gives you a thrill to look at as you crawl out of your tent each morning.

Weight

While getting blown around by a Patagonian gale can be unnerving (see p297), one thing riders universally complain about is the weight of their bike. When everything is going steadily, what can add up to 400 kilos (880lbs) of solo rider and loaded bike will trundle along as if on rails. But add in some potholes, crazy traffic, muddy diversions, fogged-up visors on the Ruta del Muerte, sinking sidestands, steps leading up to safe overnight parking or airfreight priced by the kilo – all part of the overland motorcycling scenario – and your big rig can become a handful on many levels. Is it even possible for a normal person to pick up a fully fuelled and loaded Triumph Explorer?

BIKE CHOICE & PREPARATION

RIDING THE WORLD ON AN R1150GSA

Is the R1150GSA the perfect bike? For me it's pretty damn close. I've covered over 400,000 miles on every type of terrain and the 1150 has impressed me beyond words. But if you're in for the long haul and are likely to tackle some demanding off-road riding here are a few modifications worth doing.

I got Woody's Wheel Works to fit a **21" tubeless front rim** from an HP2 using heavy-duty spokes. I honestly feel the 1150 should come with this as standard. It's still stable on the motorway and in the dirt is of course a huge improvement, especially in deep sand.

The **rear subframe** needs a few welded gussets to reduce the frame flex that a heavy load deals out to the bike off road.

One of the best upgrades have been **Touratech Extreme shocks**, built to order for the rider's weight, load and typical terrain ridden. We've yet to break one.

Touratech Zega panniers have been our boxes of choice from the start. We actually prefer that they're not the stiffest or strongest. In a fall I'd rather the boxes deformed than the subframe. After a heavy fall bang them back into shape, lay down some silicone, use rivets to resecure the panniers' integrity and you're ready to roll.

Touratech's polyamide **42-litre fuel tank** feels unbreakable and is insanely light,

enabling crossings of remote desert stages. I also eventually replaced the original instrument panel with a bombproof Touratech **IMO R300** rally computer with an easily readable digital display.

Off-road I value torque over speed so the **final drive** from an EU R850GS was a great upgrade, putting the gear ratio right where I needed it. And on motorways the higher 800rpm puts me right in the power band.

The **engine and gearbox** are standard and with basic maintenance remain bulletproof. If you prefer riding to wrenching then the R1150GSA is an awesome workhorse.

Would I take the same BMW Motorrad model if I were riding our entire six continent route again? Absolutely!

SIMON THOMAS, 2RIDETHEWORLD.COM

Cruising the pristine highways of western European and North America, such bikes are in their element, but no matter how much you hope to keep it that way, one day somewhere out in the world you'll be steaming from your ears trying to control or right your sled. I first crossed the Sahara with a guy on a BMW R80. I made it on my Ténéré (sort of); his bike is a charred wreck somewhere in the dunes north of the Niger border. Even at less-than-walking pace, soft sand and especially mud are misery to ride on a heavy bike, as effectively bald tyres slither around to dump you again and again. Bikes of 600cc or less will be more manageable, but anything over a litre can become unrideable in tough off-road conditions.

The worst thing is that like an electrocuted lab rat, you'll get scared off taking even some mild off-highway detour because you've lost confidence in piloting your tank, either due to the unconsolidated terrain or the risk of dropping it with no one else around. Without such confidence it's hard to summon up the assertiveness needed to blast through an obstacle like a sandy creek bed. And so, like R80 guy, you keep dropping the bike until you're too tired to ride it and, exhausted, you crash for good. It's not all just the bike's weight but gear too, and here again it's common to take way too much stuff. More about that later. Along with comfort, for me weight is the key issue for my sort of riding.

Comfort

You'll be riding your bike all day for weeks and months at a time. Loaded like a pit mule, the finer points of handling and throttle response promised in the brochure – things which professional reviewers get so worked up about – will be lost. What you want is to get off the bike at the end of the day without feeling like you've had a bad day on the Dakar. This is where the big touring bikes scoffed at just a few paragraphs ago have an advantage. Even loaded, they're supremely **comfortable and stable** over miles of highway, running big torquey engines and fat tyres on small wheels. Motorcycle nirvana.

Comfort doesn't just mean the thickness of the saddle (more on p73) and its relation to your footrests. It adds up to quiet, vibration-free engines with smooth power delivery, slick (or even automatic) gear-changing, supple suspension, powerful brakes and aerodynamic protection from the wind (p74). All this enables you to relax, deferring the inevitable fatigue. And when you're not tired, cramped, aching and deafened, you cope so much better with the 101 daily challenges long-distance riding throws up. Comfort also means the clothes you're wearing, and your state of mind, both covered on p115 and p29. And it also means the space and power to travel with a pillion passenger for an extended period, if that's your plan.

If you expect to be using electrically heated grips and clothing (more on p120) you need to consider your bike's **electrical output** as it's not something that can be easily uprated. Big touring bikes are typically well endowed with high wattage alternators which produce ample current to recharge the battery. As it is systems like ABS, suspension levelling and EFI all require more electrical power than older or smaller bikes which will be less able to cope. Running heated clothing at night at low engine speeds is not an unusual scenario in icy conditions, but one where the battery could discharge quicker than the alternator can replenish it. If you can foresee such a situation on your trip, ascertain that the bike you choose has the wattage you need.

Mechanical and electronic simplicity

This is particularly something which old school riders may agonise over. The bikes of their youth which they learned to maintain or fix by the roadside are no longer made (and are no longer affordable). Home maintenance is now discouraged or impossible without special equipment. Instead, an official dealer has become a vital link in maintaining your machine's composure. That's all very well if you're living a conventional, ordered life as a commuter or a weekend rider. It's not so handy once you head out into the Adventure Motorcycling Zone where your bike can be as exotic as a space ship.

BIKES TO WATCH, WAIT AND WISH FOR

Now a compact parallel twin rather than the original V, thirteen years after the XRV750 ended (the XL1000V Varadero has been expunged from the records) I'll stick my neck out and say the new **Africa Twin** (right) will become an instant classic.

Adopting both the irresistible off-beat 270-degree crank of the Crosstourers (and Super Ténéré), there's also optional 'automatic' DCT shifting and traction control, both fine tuned for off-roading. The ABS version is 232 kilos wet, but the 21-inch front wheel puts it closer to the KTM category than the GS12, while being much cheaper than both. The fact that they've 'only' given it 96hp (the same per litre as the CB500X) means they've side-stepped the giant adv horsepower race and the 18-litre tank could be good for 400 clicks.

They're even calling it a CRF1000L to capitalise on the 250's success. In that case let's hope they fill the gap with a modern day XR400/Dominator hybrid, a **rallyesque CRF450L single** with a load-carrying subframe. While we're dreaming I suppose we'll settle for an **injected DRZ450** or a similar sized **mini-Ténéré**. Isn't anyone paying attention to CCM's GP450?

Talking of which, they say in Europe new emissions regs may spell an end to the XT660Z. The ABS version may be the last gasp, but as it is the XT-Z's UK price alongside the very popular MT-07 is having the same effect. When a street scrambler-styled XSR700 was announced there was some hope the 07's brilliant 700cc, 270°-crank motor might also get Ténérised, but it now looks like it'll just be a Versys- or V-Strom-like **MT-07 Tracer**.

Instead **AJP's PR7** rally-raid clone might be out by now, last I heard using the Husky twin-cam TE630 engine and not the Minarelli-built XT660Z's motor.

We can also expect an **Enfield Himalayan** by the time you read this, an adventure styled 400 single which might see Enfield try and break from their reliance on old-school plodders.

'They say' – or should that be 'we are all hoping for' – a **mid-weight KTM parallel twin** as an alternative to the berserker V-twins. You can add a mid-weight Triumph to that wish list too, though the 800-cc triples are lighter than you'd think.

As for an adventurised **KTM 390**, some would sooner see the tasty **SWM 440** prototypes (above) reach production, even if the SWM's **RS650**, **SM650R** and **Superdual** (all based on the Husky 630 engine, like the AJP) will probably come first.

F800GS – more teething problems than
Dustin Hoffman in *Marathon Man*
but now a firm favourite.

For regular touring any bike will do. If anything goes wrong you have the potential support of recovery insurance. But one definition of adventure motorcycling is touring beyond the range of freephone roadside recovery. You can always get help of course, but it'll require organising locally. So, the further you wander and the more challenging your route, a simpler bike can mean bush mechanics, to whom 'diagnostics' is something to do with Ron Hubbard, are more easily able to fix it if it's beyond you.

It has to be said though, despite the ever more complex electronic systems found on flagship models, modern bikes are extremely reliable. Problems usually occur with a new model's 'teething problems' which can ruin its reputation for years. What's frustrating is that they're often down to using penny-pinching components not some innate flaw in the engineering.

Take **water-cooling**; it may not be essential but is now the norm, not because it's better, but because a water-cooled barrel expands and contracts less so can be built with finer tolerances to enable higher performance. Water-cooling also reduces engine noise which, as with cleaner emissions, has become an important requirement. And there's no doubt that water-cooled engines can outlive air-cooled. But radiators and fans can get damaged or clog up with mud, thermostats and fuel pumps can play up, hoses split or leak. Even though mechanical simplicity is desirable it's not a valid reason to avoid a water-cooled machine; just choose one where the radiator and water pump aren't vulnerable to falls or can be reliably protected.

Despite the impression, a machine with a water-cooled engine will **not run cooler** in extreme heat and it can certainly overheat if you're progressing slowly and revving high so the radiator fan can't cope (in soft desert sand with a backwind, for example). You'd think a water temperature gauge will warn you, but most bikes now just have a warning light on the dash. If you choose a water cooled bike consider fitting a water-temperature gauge (see p61). Better to know it's getting hot than be told.

These days air-cooled engines are really only still used on low-powered single-cylinder bikes – most modern multis have liquid-cooling of some sort, but as long as it's in good condition and well maintained, an **air-cooled** engine is no worse than a water-cooled equivalent. Choose a bike with a relatively **lowly-tuned** (low compression) engine, it'll make less heat and so be less prone to overheating in tough conditions or when running on bad fuel. One of the best ways of keeping an air-cooled engine in good shape on the road is by making **frequent oil changes** and making sure the air filter is clean. Consider running thicker oil in very hot environments.

We all managed without **ABS** for years too – it's now compulsory on new bikes over 125cc in Europe. Having ABS come on too early when riding off road (reduced braking effect) is one reason some swear by a manual disable function, though I've never noted this problem and ABS gets more refined every year. Most will appreciate it in heavy traffic or poor weather conditions. Other **electronically controlled wonders** on higher spec machines include traction control, various throttle (power) modes and electronic suspension damping. All great for lap times but on the congested and crumbling highways of India or Peru you're unlikely to be riding at the limit. Being able to detune your over-powerful adventure bike to 'rain' mode as you climb a slippery series of hairpins or seek to extend the fuel range does have a lot going for it.

Transmission and electric starts

Scooters up to 800cc use **fully automatic** CVT- or similar transmissions while Honda's innovative manual, semi-automatic and fully automatic **DCT** (Dual Clutch Transmission) lets you have your cake and eat it – and with extra jam too. It could well be the future on bigger touring bikes. An option on the one-litre Africa Twin, expect to see it on BMW's bigger GSs before long.

CCM GP450 IN SOUTH AMERICA

Normally I ride a CBR1000RR Fireblade and previous travel bikes have included Yamaha's XT500 and XT660. In early 2015 my plucky **GP450** was one of the first of the new CCMs to get tested in the field. For me its 130kg dry weight was a major factor in choosing it for a solo trip that included a section of that year's Dakar rally before riding north to Bolivia and Peru, down to Chile and back into Argentina. Over 26 days that added up to some 5000 miles, including a 1000 off-road with thigh deep river crossings, snow, ice, extreme heat, stretches of boring tarmac, altitudes up to 4500m, dodgy bio fuels, strong winds, dust and salt lakes.

I specified adjustable rear suspension, a bigger output alternator, LED spotlights, bigger bash plate, adjustable screen, an extended wiring loom and CCM's luggage and rack. The adjustable rear suspension and Marzocchi front end were truly lovely and took whatever you threw at them.

At 5'10" (178cm) and 74kg I found the seat and bar combination very comfortable for up to ten hours a day. The overall plushness and shape suited both long road stages and easy manoeuvrability off road. The Renthal bars gave a secure feel off road as well as in heavy traffic; the switchgear is minimal but functional.

As you'd expect from a 450 single, the engine felt buzzy at higher speeds. My bike ran 15/47 gearing – for adventure riding I'd raise the gearing a bit. The engine felt more than strong enough, with only a small power loss at altitude, as with any bike. Low rpm flat spots in first and second were a little annoying but I adapted to these.

The adjustable screen and wide front fuel tanks gave good wind and rain protection, permitting all-day visor-up riding. I'd advocate using the standard side stand; it's probably stronger than the combined centre stand version which broke on my trip. The standard headlight is more than adequate but the addition of the LEDs made night riding in the jungle quite fun.

My fuel consumption varied from around mid-40s mpg (16kpl) when off-road and in low gear all day or hard riding at 70-80 mph – to 60+ mpg (22kpl) at a more moderate 50-60 mph cruise. Reliability has been good as is the overall finish with high-quality components. Would I use it again on a similar trip? Yes. Now I'm confident with the bike I'm entering the CCM in a Himalayan Rally Raid.

KELSTON CHORLEY

BIKE CHOICE & PREPARATION

Final transmission to the back wheels is either by chain (occasionally rubber belt), or car-like shaft drive. Shafts are heavier, expensive to produce, absorb a little power and can make for clunky gear changes, but these drawbacks are negated by much less frequent maintenance. A lot will depend on how you ride; if you're an aggressive rider shaft may not be for you and at any time off road, a rock can kick up and smash through the final drive housing. Shaft drive benefits from a smooth riding style which bigger, heavier and less sporty bikes usually have anyway.

When correctly tensioned and oiled, chains and sprockets are very efficient and are a light and inexpensive means of transmitting power to a back wheel. Although they're exposed to the elements, modern 'o'-, 'x'- and soon z-ring chains can now last for well over 10,000 of miles with just a bit of cleaning. So when it comes to transmission, settle for shaft drive on a heavier machine or a chain-driven bike with **top quality chain and sprockets**. There's more on chains on p63.

On some bike forums they get worked up over **five- or six-speed transmission**. More has got to be better, right? Not really. Motorcycles, especially those designed for touring, have relatively flexible engines which rev over a broad rpm range compared to say, a 40-ton truck or indeed a cyclist. Both the latter examples produce most power at a certain speed engine (or cadence). Racing motorcycles are the same and extra gears allow a rider to keep the engine spinning in the optimal power range. Others suggest that six speeds spread in wide, road-riding ratios can mean an extra-low gear to tackle gnarly terrain when loaded (good for the clutch) and a high top gear to cruise at minimal rpm (good for economy and engine wear). Although I can't say I notice, there could be something to this. GS boxers have had six speeds since the 1150 of 1999, with the heavier Adventure models including a lower first gear over the standard GS. In most cases a well spaced five-speed box on a bike has been found to work as well as four speeds in a car. It's not uncommon to change sprocket sizes to raise or lower overall gearing – more on p65.

And if you happen to be deliberating over a kickstart or **electric start** only model: go for the button. Some easy-to-start 125s may still only have kick-starters but one hot day, when your bowels are in freefall and you stall on a hill in Lima with traffic blaring, you'll bless that button in getting the engine running again. Having a kickstart *as well* is a handy back-up but is rare these days. If the starter motor fails any bike can be push- or jump-started (see Troubleshooting, p180), though achieving that alone with a high-compression KTM 1190 in a muddy Amazonian trench is not so easy.

Switchable electronic ignition

On a bike controlled with an ECU and in most cases fuel injection, **switchable ignition mapping** – either literally a switch on the bike or done by replacing an electronic component or reprogramming the ECU chip from a computer – can be a very useful feature. Most bikes are reviewed on their performance figures, not how they ride, yet these are not key attributes for non-competitive adventure motorcycle touring. In the AM Zone as mapped on p11 where local bikes over 125cc are rare, chances are you'll be top dog in terms of raw motorcycle performance and ought to have nothing to prove.

Originally, in the late 1990s, something like the KTM Adventure simply had plugs you switched around to retard the timing on electronic ignition and so enable the engine to cope with low octane fuel. **Low octane fuel**, as found out in the sticks, can cause harmful detonation (see p59) especially on lean-running (as many modern bikes are) or high-compression engines. Go back another thirty years and you could alter your ignition timing with a screwdriver, but then you needed to as it was always going off. Now, as you'd expect, ECUs have become exponentially smarter and the ignition 'map' can be switched between 'sport' or 'touring/rain' or 'birthday' modes. The good thing is that electronic bike brains are getting cleverer still and at the very least, a high/low power mode suits the knee-sliding weekend warrior back home, or you on the long road to Mongolia. Benefiting from the gentler setting, something like the 109hp XT1200Z will be more than adequate, use less fuel and reduce tyre wear.

TRAIL BIKES AND ENDURO BIKES

If you come from a dirt biking or trail biking background – a trailie (or 'dual sport' in the US) or an enduro bike might seem like the best choice. A trail bike is **versatile**. There's nowhere you can't go on your trailie and the whole thrilling realm of unsealed roads (or no roads at all) becomes open to you.

Trail bikes have genuinely useful features, such as folding foot controls, bigger than average front wheels to roll over bumps and holes better, long travel suspension to absorb those bumps and more ground clearance than average when the suspension runs out. And, to a certain extent, they're designed to be dropped without suffering critical damage. But there are also **compromises**, with drawbacks including:

- High seats.
- Less sure-footed on the road due to long travel suspension, seating position, 21" front wheels, trail-pattern tyres and 'wind-catching' front mudguards.
- Narrow saddles give poor comfort, especially for passengers.

Enduro racers

If weight is such an important factor (it's the one thing that adventure motorcycling riders complain about most often), a light, powerful four-stroke enduro like a KTM, Honda XR/CRF, or Yamaha WR must make a great adventure bike, no? Well, they could be if your adventure is purely off-road. While it's true that, unloaded, these bikes are much more functional off-road than trail bikes, they differ in some key ways. The engines can consume more fuel and require more attention due to their higher state of tune. And because they're designed for regular maintenance, the **engine oil capacity** of these machines is very small. That's fine if you change it after every few hours' engine running time, as you're supposed to, but left for a couple of thousand miles is not so good for enduro engine longevity.

This no-frills nature also extends to **basic lighting** and a **narrow seat**, designed for standing up and shifting body weight rather than day-long support. **Rear subframes** are also a weak point (see p112); they were never meant to carry a load greater than a racing plate. Sure, you may be able to buy a long-range 'rally' tank but the truth is a machine like this would be all but wasted on a long touring trip. You must remember that by the time any bike is loaded up, **most traces of nimbleness will be largely eradicated** so think twice unless you're committed to off roading, or like your enduro bike too much.

Carbs or EFI

Electronic fuel injection (EFI) has become the norm on bigger motorcycles because it offers smoother and more consistent fuelling and superior economy even at high levels of tune, as well as cleaner emissions. Don't think fuel injection is new fangled – automotive diesel engines have been fuel injected for decades, only now it's electronic, like most petrol engines. EFI is also maintenance-free, something that carb-balancing BMW Boxer owners will be pleased to hear. A modern fuel injector does what a crude carburettor spent the better part of a century trying to perfect: fire a fine jet of fuel on time and at high pressure so it atomises instantly and mixes with the air to burn completely in the combustion chamber.

A fuel injector's nozzle is much finer than any carb jet and so you'd think would be prone to blocking, especially with the dirty fuel you'll find on the road. In fact, some KTM690s apart, this is a very rare occurrence with bike engines because filtration systems are up to the job, and when they're becoming blocked a warning light will probably come on.

Injectors seem to be trouble free; it's the high-pressure **fuel pumps** (usually housed in the base of the tank) and EFI management systems that are more prone to problems. Early examples of some BMW and Yamaha singles (and doubtless other bikes too) were notorious for lumpy or inconsistent fuel delivery at lower speeds, but this got dialled out on subsequent models and it's no more unusual than other teething problems exposed by online forums. The engine's electronic management computer (ECU or EMU) is constantly measuring various parameters in the engine (air and engine temperatures, throttle position, road speed and so on) to deliver an optimum fuel charge to the combustion chamber, and this alone puts it miles ahead of any carburettor – once described as 'a brick with holes in it'. Think of all the YIPS, YOPS and YAKS induction tricks they've tried over years to smooth out carburation, especially on lumpy singles – well **EFI** fixes them in one go. Ride an old carb'd BMW Funduro alongside a Sertao and you'll see the difference.

Another advantage of EFI is that it's much less affected by **altitude** (see p185) – the system compensates for the lack of oxygen by reducing the fuel, just as the pilot does in a small airplane. There's nothing wrong with carbs and **CV carbs** are much less prone to altitude woes than slide carbs once suited to racing bikes. And of course carbs can be taken apart and cleaned or repaired, unlike an injector. Like water-cooling, EFI on motorbikes may appear an unnecessary complication, but it's a real step forward and has brought a new lease of life to a lot of ropey old engine designs.

Catalytic converters

Just about all EFI bikes now also feature **catalytic converters** (or 'cats') built into their silencers to clean up emissions. Normally these work best with unleaded fuel which isn't always available in the AMZ. This is despite the confident claims of the maps featured on the UN Environment Programme website (🖥 www.unep.org/pcfv) which, since 2006, reckons that leaded petrol is no longer available in Africa because the entire continent (apart from Algeria) magically got together and agreed to ban it.

The fuel pump handles aren't necessarily greener on the other side of the border, but you can run a cat on leaded fuel for 'a few months' before lead

CHINESE BIKES?

As we all know, each year the Chinese pump out millions of sub-250 runabouts or work-horses and we're told one day we'll all be riding Chinese. Of course we're riding more Chinese assembled bikes than we'd care to admit, but Chinese *branded* is another matter. On the web you'll find tales of fearless early adopters grumbling about crummy assembly, irregular running or poor materials, just as it was in the 'Brit Shit/Jap Crap' 1970s when I started biking. To that you can add the confusion when Chinese marques get rebadged by importers. With an unfamiliar name and unknown reputation you can be sure depreciation will be crippling.

Though **Hero** in India is the world's biggest motorcycle manufacturer, China's countless factories make it the world's largest producer. But the boom has waned in recent years as India turns the screws and the Big Four fight back by dropping prices and streamlining production. Broadly speaking the Chinese have imitated the Japanese strategy in the 1960s: bang out cheap and cheerful copies then, once the world's markets for those runabouts gets saturated, tune into what affluent western buyers might look twice at. That's only just beginning to happen.

Established in the late 1990s, **Shineray** are a Chinese marque that's said to specialise in trail and off-road machines. In 2014 they bought the Italian SWM name, last heard of in the 1970s, and also acquired an Italian assembly plant off KTM, including a batch of Husky models including the TE630 enduro racer.

Shineray get rebranded worldwide as CF Moto, but in Britain are known as WK or Mash Moto in France. Right now CF Moto are unusual in being the only Chinese bike maker to produce a 'big' road bike, the **650NK** twin (to give it one of its names) cloned from a Kawasaki ER6n/Versys.

In 2015 Mash released the **Moto Mash Adventure** (above) based on an air-cooled, injected motor derived from a late-1980s 400cc version of the kick-and-electric Honda XBR500. I rode a Mash Roadstar 400 which uses the same motor (review on the website) and, while a great-looking and very pleasant 'mini Bonneville', I can't say it felt much more powerful than my old CRF250L – figures vary in the mid-to-high 20s hp. The other problem was the asking price of nearly

£4000 for the Roadstar, rising to £5600 for 'limited editions' targeting gullible hipsters. In France the Moto Mash Adventure comes with an 18-litre tank, discs front and rear, 18/21 wheels and a monoshock. It goes for €5000 (about £3500) with optional alloy panniers for another £500. That's £300 more than I paid for a year old Honda CB500X with 1500 miles. WK in the UK may have followed with a near-identical but pricier WK Trail 400 with similar luggage options, as may other Shineray outlets round the world. Capacity-wise, this Chinese bike's release is more coincidence than 'gap-in-the-adv-market' design, but there certainly is an interest in this light-weight capacity as the giant GSs and the like become the go-to tourers or weekend bikes. Right now there's only the CCM at twice the price, but probably not half bad.

The **Zongshen RX3 Cyclone** is another contender with the right looks, sold under various badges in the UK and US where it goes for US$3500 (about £2250) or the **Minsk TRX300i** (above) in Russophone lands. That price is more like it because it's just another 250 which, with its three-piece luggage set weighs a claimed 165kg (400lbs) dry. There's no shortage of suitable 250s out there. What's wanted is at least a 400's added grunt, but at a price that doesn't steer you towards a used Japanese alternative.

BIKE CHOICE & PREPARATION

neutralises the cat's fine matrix coated in precious metals. When this happens your bike will run the same but won't emit clean gases which may affect your next roadworthy test. Of course over-sensitive **electronic sensors** may have their own ideas and could flip out on leaded fuel; removing Lambda or O₂ sensors from header pipes can help. You'll find metal blanking nuts as well as electronic terminal plugs on ebay for a few pounds. As with more expensive intake air temperature sensors, they often have the effect of making the bike run better by richening the fuel/air mixture.

On any bike fitted with a cat, you can replace the stock silencer/cat with a regular – and usually lighter and nosier – aftermarket pipe. The bike's electronic emission sensor ought to adjust the fuel injection accordingly, meaning the machine should run fine.

BIKE CHOICE & PREPARATION

WHY WE ♥ OUR KTM 690s

The KTM 690R is a cult bike; nothing else comes close. Its versatility, lightness and power make it a joy to own. In five words: fun, versatile, rugged, reliable and bonkers – an overgrown, jet-propelled MTB. In a combined 65 riding years and over 50 bikes, the 690 is the most versatile we've owned. Out of the crate it's a robust trail bike. For long distance, add a Rally Raid or Safari tank, a GL Coyote saddlebag and maybe a screen or

fairing and you're ready for a high-speed, low-drag, long-haul adventure. We've covered tens of thousands of miles on ours in just about every sort of terrain and weather. They ford well, eat rocks for breakfast, carve through sand, love gnarly terrain but run fine on the open road. The engine is strong and eager; on a motorway it's got overtaking power but it'll also chug through tricky 'trials' sections at low speed. Most importantly, at 5' 6", Danielle can pick hers up unaided or help load it onto a rickety boat.

Fit road-biased tyres and the 690 gives road bikes a run for their money, especially on back roads or in traffic. With knobblies we

can set off for a weekend of technical trail riding 200 miles away then ride home. No vans, trailers or Sunday evening jams. On top of this the 690 looks great, especially the post-2012 versions.

Early models had gremlins but our 690s have never let us down; I had more problems with my 1200GS. The components are top notch; no need to worry about dented rims, worn bearings, premature rust or carrying 'just in case' spares. They're easy to work on and the high commonality of fasteners means few tools are needed. The service interval is 6000 miles and an oil change is very quick. A full service takes half the time of an F650GS single.

A true adventure bike should be able to cover the widest possible variety of terrain which means it needs to be light, well suspended and tough. A travel bike also needs speed and with the 'full fat' 67hp 690cc you have high-speed endurance that's difficult to match, plus power to romp up steep climbs or tackle thick mud at altitude.

Some say 690s can't rival bigger bikes over long-distance but we've ridden ours from East Africa to the TAT. For comfort we tried modified seats but found quality padded cycle shorts work best. A small screen reduces wind-blast and the 14-litre Safari tank can stretch the range to around 500km, though we now prefer the 4.5-litre Rally Raid rear tank. For the moment the 690 has no rivals. The discontinued X-Challenge came closest but was heavier and less well sprung. CCM's new GP450 is lighter but alongside a 690 the engine just feels weak.

Dan Ward, Dave King

Build quality and reliability

Anyone who's been riding for decades will recognise that the build quality of many modern motorcycles (and much else besides) has passed a peak, while at the same time bikes are more reliable and perform better than ever. 'Built-in obsolescence' used to be the cynical explanation as to why new things wore out early, but it's as much to do with excessive manufacturing costs being trimmed, while more attention is paid to designing a superficially good-looking machine with as many electronic gizmos as the ECU can handle. Such a product is easy to sell and wins positive reviews, even if once you look below the surface you find cheap components and a rough finish.

Just about all the major brands have models which suffer from premature wear of cheap components or poor assembly: head bearings that wear out at a

40,000 MILES ON A CRF250L

Right now in Panama I've covered about 40,000 miles on Rhonda, my Honda CRF250L. By the time it's all over this'll probably be one of the longest continuous journeys on a bike of this size. Although I'm an experienced off roader I'm also realistic and at 5' 5" knew that a simple, light and narrow machine would give me the confidence to explore off the beaten track. Riding alone, this was vital; I needed to be able to pick this thing up when no one was around. On departure I added a 12-litre IMS tank and a rack for soft baggage, a Rotopax and a metal top box. Another small rack went on the front with a screen plus handguards and a proper bashplate underneath.

The CRF wasn't designed for long journeys, but what 250 trail bike is? The seat is narrow and for me about as soft as a pickled conker. Fact is though, I've got used to it. I tried an Airhawk (see pp72-3) but found it got in the way getting on and off, plus I didn't appreciate the extra height. Still, it makes a nice camping pillow. No matter what you ride your bum will get sore, but I've found it only becomes a pain on long, uninspiring days. I try to ride less than 200 miles a day and find choosing an interesting, engaging route is the key to enjoyable long-distance travel: quality not quantity makes my day.

Obviously the modest acceleration can be a hindrance on a long day of busy, truck-filled highways – no surprise there. You have to calculate your overtaking opportunities precisely. I dropped a tooth on the front sprocket for a brisker response and it made a big difference.

I've replaced the chainset about four times, the tyres five times and the oil every 4000 miles or so. The oil consumption's still negligible. The fork seals went at around 32,000 miles, as did the head bearings. The CRF has a skinny subframe and mine snapped in Indonesia around 20,000 miles in (see photo, p112) but was easily repaired in a day. Other than that, it just keeps on running. Parts like oil filters and sprockets have

been easy to find with the exception of Argentina, where I had to ship in from the US, taking three weeks and costing double.

Along with camping and people's generosity, the light shipping weight plus fuel consumption of around 25kpl have all helped keep costs low. While there were a few occasions I would have loved a V-Max with an Electra Glide seat, there were many other times I thanked the stars for my nimble 250. My priorities were reliability, off-road agility and weight. Rhonda has ticked all those boxes.

STEPH JEAVONS ONESTEPHBEYOND.COM

HONDA BUSHLANDER IN SOUTHERN AFRICA

I'm a firm believer in keeping it simple and so for my nine-month trip around Southern Africa I initially considered second-hand Transalps, KLRs or XR250s. I wanted a simple, cheap and reliable bike that wouldn't require much modification to do the journey but buying used and preparing the bike myself wasn't something I'd any experience with.

When I came across the CTX 200 Bushlander (see p70) in a Honda dealership in Cape Town it seemed too good to be true (It was: the CTX is no longer sold new in SA). It cost me R35,000 (roughly $3500 or £2200 back then, now less) and included a two-year warranty and a year's breakdown assistance which gave me peace of mind.

This farm bike comes standard with front and back racks, bash plate and handlebar lever protection. I replaced the knobblies with some Mitas E07s and added 4mm-thick tubes. On the light CTX these tyres actually lasted the whole 29,000 kms, and with only two punctures!

The CTX only weighs 126kg dry so even full of fuel and with 30 kilos of luggage it's easy to pick up in the sand when you inevitably fall off. It's essentially a Honda XL200 with some agricultural extras and has been in production for over thirty years so parts were easily obtainable. I replaced a snapped speedo cable in Mutare, Zimbabwe and one of my side stand springs (yes, the CTX has two side stands) on the border of Zambia and Malawi.

I found the best speed for fuel economy and comfort was 80kph and with a top speed of around 100kph I wasn't that far off the legal limit of 120 anyway (or only 80kph in Malawi). As it was, speeding down highways wasn't for me. I was more interested in meandering slowly up across southern Africa, and often on tracks – which the CTX handled great.

The 8.5-litre tank could be an issue in some remote areas, but a cheap 10-litre jerrican increased the range to around 4-500kms which was plenty.

At the end I sold the CTX for R20,000 meaning I had a brand new bike for nine months and nearly 30,000kms for only R15,000. I regret nothing about choosing the Bushlander, even those 500-km slogs across Mozambique when I was running out of time towards the end. It took me to some great places like Messum Crater in Namibia, Makgadikgadi Pan in Botswana and Honde Valley in Zimbabwe with negligible cost or mechanical issues. Some may turn their nose up at 14.5hp but as I read somewhere 'You only need 12hp to travel the world. The rest is just wheel spin.'

JAMES MORRISON, WHEREISJAMES.COM

few thousand miles, as do chains or electrical components like rectifiers, due to hasty assembly or poor wiring. So while your modern bike is unlikely to be handed down to your descendants, as long as it runs it will do so as reliably as any machine ever made, particularly once you've replaced possibly cheap original equipment (OE) such as chains and suspension, as well as headstock or wheel bearings. If you're serious and have the means, check that the swingarm and suspension linkages have been properly greased out of the factory, too; it's a common complaint.

Nowadays more than ever it's possible to get abreast of a particular model's foibles with the mass of information found online. Owner-enthusiasts' forums and wikis will minutely dissect the beta on their machines, suggesting which upgrades and accessories work best.

Parts availability and fuel economy

Plan for the worst: **leave with new consumables** (tyres, chains, brakes), some key spares and maybe send some stuff on. Recognise that your adventure includes unpredictable events which will require resourceful solutions. If something can't be fixed or diagnosed locally despite all your efforts, then consider using DHL and the like, having someone fly out what you need, or even flying to a nearby country where the component can be bought. Remember, parcels sent by express couriers can get bogged down with customs clearance which can drag on for weeks. And depending on where you are, that wait may well exceed the cost of simply flying somewhere to get what you need.

Parts availability is a quandary, but the best attitude to take is that out in the AMZ there won't be any specialised parts to be found, especially in Africa north of the Zambezi. The richer countries of South America may be better off, with much of Asia falling somewhere in between. And what you do find out there in terms of **tyres and chains** will be of a lot lower quality than stuff back home, and often not of a size that fits big bikes.

Even with current fuel-injected engines, advances in **fuel economy** are only occasionally on a par with cars, partly because to most users in rich countries, motorcycles are for blowing away the cobwebs on a weekend. As it is, economy is a preoccupation more prevalent in places like Europe where fuel is costly. But once on the road in foreign lands, your bike's fuel range *will* become a preoccupation, and the cost of filling the tank a daily expense.

'Two wheels and an engine'

Over the page there's a closer look at **ten bikes** that tick most of the boxes for overland travel or that are otherwise worth considering. It's not a 'top ten' so don't get fixated on them and their alternatives. Bikes like the big GS BMWs are becoming so obvious that some riders go out of their way to be different. In the end anything that has two wheels and an engine could be the star of your biking adventure. If you're new to this game sticking to the well-known or popular machines makes sense.

Only across western equatorial Africa might you *need* some off-road utility, but even here such stages are becoming shorter by the year. Unless you're purposely seeking off-road challenges, for trans-Asia or the Americas any **road bike** will work most of the time. **Dual-purpose** tyres will make your road bike more secure on dirt roads while keeping it steerable on the highway.

Otherwise, think about **buying abroad**. If you want to start your ride in North America but aren't from there, buying there saves a whole lot on shipping costs and bikes cost less. Your KL650s and so on are incredible bargains by European standards, with plenty of kit and know-how around.

Meanwhile, in **Brazil** you can pick up an NX 400i Falcon (mini Dominator) or an XRE 300 with a beak to die for, as well as Yamaha Ténérés from 250 to 1200 (though check you can legitimately roam the continent first). Check out the **HUBB bike sales and swap forum** too. Many riders seek to sell their bike or buy yours, especially in South America.

If you like to be different or have experience the following selection may be rather conservative. In that case the only limit is your imagination, your budget and Newton's Three Laws of Motion.

BIKE CHOICE & PREPARATION

BMW OILHEAD AND HEXHEAD GS BOXERS

Manufactured	1150 '99–'05; 1200 since 2004, water-cooled since 2013
Engine	1130/1170cc four-valve flat twin
Kerb weight	from 229kg/505lb to 260kg/573lb
Fuel capacity	From 20 ltr/5.3 US gal
Max range	At least 400km/250 miles @ 21kpl/50mpg US
Riders like	Image, poise, power, ready for RTW
Don't like	Weight, ubiquity, some component reliability issues

Who would dare skip the GS Telelevers and risk mass book burnings? Not me. Right off the bat the 1100 was a hit, but the heavier 1150 was a whole lot better and the 1200GS better still, managing to lose 30kg (regained on the Adventure model). The air-cooled 1200s (left) are 'hexhead' engines: smoother, more powerful and managed by electronics.

Since the 1150 the **Adventure** or 'GSA' versions feature a lower first gear, switchable ignition for poor fuel, a 30-litre tank, a little more suspension travel plus, spoke wheels, hand guards, crash bars and other protective features as well as some 20 extra kilos and OE luggage which may not be up to the job. Commonly chosen for two-up tours and loaded down like a yak on market day, even custom-tuned Ohlins shocks have been known to fail – Hyperpro seems the way to go but even then it's as well to remember the pressure that rear shock's under. The dive-free telelever forks are trouble free and a revelation. **Final drives** wear out prematurely, the notorious 'ring antenna' can fail and immobilise you ('05–'09 models), as can a fuel pump controller and, less drastically, the fuel level sensor strip. Check out the wheel flange recall too, covering 2006-10.

In 2013 the GS gained water-cooling, a wet clutch and an 'electronics package', producing a big increase in smoothed-out power and rideability. 'The best GS ever' rose the cry and even at $20,000 sales didn't skip a beat.

Confounding their bulk, a GS outgrows any 'LWR' kudos to remain the definitive global mile-muncher.

Alternatives In sales terms, competitors in this 'hammer-a-walnut' sector can only pick at the crumbs. The Super Ténéré never really cracked it, nor has Triumph's shaft-driven Explorer 1200 and nor will the CRF1000L. The GS remains *über alles*.

HONDA CRF250L

Manufactured	from 2012
Engine	249cc water-cooled single
Kerb weight	145kg/320lb
Fuel capacity	7.8 ltr/2.1 US gal
Max range	265km/165 miles @ 26.5kpl/62.4 mpg US
Riders like	Looks, Honda reliability, cheaper than competition
Don't like	Tiny tank, skinny subframe, basic suspension

As soon as it came out, Honda's 250L became a hit around the world. Cosmetic similarities with the dirt racing 250R and 250X enduro helped, but those are completely different competition machines. Others celebrated the 'return of the humble trail bike', not a snorty enduro or supermoto.

The CBR250R roadbike engine is not the lightest around and the L's suspension gets shown up once roads deteriorate. Like any 250 they'll run low on puff on long climbs or at altitude, with little left to pass traffic at 100kph, but in the ragged corners of Adventure Zone that's flat out anyway. And although you'd not always want to stretch it that far, the 8000-mile (12,000km) oil change intervals sure help.

Dealing with the puny tank is probably top of the list. Unfortunately the after market jobbies are still no more than 50% bigger and so hardly worth the bother. I managed with a 5-litre can in the US (averaged 87mpg or 30.7kpl once I retuned the EJK black box). Don't fret over the engine – you bought a 250 –, instead consider better suspension and think about how to make the subframe last by avoiding heavy loads strung out way past the axle. Unsupported, it will flex from side to side and may snap behind where the two tubes join.

Alternatives Some adapt the CRF250M (for Motard) with its slightly lower seat height. You'd think Kawasaki's once pricier but better sprung KLX250S or Yamaha's sportier WR250R would get a look in, but they don't. However, if you can get a ride on the Brazilian-built **XR250R Tornado** – most easily in South America or South Africa you'll be surprised: lighter, better sprung and with an 11-litre tank (but similar 30kpl potential, despite the carb). Only thing they're taller and have a similar, thin-tubed subframe.

© STEPH JEAVONS

YAMAHA TÉNÉRÉ XT660Z

Manufactured from 2008

Engine 660cc water-cooled single

Kerb weight 206kg/454lb

Fuel capacity 23 ltr/6.1 US gal

Max range 577km/360 miles @ 25kpl/59mpg US

Riders like smooth EFI, fuel consumption, comfort, looks, heritage

Don't like Weight, height, build quality, not in North America, price rise

Now in its fifth iteration and fourth decade, the Ténéré came back after a nine-year break and arguably was the best ever. All you had to accept is that this is how the Japanese build some bikes these days: good looks covering cheap components among mandatory emissions claptrap. For the minority of owners who'll take it to Kathmandu via Timbuktu, it was initially one of the best platforms in its category until prices shot up from £4500 to nearer £7000. The Italian-built EFI motor derived from the XT660R and X wasn't new, but Yamaha finally nailed low-speed fuelling issues – a common complaint with many bikes at that time.

They didn't put any effort into making it light or using quality components – a common ploy with low-end Jap bikes to get a new model off to a good start. As far as the chassis goes, the heft in the vital subframe is a good thing, but the mufflers are high and way out back, ruining the centre of gravity, and the double-disc front end weighs a ton; one big SM disc and caliper could do the job. The OE screen is a bit low for six-footers and they say cush drives wear out (another common complaint on big singles; stuff them with inner tubes). Low 10:1 compression means it'll live on low octane fuel. You'll need a full bash plate, but apart from a rack and luggage, you're good to go.

Alternatives In the XT660Z's home markets of Europe and Australia there's

still not much in injected, faired and big-tanked singles, unless Suzuki, Kawasaki and Honda snap out of it. Of the old air-cooled XTZs, choose the twin-lamp 3AJ or a younger XT-E which'll need 'Ténérising'. Avoid the five-valve, water-cooled XTZ660 they made in the 90s. Or take a high jump and go for a KTM 690 or a Husky Terra (left) if the price is good.

KTM 690R

Manufactured from 2008

Engine 654cc water-cooled single; from 2012 690cc

Kerb weight 152kg/336lb

Fuel capacity 12 ltr/3.2 US gal

Max range 300km/3186 miles @ 25kpl/59mpg US

Riders like Suspension, power modes, economy, weight. What else is there?

Don't like Pump and injectors, height, adventurising costs, seat, filler cap

The 690 E came out in 2008 with the slightly taller R a year later. Engine was 654cc and only in 2012 did it become true 690cc, the E was dropped but then so was the height of the R. You get a close-ratio but tall geared six-speed box and the 12-litre tank under the seat is the subframe (no metal superstructure). You may want to uprate the bolts on that.

© JUSSI HYTTINEN

The 690 (and all KTMs for that matter) is the sort of big single dirt bike you'll never get from Japan – light, focussed, hardcore – but with issues. Some get saddled with outright lemons, others cover tens of thousands of kilometres with nothing but a mile-wide grin. If only they'd made a travel-ready version like the old Adventure 640R. Out of the crate it's in a class of its own in terms of off-road performance – Ténérés, XRLs and KLRs are from another planet where they still live in caves. You need to spend another couple of grand to make a 690 a decent travel bike: screen, seat (see p71), lights, fuel range, a Shindengen reg/rec. Step in Rally Raid Products with things like hex bolt conversions for the dodgy injectors; carry a spare and even a fuel pump. Keep an eye on the exhaust rocker bearing – frequent changes with good oil help. You need to look after a 690, not just ride it day in, day out.

On the plus side the suspension is good to go and the 690s are actually amazingly economical – matching an XT660Z which is some 50 kilos heavier on a wet day. The page you need:
🖳 **welikebikes.be/KTM690Wiki** or
🖳 **rollinghobo.com/690r**.

Alternatives The 450 CCM or discontinued BMW XChallenge or a worked over XR650R. The forthcoming AJP PR7 looks like it might be more ready out of the box or downscale drastically to a DRZ400 if the mission is gnarly.

SUZUKI DL650 V-STROM

Manufactured From 2004

Engine 645cc, water-cooled, 90° V-twin

Kerb weight 220kg/490lb

Fuel capacity 22 ltr/5.8 US gal

Max range 500km/310 miles @ 23kpl/54mpg US

Riders like Price, engine, fuel consumption, overall comfort

Don't like Not much at all, a bit low but top heavy

© C. SEIWALD

BIKE CHOICE & PREPARATION

Equipped with a great engine that has been around since the last century in the road-oriented SV650, like the SV, the inexpensive V-Strom is nothing more than a great all-rounder. It's the smooth engine that makes it much more popular than the bigger, one-litre DL, and as with any bike in this category, a good engine that you can ride all day is the key while suspension is far easier to adapt according to your weight, payload and riding preferences. Fuel range and comfort come next and the DL delivers here too. Some find it a bit plasticky and say it's top heavy, but at least you can get alternative seats and aftermarket bash plates.

Wheels are 17-inch and 19-inch, the bigger front implying that the bike is suited to off-tarmac scenarios, but tyre tread will have a lot more impact than wheel size. ABS became an option in 2006.

In 2011 the V-Strom received a makeover with better looks, a more refined and economical engine based on the SVF Gladius, some firmer suspension and even a few kilos were lost on the way. At the same time they released the 650X version with a lot of the accessories you'd fit anyway, but not necessarily what will work best out on the road.

© DANIEL

Alternatives The obvious comparison is the less well-loved Transalp from Honda; not quite as comfy or long ranging even if it might have the edge on dirt roads. There's the more obscure (for overlanding at least) Kawasaki 650 Versys with a harder revving and juicy parallel twin engine that's less suited to prolonged touring, or of course the 800cc F650/700GS from BMW.

KAWASAKI KLR650

Manufactured From 1987 – significant upgrade 2008

Engine 651cc water-cooled single

Kerb weight 195kg/432lb (2012 model)

Fuel capacity 23 ltr/6.1 US gal

Max range 480km/300 miles @ 21kpl/50mpg US

Riders like Know-how and aftermarket goodies, price

Don't like Seat, cam chain tension issues

Soon this bike will be older than me but is still going strong in the US and Australia. Banged out in Thailand, up until 2008 all they did was change the colours each year. Then came a signif icant if more road-oriented upgrade: chunkier spokes and forks (at last), more power, a new look with better brakes and firmer seat plus revised suspension and an alternator with a bigger output.

KLR650s are the Ténérés North America never got and have been refined by enthusiasts and small-time engineering outfits who've fixed every last crease that Kawasaki didn't or wouldn't iron out. With a 9.8:1 compression ratio, it laughs off low octane fuel and on a run can easily top 21kpl (50mpg US) on its old-fangled carb. If only your butt could outlast the tank. Other seats and roadside rest areas are available – and it's hardly unique to KLRs.

The big tank, small fairing and the 650cc water-cooled engine gets the KLR off to a great start, but pre-2008, unless you like steering with oars, brace the front forks. Balancer chain tension is a weak point and it's said the 2008 upgrade saw a lame fix to the spring, so fit a 'doohickey' (google it). Another problem on old models was the stock idler shaft adjustment lever, but you can buy a re-engineered replacement for just $40. And disconnect the sidestand and clutch cut-out switches before they do it themselves. Any other questions? ⌨ **www.klr650.net** are at your service.

Alternatives KLR users are mostly from North America where true alternatives are few. The unchanging air-cooled Honda XR650L is similarly well known there, a taller, dirt-oriented machine that needs a tank and fiddling with the jetting to run right. A Suzuki DR650SE is also an option, but all these carb'd big singles could be reaching the end of the line.

BMW G650GS SERTAO

Manufactured	from 2011
Engine	652cc water-cooled single
Kerb weight	193kg / 425lb
Fuel capacity	14 ltr / 3.7 US gal (17 ltr on F models)
Max range	400km / 250 miles @ 23kpl / 56.5mpg US
Riders like	Great economy, smooth EFI engine, comfy seat
Don't like	Weight, old surging and stalling issues, water pump leaks

After seven good years, in 2007 the original and proven EFI Rotax 650s were dropped, presumably to push the new 800cc twins or the X-series singles. Though there was nothing very wrong with them, the lightweight X singles were a flop in most places and the similarly named F650GS and F800GS twins got off to an inauspicious start. And so the 650 singles returned to the fold in 2011 with a road-oriented G650GS model with cast wheels (19" front), and a few months later the original F650 'Dakar' was reborn as the snazzy 'Sertão' with 20% more suspension travel, spoked wheels (21" front) and switchable ABS and heated grips as standard. Though heavy for a single (what isn't these days), all the BMW 650 singles are ergonomically sorted and comfy, with a 400w alternator although fairly high 11.5:1 compression which requires 91 octane fuel. The tank is smaller but it does look like it's the same old 650 which is no bad thing.

The first generation had early issues with **surging** and **stalling** but software updates and new injectors have surely fixed that by now. The underseat tank may only be 17 litres but that's equivalent to at least a 20-litre 'carb' tank and is big enough. The plastic bashplate is another sign of the times; alloy works best to protect the hoses and water pump (some leaked). You'll find a mass of detail (if not so much on overland preparation) on the web-

site formerly known as Chain Gang: 🖥 **www.f650.com**. Other than that try 🖥 www.ukgser.com.

Alternatives Don't write off the old models pictured here. Just be ready to deal with leaking water pumps and worn head bearings. Otherwise it's the usual suspects from Japan or the overlooked Husky (and soon SWM) 650s.

HONDA CB500X

Manufactured	from 2013
Engine	471cc water-cooled P-twin
Kerb weight	196kg/434lb
Fuel capacity	17.5 ltr/4.6 US gal
Max range	550km/340 miles @ 26kpl/61mpg US
Riders like	Inexpensive, 8000-mile services, fuel economy, RRP kits
Don't like	Basic suspension, 17-inch wheels, bland

Did the recession of 2008 induce some of the big manufacturers to come up with inexpensive and eco-nomical motorcycles? Possibly. Honda's innovative 700cc Runners were one, the CB 500X, -F and -R twins were another less innovative take, and the Adventure-styled X was the pick of the bunch because it looks as good as it goes.

© JENNY MORGAN

Of course it's just another road bike with a beak, wide bars but the same old 17-inch wheels and basic sus-pension, but like the XT660Z when it came out, the price of the Thai-built machine was unbeatable; in the UK they sell used from £3500 and doubtless less in North America. You get a small, easy to handle machine with a low cen-tre of gravity and a relaxing engine with fuel consumption close to a CRF250L, but enough poke to overtake anything and sustain legal cruising speeds where possible. Honda build quality and reliability can be taken for granted and the subframe is ready for the load.

KTM 690 specialists Rally Raid Products saw the potential to improve the CB-X into a gravel roader, manufacturing or commissioning bits like a spoked 19-inch front wheel, a spoker for the back (with a sealed-for-tubeless option), proper bashplate, racks, bigger pegs, extended forks and a Tractive shock plus a linkage – all easily reversible home DIY replacements or add-ons. At 200kg plus payload, it won't turn your Honda into a BAM-bashing 690, but it will enable dirt road excursions where the standard bike may struggle. See how I got on with my RRP CB-X on the AMH website.

Alternatives   Like the CRF, Honda seem to have reinvented the light-weight 500 twin category. The age-old V-Stroms, Versys and XL-V are sub-stantially bigger, heavier and juicier but won't cost much less, used.

EIKE CHOICE & PREPARATION

BMW F800 and 650 (700) GS

Manufactured	from 2008 (F700 from 2012)
Engine	798cc water-cooled parallel twin (all models)
Kerb weight	207kg/460lbs (199kg/440lbs)
Fuel capacity	16 ltr/4.22 US gal
Max range	385km/240 miles @ 24kpl/56.5mpg US
Riders like	Class-leading economy, weight, looks, it's a BMW
Don't like	Early issues, 800's engine characteristics, it's a BMW

For those resisting the GS Boxer cult, the parallel twin F-GSs were a breath of fresh air. One initially inoffensively plain and dubbed a '650' (left) in a muddled twist of marketing back-projection. The other a snazzy evocation of the old Paralever bumble bee.

Weighing in around 200kg wet, here were a pair of Bavarians without the beer gut, although the twins got off to a bad start with other health issues. The modern malady of great design masking cheaply sourced components and inconsistent assembly saw some early adopters pulling their hair out and may well have led to BMW re-introducing the GS 650 singles. It's all on the web, just remember, 'the squeaky door gets all the oil'; many riders of early models experienced no problems in tens of thousands of miles.

Most will be drawn to the flashier 800, but I believe the '650' is the choice for overlanding. At 71hp, it's 18% less than the 800 but is only 10% down on torque which also peaks 1250rpm lower. The result is a milder engine, better economy as well as road manners from the single-disc, 19-inch front end. The (terrible) seat is lower and cast wheels run tubeless – a huge benefit (see p85). It ran fine on 91 octane and I averaged 68mpg (24kpl) over 4000 miles. The '650' was renamed and retuned 'F700GS' (below) in 2012 to end confusion with the single, but the word is it lost the 650's torquey attributes. All models need a bashplate, radiator protection and can be remapped to run on low octane

fuel. The website 🖥 **www.ukgser.com** has the drum on the twins.

Alternatives Triumph's Tiger 800s are more powerful and probably more fun, but juicier. Honda's NC750X is at the other extreme with the 650 V-Strom or Yamaha's Tracers in 700 twin or 900 triple form. And by now there may be an F900GS with DCT and maybe something from KTM.

TRIUMPH TIGER 800

Manufactured	from 2011
Engine	799cc water-cooled triple
Kerb weight	195kg / 430lb
Fuel capacity	19 ltr / 5 US gal
Max range	430km / 270 miles @ 23kpl / 54mpg US
Riders like	Stonking motor, 645w alternator, name on the tank, sound
Don't like	Ticks fewer boxes than BMW 800s, except the one that counts

One problem with trying to break out and take to the road on a Triumph 800 triple is that it will take months to get over the fun of the howling motor, by which time the world's fascinating cultures, exotic wildlife and awesome scenery will have passed by in a blur.

The formats of the two Tiger models closely mimic the 800cc BMW twins. The Tiger (now 'XRc') has cast wheels with a 19-inch front and slightly less suspension travel, and the 800 XC has spokes with a 21-inch front, an inch more travel and seat height (though both adjust by an inch). Plus you get a cheeky beaky at a near ten per cent premium over the 19er, just like the BM. But unlike the BMs, the motors' characteristics are identical – the same 95hp and flat torque curve that pulls right across the rev range or mountain range.

In 2015 the Tigers got a revamp, more singing and dancing traction-, mapping and ABS electronics, and better or more equipment in the XRx and XCx versions with improvement in fuel consumption and notably, less weight. As with the F-GS twins, the 21-incher looks more purposeful but with your speed and cornering potential, the 19er will be more secure on the tarmac and with the right rubber manage fine on the loose.

Teething problems on the Thai-built machines appear to be less prevalent than the BMW equivalents and reliability better than a KTM. But unlike KTMs you'll benefit from a suspension makeover and a clearer screen. A centrestand is an extra but propping up a hefty Tiger on a roadside stick is a bit cheap. Other than that, knock yourself out!

Alternatives The BMW 800s are the obvious comparison, more economical but more boring too. The as-yet untested 900 Yamaha Tracer could be another triple contender and is cheaper, or one of the smaller KTM V-twins.

Bike preparation

There's a difference between going on a fortnight's touring holiday or ticking off a BDR in the western US, and setting off across Asia, Africa or Latin America, in other words, the 'Adventure Motorcycling Zone' or AMZ. Riding in the latter is this book's definition of adventure motorcycling and assuming that most readers don't live in those three continents, it can be summed up as 'exposure'. Among other things we'll get to later, you'll be a long way from the traditional support networks of motorcycle dealers, warranty claims, insurance, formal vehicle recovery and clinical repair. Of course recovery, repair and maybe occasionally a dealer can all be tracked down or arranged, but you may still be in a place where you don't speak the language and have the clock ticking on your visa or other pressures.

Because ordinary problems can become complications in the AMZ, it helps to simplify things and be ready for the worst. Piles of money is no help because a trouble-free ride is not guaranteed by buying the most expensive adventure motorcycle and festooning it with the most expensive kit. What counts is some experience running your bike with as fool-proof a set-up as you can manage, and then the ability to deal with the issues as they arise. Whether you're buying at home or abroad, **thorough preparation** of your machine is just about the best insurance you can get to guarantee a mechanically trouble-free trip. And because a long-range adventure bike will require modifications, the more time you spend riding your modified machine before you leave the better.

The great thing is that in the past few years, just as with bikes, the range of equipment for motorcycle overlanding has expanded greatly. There have been few actual innovations – low-draw, high-output lighting might be one of them (see p76). What counts hasn't changed and **what follows is what works for most people**, backed up by experience. It's not a tablet brought down from the mountainside. You may well have your own creative solutions because coming up with them is all part of the big adventure.

Pre-departure suspension testing programme.
© James Morrison

Testing, testing

If you're heading overseas with a brand new set up like metal boxes and modified suspension, a short **test run** to see how the whole rig handles is very worthwhile. The fewer surprises you encounter in the nerve-racking early days of the actual big trip the better, because you'll have enough on your plate without finding that with your fully packed alloy luggage suite causes the bike to handle like a beached gondola.

Try and do as much of the work as possible yourself, or under close guidance so that when something gives trouble, you have a clue how it all went together. Complex things like engine rebuilds, fabricating or welding have to be left to competent mechanics (which could include you), but basic repairs and maintenance tasks like fixing punctures and changing tyres (see p92) and engine oil, or inspecting and cleaning air filters are elementary tasks you should be able to do before you go.

As a rule, if you doubt whether any consumable component will last the entire length of your planned trip, **renew it** and finish off the partially-worn item later or take it as a spare. This applies especially to things like **tyres, chains and sprockets** and **brakes** which wear faster on fully-laden bikes ridden on bad roads, but it can also include wheel bearings, cables and other consumables. And lastly, bear in mind that **modifications other than those recommended here** may be necessary or useful on the machine of your choice.

ABOUT FUEL

In 2006 the United Nations Environmental Program (UNEP) announced that leaded fuel had been eradicated from Africa. From Casablanca and Cairo via the Congo to the Cape, every fuel station (except in Algeria) was selling unleaded petrol which modern bikes require. I thought this claim was far fetched at the time, and years later there are still plenty of places in central Africa and Asia where you won't find a green-handled petrol pump.

Leaded fuel, octane ratings and compression ratios

A petrol engine works by compressing a fuel-air mixture, igniting it at the right moment and allowed the resulting explosion to turn a crank, much like an old steam engine. The problem is pressure and heat can cause as-yet-unsparked gases on the far side of the combustion chamber to spontaneously ignite, something known as **detonation** or 'knocking'. Signs of knocking are a light tapping from the cylinder head, worst in high gears or under heavy throttle loads. The fuel is igniting in two places; one caused by the spark, the other because low octane fuel has caused unburned gases to ignite. It won't ruin your engine the way much more damaging **pre-ignition** can, but it's certainly inefficient and results in power loss.

About a century ago they discovered that adding **lead** (or tetra-ethyl lead*) to petrol reduced knocking – it effectively increased the fuel's **octane** or anti-knocking properties. This is what 'four star', 'premium' or 'super' refers to in fuel; an octane rating of 95 RON (Research Octane Number) which as we know costs a bit more than 'two star' or 'regular' where the octane can drop below 90 – in outback Mongolia you'll be lucky to find anything above 90 RON. It took about half a century and the exponential increase in motor vehicle use to recognise that the lead in exhaust emissions was a serious health hazard. It's been banned for road use in much of the West for decades.

So while combustion chamber design has a lot to do with it, in general a high-compression engine – say anything with a CR of over 11:1 – is more prone to knock on low octane fuel which you'll find in poorer or rural regions

* A bi-product of tetra-ethyl lead in fuel included the lubrication of the valve seats in the combustion chamber. Since at least the 1980s, alternative additives have been included in petrol and engines have been designed to not prematurely wear out their valves seats on unleaded fuel.

BIKE CHOICE & PREPARATION

of the world, places where emissions standards are less a priority than keeping the road open and an old banger running. A Honda 250 Tornado runs 9:3, an KTM690 is 11.7:1 while 800cc BMW twins are 12:1.

A **lean-running** engine is more prone to detonation, and lean mixtures – a relatively high air-to-fuel ratio – are the norm these days because they burn hotter encouraging complete combustion which lowers exhaust emissions, more of which below. At the cost of longevity and smoothness, increasing the compression ratio is an easy way of getting more power and also ensuring more complete combustion – it's one reason why diesel engines are more efficient; they use a much higher CR to 'auto-ignite' the charge without a spark and which then burns more completely (an 18:1 CR also explains why diesels have to be more heavily built when compared to a similar petrol engine).

To reduce pollution, in recent decades increasingly strict **emissions standards** (Euro 5, Euro 6 and so on) have been imposed on vehicle manufacturers, including motorcycles. It's partly the reason **fuel injection** has replaced carbs on bikes, while parallel advances and price drops in digital technology have made electronic fuel injection (EFI) much more precise and efficient. Meanwhile, on the hot side of the cylinder head, **catalytic converters** featuring a matrix coated with precious metals, have become incorporated into exhaust systems as a way to further reduce toxic emissions.

The problem is the world is not equal. The three continents which add up to the AMZ are economically less well off than the other two or three continents from which most AM riders set off on their moto adventures. In many of these places the fuel available might be leaded and/or of a lower octane, while the vehicles sold in that country come with less refined engines suited to running on this kind of fuel (the ethanol-based petrol made and sold in Brazil is another issue, see p306). So we have sophisticated bikes primarily sold in rich countries running on the crude fuel found in developing countries.

In the old days low octane fuel was most easily managed with octane booster, a fuel additive containing tetra-ethyl lead. Today sophisticated electronics are either switchable or just simply flexible enough to cope with low octane fuel. A BMW F650GS twin I used didn't blink on a tankful of Moroccan two-star despite its relatively high compression ratio.

We're emerging from an analogue-to-digital transition where sophisticated technology has filtered into the mainstream. ECU-managed engines no

longer shut down or go into 'limp-home mode' just because a light bulb blew. At the same time a parallel industry has grown in reprogramming or outwitting an ECU's web of sensors. Some can increase performance, but more commonly these widgits reduce the harshness of over-lean engines by repositioning air-intake temperature sensors, eliminating O_2 sensors or fitting tunable fuel controller 'black boxes', all now as normal as jetting a carb.

Tunable underseat fuel controller.
A lot less aggro than swapping jets.

ENGINE TEMPERATURE

With the prevalence of water-cooled engines, the old school dodge of fitting an **oil cooler** is less necessary and really, if the engine runs correctly an oil cooler shouldn't be needed. But when did that ever stop anyone meddling with their bike? If you do decide to fit one, **dry sump engines** with separate oil tanks lend themselves more easily to this modification as any of the external oil lines can be cut and a cooler spliced in with extra hosing.

Fitting an oil cooler reduces the oil pressure and increases the capacity a little. However, having an oil cooler (or water-cooling for that matter) doesn't mean that important things like oil level, quality and cleanliness, valve clearances and fuelling (where adjustable) can be neglected if the bike is to run well in hot and demanding conditions. Mount an oil cooler up high and in front of the engine. If you move into a cooler region or elevation, cover the oil cooler (or part of a radiator). Over-cooled engines wear quickly and run badly.

If a water-cooled engine is **overheating** there's something wrong with the cooling system or quite simply the conditions are too hot: most likely in desert sand where you're revving the engine hard at low ground speeds with a tail wind creating a minimal flow through the radiator. In this case **stop but don't switch off** and **park into the wind** to let the running motor cool down. Unless it's running and parked into the wind, when a bike stops moving the lack of airflow over the motor or through the radiator causes the temperature to rise momentarily. Turning the engine off at this point causes the temperature to rise dramatically which could send it over the edge and crack a barrel or blow a head gasket. Keep the engine running during short stops on hot days so the oil (and water) continue to pump round and cool the engine. Should your radiator boil right over, refill it a little at a time; pouring cold water into the baking barrel's water jacket could also crack something.

Although most water-temperature gauges are pessimistic don't get into the habit of running close to the red zone. On air-cooled bikes with no gauge it's also good to know your normal engine temperature. **Oil temperature gauges** which screw in in place of the oil filler cap or dipstick are a handy way of gauging engine temperature.

Better still is a proper oil temperature gauge. Touratech and others make a sender that replaces the sump drain plug on many bikes and which wires into a Touratech IMO or Voyager computer. I once wired it to a regular oil gauge but the results were not so legible. But because it's all relative it doesn't have to be the exact actual oil temperature; a sensor attached to a spark plug will give you a reading that'll also stabilise at a normal operating level. Being able to see how much above normal that reading might get is very useful in that it shows how hot your engine might be getting and when it might be an idea to back off a bit or stop let it cool down (into the wind) and maybe see what's wrong.

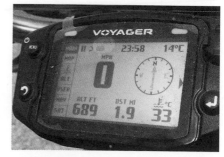

Spark plug warming up at 33°C. Establish what's normal and watch for aberrations.

BIKE CHOICE & PREPARATION

FUEL FILTERS

Today's prevalent **fuel-injected** engines have sophisticated and effective fuel pressurisation and filtration units built into the tank which can't be cleaned and – amazingly – rarely need it. They're also immune to vapour lock and adding an inline fuel filter may disrupt the sensitive fuel induction process, so unless you know better or your bike has a well-known weak point here, leave things standard.

In a carb-engined bike it's a good idea to fit an **inline fuel filter** into the fuel line(s). The inexpensive translucent, crinkled-paper element type (pictured below left, inset) work better than fine gauze items, which most bikes already have inside the tank as part of the fuel tap assembly. Make sure you fit it in the right direction of flow – there should be an arrow moulded into the filter body. These filters can be cleaned by simply flushing in the reverse direction with fuel from the tank, or spare ones take up little room.

In desert areas dust is always present in the air and even in the fuel, and in Iran or Pakistan it's common for roadside fuel to be dished out from a drum with a ladle or jug (picture below). The fact that they pour it through a pair of grandad's underpants is of little consolation. Better to pre-empt with something like a fine fabric sock which sits in your tank's filler mouth (as pictured below left). The problem is these usually only fit aftermarket plastic tanks with unrestricted mouths. Modern factory fuel tanks have a filler hole just bigger than the size of an unleaded petrol pump nozzle. The sock idea won't work unless you adapt it within a cumbersome pre-funnel.

In hot conditions inline filters can create **vapour lock**: the evaporation of fuel in the filter body before it flows to the carburettor which leads to fuel starvation. The engine cuts out but as it cools the fuel will eventually recondense and flow into the carb and the bike will run until it gets hot again. Vapour lock is worse when your tank fuel level is low and the filter body itself gets hot – we're talking temperatures of over 35°C. To get round it top up your tank and pour water over the fuel filter – you should see it fill up with fuel. Wrap it in a damp cloth and think about more permanent insulation. I had vapour lock on a Funduro in Libya once and taped a piece of cardboard alongside the barrel to keep the heat off the inline filter. It worked for the rest of the trip, even when temperatures got well over 40°.

Left: Fuel filter sock for wide-mouthed tanks will always catch something. © amsterdamto anywhere.nl. **Right**: The reason to use one (or an inline filter on carb bikes).

Dusty groups clog filters. Paper elements work better but oiled foam can be re-cleaned.

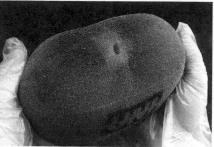
Freshly-oiled Uni filter. Latex gloves are handy or just oil-squidge it in a plastic bag.

Air filter

Carb or EFI, an air filter may require daily cleaning during high winds, sandstorms or if travelling at the back of a dusty convoy. The **reusable multi-layered oiled-foam types** such as those by Twin-Air, Multi Air or Uni Filter are best. If you think it'll have a hard life, carry a **ready-oiled spare** in a plastic bag that can be slipped in as necessary while the other gets cleaned later. You can rinse a re-usable foam filter with petrol and then soak it with engine oil, but proper **air filter oil** does the job much better, remaining sticky while not draining under gravity or drying out, as engine oil does. But if you run out, engine oil is better than nothing. Make sure you seal the airbox lid correctly, too.

Greasing the inside of the airbox is messy but catches more airborne particles and keeps the surface of the air filter cleaner for longer; a stocking over the filter is another way of extending the maintenance periods. If you're *pushing* your turned off bike through deep water, seal a plastic bag around the filter with an elastic band or tape then refit it to keep water out of the engine.

Some bikes have poorly positioned **air intakes** that can cake the filter in one sandy day or drown an engine if you go too deep in a river. Check your bike's snorkel/air-intake and which way it's pointing. After modifying the seat on an XR650L I found sand spinning off the back tyre would've got shovelled straight into the airbox – an alloy baffle plate and duct tape fixed that.

CHAIN AND SPROCKETS

Enclosed from the elements, **shaft drives** are virtually maintenance free – at the very worst the final drive bearing on a hexhead BMW might require changing at 25,000 miles. In this respect shaft drives are well-suited for overlanding, though they're usually fitted to heavier machines.

Chains – making them last

Most bikes are fitted with lighter and less expensive roller **chains and sprockets**. Dry-running **belt drives** are found on some mopeds, lumbering cruisers and as camshaft drives in the engine, but don't really seem to be catching on with bikes. Lighter, quieter, lube-free and very long wearing, they're even beginning to exceed the breaking strain of comparable chains. Their only drawback is the cushioning effect makes them slightly less efficient, they need a relatively large and wide rear 'sprocket' and altering the gearing (as explained over the page) is less easy.

BIKE CHOICE & PREPARATION

O-ring chains have grease between the outer rollers and inner pins, sealed with tiny rubber rings between the rollers and side plates. Only when these rubber seals begin to wear out after many thousands of miles will the chain begin to wear out like an ordinary chain. Manufacturers have since come out with somewhat gimmicky 'X-' and 'W-' ring chains (effectively, multiple seals), some of which are guaranteed for 12,000 miles. For *Desert Riders* we were testing various systems; the other two guys fitted DID 'gold plate' x-rings while I tried out a similarly-priced RK 'XW' ring, also made in Japan. Result: the DIDs barely needed adjusting while my OK RK needed about three or four adjustments in 5000km. To cut a long story short, you can't go wrong with a DID gold plate, or whatever brand is said to be as good.

Chain tension

Your bike's manual will give exact instructions, but in most cases a chain should be adjusted to provide **40mm** (1.5") **of slack** measured midway along the bottom run of the chain, *loaded up but without you on the bike*. On most trail bikes with long-travel suspension, this'll give an impression of an overly slack chain when the machine is unloaded and at rest, but this slack will be taken up once the suspension is compressed to the correct level when the bike is on the move. I've found you can expect a certain amount of tightening and polishing of the chain towards the end of a hot day; this will slacken off to the correct tension as the chain cools overnight. Make sure you adjust it correctly: an over-loose chain is less bad than an over-tight one, but correct adjustment is best. Realistically, with a quality chainset and moderate riding habits, you can expect to have to make adjustments every few thousand miles.

Aerosols and automatic chain oilers

Chains are obviously exposed and external lubrication will attract grit and accelerate the wear. An enclosed chaincase like on old MZs and CG125s is best, but has long been unfashionable. Modern o-ring chains actually cope well with minimal oiling, but still benefit from a **daily lube** to oil the chain-to-sprocket surfaces. Chain lube **aerosols** are easy to use but are bulky, relatively expensive, will run out and may not be available on the road. A cheaper but labour-intensive alternative is a small bottle of thick gearbox oil applied along the inside of the rollers with a toothbrush. For the chain it's like sipping an ice cold beer in Alex and will help stop corrosion which could wreck the o-rings.

After too many days of diligently doing that, you'll dearly wish you had an **automatic chain oiler** – they're well suited to bikes without a centre stand where properly spraying a chain is awkward. Scott Oilers are well known but some models go out of their way to complicate a simple procedure. Loobman's at the other end of the scale but doesn't differ greatly from something you could make yourself. Like other units, it requires manually turning on once in a while which can equate to 'forgetting'. The OSCO unit falls somewhere in between: with the reservoir in arm's reach unscrew and lift the plunger to give the chain a shot as and when. But that still requires remembering.

A unit that's out of the way, automatically oils on the move, stops at rest but doesn't get caught up with the bike's electrics or induction vacuum is ideal and I've found **Tutoro** ticks all these boxes. Delivery is activated by a motion-sensitive weight in the reservoir which cuts the flow when at rest. A knob

Left: Out of the way Tutoro auto oiler: fit it and forget it between top ups. Inset: sprocket ruined by a cheap chain and Libyan sands. Use well-known brands and *steel* sprockets. **Right**: OSCO (One Second Chain Oiler) requires manually delivering a shot of oil once in a while.

adjusts the flow rate – back off in warm places when the oil's viscosity drops. In sandy conditions you might want to close off the flow altogether. Get the twin-nozzle feed option and carry a spare. The reservoir lasts about 2500 miles using Tutoro's oil which is nice tacky stuff; you'll want to make it last before resorting to thick truck oil. It can be vulnerable to a carelessly swung leg or debris kicked up by the tyres so think carefully where you mount it. Tucked in between frame rails as close to the rear sprocket is best.

Sprockets

Good quality **steel sprockets** are the best way to get long service life from an o-ring chain. Avoid lighter alloy versions which are for gram-saving racers – they won't last no matter how 'hardened' they say they are. And beware of buying obscure chainkits with inferior steel sprockets for the same reasons. **Original equipment** (OE) sprockets matched up with a quality chain will last at least 10,000 miles on a 650 – double that with daily oiling or a chain oiler. Both items are well worth the extra expense for a longer service life.

Final drive ratio

The good thing with chains is you can easily alter the final drive ratio. Road bikes are often too highly geared, good on the open highway, less so when stuck with a full load in the mud on the Rhotang Pass where the tall first gear forces you to slip the clutch – not good, especially with powerful bikes like 690 KTMs. A good way to check is see what speed your bike does trickling along in first at tickover. Anything over five mph will be on the high side. On some bikes **swapping the front sprocket** for at least one-tooth smaller can take as little as ten minutes (don't go smaller than twelve teeth as it's too acute a turn for the chain). Doing this you'll gain better control at walking pace without slipping the clutch, as well as better response from the lower gears when you most need it, though rpm will climb at cruising speeds.

Smaller sprocket fitted for gnarly ops.

BIKE CHOICE & PREPARATION

CARRYING EXTRA FUEL

Without fuel you're going nowhere but first ask yourself, does your motorcycle really need what is usually the considerable expense of a **larger tank?** There are few places in the world where a fuel range of more than 300km or nearly 200 miles is needed on a sealed highway, and that translates to just 15 litres or just under 4 US gallons if riding at **20kpl** (57 mpg; 47 mpg US or 5ltr/100km; conversion table on p331). In fact that figure's pretty conservative when you think of today's fuel-injected bikes and was close to the lowest I recorded on an XT660Z a few years back. The *average* over 5000 miles was 35% higher and all my travel bikes since: F650GS; XCountry; CRF250L and CB500X have been more economical. So a range of about **400km or 250 miles** should see you through when a remote station is out of fuel, and that adds up to a need for just 20 litres or 5.3 USg.

Besides the expense (some special oversized BMW tanks can cost over €2000), think about the extra weight in proportion to your bike's size. On *Desert Riders* we used '40'-litre XR600 tanks for our XR-Ls but they made the bikes very top-heavy in some off-road situations even though we actually needed that range and a whole lot more. Far better of course to have a bike which uses very little fuel in the first place. The first fill up on my Honda CB500X returned 92mpg (32.5kpl) – that adds up to a potential range of 350 miles or 550 kilometres on the 17.5 litre tank.

That said, buying any bike with a good-sized OE tank is one reason why KLRs, V-Stroms and GS-As are so popular; it's one less thing you have to buy, and on the odd occasion where you might need extra range, a plastic fuel can or bladder will see you through, and weigh next to nothing at other times. There's another time where you might want to fill up a huge tank and that's when crossing from somewhere like Venezuela to Brazil or from Iran to Turkey. In these neighbouring countries the price of fuel has among the biggest disparity in the world, costing up to ten times more. In a diesel truck it may be worth filling an oil drum – I've done that myself on occasions – but on a bike the savings are not so spectacular.

Big plastic tanks

Up to 25 litres is ideal up front. Laws have changed and so bikes now come with **plastic tanks** which combine the best in strength, lightness and durability while being rust-free and resistant to vibration. If necessary they're easily repairable with glue. Acerbis have made replacement plastic tanks for years, mostly to adapt dirt bikes into desert racers, though the range includes 22 and 25-litre tanks for 650 DRs and XR-Ls. IMS, Clarke and Safari in Australia do the same with a 38-litre IMS tank for the KLR costing $550 and an 11.7L for a CRF250L for about half that. Safari do a 32-litre for KLRs and the KTM 690 pictured, and now even cover 800cc Triumph Tigers with a 30-litre job.

Supplementary tanks or containers

There's something to be said about not having the most gigantic tank you can get your hands on. When you're reluctantly forced to top up your 38-litre tank with rancid donkey piss on the Pamir Highway just to be on the safe side, you risk contaminating your entire fuel system and paying the price when, for example, the fuel pump has a cardiac arrest. With a normal-sized tank and

Left: A 14-litre Safari front tank on a KTM 690 is a good place for extra weight.
Right: At a fraction of the cost this Aprilla Pegaso has a well-protected 10-litre jerry on each side.

say, a potential to stash ten litres on the side, you can put the donkey fuel in there and possibly get away with not using it. Compartmentalising fuel is a good idea and can be much cheaper to do.

It's now less unusual for bikes to have **underseat tanks**. They lower the centre of gravity but as you can imagine, enlarging them is awkward. BMW's G650GS single (14L) and the standard 800cc twins (16L) do it this way but will still give you 300km; a KTM690's 12-litre rear tank is good for more like 250km. **Supplementary tanks** or storage is a solution.

Metal jerricans were the old way of doing it. The 20-litre ones are too bulky for a bike but the slim 10 or 5s make robust containers that can be fitted on either side of the engine (as above), keeping the weight central and making handy crumple zones. Tough, **plastic fuel cans** are even cheaper but tend to be boxy to cope with expansion pressures. On a bike slim is best. Rotopax cans start at 3.8 litres, FuelFriends from Germany go up to 1.5 litres. Rotopax are 'the look' and have a neat system for secure mounting but are only around sixty per cent efficient for the space they take compared to a regular can.

Fuel bladders are another way of doing it. They take up less space when not in use but can be awkward to lash down unless there's room in your luggage, especially if they're over ten litres. In Europe you can buy a TUV-approved disposable 5-litre Jerri-Flex **fuel bag** for €10 which could be handy for a one-off long stage, but aren't endlessly reusable. The last resort are regular plastic drinks bottles you're quite likely to find by the roadside. Most

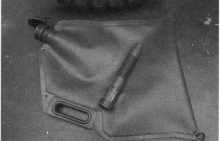

Left: The small 3.8-litre Rotopax takes a lot of space for its volume. **Right**: a similarly rugged 7-litre bladder from Liquid Containment. Cap seals can fall out, carry spares.

BIKE CHOICE & PREPARATION

Keep visual tabs on your **throttle's position**, and so fuel consumption with an index mark on the throttle housing and three on the twist grip: shut, halfway and wide open, as above.

useful are two-litre ones which held something fizzy as they're more robust than regular still PET water bottles. With any sealed petrol container, heat and shaking will create pressure like a fizzy drink; this is why fuel tanks have breathers. That's undesirable when hammering down a corrugated backroad to Persepolis in July, as some plastics become softened by petrol, so decant that unsafe fuel into your main tank before the container disintegrates and decants itself all over your hot silencer. It could happen in a matter of hours.

Even with a proper fuel bladder, resist the temptation to fill it right up. An **air gap** allows for fuel expansion and lessens the pressure on seams and seals. There's not much you can do about shaking on a rough track, but keeping a fuel bladder or a temporary container out of direct sunlight or draped in a wet rag will slow heat build up. Remember too, that assuming the seal has held, fuel may be under pressure when you come to opening any sealed fuel container, so it's not the time to have a roll-up drooping from your lower lip.

ENGINE PROTECTION

Even if you're planning a road ride, protecting your bike's vulnerable underside from tumbles, kicked-up rocks and bottoming-out is a good idea. These days many adventure-styled bikes feature what look like sump guards but few are up to the job. They're either too small or at worst are made from brittle alloy-coloured plastic. The good thing is, because this is such a vital accessory in terms of looks as well as function, there are plenty of aftermarket fabricators out there ready to fill your needs with a **plate of 4mm alloy or 2mm steel**. If not, then it's an easy home fabrication job or modifying a plate from another bike. These plates aren't only protecting what's under the engine but possibly also exposed suspension linkages, oil filters, water pumps and so on. Make sure yours is the width of the engine including coming up the sides, and covers possible frontal

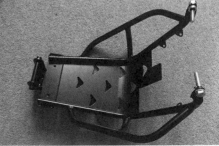

Left: Only a week old and already you can see how this ally plate has paid off on a TTR250.
Right: Steel plate and bars from Rally Raid Products. Additional alloy panels fill the gaps.

Left: Carry a tube of Chemical Metal hardening putty or, better still, two-part JB Weld. Right: Engine bars – one less thing to worry about when the inevitable happens; good for lashing, too.

impacts. The underside of the engine certainly needs protection – a suspension-bottoming bounce onto an inauspiciously protruding rock can easily punch a hole – a tricky repair in the vertically split crankcase of a typical Japanese bike. In the field I've fixed small cracks with Chemical Metal or JB Weld hardening paste – it's worth carrying some with you.

Engine crash bars like the well-supported bar above right is more weight and expense but means you'll know the fragile alloy engine casings – and even foot control levers – need not get mashed in a crash. They also make excellent attachment points or front racks (see photo, p67), or something to grab as you haul your bike out of a trench. On the back your baggage can also act as bike protection, but thin metal boxes can become irreparably deformed.

Next, fit some proper **hand and lever protectors** – a broken lever mount can ruin your day. Again don't rely on OE plastic items which can be little more than unsupported wind deflectors. Large plastic cowlings molded onto thick alloy bars which clamp solidly to your handlebars are what's needed – my Barkbuster Storms (below left) are now on their fourth bike. Without such protection, keep your lever mounts a little loose on the bars; that way the mounts may turn on the 'bar and spare the lever when the bike falls.

With the whole CNC craze **radiators guards** have become fashionable add-ons. Radiator fans are vulnerable for sure, but I suspect some of these guards also limit airflow at low speeds. Whether they're designed that way or not, I'd space such guards at least an inch in front of the radiator fins.

BIKE CHOICE & PREPARATION

Left: Lever and hand protectors keep the rain off too. You may need to saw the lever ends off.
Right: radiator guards look cool but space forward for good air flow and easier fin clearing.

SEATS AND SCREENS

One of the biggest complaints riders have about their bikes is that seats which – besides being too high for shorter riders – become uncomfortable after just a couple of hours. We've all been there; shuffling from one cheek to the other, trying to relieve the pain and stimulate circulation. Narrow trail bike seats are notorious in this respect and pukka enduro bikes even worse – one reason they're not suited to long travels.

Regular saddles are hit and miss because everyone's different and what might suit one will be agony for another. Up to a point your butt can adapt over several weeks, and some days might be worse than others. The key – just like in any sedentary scenario – is not to just sit there for hours, even if you have the range. Provided it won't set your bike off into a wobble, slow down and stand up occasionally or **get off every two hours** and do some stretching.

AG BIKES FOR OVERLAND – MILKING THE POTENTIAL

Although emissions regs may be finally catching up with these motorcycle fossils, in South Africa, Australasia and a few other markets, you might still be able to buy a crude Japanese 'ag' or 'agricultural' bike: functional, no-frills farmers' hacks of around 200cc and featuring the white heat of 1970s technology.

Your average farmer's sled is a parts bin special not unlike the BMW Basic/Kalahari (itself a bit 'ag' some might say). Old production lines have been quite literally farmed out to overseas factories where labour is cheap so that the development of next year's crotch rocket is not disturbed.

The Honda **CTX 200 Bushlander** is one good example, costing 35,000 SA rand or AUD5200. For that you get what looks like an old XR200 with electric start and a back-up kick. They don't waste alloy on ag bikes; rims and swingarm, bars and racks are strictly ferrous for extra ballast.

Crude handlebar lever protectors come as standard, part of a frontal rack which is matched by a similar 'sheep rack' on the back. There are also rudimentary engine protection bars and a tinny bashplate; tyres are 18- and 21 inchers. Along with the 136kg (330lbs) weight, oversized 'mudshrouds' and 9:1 compression help keep the speed down, and what other bike comes with a clutch lock for those sudden stops and *two* side stands: add two rocks and you got a centre stand!

Downsides include the tiny 7.8-litre tank with a range of 200km. Cruising speeds are in the Enfield Bullet category but with fewer roadside repairs. More on p46.

© WWW.WHEREISJAMES.COM

Yamaha produce the similar **AG 200E** (electric/kick, 12-litres, all-drum, enclosed chain, 127kg/280lbs wet. Suzuki's 200cc **Trojan** (below) weighs the same but has a 13-litre tank, front disc and an oil cooler.

All of these bikes make rugged, low maintenance, low expectation crash-proof rides suited to a slow pace for places like Indochina, Central Africa, the Darien Gap or other low-speed, short-range, low altitude environments where transportation on or along rivers will be an option.

Left: Corbin aftermarket saddle. Actually not so plush but wide enough.
Right: Selle Valle seat on a 690. Suede looks good but on the narrow side.

Improving your saddle

Traditionally, what feels soft and compliant in the showroom may not reflect your mood at the end of a 400-mile day, especially in the more **upright** seating stance of a typical travel bike which transfers the weight directly down the spine. It's common to assume that this discomfort is caused by a saddle being too hard but it's usually foam that's **too soft** or has lost its springiness so you sink straight down to the seat base. I distinctly remember sensing this later transition on a 2000-mile ride on an XCountry with only about 9000 miles on the clock at the time. The factory foam went, never to return, like a tyre slowly going flat. Most seats use ordinary open cell polyurethane foam that'll do the job for weekend burn ups to the bikers' cafe, less well for a heavier rider on a long, rough ride. Problem is, it's not something you can find out without first doing the miles. Seats are like tyres: opinions vary and everyone has them.

    Too narrow is a more obvious cause of discomfort. After all would you expect to spend a day at work sitting on an 8-inch wide piece of vinyl-covered foam? A bike intended for off road use requires you to stand up and grip the tank/seat area with your knees for stability so saddles have to be narrow. Another limitation here is that for shorter riders a **wide seat** can be as bad as too tall in terms of reaching the ground. Harley can get away with a saddle as wide as the Dakota prairie because the height is low enough to step over.

    Lack of all-round support can be another reason, exemplified by the popularity for capacious bucket seats in the US. Intuitively this looks plausible:

Left: Roadside emergency foam. I could not face the F650GS ride home without it.
Right: Why settle for sheepskin when you can have a bear rug? Food chain oneupmanship.

humans aren't made of Lego so **spreading the load** over an anatomically con-
toured perch makes sense, but such a seat sure looks odd on a KTM 990 with
TKC 80s. Some believe a flat seat which allows you to move around is better.

It's said the **breathability** of the seat cover comes into it too, reducing heat
and sweatiness. Clearly, sitting all day on an impermeable vinyl cushion does-
n't add up; the only reason a bike seat is made of vinyl is to stop the foam
inside getting soaked in the rain. But online blurb on breathable seat covers
isn't so convincing, or at least breathability is just one element in seat comfort.
Breathable seat covers with a Gore-tex-like membrane are the latest add-on for
your big adventure tourer and cost from $600. Where will it end?

What you're wearing also has a bearing. I find leather trousers extend my
in-saddle duration, though I doubt they're especially breathable, just less
slidey which may mean less friction. Padded **cycling shorts** are said to work
too. It all just goes to show that whatever works for you is your answer to day-
long comfort. Two of the least uncomfortable seats I've used were on a Suzuki
GS500 and also an XT660Z which had its fair share of detractors.

Airseats, sheepskins and gel pads

The good thing is a seat's foam, profile and covering can all be modified by
you or a motorcycle seat specialist. Most people seek to add firmness and
width and either reduce any step or, less easily, dish the seat anatomically.

Height permitting, adding something to the original saddle is the simplest
way of reducing discomfort. Strap-on Airhawk seat cushions are well known
and inexpensive, using air's compressibility in individual air cells. As with an
air-bed, you want to inflate it just enough to lift you, any more and you'll wobble around like an electrocuted Space Hopper which doesn't feel safe at all.

16,000 MILES ON A YAMAHA TTR250

I'm 5' 4" so the seat heights and fully-loaded
weights of the traditional overlanding
machines can be intimidating. I used a XT225
Serow for my ride from Alaska to Argentina;
a sturdy little trail bike but it did suffer at the
higher altitudes. A few years later for
London to Cape Town I decided I was ready
to step up to a Yamaha TTR250.

TTR Good

The TTR was taller than the Serow so I fitted
a Kuba lowering link but because it wasn't a
UK grey import there were more parts like
bash plates and tanks available. My TTR took
a beating crossing the Sahara and the
wrecked roads of the Congo and Angola but
I didn't have a single mechanical problem
except dust in the switches.

I changed the oil every 2000 miles and
washed the air filter, but that was about it.
On departure I replaced the chainset, cables,
bearings and brake pads with original
Yamaha parts and I'm sure this helped the
bike's reliability. The 22-litre tank was good
for up to 400 miles, depending on the terrain.
I didn't even adjust the chain until the day
before Cape Town!

In 2013 another secondhand TTR took
me over three thousand miles around Iran
where it had plenty of oomph to dodge what
they call driving out there, was light enough
to pick up and could cruise at 60mph.

TTR Bad

The worst thing about my TTR250 was the
seat. I had my seat remodelled by
www.motorbike-seats.co.uk then added the
trusty sheepskin.

The 250cc engine was mostly fine; a couple of times I had to push in deep sand.
Because I had lowered the suspension, back
in the UK I noticed all that bashing up had
worn away the front of the swingarm.
Another swingarm on ebay was £150.

LOIS PRYCE
Lois' TTR book: *Red Tape and White Knuckles*

A little springiness and air circulation is also the idea behind a **sheepskin** though they'll get soaked in the rain and tend to lose their springiness after while. It's hard to think how a **gel pad** can improve a motorcycle saddle, but different solutions suit different people. Gel doesn't compress like open-cell foam or air, it merely displaces, rather like human tissue. But just because it resembles human tissue (as some gel pads boast) that doesn't mean it's a comfortable medium for

Airhawk seat pad – easy way to improve comfort but adds height and can wobble.

sitting on, unless you find sitting on other people agreeable. Gel also tends to retain heat rather than disperse it as internal foam, wool or air pads can do.

'Bottom' line, no matter what you ride you'll be doing a lot of it for weeks at a time, and even if most overlanders won't be engaged in 1000-mile day Iron-Butt epics, addressing the age-old motorcyclist's complaint of saddle soreness is crucial. The dynamic elements of the bike you choose – power, braking, handling and looks – will appeal to a broad range of users, but a seat can't be expected to do this. Because comfort is such a subjective matter only a few guidelines and principles have been given here. If you think you need a better seat, don't hold back from investing in something you'll depend on every second of your ride. As mentioned, addressing your **comfort is important** because once you're fatigued through discomfort or even in pain you're much more prone to making mistakes or can be slower to react to hazards.

SIT ON THIS

Over the years I've made ten saddles for my TTRs, from chopping bits out to totally remodelling the base, foam and cover. I find half-inch rolls of open-cell upholstery foam or Millets camp mats glued in layers work well for building up a shape. Then surform smooth and add denser closed-cell roll mat ('karrimat') for the sides. Using karrimat alone makes for a firm seat – these days I add a softer layer on top. For the cover I make a paper pattern then sew using breathable polyester micro fibre, not just patterned vinyl. Looks like cheaper PVC but much less sweaty – there's a reason rally bikes use suede saddles. Tools: staple gun, surform, gaffer tape, scissors, screw driver, bread knife, glue, heavy duty sewing machine.

ROBIN WEBB

Windshields

However small or slow your bike, consider fitting some sort of windshield or improving what your bike might already have. With city riding or commuting such protection has little effect, but out on the open road all day, the relief from the wind pressure at anything over 80 kph will greatly reduce fatigue, just as long as it does so without causing unwanted turbulence.

Most riders fit screens that are too high to work well at speed; there'll always be some turbulence behind the lip, what you don't want is for your helmet to be in that zone. Getting this right can be tricky which is why some riders are happiest replacing a factory-fitted screen.

Avoid trying to replicate a car-like windscreen which measures up higher than your head – some aftermarket screens like this come with a high-speed safety warning. Something that's just a foot high and as wide clamped to the 'bars can be adequate and will help reduce the wind blast and effects of pelting rain against your jacket. All you need to do is adjust it just right. That can take some experimentation.

If your bike has no frontal protection, the simplest windshield **clamps to the handlebars** with as few as two struts and as much angle variation as the surrounding parts allow. Some assume bar-mounted screens can cause instability; that may be so on a supercharged XJR13 lapping the Nürburgring, but the 15-inch high Slip Stream Spitfire (below left) worked fine on my more modest CRF250L and later XCountry at speeds of up to 80. Though I never made use of it, its quick release facility can help on hot, slow days or when off road. One flaw with some bar-mounted windshields is they can crack when the bike falls and bars bend. Rubber grommets in the screen and elsewhere in the mounting system can reduce the chances of this, as can fitting tougher motocross handlebars or mounting close to- or off the bar clamps.

Your next option is **replacing the fixed OE screen** on your bike, usually for something taller or better still, adjustable. Be wary of fellow owners claiming they found so-and-so aftermarket screen to be as tranquil as a sunny afternoon back in the womb. Just as with seats, what works for one rider, even the same size, may not work for you.

There's a certain need to accept that on a motorcycle you can't expect to feel entirely cocooned from the passing wind rush and noise, and your type of clothing as well as modern helmets with clever air vents can all contribute to

Screens – they don't have to be anything flash, especially at typical AMZ speeds.
On the **left** a dinky $80 Slip Stream Spitfire on a CRF. **Right**: home improved screen on a KLR.

Left: Touratech's universal clip-on spoiler adds height. **Right**: for the same price a Palmer Products windshield adapter fits between screen and mounts to give three height and three angle positions, plus whatever your bike's mounts might provide. Knobs enable tool-less adjustment.

noise and buffeting. However, you can certainly hope that a screen will appear to lift the air stream just over your helmet at cruising speed without your head bobbing around like a ping pong ball on a jet of water. That's quite a tall order with any fixed screen which is why **adjustability** is more useful than outright height. From the factory, screen adjustability's only beginning to become an option on non top-of-the-range bikes and is often just 'high' and 'low' but it's handy not only for different sizes of rider but also for different types of riding: you may like a highway rain-cruising position and a lower one giving better visibility or less distraction when off road.

MRA from Germany produce Vario screens with a wide range of adjustability and in the US Madstad do the same. Both have found favour with many riders while on my CB-X which had 'high' and 'low' mounts, I thought my screen was good enough but angled too far back. The Palmer Products adjustable mount (above right, similar to the Madstad) met my needs.

MRA also do an 'air deflector' for the top of their screens to 'layer' and help lift the air rushing over the lip. It's common now to see fitted screens separated a little from the surrounding fairing (below right) so as to allow air to flow under the screen and reduce the pressure imbalance which otherwise forms behind the screen and which causes turbulence. The thing to remember is you need to experiment to find what suits you and that can happen quicker and cost less if you buy something with a good range of adjustability.

BIKE CHOICE & PREPARATION

Left: Widely adjustable Madstad screen clamps off bar mounts but owner concurred: too much in-your-face metal. **Right**: airflow passing *under* an Explorer's screen helps reduce turbulence.

Auxiliary spots may be written off as bling but have uses for day-riding and back-ups.

LIGHTING

Never ride at night they say, and that's good advice on the back roads of the AMZ (more on p124) until you need to, even for just a couple of hours and for whatever compelling reason.

Modern motorcycle lighting has improved massively over the years, though you may not think so hopping off a £15,000 shaft-drive landship onto a Binqi 125 Splatblast.

In the old days it was the reflector and glass lens area where aftermarket improvements could be made. Recently the advent of high output HiD (high intensity discharge) and until recently slightly inferior LED (light-emitting diode) bulbs have transformed illumination while also significantly reducing the power draw on your bike's generating system. When you factor in the much longer bulb life, this truly does appear to be a win-win-win situation: brighter lights that last ages and reduce the chance of a flat battery when darkness sees things like heated grips and vests draw on the battery.

It's not all about brightness

The bling aspect of strapping a bank of spots across your rig is old news for fourwheelers and today the range of nifty little spots that can stun a bat back into the Stone Age has not been overlooked by members of the adventure motorcycling community. They're now as much a part of the look as a Arai X lid. It's easy to get worked up over thousands of claimed lumens (which does have its uses as a day-riding light) but if you're looking to get beyond the 'look', first ask yourself does your bike actually need a better headlight. Many riders are now choosing to simply replace conventional incandescent (filament) bulbs with an **LED bulb**. Little extra wiring and no extra bracketry required. If one's not available for your bike it'll have to be **auxiliary lights** which do have a useful **redundancy** element should your main light gets smashed in.

I never got round to fitting mine, but was told the narrow beam Vision X unit (pictured) is a good choice: durable, easy to fit and, unlike a Rigid

Vision X 2000-lumen lazer mounted under the clocks. Similar Chinese kits on ebay.

Industries unit I tried once, with cable lengths and switches suited to bike mounting, not a fourbie's roofrack. Set them up for a brighter beam pattern as far ahead as possible; illuminating just ahead of your wheel has little value.

Don't forget, day or night it's as much about **being seen** as not riding off a cliff, as well as riding to suit the conditions, no matter how bright your lights. Hi-viz vests and LED rears all help among inattentive traffic unused to big bike speeds.

SUSPENSION

Your average bike comes with average suspension that's fine on smooth roads at steady speeds – push it in terms of speed, surface or payload and it all goes Pete Tong. At its most basic there'll be no adjustment on the forks and only spring preload adjustment on the back. Higher end adv bikes like KTMs and the big GSs score over their Japanese equivalents because as much attention is paid to suspension as power delivery. Riding such a bike can be a revelation, especially off road where it's all put to the test.

Full adjustment can mean ride height (shock length) and damping rates which the latest bikes do electronically or from the 'bars. It may also include rebound damping plus high- and low-speed compression damping too. Multiply those variables, front and rear, by changes in temperature, surface, payload and speed and the set up gets mind boggling. But when it's right, you'll know; the confidence born of composure and control can be magical.

Generally, on a travel bike you're buying the motor while getting the suspension, because suspension is easier to improve than an engine. With online forum know-how it's not so hard to track down a more sophisticated used OE shock that may fit in place of your basic units (for example: R1 shocks on a Versys, V-Strom on GS500). With the front, fitting a **complete front end** from a dual sport or dirt bike (as below) is easier. Just remember: you're looking for better suspension not simply more travel.

The key is better quality travel, not more travel

Start by setting up your rear preload to give **35-50mm of sag** over the rear spindle with you on then off the loaded bike with shock fully extended (you may need assistance to do this). Where present, adjust the damping one or two clicks at a time to find the sweet spot that's neither harsh nor bouncy – or better still, let a suspension specialist sort it out. Hard-working shocks and fork seals can wear out so carry spares or have them ready to send out.

If you have the cash then the big names include Hyperpro, Ohlins, Progressive, Wilbur, WP (now KTM) and Tractive (WP breakaway). Most will do **fork springs** too. On both ends **progressive** springs or damping respond better to small movements but resist bottoming out. Otherwise, a shock refurb' (new seals, oil, maybe revalve and re-gas plus **firmer springs** might do it. With a set of front and rear Hyperpros that's about £250 with oil.

Left: Adjustable Showa DRZ400S forks – great budget front-end makeover once you sort the steering head. **Right**: Hyperpro 461 had every adjustment but for me the best thing was the easy-to-use hydraulic preload knob; no more skinned knuckles and slippy C-spanners.

WHEELS

Motorcycles wheels are either spoked 'wire' wheels or one-piece – these days most often cast from aluminium or made from some fancy space shuttle composite. With any wheeled vehicle the mass of its wheels has a disproportionate effect on acceleration: the lighter the wheel (and tyre/tube for that matter) the faster the machine accelerates and brakes.

With motorcycle publications comparing acceleration times down to the nearest nano-second, you can see why sports bikes have the lightest possible wheel, brake and tyre combinations. 'Unsprung weight' – the part of the wheel and suspension that moves up and down – is another motivation for light wheel assemblies on all types of performance-oriented bikes. If you're logging lap times on your Panigale you'll want a set of BST carbons for around £2,287 including tax to save a couple of kilos. If you're on a multi-day rally you'll be running heavy-duty spoked rims which flex a little and so absorb the impacts of hard off-roading without cracking.

Spoked or one-piece wheels

So where does that leave the overland adventurer faced with bikes shod with spoked or 'cast' wheels and a mixture of road surfaces from pristine tarmac to rock-strewn trails? As is so often the case the wheels on your bike are defined by image and price – 'intended use' matters only at the extremes: you'll never see a motocrosser with cast wheels nor (these days) a superbike with spokes. BMW's standard GS1200 comes with cast wheels while the 'Adventure' version has spokes. Most Japanese adventure-style bikes come with cast alloy wheels but, apart from their 'entry level' 1050, the more dirt-sport oriented KTM V-twins all have spokes, so does the new Honda Africa Twin. It's the same with BMW GS700 and 800s, Triumph Tiger XCs, Husqvarna's short-lived Terra and Strada 650s. 'Street' models runs cast wheels including a 19-inch front; the hardcore one will have spokes with a 21-inch front and cost up

Left: Suzuki GS500's 17-inch cast wheels replaced with identical 19-inch SM Pro rims on DR650 hubs. The rationale: a single spare fits both ends, and in Asia sourcing a 19-inch replacement would be easier. **Right**: Bruce Smart's GSXR: 74,000 miles RTW on 17-inch alloys.

to 20% more. So ironically, cast wheels have now become a low-spec option on big adv bikes because spokes have come to signify 'off road' and therefore 'adventuresome' which (like black), obviously costs more.

A few myths about spoked wheels: they're not necessarily **lighter** than cast. The 19-inch alloy front wheel of a V-Strom 1000 weighs just 4.1kg, only 600 grams more than the two discs clamped either side, and this is not a high-spec machine in the GS or KTM category.

Spoked tubeless wheels on a GSA12. Big KTMs have similar wheels.

And the much vaunted '**repairability**' of spoked wheels is exaggerated and can as easily be described as 'need for maintenance'. If you're unlucky enough to have a Peruvian bus run over your spoked rim, finding a replacement, let alone having the skill to lace it all back together correctly will be no easier than replacing a similarly mangled cast wheel (most probably from a breakers outside the AMZ).

In the early days cast wheels were brittle or soft or crack-prone and some mag wheels on early Ducatis were said to have such a high magnesium content they could burst into flames if scrapped along a kerb. Although occasional problems with alloy wheel components still occur (as BMW's 2015 recall of 300,000 bikes proved), one-piece wheels themselves are much better than they used to be and are well suited to mainstream overlanding.

It's said you can't knock a dent out of a one-piece wheel's rim because alloy weakens on bending much sooner than steel. On a cast wheel this **rim-dent** repairability becomes more of an issue because nowadays one-piece wheels all run tubeless tyres, and as you'll read over the page, that's a good thing. For overlanding the benefits of tubeless tyres are far greater than the risks of denting a cast wheel's rim to the point where the tubeless tyre's seal is compromised. Faced with that problem in the middle of nowhere, a judicious whack with well padded rock will restore normal service – and if that doesn't work, see p90.

Once a bike gets saddled with an overlanding load some rims may not be up to the heavy beating from potholed roads and corrugated tracks. Rear wheels carry maximum loads so are prone to loose or broken spokes or rim dents. It's one reason to keep tyre pressures on the high side and let good quality suspension take up the slack. Carry a **spoke key** and check tension after rough stages: tap each spoke to get a clear 'ding'. The more frequently you do this, the less likely a wire rim gets too far out of true (more on p182).

Cast or wire, many motorcycles are produced with cheap components to hook you with a low purchase price. Something like the Triumph Bonneville series is a good example; a great-looking bike that's fine for the intended use. Should you choose to take it or a similar machine on an adventure, consider **heavy-duty spokes** or better still, upgrade to quality rims from SM Pro, Excel or DID. The benefit of doing this is the difference between having to check your standard wheels regularly or largely ignoring the strengthened items.

Wheel sizes

Just about all full-sized bikes have rear wheels 17 or 18 inches in diameter with fronts in 17, 18, 19 or 21 inches. Trail bikes traditionally had 18/21s because a bigger diameter wheel gives more ground clearance and the large and narrow front both flattens out irregularities and cuts through loose dirt better. On road bikes quick steering is more valued so small, wide 17s have long been the norm at both ends. But on any wheel the **tyres' tread pattern** will have a greater bearing on how well a machine grips on different surfaces, while the wheel size will determine what's **available locally** to fit your bike. On a long trip this is important, especially on a powerful, heavy bike which may get through a rear tyre in less than 5000 miles.

Most modern road bikes over 600cc run **17-inch wheels** front and back. Some in the adventure category like V-Stroms, Triumph 800XRs and BMW GS700s and all 'non-R' KTM Vees have a 19 up front to look the part or for the 'bigger rolls over bump better' reason. On the road 17s work best because the reduced centrifugal force from the small diameter makes flicking through bends easier. The thing is, out in the world most poor locals don't ride ZZR1100s in full leathers, they ride four-up on handed-down versions of Honda's CG125 or similar which run skinny 18 or even 19-inch tyres. It's changing now as larger capacity leisure bike production expands in the formerly 'workhorse' markets of the developing world, but 17-inch tyres can still be hard to come by or expensive to buy in outback Asia, Africa and the poorer Andean countries. That is why you see round-the-worlders as pictured on p84 setting forth with a spare tyre slung over the bike.

Generation 2 Versys: 'a road bike with adventure styling'. Where have you heard that before? Seventeen-inch front 'drops in' predictably on the road but can be a handful on loose surfaces.

Changing wheel sizes

Changing 17-inch cast wheels for 18s or 19s (as on the GS500 pictured earlier) can be quite an expensive and complicated undertaking. If it's that important you might be better buying a bike with such wheels in the first place – but we bikers do like to mix it up. Spoked wheel sizes are much more easily modified because all you're doing is lacing on a bigger rim to the original hub with the critical suspension and brake rotor clearances all unchanged. If you're going down that road then (as mentioned on p77) fitting an entire front end (triple clamps, forks, brakes and wheel) from a donor bike with a usually bigger wheel (again, as on the DR650-fronted GS on the previous page) can be less aggro than finding a bigger cast wheel to fit your forks, although a front 19-inch DL1000 cast wheel will fit onto a Versys as pictured left (once you skim 5mm off the Suzuki's rotors).

You're unlikely to notice the difference in a 17- or 18-inch wheel on the back but there's no doubt that at the sharp end size makes a difference. On the dirt a 17-inch front will feel less secure (tyre tread notwithstanding), but so will a wandering 21-inch knobbly once doing a ton on your CRF1000L. It's fair to assume the bigger your bike the heavier – and so less agile – it'll be on the dirt giving you fewer chances to push it to the limits there. On bikes unable to sustain three-figure speeds, 21s are seen as less of a drawback on the road and certainly help the bike in the dirt.

Overall then, for a bigger adv bike a **nineteen-inch front** is a good all-road **compromise** which is why you'll see 19s on the big bikes listed earlier. If you're running tubes there's also the benefit that, especially if you have an 18 on the back, you can get away with one size of inner tube for both wheels.

Thirty-five years earlier, my first travel bike: an XT500 with a RM370 front end and a steel 19-inch rim (alloy hadn't been invented back then). It got me there.

TYRES

No other item gets prospective adventure riders in such a lather. And quite right too because rain or shine, your tyres are out there on the front line, rolling over whatever surface while supporting 250-500kg and responding to your inputs to speed up, slow down or turn. We ask a lot of our tyres because the consequence of them not performing when it comes to traction, longevity and durability can be serious, and yet choices can often be governed by price and looks – and once on the road, by whatever fits.

We're supposed to be on an adventure which by definition includes unpredictability – not least on the highway infrastructure of the AMZ. You won't always be gliding along pristine, autobahns lined with Armco from one franchised service area to the next. Instead, at times you'll be darting for the edge of the road to dodge brain-out drivers on crumbling 'national' highways awash with monsoon deluges or windblown sand or jumpy livestock. But one day on your big adventure you'll come to a junction: right leads directly to your destination via the highway, left is a dirt road excursion through the mountains. Even if it's a shorter distance it may well take you longer, but saving time is not always what the ride is about. Along that road you may come to a breathtaking panorama, spend the night in a friendly village that rarely sees tourists, or camp overnight in total solitude under the shooting stars. You can do this on a highway too, but the chances of having memorable adventures are greatly increased by taking the road less travelled. It'll be a shame to think 'Looks interesting but with these tyres I won't risk it'.

Choosing tyres

Unless you set off on a real lemon, chances are **punctures** will be your most common breakdown; your tyre's **tread** pattern will be the most likely reason for coming off; and finding **replacements** will be the most frequent service item. That's why tyres get all those forum inches. Choosing the right tyre won't have you fiddling from the rooftops or singing in the rain, but buying a sub-optimal tyre could be galling for all the above reasons.

At the outset do yourself a favour by choosing an established quality brand: for motorcycles this adds up to tyres made by Avon, Bridgestone, Continental, Dunlop, Metzeler, Michelin and Pirelli, and lately less established brands like Heidenau, Mefo Sport, Mitas and Shinko. None of them make bad tyres, but any could be inappropriately fitted, used or maintained. The whole Bridgestone 'Death Wing' was an online urban myth – or if it wasn't it could have been applied to any number of other OE tyres. In the UK there are over twenty types of 'Trail Wings'. The Heidenau K60 Scout was another tyre that got people worked up – one rider blamed his K60 for dumping him at 115kph in the rain on an oily Guatemalan road. Then there were the deadly cracks in similarly long-lasting Mitas E07s, and an E09 that exploded into a ball of flames and destroyed a village in Laos. Some are even convinced Continental vary tread compounds for different markets because reported user wear rates are so inconsistent. It's the way it is with online tyre talk.

For motorcycle overlanding, tyre choice is a balance between **street-oriented tyres** offering long wear, secure road manners but poor grip on loose surfaces. Or more **dirt-biased road legal tyres** with a more aggressive tread

TYRE SPEED RATINGS (LETTERS) AND LOAD INDEX CODES (NUMBERS)

Speed symbol	K	L	M	N	P	Q	R	S	T	U	H
Speed (kph)	110	120	130	140	150	160	170	180	190	200	210
Speed (mph)	68	75	81	87	93	99	106	112	118	124	130

Index	lbs	kg	Index	lbs	kg	Index	lbs	kg
36	181.7	125	50	276.2	190	64	407	280
37	186.1	128	51	283.5	195	65	421.5	290
38	191.9	132	52	290.7	200	66	436.1	300
39	197.7	136	53	299.4	206	67	446.3	307
40	203.5	140	54	308.2	212	68	457.9	315
41	210.8	145	55	316.9	218	69	472.4	325
42	218	150	56	325.6	224	70	487	335
43	225.3	155	57	334.3	230	71	501.5	345
44	232.6	160	58	343	236	72	516	355
45	239.8	165	59	353.2	243	73	530.6	365
46	247.1	170	60	363.4	250	74	545.1	375
47	254.4	175	61	373.6	257	75	562.5	387
48	261.6	180	62	385.2	265	76	581.4	400
49	268.9	185	63	395.4	272	77	598.9	412

Tyre sizes With a front tyre stamped 110/80 B19 the '110' refers to the notional tyre width in millimetres and the '80' refers to the equally notional height of the tyre as a percentage of width; in this case 88mm, the 'B' refers to bias belt (cross ply) construction as opposed to radial; see box p85, and the 19 refers to the diameter of your wheel. Just remember a 110/80 from Heidenau may not be identical in size to a Michelin, but it will be very close.

All road-legal tyres are **speed-** and **load-rated** by the manufacturer, though it's better not to push this to the limit: a tyre branded '59T' is designed with a maximum speed of 190kph while carrying a load of 243kg. Travelling loaded and two-up will probably put your machine near such a tyre's design limit. The ply rating is an outdated way of rating the load on non-radial tyres – more being better. You can also tell the **age of your tyre** by deciphering a four-figure stamp which should be something like '1812' which means it was made in the 18th week of 2012. This can be useful to know if buying used tyres; anything more than five years old may be getting past its use-by date for heavy adventure touring.

If you find a tyre you like that you can't buy locally, send them ahead. These K60s are actually on the way from a port to a nearby post office. © Margus Sootla

which will wear twice as fast on the highway, won't grip or corner well in the rain and, to some sensitive ears, may even be noisy. Then at some stage in your travels you may have to rely on obscure Asian 'black cheese' brands, or a tyre that's not intended for your big machine and which will wear out in no time. This is why riders choose to post trusted tyres onward, or cart them around for months.

Tyre performance depends on your route, your riding style and your bike's power and weight: **gentle acceleration and braking** greatly increase tyre life and alert and responsive riding off-highways (especially in rocky terrain) will also mean fewer punctures and less grey hair. In the end anything **black and round** that keeps your rims from scratching the bitumen will do the job, and in the dusty corners of the AMZ you may have little choice.

Tread patterns and compounds

Despite tyre manufacturers' proclamations about cunning, computer-designed knobs, sipes and grooves, this is mostly marketing hype. Actual function may be no better than a Dunlop K70 from the 1970s. What really matters in a tyre – the **compound** and the **construction** of its carcass – is impossible to evaluate just by simply looking at it, or even by doing some research.

Biking lore states that a soft compound tyre grips well wet or dry but doesn't last, while a long-lasting, hard-compound tyre can be skittish on wet roads, as will any tyre with a knobbly tread pattern, especially when new and at maximum pressure. Construction technology has evolved greatly to control flex, as has varying compounds across the tyre width, load indexes and reduced weight, but **tread patterns** have not evolved much. A farm tractor tyre looks the same as it did 77 years ago because it works, just as slicks would work best on smooth, dry, paved roads. In the real world **tread** is needed to expel surface rainwater where a slick would aquaplane, or of course to grip on loose or soft surfaces, just like a spiked running shoe or a pair of lugged hiking boots. It's as simple as that.

Heat, pressure and traction

Harsh braking and acceleration take their toll, but it's the **heat build-up** in the body of the tyre that accelerates wear during normal riding. Every rotation of a tyre causes the sidewall to compress and flex as it's pressed down against the road, and then rebound as the wheel rotates and the weight is released, just as each step you take compresses your feet momentarily. Except at 60mph (100kph) a bike tyre is doing this about thirty times a second. These days clued-up sports bike riders will warm up their high-performance tyres before going for it, but once any tyre gets too hot it'll soften dramatically, become more puncture prone, wear more quickly – and at high speed may even start to disintegrate.

TUBELESS TYRES AND RADIAL CONSTRUCTION

Tubeless tyres and radial construction are both real steps forward for motorcycles. If these sorts of tyres fit your bike, so much the better. Without an inflated inner tube rubbing against the inside of the tyre as it flexes, tubeless tyres **run cooler** and so last longer. And when a tubeless tyre punctures, it deflates *gradually* as the air leaks out through the tiny hole in the carcass, not an inner tube potentially bursting like a balloon. The tyre usually stays on the rim too, which gives you a chance to safely bring the bike to a stop.

To make your own **roadside repairs**, assuming the tyre's still on the rim, you just plug the hole from the outside with a ramming spike tool fitted with a rubber bung covered in glue – a five minute job. It is illegal in some countries where you must get the inside of the tyre vulcanised at a tyre shop but ram-plugging is unbelievably easy compared to repairing inner tubes, and in my experience reliable, even off-road, providing a rim is undamaged. Even if there's a slight ding it's easy to knock out, and if not, fit a tube until you can make a proper repair.

The bead of a tubeless tyre seals by being located in a **groove** in the rim (see diagram). Should you need to remove a tyre in the field you need a lot of leverage to 'break the bead', and then some fast and high air pressure to remount it. You can use another bike's sidestand to press down on the tyre to break the bead (below), get a friendly car driver to drive over your tyre, or use tools like Motion Pro Bead Pro. Then you need a CO_2 cartridge or an electric pump plus lots of tube lube to remount it. Even water will work.

Practice at home so you know what to do in the very unlikely event of having to remount a tubeless or safety-rimmed tyre by the roadside.

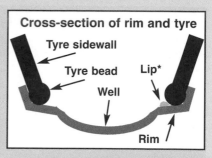

Cross-section of rim and tyre

Tyre sidewall
Tyre bead
Lip*
Well
Rim

*Lip and locating groove on tubeless or 'safety' rims, found even on tubed wheels.

Constructed with parallel rather than cross plies, a **radial tyre** (aka: '0° belted') has more flexible sidewalls than a cross ply- or bias belted tyre. This enables the tyre to deform as you lean and so maintain a larger contact patch without generating the heat friction of crossed plies. More contact means better grip; less heat means greater longevity. Many tyres for the bigger adventure-styled bikes are radials now, such as Metzeler's Tourance, Michelin's Anakee and the Conti TKC70.

There is something to be said for the lower cost, stiffer sidewalls and greater size range of bias-belted tyres which are more suited to off-road riding where rocks can damage an otherwise thin radial sidewall, but assuming you've bought a quality tyre and watch your pressures and speed in rocks, that shouldn't happen.

BIKE CHOICE & PREPARATION

© ROBIN WEBB

Above: Tubeless conversion of spoked wheels. 3M 5200 mastic sealed each spoke nipple. Worked on the back, less well on the front because the rim lacked a 'tubeless lip', as shown above. Full story on the website.

[keep tyre pressures] as high as possible and as low as necessary

Under-inflation is clearly bad for longevity, but **low pressures** can dramatically improve grip in sand and mud. In this part-deflated state the contact patch or 'footprint' of a tyre *lengthens* significantly to work more like a tank track. Even a regular road tyre will grip better and feel more secure in this state, but with the greater flexing the tyre will quickly get much hotter. So balance any pressure drop with the gross weight of your machine, **keep your speed down** and reinflate as soon as possible. One good thing about choosing knobbly tyres is they'll grip off-road even at road pressures. In mixed terrain that's a great way to avoid punctures.

Over inflating tyres just 'to be on the safe side' won't make them last longer and quite possibly the opposite. An over-inflated tyre bulges away from the rim, the contact patch is reduced (affecting traction), and the smaller contact area will wear quicker. This is why closely **managing your tyre pressures** will give greater mileage. Increase pressure as payloads or speeds increase (for example, an unexpected passenger), and reduce them a bit on loose tracks for better traction. As high as possible, as low as necessary.

You can't have it both ways

For most adventure riders, a typical unsealed road would be a gravel or sand track, either graded smooth or corrugated into a 'washboard' surface by the passing of heavy vehicles. Riding in the dry at sensible speeds in a straight line your tread pattern won't come into play much; any tyre will do as steady traction propels you forward.

Excepting a couple of punctures, this Husky Terra managed two weeks of rocky Moroccan trails on Dunlop TR91 Trailmax 'road' tyres (similar to TrailSmart) with no problems.

It's when braking into **loose surface bends**, negotiating soft **ruts** carved by passing traffic or when it **rains** that tread comes into play and tyres without pronounced edge knobs skitter about or make a bike unrideable. Learning to handle a heavily loaded bike on this sort of surface will be part of your adventure and you'll be surprised what even a regular touring bike can manage.

With a more blocky tyre, the knobs that bite into unconsolidated surfaces so effectively are the same knobs that will flex, squirm and eventually let go as you lean into a bend at too high speed on the road. And over many road miles those knobs will wear unevenly, especially as the leading edge deforms from braking forces on the front tyre (sometimes referred to as 'cupping'). This'll impair traction on the highway, as well as produce vibration and noise.

Tyres for your adventure

As with bike manufacturers, some tyre makers have responded to the current trend by reclassifying dual-purpose tyres as 'adventure tyres' to suit the ever-faster and heavier adventure tourers like XT1200Zs, big GSs and KTMs and Triumph multis. When new, these bikes must be sold with a tyre that looks the part, must survive being pushed hard by road-biased road testers but, for safety ('read 'liability') reasons your 160hp, 250kg KTM 1290 must come with tyres that match its staggering performance potential on the highway. Putting a set of Michelin Deserts on a 1290 will make it great in the sand and look cool at an HU rally, but will also be quite a handful on a sleety Andean pass.

I've divided tyres into three categories: what are essentially **road tyres** which might come fitted as original equipment (OE); **do-it-all 'adventure travel' tyres**; and **off-road biased tyres** which look the business but wear fast.

Road tyres will have a token shallow and wide blocky tread pattern but on gravel roads, let alone sand and mud, the tyres below will be no better than a street tyre. Indeed you may well be better off with a regular, hard-wearing road touring tyre, even if it doesn't look sexy. They include: Avon Distanzia and Trailrider; Bridgestone Battle Wing 501/502 and Trail Wing TW 110/152; Continental Trail Attack 2 and TKC70; Dunlop Trailmax and Trailsmart; Heidenau K76; Metzeler Enduro 1, 2 and Tourance; Pirelli MT60 and Scorpion Trail; Michelin Anakee, Mitas E-08 and MC24; Shinko Trail Master E705.

All these tyres, especially the radials from the more established brands will be found fitted new on the biggest and heaviest adventure-styled bikes.

Left to right 1: The very popular Tourance radial at home on a 1200GS. **2**: Similar Michelin Anakee. **3**: Conti TKC70 radial on KTM 990 – 60/40 road/dirt they claim. **4**: Scorpion Trail on a CB-500X.

Left to right Metzeler Enduro 3 (photo **1**) and Michelin T66 (photo **2**) offer a little more bite on gravel while delivering good mileages. Same with the Maxxis E-07 (photo **3**) on an XCountry and Heidenau K60 (photo **4**) on an F650 twin; both less than half worn after 5000 miles to Morocco and back.

The next category is '**Adventure travel tyres**', something that can work OK on a gravel road but still has the potential to last 10,000 miles – in other words the kind of tyre you'll want. As long they come in the right size they'll work on bigger and more powerful bikes too, but may not handle fast roads quite as well as the best radials mentioned above. On a lighter, less torquey bike like a 650 single or 500 twin they can last for ages. Your mileage may vary but they include: Avon Gripster; Bridgestone's Trail Wing TW301/302; Continental ContiEscape, the chevron-patterned Dunlop Trailmax; Heidenau's similar K60; Metzeler's Enduro 3 Sahara and Karoo 3; Mefo Sport Explorer and Super Explorer; Michelin's Sirac and T66; the Mitas E-07 and Shinko 804/805.

The final category are **dirt-biased tyres** or street-legal knobblies of which the **Continental TKC80** Twinduro is a favourite. There's nothing special about a 'TKC', the usual spread of square knobs but *less high* than a motocross tyre so your 100hp-plus rig won't squirm around like Pan's People on rubber stilettos. TKC80s are confusingly designated 70/30 road/dirt use but which sounds right. Alternatives include the more conventional Bridgestone Trail Wing 301/302, Dunlop's D606 or their D908RR rally tyre – both street-legal knobblies that when new on the road will feel edgy until they've worn down a bit (as with all street-legal knobblies). Michelin's 'Desert' pattern T63 has been around for donkey's years, so has Pirelli's more aggressive MT21. Neither has

Left to right 1: A TKC run tubeless after 4500 miles on an XT660Z. **2**: A slightly OTT Maxxis Desert was all there was to replace a CRF-L's OE IRC GP22R. Similar to a TW 301, the IRC was shot and split in just 3200 gentle miles. **3**: MT21 on a Funduro – a bit hairy on the road until you get used to it. **4**: Mitas E-09 'Dakar' on a KTM 990. Can require a hydraulic ram to break the bead on some wheels.

TYRE CREEP AT LOW PRESSURES

Riding at the low pressures required to improve traction in deep sand or mud can cause a rear tyre to get pulled around the rim by the engine torque (and less often the front due to hard braking). This isn't a problem with tubeless tyres, but as an inner tube gets dragged round, the valve may get ripped out, destroying the tube.

If running tubes at low-pressure, **security bolts** (aka: rim locks) are a good idea on the rear to contain tyre creep. They clamp the tyre's bead to the rim and, if not already there, require a hole to be drilled into the rim.

In the early days when running low pressures keep an eye on your valves. If they begin to 'tilt over' as pictured below, it means your security bolt may need tightening or your tyre repositioning (some creep can occur even with rim locks). Always keep the 12mm nut at the base of your valve **loose**, or don't use it at all. They're only useful as an aid to refitting tubes when fitting tyres.

If you're running tubes at low pressure, keep an eye on your valves. If they begin to lean it means the tyre is creeping.

Rim locks; they ought to be fitted as original equipment to most trail or enduro bikes running tubed tyres.

changed just because adventure motorcycling has now become fashionable. One newish-comer is the Mitas E-09 or -10. The 'Dakar' variant has four-plies for stiffer sidewalls so, like a classic Michelin Desert, you can almost run it with no air. Some bikes will be too light to make the tyre spread and grip properly in the dirt but the 1100GS on p84 covered over 10,000kms two-up from Namibia to Europe with tread to spare, while another KTM 950 rider told me his '09s were shot in just 500 miles.

Finally Shinko's 804/805 is another TKC clone worth a look as these obscure brands can be cheaper. Remember, the more powerful your bike, the less high knobs you want; typically around half an inch (12mm) or less. Big knobs won't necessarily last longer on a loaded Africa Twin they'll just squirm, get hot and fly off in someone's face. There's a reason why some manufacturers specifically don't make some tyres to fit certain big bikes.

You can **mix tyres from these categories**: most put a more dirt biased tyre up front where wear is less, and a roady tyre on the back. On the dirt the back end can spin and slide a little, but the more important steering and braking will be better. Just hope you don't have to make an emergency stop one wet night because your front TKC or similar won't behave like an Anakee. Although I've yet to test this theory, up to a point you can get away with less road-oriented tyres on bikes equipped with **modern ABS**. Assuming an off-road biased tyre locks up sooner than a road tyre, the clever electronics should catch it.

It took a lot of paddling to get up this creek during which time the tyre picked up a collection of acacia thorn tips which worked their way into the tube over the next few weeks.

PUNCTURES

You need to be confident you can fix punctures yourself – it won't always be practical to get to a tyre repair shop. **Practice tyre removal at home** so when the inevitable occurs you can be sure that you've done it before so you can do it again. Any emergency repair undertaken in a remote location can be unnerving; the better prepared you are the less chance you'll make absent-minded mistakes like forgetting to align the chain, leaving your tools by the roadside or, as I managed one time, leaving a tyre lever *inside* the newly mounted tyre.

Avoid labour-saving aerosols which are messy and unreliable. **Puncture-sealing fluids** like *Slime* or *Ultraseal* (in the UK) are worthwhile however, and do an amazing job of nipping punctures in the bud, as well as dynamically balancing and cooling both tubed or tubeless tyres. Whenever a tyre is punctured the pressure and centrifugal force in the tyre or tube forces the fibre-laden fluid out through the hole where it solidifies and seals in seconds. It doesn't always work but for the small cost is well worth it.

If that stuff doesn't work for you, the best way to repair a puncture is to plug a tubeless tyre – it takes two minutes – or remove the tyre and repair or fit a new tube. The key is ensuring there's enough slack in the bead (picture 4, overleaf) so you're not applying extreme force on the levers. Electric or manual, **protect your pump** from dust and loss; it could be vital.

If you can't repair a puncture, try stuffing the tyre with clothes or anything else that comes to hand to vaguely regain its profile. If you do a good job, you can carry on without too much difficulty, but if the tyre is damaged or starts to disintegrate and tear you're better off getting a lift somewhere to sort it out, or if desperate, carry on on the rim.

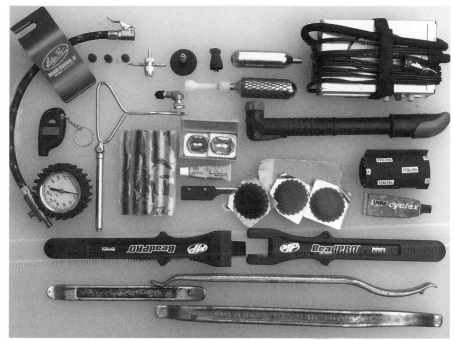

From top left: Motion Pro Bead Buddy II, spare valve caps; 3 valve extractors (or integral with some valve caps), CO² cartridges and attachment hose, 12-volt compressor. Cheap digital pressure gauge; tubeless ram/reamer; right-angle tubeless valve, mini handpump. Bulky analogue pressure gauge, slim 'pen' pressure gauge; tubeless string plugs; tubeless ring plugs (in box); cement (glue); small knife to trim off plugs; tube patches on sandpaper; roll of thick patch material; more glue. Motion Pro bead breaker/tyre levers; short BMW lever; Buzzetti Pro levers.
Not shown: talc to dust over a drying patch and to 'dust-lube' the inside of the tyre.

Puncture-repair kit

Assemble your items of choice from the picture above. Not all the items are needed and there is some duplication to show all options. Carry at least one spare inner tube per wheel. A **mini air compressor** is well worth the space but run the engine if you use it for more than a few seconds to spare the battery and give it more power. I don't bother with CO² cartridges anymore but carry a **mini hand pump** as back up. In my experience a good **tyre lever** is a blade no more than 20mm wide, up to 5mm thick and 300mm long, just like the Buzzettis above, in fact. As mentioned opposite, whatever lever you use, take care in the last stages of tyre mounting (photo 11, next page). Avoid brute force which can pinch a tube.

Basic puncture kit
• One spare tube per tyre
• At least two tyre levers
• Patches, sandpaper, rubber solution, a valve extractor (if not in valve cap)
• Or tubeless plugs, glue and ram/reamer
• Electric compressor and air pressure gauge

1. Find a flat spot well away from the road. With no centre stand, use a pannier or rock opposite the sidestand, or just lay the bike on its side. Work on a sheet and use a bowl for loose fittings.

2. Remove the valve cap and valve base nut and loosen the security bolt if present. Unscrew valve core with special tool, releasing any remaining air and push the valve (and security bolt) into the tyre as far as they'll go.

5. Getting the second lever in is hard unless you release the first lever a little. Once in pull them both up in close succession. Note how the disc holds one lever down. Keep working round the tyre until one side is outside the rim.

6. Stand the tyre up, push the valve in and drag the tube out the side. Carefully examine the outer tyre and pass your fingers over the inner surface to feel for thorns or whatever. You may have to take the tyre right off.

9. Clean off the rubber dust with a petrol rag, apply a thin film of adhesive over a broad area and let it dry to the touch. Apply the patch, foil-side down. Knead the patch down firmly with a tyre lever then sprinkle with talc.

10. Stand the wheel up, push the tube back into the tyre by first pushing the valve through and fitting the 12mm nut. With stiff tyres, lever up the other side to make room for your fingers to work the valve in.

3. Put your weight on the tyre to push the bead off the rim, use bead breakers or with another bike do the sidestand trick (p85). Check again that the valve and rim locks are pushed right into the tyre so they're out of the way.

4. Crouching or kneeling on the tyre to keep the bead in the well, push the first lever on the opposite side under to hook under the tyre's bead.

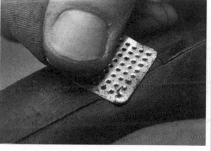

7. Inflate the tube to locate the hole. If you can't hear a hiss, pass the tube over wet lips to feel for a cold jet of air or submerge the tube in water and look for bubbles. Don't assume you only have one puncture.

8. Release the air, place the tube on a firm surface and roughen the area around the hole with sandpaper or a grater. The rubber surface around the hole should have a scratched, matt appearance.

11. Standing or kneeling, position levers at 10- and 2 o'clock and start levering them towards 12 o'clock. As you lever, kick at the tyre to make sure it's in the well to give you the necessary slack for the final satisfying 'pop'. Take it easy as this is where tubes get pinched.

12. Re-inflate until bead remounts the rim evenly. If not, keep inflating/deflating with soapy water. Check pressure, tighten rim lock (if present), fit valve cap and refit the wheel. Check all nuts are tight, pack up tools, recheck pressure, pump up the brake and ride on.

EQUIPMENT CHECKLIST

It's unlikely that you'll take just these items, but consider this as part of a useful checklist to give you ideas on essentials you may have overlooked.

Documentation
- Passport
- Vehicle registration document
- Carnet
- Cash in hard currency
- Debit and credit cards
- Travel tickets
- Travel insurance
- Green Card and/or Third Party Insurance
- Driver's licence (including IDP)
- Several spare passport photos
- Address book (paper or digital and online)
- Photocopies and online images of all important documents

Clothing
- Helmet
- Boots and light shoes
- Socks and underpants
- Thermal underwear
- T-shirts or shirts
- Shorts
- Fleece
- Riding jacket
- One-piece waterproof riding suit
- Gloves, plus spare pair
- Trousers or riding pants, plus spare pair
- Balaclava or sun hat
- Handkerchief or bandana
- Sun glasses

Camping and sleeping
- Tent or self-supporting mozzie net
- Sleeping mat
- Sleeping bag
- Collapsible stool or chair
- Ear plugs
- Head torch plus a back-up light source.

Cooking
- Stove and fuel (if not petrol) plus spares
- Tea towel and pan scrubber
- Lighter or other reliable fire source
- Spoon and fork
- Cooking pot(s) with lid and pot gripper
- Swiss Army knife or multitool
- Mug
- Ten-litre water bag
- Basic food items like salt, pepper, oil, sugar/sweetener (more compact)

Toiletries
- Soap and towel
- Toothbrush and toothpaste
- Toilet paper
- Skin moisturiser and insect repellent
- Universal basin plug
- Needle and thread
- First-aid kit (see p157)

Navigation and orientation
- Paper maps
- GPS or Satnav with relevant maps loaded
- Pocket compass
- Guidebook(s)
- Useful waypoints (online or on a device)

Miscellaneous
- Smartphone with GPS feature
- Basic mobile phone
- Laptop, tablet or iPod
- Camera and memory cards
- Spare batteries for everything
- Cables/adapter plugs to recharge gadgets
- Adapter wall plug for your regions
- Waterproof bags
- String or cord
- Elastic bands

FIT NEW AND KEEP THE SPARES

It has been said already but get familiar with your bike by fitting good-quality new consumable items like tyres, brakes, batteries and chain and sprockets and keep the part-used-but-still-serviceable items as spares.

Taking new spares is not the same because anyone who's worked on their own bike will be familiar with the discovery that the replacement oil filter you spent half the morning tracking down and carried halfway across Africa doesn't fit. It's something better found out on a quiet Sunday morning on your drive with a steaming mug to hand, than by the roadside on the outskirts of Istanbul on a Friday evening. Fit new stuff now, keep the used item as a backup so you'll know for sure it will fit.

SPARES AND MAINTENANCE PARTS LIST

This list is a start. Special tools and spares for your bike will be as essential.

Tools
- Allen or Torx keys
- Junior hacksaw with spare blades
- Multimeter, electric
- Oil filter removing tool
- Pliers with wire cutters
- Screwdrivers, selection
- Spanners and mini socket set to suit every fitting on your bike
- Tyre levers, pressure gauge and mini compressor
- Puncture-repair kit & inner tubes (see p91)
- ECU diagnostic tool (requires smartphone or laptop)

Spares
- Bolts, nuts, washers & self-tapping screws
- Spare bulbs
- Electrical connections, fuses, wire
- Old bulb in a socket with wire (for continuity testing)
- Filters: fuel, oil
- Mini jump leads
- Keys, spare
- Pipes: fuel (rubber), siphoning (clear plastic)
- Spark plugs
- Tyre(s)
- Air filter, pre-oiled in a plastic bag

Sundries
- Cable (zip) ties, wire, duct tape
- Grease
- Jubilee (hose) clips
- Radiator sealant
- Epoxy glue and metal repair paste
- Instant gasket
- Thread-locking cement (Loctite)
- WD40/GT85 or similar
- Connecting link(s) for chain
- Control levers and cables (run cables alongside current ones)
- Diaphragm for CV carbs
- Spare bungees, straps and inner tube strips
- Spoke key
- Top-up oil and rag
- Thin wire and wire coathanger

BIKE CHOICE & PREPARATION

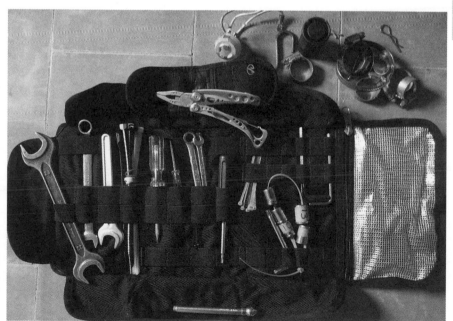

Some tools: From the top, bulb on a wire for circuit testing (bulb is in the film cannister), hose clips. Next includes back wheel spanner, mini sockets and zip ties, all in a nifty Kriega tool roll.

Load carrying

Total overload – and all the wrong junk too. Next trip was too much the other extreme and the third wasn't much better. By the fourth trip I had the luggage system nailed.

Just like a big trip needs a big bike, a long ride needs a lot of stuff, right? That's what most first-timers think, but part of the satisfaction of two-wheel travel is discovering how little you actually need to get by. **Overloading is by far the most common mistake**. You can take my word for it or learn from experience. Second time around, everyone takes less stuff.

Much of this is down to the realisation that just because you've left home, it doesn't mean you've landed on the dark side of the moon. The world out there has all the things you need to keep moving, from food and fuel to lodgings and yes, even wi-fi.

Riding or even just getting on an overloaded bike can be demoralising, and yet we're still talking about a tiny amount of gear – in volume it adds up to the typical allowance for an international flight – and all this to sustain yourself for months on the road. We all have different needs of course, but with a full tank and a typical 30kg/66lb payload your machine may handle like a piano on anything other that the smoothest highway and be impossible to pick up without help.

LUGGAGE SYSTEMS

On a motorcycle there's not much choice about where your baggage can go: behind you and alongside the back wheel, with a tank bag or tank panniers in front and a small backpack on your back. The most basic level of motorcycle baggage is a **rucksack** or kit bag strapped across the back seat – something that many a young, cash-strapped motorcycle traveller has tried – and also what some worldly purists return to after many years on the road. It may not be secure in both a thieving and a fitting sense, but short of a pair of carrier bags, is as cheap as it gets and can easily be carried when off the bike.

Einstone's Theory of Relative Space states that no matter how capacious your set up, it will be filled to bursting point. Keep it small and you'll take little; use big containers and you'll still cram in a lot of stuff. It's tempting to assume that the former method is superior but the fact is, just as some riders like lightweight machines and have baggage strategies verging on OCD, others feel comfortable on a massive machine clad in an elephantine mass, ready for anything. Each to his own but few riders come back saying they sure wish they'd ridden a heavier motorcycle.

General principles

Soft, hard or firm, whatever you choose, **convenience** of access, **ease** of removal, **robustness**, **durability** and **security** are the key considerations – see the table below. Visualise how your system will stack up in a day-long downpour, a shunt or an opportunistic theft, but recognise that surviving a heavy crash, ten years on the road or a determined thief is not always possible.

BIKE CHOICE & PREPARATION

LUGGAGE CHOICES – SOME FACTORS

For	Against
SOFT FABRIC BAGS	
● Light and relatively inexpensive	● Can tear, burn and sag
● Light rack sufficient, or useable without	● May not be weatherproof without a liner
● Contents immunised from vibration	● Can get grubby; hard to clean
● Absorb impacts, sparing the subframe	● Where present, zips will fail eventually
● Less risk of leg injuries	● Less secure against ransacking or theft
● Can be easy to mend	● Fragile contents can get crushed in a fall
FIRM PLASTIC CASES	
● Robust, weatherproof, abrasion resistant	● Large cases are heavy for what they are
● Don't dent or deform like alloy	● Hinges/seal weak points on sideloaders
● Some top loaders have wheels & handles	● Not actually designed for motorcycles
● Some brands claim a lifetime guarantee	● Require a solid rack and mounting
● Inexpensive clones available	● Sideloaders spill out when opened on bike
● Rounded corners and edges, unlike alloy	● Unlocked latches may fail on impact
HARD ALLOY BOXES	
● More secure, depending on locks	● Can be heavy, wide and expensive
● Best examples are very robust	● Require a solid rack and mounting
● Weatherproof (until lid edge deformed)	● Not suited to hard, off-highway riding
● Can act as rear 'crash bars'	● Hard edges and corners can injure in a fall
● Easy to paint, sticker (and sit on if q/d)	● Hard to straighten once badly deformed
● Easy to bolt on external mounts & holders	● Tough boxes transfer stress to subframe

Compartmentalisation – coloured bags, boxes or dividers – all aid organisation and help you remember where things are which can be handy in the early days. Keep regularly used items on top or outside, overnight stuff elsewhere and rarely used items buried, with valuables on your person. While being securely mounted, whatever system you use should be **easily removable**. That needn't mean dismounting the entire container; pulling out a liner bag to take indoors is much more convenient, even with soft bags.

When it comes to strapping things on the outside of your containers or on to your bike, don't rely on elasticated bungees – something like **Rok Straps** cleverly combine tough elasticity with buckle-fed adjustability. Carry spares including regular adjustable straps or strips of inner tube; straps get lost, damaged or pinched but have other uses like clothes lines or belts.

Distribute your load as **low and centrally as possible**; the same principle as mass centralisation used in vehicle design. A loaded bike's **centre of gravity** (CoG) with you on it is more or less where the injectors or carb usually sit. In motion a centralised mass is more agile (able to change direction) than a dispersed one, be it a motorcycle, pushbike or airplane. Heavy weights want to be as close to the CoG as possible, while light things like clothes, sleeping bags or empty containers can go out on the back of the seat or even in front of the headlight. Avoid heavy weights **behind the rear spindle**, something that tail racks encourage. It's easy to keep piling it on but the rider who packs thoughtfully will reap real benefits in balance and steering, especially when fully loaded off the highway. How much volume? About **30 litres** for each pannier to keep the bulk of the weight low and as little mass and volume on the back seat and tail rack. This allows **expansion capacity** for days when you'll want to stash your jacket or load up with provisions.

Hard, firm or soft?

This debate is often simplified to 'hard vs soft' while overlooking the nuances of 'firm' luggage. In truth most bikers combine all three and anyway, it usually refers to the panniers. Beginners are often drawn to shiny alloy boxes for the same reasons that most of us live in brick houses with cupboards and not tents with bags. A solid box looks weatherproof and can be locked securely to itself and the bike.

Left: Mixing soft Ortliebs with firm plastic and rigid fluid cans underneath. © Sean Flanagan.
Right: Sawn-off 20-litre jerry; cheap but a bit small, especially when using Touratech 'disc' mounts which take up inner space. © Robin Webb

The bigger the bike the harder the luggage. We once used alloy boxes from Touratech and Tesch for a desert trip on XR650Ls. Even before it was over we agreed they'd been a mistake. The convenience was handy but they were **too wide** on narrow mountain tracks, and the hard edges and sharp corners were intimidating. For that trip away in the wilderness a light rack with soft bags would have been much better. But most overland rides aren't like that, they follow roads between towns and cities through all weathers where the benefits of solid luggage are appreciated daily.

HARD LUGGAGE

The first thing to acknowledge is that most proprietary touring hard cases as found on your bike manufacturer's official accessory list may not be up to the demands of bad roads, dust, vibration and occasional overloading, as well as shock loads, shunts and spills. They're more often used as free bait when a new model's sales are flagging. What works for Mr & Mrs as they pull up outside an Andalucian parador to be handed a chilled apéritif, won't survive the rugged ride from Lahore to Kathmandu via Srinagar. The couple are touring; you're engaged in what's come to be known as adventure motorcycling, a less predictable endeavour ill-suited to bulbous, clip-on cases. Some Givis – a byword for sedate road touring – are rated to carry just 10kg each.

Alloy boxes

Aluminium boxes were originally handmade by riders until outfits in Germany like Därrs, Hepco and Tesch started producing them. The idea caught on, with Touratech, Metal Mule in the UK and Jesse Luggage in the US among the best known. But with prices up to a staggering £400 for a 30-litre-plus box, copies and all-out knock-offs have hit this booming market.

For hard use it does appear you get what you pay for: cheaper boxes will look the part – it's only a metal box, after all – but may fall apart, too. Pricier gear should last, but may not. Jesse Luggage's Odyssey II system is among the most expensive out there but the engineering and attention to detail – including slimness – is sound. In the UK Metal Mule has a similar reputation for bomb-proof cases. Buying a set of either may cost 10% of a new bike but they're an integral part of your set up on which you'll be relying daily for months.

BIKE CHOICE & PREPARATION

Left: Jesse outfit with toast racks. Jesses are notable for trying to stay close in to the bike but retain useful volume. Odyssey IIs slide forward when solo. **Right**: Hepco & Becker (near identical to pricier Krausers). Top box takes a full face lid, but that can be U-locked anywhere on a bike.

It's a box

At the very simplest level you get a six-sided rectilinear box and lid in **1.5 or 2mm** alloy that's either **welded** or **riveted and sealed** (or a bit of both). Making one isn't exactly rocket science which is why riders are attracted to less expensive options from eastern Europe. On a heavy bike with a long ride ahead, thicker is best. Riveting may look cheap but can be stronger than a plain, welded 1.5mm box. We're talking blind rivets as used on aircraft, not hobbyists' pop rivets. Any curves or bevels increase costs, but add rigidity and so resistance to deformation in a crash (as does a box-section rim around the top where the lid closes). Any rigid vessel with a curved or multifaceted cross-section is more robust than a slabby, rectilinear one. There's a lot to be said for not having a **sharp corner** on the forward outer edge to dig in as a falling bike slides. The payoff with bevelling is a less efficient packing space.

All alloy boxes are **top-loading**; not so handy for access but you can get round this by using lift-out trays or inner bags. As it is, most alloy box makers (as well as Kriega or Hein Gericke) offer **lift-out holdalls** to carry inside without having to remove a clanky, dirty box. A stout shopping bag or cheap sports bag does the same job. Don't even think about it: get a pair. Something is needed if the inside of your box isn't anodised, powder coated or painted, otherwise you'll get a smeary residue on anything that rubs. A thick layer of powder coating works best. On any case lid **strap rings** are a good idea for optional top loading, as is a smooth top and recessed handles (if present), so you can use the case as a comfortable camp seat, once removed.

> The peace of mind offered by a secure lid should be the main reason for investing in an alloy box

The way these lids open, clamp down, **lock** and **seal** is another thing to inspect closely. It's not too much to expect your alloy cases to be watertight to the point of submersion and have clamps that can't be prised open by a 12-year old with a big screwdriver. Any bent wire hasp that levers down on a curled up tab – whether locked with a key or with a padlock as shown below – won't take much to prise off or whack open, but many box makers still use these cheap clasps. The peace of mind offered by a secure lid that discourages opportunists should be the main reason for investing in an alloy box.

Left to right – Clamp close-up 1: Touratech Zega Pro integrated lock: lots of leverage for opportunists. **2**: Key clamp on a Hepco & Becker case. **3**: Padlock and rivetted tab acceptable if home made, not off the shelf. **4**: Jesse clasp and padlock rings; no one's getting in there easily.

Left: Touratech: lower mounts take the weight, upper tabs swivel to secure behind the rack. **Right**: A tougher Metal Mule case with no metal-to-metal contact with the rack is better. Location locking lever is held down by the lid. © Dan Ward. **Inset**: chunky silicone seal should last.

Jesse use chunky locking clamps that at least look like they'd be hard to lever open; Touratech Zega clamps are notoriously flimsy and have been that way for years; the later Zega Pros don't look that much better with all sorts of ways to get in there and lever away. A plain key lock with the locking mechanism hidden **inside** the lid (as on Metal Mules – above right) is less of an invitation and a rubber silicone seal will eliminate rattles and leaks.

Firm 'plastic' cases

An alternative to the blinding sheen of alloy are cases made from either roto-moulded polyethylene (like a cheap kayak or canoe), or from denser and heavier injection-moulded polycarbonate resin. Both materials are tough and very resistant to abrasion and knocks. As such they're well suited to moto-overlanding, unlike more brittle touring cases made of thinner ABS plastic. Moulding these sorts of polymers enables various colours as well as complex shapes like rounded corners and ribs to add rigidity to the structure, just as bevels do on metal boxes. The **weight** compares with the toughest alloy box.

On the side of a motorcycle, this stuff slides down the road a lot better than thin alloy or most fabric bags. Cases like those made by Peli come in all sorts of sizes and are well known for their suitability to rugged applications. For use on a bike, the Peli Storm iM2600 gives an ideal 35 litres of volume and weighs only 3.8kg (8.4lbs). Peli's original 1550 is a tad smaller, a pound heavier and another brand is Nanuk who's 940 case is a little larger but weighs the same. Seahorse is another US brand but with nothing in the 30-litre size.

Caribou, also in the US, were among the first to capitalise on converting Peli cases for use as motorcycle luggage, adding one-key lid locks and mounting systems which now use Hepco & Becker racks and which spread the load better than some proprietary touring mountings for which they also make kits. You can also buy DIY kits and cases fitted with locks. Just remember in dusty conditions key locks on any container at the back of a bike are prone to clogging and jamming with dust. Tape over them if conditions require or keep some lube handy.

The lids on the cases listed **open outwards** like a suitcase on its side which can be nuisance, especially when the bike's leaning on its stand. Load retain-

Left: Peli Case 1440; tough, top opening and with wheels and a handle, but at over 7kg, very heavy.
Right: side-opening Peli Storm iM2600, at 35 litres a more conventional size for a bike. Both will
need solid rack mounting systems, maybe even permanent fitting but with removable bags.

ing straps limit that, as do Caribou's liners up to a point, but the lift out bags are the real solution to stuff falling out, if not for quick roadside access.

The lids **seal** with an o-ring in a groove that can be easily repaired or replaced, although it's more exposed than an alloy lid. Another drawback is that it's the lids and their hinges that take the impact when a bike hits the deck. Caribou claim the Peli guarantee is for life which is reassuring, but you wonder how many times a big, heavy bike can fall onto its sidecases. Probably more than the tinniest alloys, but if you're not convinced then the ribbed and **top-loading Peli 1440** might be a better choice (see above left). Around 42 litres, it weighs a hefty 6.6kg (14.5lbs) and is nine inches wide, but that includes wheels and a handle for when you rock up at the Hilton.

As well as the usual range of alloy boxes Hepco make the double-skinned, rotomoulded 37-litre, top-loading **Gobi** which was an option on the original KTM 950 Adventure before KTM made their own similar luggage (see below). A moulded back spreads its weight over an H&B rack, but if the single mounting latch lets go (like the notorious ABS Krausers of old), the whole thing goes tumbling. Gobis incorporate a not-so-usable 3.5 litre water reservoir but at 25cm that just makes them extra wide. They weigh six kilos each (without the water) but are only rated to carry 10kg. If you're unsure about a clamping system on any heavy case use a **back-up strap**.

Left: KTM branded luggage: 31 and 42 litres per side but not all owners are impressed. Top box is a metal Zega Pro. **Right**: BMW Varios clip on in a jiffy too but also slide out, increasing capacity by up to 10 litres per side. The question is: can these factory options hack life on the road?

SOFT BAGGAGE

Soft baggage usually signifies some kind of fabric pannier as well as a duffle bag or kit bag across the back and, as with alloy boxes, these are all variations on the same thing and whose range has expanded greatly over the years.

Materials and closures

The best panniers are **double-skinned** with the outside bag in rugged, abrasion-resistant fabric, and with (in most cases removable) **waterproof liners** inside. This is the way to do it because small tears or other damage to the exte-

Soft set up: ex-army rucksacks have handy external pockets but need waterproof liners.

rior won't necessarily compromise the liner's waterproofness, as it can with a one-piece vinyl pannier. Should a liner fail (or not be up to it in the first place) it can be easily replaced, even with chunky bin bags, while the main body of the weather-beaten pannier lives on.

Cordura is actually a brand name of DuPont who manufacture many types of synthetic cloth, but most understand it to be a chunky, canvas-like woven nylon fabric also used in riding suits. Note that although 'canvas' means a stiff, plain-woven cloth originally made from hemp and later cotton, some baggage makers use this word to describe synthetic fabrics. Another fabric buzz word is ballistic nylon which sounds flash and has better abrasion resistance than Cordura, but won't actually stop a slashing knife, let alone a speeding bullet.

None of the above fabrics are waterproof unless coated with polyurethane (PU), and even then they'll leak at sewn seams unless they've been laboriously sealed with tape. 'Vinyl' is a vague word but in most cases refers to now-unfashionable PVC or similar thermoplastic polyurethane (TPU) coated nylon or polyester fabric. The strength of the underlying fabric weave, as well as the thickness and pliability of the TPU coating creates the stiffness and durability of the final material at a given weight. This stuff is **waterproof** and better still, panels are heat- or RF-welded, sealing it like a bucket. The problem is it slides down the road less well than Cordura and attaching external fittings like D-rings and pockets is hard or expensive to do well.

To sum it up, you want woven, abrasion-resistant Cordura or similar on the outside to take the knocks, and an equally rugged waterproof liner inside. Avoid anything with **zips** for important closures. Even if you remember to keep them clean, zips will jam or break through over-filling, hasty yanking or dirt, and are a real pain to repair. And in case you haven't guessed, avoid any bag with a giant 'shower cap'; this isn't a sustainable solution on the road.

The best closures are **roll up and clip down** derived from TPU kayaking dry bags. Not surprisingly, smooth, malleable surfaces coated with TPU on both sides will seal better than coarse Cordura or nylon coated on one side, another reason to use soft vinyl liners. Only a day of pelting rain may work its way through a closure rolled up tightly without creases, then cinched down. The other good thing with any roll top bag is that it's only as full as it is; a half empty bag will roll down smaller, unlike a rattly box or zipped bag.

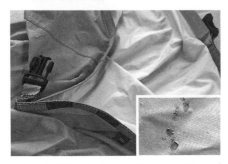

Exped 40-litre dry bag makes a good liner.
Inset: another near new liner already peeling.

Waterproof liners

Lighter and less stiff coated nylon liners will do the job, but as mentioned, unless sealed at the seams, they'll leak and eventually the proofing or seams will rub or peel off, as I found with a Kriega rucksack liner. Small holes are repairable with Seam Seal or similar.

If you're choosing aftermarket liners, consider a **light colour**; it makes digging around for stuff inside less murky than with anything black. The light blue Exped 40-litre XXL UL makes a good side bag liner while it lasts. Otherwise, thinner TPU liners remain malleable to roll up and fill the space, especially when temperatures get low. Problem is they're usually tube shaped. Ortlieb's 30-litre Messenger Bag rolltop backpack looks like it could do the job, especially if you're pulling the liner out nightly and leaving the outers on the bike, as opposed to demounting the whole bag. Or see if anything from OverBoard suits your needs. Some mounting systems are better than others, but if you can leave the outer bag securely lashed to the bike or the rack, the less chance there is of inadvertently getting it wrong one day and having something come loose. When done daily, dropping a liner into a pannier offers less room for error. Many integral liners are velcroed to the inside rim of the outer bag so both get rolled up as one when you close the bag. But, assuming they have clips (as above), you can roll and clip each separately and when clipped together, the liner has a useful carry handle.

Backing plates and racks

Loaded bags will sag or shift and many riders will have had a throwover pannier melting on a pipe or canvas panniers catching fire. High speeds, rough riding or just hasty mounting has seen me burn or melt bags on at least four occasions. A plastic side panel – even one coated inside with aluminium foil and flame-proof material – isn't enough to keep a fully loaded, jiggling pannier from pressing down and something melting. Nor I suspect are the rubber back panels on the back of some panniers.

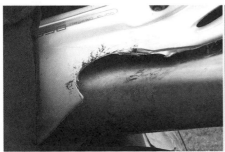

This is how it starts (left) when throwovers press on a pipe, then things can escalate ...
Use a rack or pipe guard or face an irate farmer and his charred field of maize. © Austin Vince

Left: Homemade (no, really!) pipe guard and bag rest, or buy something slicker in CNC from GL.
Right: Ortliebs Side Bags: faff-free QL2 mounting but only 28ltrs, single skin and no external pockets.

Bike designs vary and some may be immune to a throwover set up, but the only way to ensure your bag doesn't melt is to **keep it away from pipes** by mounting it on or against a rack, or using a guard if one isn't part of the silencer. Giant Loop, Mosco and Enduristan sell these guards, or you can make something far uglier from 4" channel jubilieed to the silencer, as above.

Lately fabric pannier designs are improving on Ortlieb's elegant QL2 by fitting rigid backing plates to mount securely on racks. Some systems look better thought out than others: SW Motech's Dakar bags slide and clip *upwards* onto their own wedge rack but clearly need the throwover straps to stay put. Conversely, Mosco Moto's Backcountry bags drop onto a similar wedge-plate arrangement of their corresponding rack plate which will fit most flat-sided racks, and Jesse make a Soft Plate mount for Ortlieb Saddle Bags. On rough terrain with heavy loads, forces get concentrated where the backplate meets the fabric; that's where an unsupported bag will begin to tear, just as throwover straps can tear where they join the main bag.

A **rack** doesn't have to be the hefty structure fit for an alloy pannier. Even a single, well-shaped **bar** will help retain throwovers, although mounting bags securely to a rack is the best solution. Granted, a rack might be another thing to bend in a crash, but soft bags (and their contents) absorb some of the impact rather than transfer it to a rack and subframe, so this is a less-likely-than-usual scenario. The rack mounts will also be less prone to vibration from hard boxes and so as mentioned, don't need to be so bombproof.

BIKE CHOICE & PREPARATION

Left: Lightweight softbag rack for BMW XCo (with auxiliary tank behind) from Hot Rod Welding.
Right: Wolfman rack – chunky tubing eliminates a back brace but may not be lighter.

Left: A 90-litre duffle drybag lashed to the rack – a great way to get the volume in, if needed.
Right: More boxy roll-top 30-litre Enduristan Monsoons on a third-party rack. Cordura lowers,
PVC upper and removable liner but no pockets outside.

Soft bag selection

Many a rider started out with a 26-litre Ortlieb roll-top throwover **Saddle Bag** which can be adapted to fit a rack, or at least lashed to it. But for most this capacity is a minimum, perhaps to limit loads. Most backpackers will carry a bigger rucksack. Without getting too wide, the bigger the better on the side as that's where the weight wants to be, with little or nothing behind the tail light.

Ortlieb's 28-litre **Side Bag QL2** uses a clever rack attachment system (previous page) adapted from their pushbike panniers. I've used those in the Himalaya and the ease of grabbing the handle and simply lifting them bags off can make your day. But for some reason the sprung rack attachment hooks are 16mm or 20mm, when the industry standard for racks is 18-mm tube.

Also from Switzerland, Enduristan make the cubular 30-litre **Monsoon** throwovers, but with the now more common Cordura outer (onto which you can sew or rivet), and a sewn-in vinyl liner. The capacity is in the ballpark but I found they stuck out a lot on an F650GS's wide Metal Mule rack.

Wolfman in the US make the 32-litre **Rocky Mountain** bags in a mixture of PVC and ballistic nylon. They lash down solidly with more straps and buckles than an episode of *Fifty Shades*, either to their own racks or others with adaptors. But that's all usually too fussy for daily demounting so just whip out the PU-coated nylon liners instead.

Left: There's low-tech and there's subterranean. Ex-army rucksacks are cheap and some come with integral frames. **Right**: Giant Loop Siskiyou throwovers use zips. May need a pipe guard too.

Left: SW Motech Dakars use optional backplates to slide up and clip onto a basic, unbraced rack but still rely on over-saddle strapping to take the weight. **Right**: Mosco Moto Backcountry (25- or 35L) takes the weight on a more intuitive drop-down wedge plate – no need for saddle straps.

Giant Loop's U-shaped Coyotes are well known among dirt riders but the design and the zips don't make them well suited to long term overlanding. The more conventional **Siskiyou** bags are closer to the mark, mixing Cordura with PVC and with a novel foam sandwich in the bag body to protect contents and help give them some shape. The large vinyl throwover panels are less of an innovation, nor is the small 'wedge' outer pocket; a box shape works much better. Both outer and inner roll-tops use zips, but if they pack up the bags will still seal well enough. They cost a staggering $700.

At the other price extreme **21 Brothers** from Poland make something less rugged but broadly similar to the better known bags featured here. Strap-on 1.5-litre exterior pockets are optional, red Monsoon-like liners are sewn in and capacity is about 30 litres. They also closely copy Giant Loop's Coyotes.

SW Motech make lots of everything for bikes but with their Bags Connection luggage and racks choose carefully for rugged overland operations. The roll-top **Dakar** panniers are inexpensive and claim a useful 32 litres, but the maximum stated payload is just 5 kilos (11lbs). The formed bag has an internal stiffener to limit sagging, a separate proofed nylon liner and handy external lashing points. They can attach Wolfman-style with cinch straps to any tubular rack (some more securely than others), or take a screw-on plastic backing plate which slides up onto their wedge rack which, once you see the untriangulated mounting arrangement, may explain the modest load rating.

Left: Kriega Overlanders allows modular mounting (including Rotopax; p67) on a q/d back plate that fits any rack. **Right**: 21 Brothers throwover with added frame attachment straps. €150 with pockets.

THE TRUTH BEHIND SOFT BAGGAGE CAPACITY

With any rigid rectilinear container, capacity is easy to calculate: internal width x length x height in metres = volume in litres. I used to think that for a box-shaped bag it would be more or less the same. Not anymore.

As a flexible (but non-elastic) bag bulges outwards in one axis, you'd assume it compensates by contracting in the other to maintain and equal volume. Wrong.

Like so many things in the universe, 'suitcase-shaped' panniers seek equilibrium when under pressure, and that is found by striving to attain sphere-like proportions or, in an edged flexible container, a cube which is the next best thing.

Strapped up, my Adventure Spec Magadans measured up at just 24 litres using a tape measure (external pockets not included). But filling them with water they bulged out to take no less than 40 litres.

Another way of looking at all this is that a cube-shaped bag uses less fabric than a rec-

tilinear one of the same volume and so weighs less (and presumably costs less in materials). But on a bike, a flatter, 'suitcase-shaped' container of the same volume is more practical in terms of greater surface area (ease of access) and of course reduced width. To me 20cm or 8 inches is a practical width limit for a bag or box, once you factor in fat pipes and so on.

All this matters when comparing stated soft luggage volumes with hard cases. The latter should be immutable (even if it may be stated inaccurately from one source to another, as with Peli cases); with soft bags it all depends how it's measured: WxLxH or, as Giant Loop say they do, with jugs of beans. Few of us are riding around with panniers full of beans or water, pushing our soft bags to their maximum potential volume, so the true practical volume of a soft pannier is somewhere in between.

Long version: see 'Resources' on the website.

L x W x H = 24L + pockets
AS spec

40 litres of water

Kreiga's tailpacks are well known and their **Overlander** pannier system (previous page) mounts up to four 15-litre packs onto a pair of chunky plates. Each side weighs from 2.4kg empty, and the plate in turn clips to any 18mm rack with a bit of fiddling. Some riders may like this modular concept but that's something that's as easily done inside a single, large bag.

Other zip-free throwovers include Andy Strapz **Avduro Pannierz**, a four-pocket update of their old 25-litre Expedition model and which takes some cues back from the larger Magadans. Their fabric is described as '12-13oz reinforced canvas' but shouldn't be mistaken for rugged Cordura far less melt-proof cotton canvas, as I found to my cost one time. But at A$500 the price is good.

In the UK Adventure Spec produce the '30-litre' **Magadan** velcro throwovers (£350), developed by Walter Colebatch. Based on a former Australian design, the double outer shell includes a slash-proof aramid liner plus thick, taped PVC inner bags and four big external pockets. Read Walter C's design statement at ⌨ adventure-spec.com and you can see he thought it all through. It doesn't have to be complicated or covered in straps and buckles to work.

 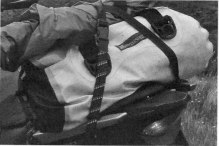

Left: Topbox; irresistibly handy and secure and just the right height. **Right**: Watershed Chattooga uses tough fabric and a fat rubber seal like a zip-lok freezer bag, then clips. You can float on it.

On the back

If not using a lockable top box, across the back of your seat or on a tail rack a soft duffle bag or holdall is ideal for light items like camping gear. The 49-litre roll-and-clip **Ortlieb Rack Pack** is still popular and about as big as you want. The **top loading** makes it easy to chuck in your tent, mat and sleeping bag each morning. It can rain all day on a Rack Pack and if done up right, it'll take longer than that to seep in. Bags opening **at the end** like a tube of Pringles are less useful, and drybags that open at *both* ends are a solution without a problem.

In the UK, Lomo or OverBoard make cheaper options to Ortlieb and many side bag makers will supply some sort of matching duffle. If you're engaged on an outlandish Siberian wet-fest I recommend **Watershed**'s tough PU fabric, genuinely submersion-proof drybags. You can squeeze a tent, sleeping bag and a mat into the 30-litre Chattooga model (above right).

Tank bags and backpacks

That's your main loading covered but there are additional ways and means of stashing your knick-knacks with scores of outfitters offering cunning solutions that would have Batman flitting back to the cave with a roll of Cordura and some clippy-clips. These baggage accessories all help to **compartmentalise** your gear which adds up to faster and more convenient access, just like a well-organised work station. Just remember that even if it isn't your first time, you'll still find it takes a couple weeks on the road to optimise your system for access, security and weather-proofness. It will sort itself out.

Left: Ex-army chunky canvas pouches for bottles. **Right**: Tool tubes can maximise space behind boxes.

Backpackers: handy for hydrators and easy to carry off the bike, unlike over-large tank bags.

Tank bags are a tried and tested way of keeping frequently used and high value gear handy and in view. Much of course will depend on your bike's tank (or area where tanks used to be) offering a stable base, although cut foam pads can get round this. Don't make the mistake of using a huge tank bag. It can get in the way of seeing your instruments, including accessories like GPS. And anyway, you want a bag you can remove and carry easily when it comes to leaving the bike and going for a wander. Some tank bags can convert into backpacks and all should include a shoulder strap.

The tank can also be a place to sling over a pair of **tank panniers** providing there's enough room for them in front of your knees. In this position they also offer a bit of protection to the bike as well as very handy access. BMW boxers are well suited to such tank saddle bags, providing the tank isn't huge.

Kreiga and Touratech make all sorts of handy **pods and pouches** you can attach to the outside of your hard boxes. At the very least it's useful to have an external container for engine oil or a water bottle where they can leak harmlessly. After that it's up to you to suit your own needs. I like a jacket with an array of big pockets plus maybe a backpack or a waist pack because, depending where you ride, more stuff lashed to the bike is more stuff to fall off, get damaged or get pinched.

If there's room on your bike to stash spares and maybe a hidden back-up phone plus a set of keys then so much the better. That way you can forget about these things until you need them, and it makes for less clutter and more room in your main baggage. You'll never have enough of that.

Left: Ex-army Rotax-engined Harley with side panniers. A much better position than hanging off the back on a tail track. **Right**: Cunning but note the additional fender support.

Rectangle in 18mm tube (Touratech p# 01-051-0300-0), your standard hanging rack from On The Road: 16/18mm tubes, 6 attachment points and the all-important back brace.

RACKS

For a long overland ride a **strong rack** is highly recommended to support not only hard/firm but also soft baggage. If you happen to possess unusual self-restraint you might get away with using soft luggage without a rack. I tried it on an old Ténéré, but even with just a ten-litre jerrican sat on the back seat the rear subframe flexed, inducing a weave on loose surfaces, although the Metzeler Sahara tyres didn't help there. And later on the whole lot caught fire. If your baggage is much heavier or the roads rough, subframes can bend or crack – and as shown on p104, bags pressing on pipes have grave consequences.

These days many pannier sellers offer racks for popular adventure bikes, even ones who formerly eschewed racks. You'd assume they're built to take the hammering, but don't count on it. Just as with adventure bikes 'visually rugged' is a phrase to fear. You'll still read reports of racks breaking out in the field which is why people get their own made to suit their needs.

Err towards racks where a tube end hasn't been flattened and drilled to make a fitting. And stay away from quickly detachable racks using Dzus-like fasteners (and probably Triumph's 'Dynamic Luggage System' come to that). SW Motech's EVO racks do this, so do Givi/Kappas. I bought one for a Versys and was initially baffled until it was explained that your image-conscious biker likes to whip the rack off their Hyperbusa when out for a burn-up-and-latte, then refit it for their hols. Easily removable baggage makes sense wherever you ride, but for overlanding the whole point of a rack is to provide a **solid base** on which to support or mount heavy loads for rough roads.

BIKE CHOICE & PREPARATION

Left: A Dzus mount for a rack? John McEnroe's famed exhortation springs to mind.
Right: Hard to see where this Metal Mule rack ends and the 1200LC starts.

Left: Unbraced rack needs to be chunky so won't save weight but looks neater. Stashing space behind too. **Right**: Mount anywhere between A and B, including the pillions. The less inline the better.

Stronger rear subframe

A subframe is more or less a right angle triangle with the 90° angle under the seat reaching down to the footrests and back at the tail light. Loading the back end stresses the diagonal leading to the footrest, or the unsupported beam when this triangle is partial, as above right. Here you can see the unsupported rear spars have been curved so they can be gusseted with plates to add rigidity and increase loads. Gusseting and bracing may be necessary on your frame too even before you start thinking about a rack – but doing this intuitively can make things worse. Few people really know what they're doing here, how can they without expensive testing? When meddling with a subframe design that may be more sophisticated than it looks, it's not impossible to amplify stresses or simply transfer them elsewhere.

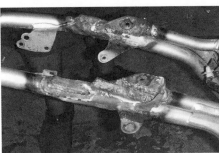

Left: Seamless subframe repair on a CRF250. © Steph Jeavons. **Right**: Swapping out an alloy for a later steel subframe on a BMW XCountry. I was lucky to have this option.

Building a rack

As already said, mounting heavy racks and boxes on bike subframes isn't an exact science, partly because each bike is different; the alloy subframe of an old KLR or XR650R is weaker than a new Ténéré or 650 Sertao. Mounting a heavy rack onto the unsupported beam or cantilever that is a motorcycle subframe may just see the whole thing droop before you even load it. Slapping on metal willy nilly is not over-engineering, it's bad engineering.

With the subframe attended to, by adding a rack you're augmenting the triangle with a notional spar running from A to B on the subframe pictured

Left: Bent strips easy to fabricate and weld but are less rigid than tube and not much lighter. Think carefully where racks attach – especially on alloy frames. **Right**: Home-made 4-point platform rack for a DR650. Cut back corners don't dig in or snap at your shins. © Sean Flanagan

top right on p112. This transfers compression down to the 'A' mount – a key area of stress, at its height when your suspension bottoms out, (a good reason to fit a progressive spring). A diagonal tail light-to-footrest spar may keep your throwover from flapping around like an untended fire hose, but it will barely support the bag.

The frames shown above and on p111 are doing the same in a less obvious way by using **three or more** mounts and a more practical rectangle between A and B to which you can more easily mount boxes or cases. I happen to believe that, especially with a rigid case, **separating the mounting from the load is a good idea** which is how the platform rack above right works, even if just about everyone these days makes or buys 'hanging racks'. Most off-the-shelf racks are also **too far back** to make room for a pillion's legs with a box mounted. Here are some other points to consider and your chance to do it right.

- Use easily re-weldable and sourced **steel**, not aluminium.
- **Round tube** is stronger than same-sized square section, but square is less work to weld. Minimise curved sections in either.
- Solidly **bolt** the rack in three or more places per side.
- Use **same sized bolts** for all mounts and check in the early days or after tough stages. Carry spares in case they shear.
- Where applicable, make sure there's **enough room** for wheel removal, easy chain adjustment, full suspension compression and the swing of a kickstart, if present.
- A **brace across the back** will stop inward flexing to create a more rigid 'cube'. Straight or 'V', the lower the brace the better. Some soft luggage racks dodge this, but can end up heavier to resist the flex.
- Don't simply crush, drill and bolt tube ends. Weld on a **tab** and drill it as this point is often prone to failure.
- Don't expect total rigidity. Fully loaded, everything will **flex** (especially side-to-side) but that's better than bending or snapping.

Because of the complex forces going on here, forces from all directions which weren't necessarily anticipated when the bike was designed, the simplest way to ensure a rack – home-made or otherwise – doesn't lead to frame problems is to **keep your payload light**.

BIKE CHOICE & PREPARATION

Left: Hot Rod Welding's 'sheep rack' for 650X BMWs doesn't hang out like a bunch of teenagers at a shopping centre. Worth imitating. **Right**: Tiny plate rack on its way to ebay.

Tail racks and front racks

Even though you can use the back of the seat and grab rails (where present), a tail rack is an almost universal addition on a travel bike. A flat, solid surface on which to lash a bag or fix a box makes sense, less good is the tendency to overload this convenient patch to the detriment of both centralised weight and subframe longevity.

The advent of cheap computerised metal cutting machines has led to a craze for **plate racks** as pictured above right, along with any other number of CNC derived 'hard parts'. Watching a machine zip off a form while you have a rollie is a lot less work than bending and welding tube, but I still think **a tube-based rack is better**. It has no nasty edges, is easy to lash things to (including a plywood base) and gives you something to grab on to, or to lash down a bike.

I've long admired the idea of wide 'sheep racks' (as I call them), similar to what you find on the back of a farmer's quad bike. Walter Colebatch, the man from Magadan, also helped develop an ingenious 'sheep rack' (above left) for BMW 650X bikes. It provides the width and so stability, but cleverly wraps round the back of the seat for all the right reasons, while still accommodating passengers. My last few bikes all had grab rail mounts which could have easily been used to fit a wrap-around sheep rack.

A **front rack** is a less common. There may be a rationale to spreading the load around the bike, but adding weight above the light is about as desirable as doing the same on your crash helmet. I've even seen front racks with a pair of Rotopaxes proudly hanging from them. If you're going to put a rack up here, keep it small and the load light, or just lash a bag directly to the bike.

Test run

When all that's done, take your fully-loaded bike for a **test ride**. As you wobble down the street you'll wonder how on earth you're ever going to ride from Anchorage to Brazzaville and your first ride on the dirt will be the same again.

While loaded up, lay the bike over and try to **pick it up**; if you can't it's really too heavy, and unless you're certain there'll always be someone around to help you, consider reducing the weight or repositioning the baggage. This may be your last chance before D-Day. Many first time riders send stuff home in the early days of a big trip.

Clothing for the long ride

As much as any of the advice given in this book, clothing is a matter of personal taste but, whatever image you decide to cultivate, you'll need to protect yourself from wind, sun, heat, cold, dust, rain, stones and crashing. All up it's a lot to ask of your clothes when on the road for months at a stretch. **Comfort**, **lightness**, **utility** and **quality of construction** are all important features to consider as you'll probably end up wearing the same kit most of the time.

You don't need masses of **spare clothing**. Instead make do with one change and launder every few days until it wears out, then replace it locally. Save space by opting for multi-functional items that are light and quick-drying, and resist the temptation to pack a smart outfit 'just in case'. In the unlikely event of an invitation to an embassy soirée, you'll create more of a stir in your weather-beaten leathers than crammed inside a crumpled shirt and tie.

Jackets
The adventure motorcycling boom has hit jackets and just like everyone else, clothing manufacturers are tying themselves in knots trying to reinvent a modern day oilskin. One jacket I had came with no less than ten tags proclaiming 'seam-tech', 'reflek-teck', dry-tek and the latest jackets mix all sorts of NASA-certified fabrics, textures and features to the point where the eleventh tag can boast a four-figure sum.

All you're asking is the jacket combines a feeling of protection and security with comfort and utility at a price you can afford and with a look you can

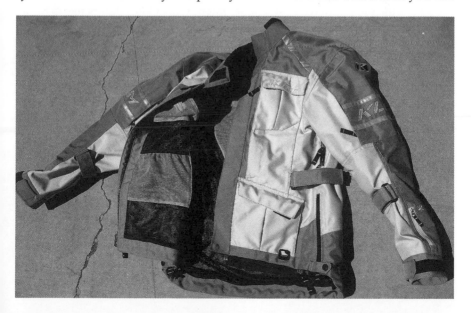

Left: Aerostich Darien Light, an all-time classic. **Right**: ARMR Moto Kiso cheapie. Smart looks, has 'armour' but waist band too high, pockets too small and a liner clammy (but removable).

BIKE CHOICE & PREPARATION

admire. It wants to seal up snugly around the neck, wrists and waist for cold days, while being adjustable with zips and vents as days or climates warm up. Velcro bands or a belt at the waist helps seal your core warm on a cool morning while being easy to release on the move.

A good jacket wants to have all the above qualities and also have enough **good-sized pockets** to carry valuables (something that's often merely enumerated in descriptions and reviews). Keeping valuables on your person is the best way of ensuring they stay with you, so look for big zipped pockets, at least one of which is inside. Make sure the ones on your chest aren't so high or so small that you can't easily get your hand in. Side entry often makes for a bigger pocket to hold a map or documents, while on the back, pouches for a hydration bladder and another below at hem-level are all handy.

The best jacket to fill all the above criteria most of the time is a **touring jacket** based on Cordura, a tough woven nylon that's light, looks good, abrades well as you slide down the road, is easy to clean and forms a tough shell on which to **laminate** a breathable membrane. Other things like ceramic superfabrics and aramid-infused Cordura are increasingly used. Aerostich, Dainese, Klim, Lindstroms, Rev'It and Rukka are some well known names. You need to spend at least £250/$400 to get something decent, but you can pay from half that or up to four times more.

Elements of a good touring jacket

Apart from budget and nailing the right look, what you choose will also partly depend on **where** you're going. Most of us are looking to ride somewhere warmer like Africa or Central America. Here venting may be more useful than waterproofing but as we've all learned: **it's always colder than you think** on a bike. Even then, avoid removable thermal liners, they're often cheap addons. You probably already own a draw full of fleeces or will get a heated liner.

Comfort and fit With online shopping it's easy to order something that looks cool, has great online reviews and is 35% off in a sale. Doing so with clothing is a gamble, so make sure they do returns or better still see what's going at a big motorcycling show where you'll have everything from price-slashed junk to outfits that would make Neil Armstrong look like Columbo. Sit on a bike if you get a chance, or if at home wear it for a couple of hours. Play with all the zips, adjustments and pockets and move around to assess how it actually feels.

Rukka PVC one-piece. Not made for years but bone dry in an all-day downpour. Current proofed nylon onesies are inexpensive. But all can get clammy as a bin bag, especially with a heated liner.

Waterproof/breathable As explained below, don't be too hopeful that so-called breathable fabrics will stay waterproof forever. Cheaper jackets have removable liners rather than having the membrane laminated to the outer shell. It may sound like the best of both worlds – breathable and airy in the sunshine; zip in the liner when clouds roll in. In fact it's purely a cost saving measure, allowing any number of flash-looking shells to be designed to take an off-the-peg liner and in my experience, play it safe by being more waterproof than breathable. Laminated directly to the shell works best because it won't 'wet out' and clog the whole system. All your top-end jackets are made this way.

Ventilation is an admission that breathable membranes don't work so well, for 'passive' motorcycling (as opposed to hiking up a hill with a full pack). Zipped vents or panels which pin or roll back appear on the chest and arms, with exhaust vents across the back. The main zip open is the best vent of all, but will flap annoyingly so venting is worthwhile as it encourages you to always wear your jacket properly. Just don't expect miracles in airflow or waterproofing.

Quality zips Zips have a hard time, being stressed, folded, caked in filth, ill-maintained and yanked upon. Do yourself a favour and make sure your jacket is fitted with chunky, quality items. A regular zip isn't waterproof. The so-called water-resistant zips that appear on some jackets are, as far as I can tell,

BIKE CHOICE & PREPARATION

BREATHABLE FABRICS

The efficacy of breathable membranes like Gore-Tex is much discussed when applied to motorcycling. The micropore film laminated to your jacket shell (or less effectively, a separate liner) releases the condensation vapour formed by sweat, while miraculously resisting the ingress of water (aka, rain).

Thing is, for such fabrics to work a certain amount of 'thermodynamic pressure' and heat must build up inside the jacket for the vapour to start purging. This heat can be easily generated climbing Nanga Parbat, less so sat on a motorcycle at 70mph.

Some condensation is not so bad and can be dealt with by vents or stoicism, but a garment failing to keep rain out is a real drag.

Breathable membrane garments need to be **washed regularly** in special soaps and then re-coated or even cured in a hot dryer with a solution called DWR to help rainwater bead and run off the jacket, rather than soak in. Such maintenance is easily done with your weekend hiking cag and helps maintain breathability, but out in Lubumbashi, Olapoque or Krasny Ogurek, getting hold of that sort of stuff will not be so easy.

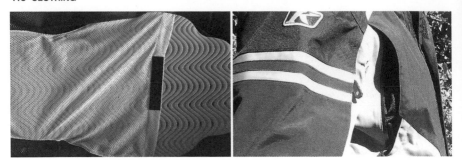

Left: Go for supple molecular CE *approved* armour. Right: Jacket vents can help up to a point.

BIKE CHOICE & PREPARATION

merely fine-toothed and therefore less robust zips which bind a rubbery plastic edging together as they zip up to seal out rain. That may work for hill walking, but belting along at 110 clicks into a storm, such a closure can't be expected to resist water. Rukka still use Gore-tex's Lockout 'rubber seal zip' but a regular robust zip with a double storm flap is the best protection against oncoming rain.

Impact and wear protection has got much cleverer over the years and now includes polymers like D3O or Seeflex armour 'approved' (rather than 'certified') to so-called Level 2 CE – European Union standard that relates to many safety features like armour. (A similar logo indicating 'China Export' is not the same thing.) This armour is soft, malleable and therefore unobtrusive to wear until an impact when it locks up hard at a molecular level – perfect for crashing from motorbikes. You'll want it on the elbows, shoulders and maybe the back, while points of high wear like elbows and shoulders benefit from a panel or second layer of kevlar or some superfabric.

Other features include cinch straps on the arms – I managed decades of biking before I realised I was missing those. Reflective stripes are now a legal requirement in some countries and appear on most jackets. And lately integrated but removable kidney belts have made a reappearance on some adventuresome jackets. I used to wear them in the 80s because *Dirt Bike* said I should. The idea is they stop your innards getting jumbled as you hammer across the piste, but I never really found them that comfy or noticeably effective.

Trousers – alternatives to jeans

With trousers the accent is on comfort and protection, pockets are less important as sat down on a bike what's in them will get in the way. Many jacket makers produce matching riding pants with similar features. Look for articulated knees, long- or even full-length zips for easy removal, vents I suppose and a non-slippery seat. Again, avoid cheap loose or zip-out liners which will snag.

Leather trousers are hard-wearing, low maintenance, crash well and look good when filthy. Look for soft supple cowhide and one piece legs (no seam across the knees) which jacks the price up. They're not waterproof and heavy so tuck into boots and use strong braces to hold them up to stop the crotch splitting in the countless times you swing your leg over your bike.

Riding jeans include kevlar linings or patches, as well as pockets for **knee**

Left: No need for full-on MX bricks, just solid ankle protection. **Right**: two pairs of gloves essential.

protectors or pads a good idea whatever trousers you choose. If nothing else they make kneeling on the ground when working on the bike a whole lot more comfortable. Whatever you buy, remember you'll be wearing it constantly so think about durability, wear and comfort right across a range of climates. As a rule it's easier to cool off than warm up so a dependable outer shell is the key.

Boots, gloves and helmet

Invest in a pair of **boots** that will last the trip and protect your feet and ankles in the frequent low-speed tumbles. Full-on MX boots can be over the top and heavy; choose something that offers protection while still being suited to walking around the ruins of Machu Picchu or a spot of shopping.

Gloves are important, not just for crashing but for warmth, protection and carting luggage around. Take **two pairs** as they're easily mislaid. Pick some thick ones for long, cold and wet days, and a thinner pair of 'day gloves' which you'll use most often, especially off road. Being able to operate a camera through the thin pair saves a lot of faffing. You'll get the usual claims from waterproof membranes as well as rufty-tufty knuckle armour. Better to leave bad weather to either some muffs, big hand guards or the screen. Waterproof mitts may have fewer seams but are more suited to ice climbing than motorcycling where you do need fingers.

With **helmets** you want comfort, quietness (from a smooth exterior or earplugs) and good visibility in a light weight package. Ventilation can work but adds noise. Take your pick with the flip-ups which open like a Ro-Ro ferry, the peaked 'adventure' style of Arai Tour X and its many clones or open face, perhaps with a big visor like the X-Lite (below).

Whatever you get, look for a **liner** that comes out easily for regular washing but won't fall apart in doing so, tool-less main visor removal for easy and possibly daily cleaning (on the road try to minimise rain swipes with gritty gloves). And **integral sun shades** are much more versatile than sunglasses, just as long as operating action is smooth. Up to a point at low sun angles they can make noise-inducing peaks redundant.

Left: Heated grips trounce bulky gloves. **Right**: Aerostich Kanetsu inflater tube presses elements against you; other jackets do the same with a stretch fit. Either way, get a heat controller.

Cold-weather clothing

It can't all be one long holiday, especially for genuine round-the-worlders who'll want to face a cold season or sustained high altitude with smug optimism, not dread. Retaining and maintaining body heat is what counts. Fairings, windshields and handlebar muffs – bodged from roadside rubbish if necessary – are the first line of defence. Keeping warm also means **regular stops** to stimulate circulation as well as to take on hot food and drinks. When under-dressed the body involuntarily tenses up and shivers to try and generate heat and old hands will know that a stiff, chilled rider loses the suppleness needed to control a motorcycle proficiently. Add in a chilly night's added hazards and warmth becomes imperative for safety.

Insulation is the next step as it's the trapped, still air heated by your body that keeps you snug, not bulky materials per se. Use a thick fleece under your outer shell and wear a neck tube and a balaclava. **One-piece** fleece or thermal base layers and/or outer shells (like Aerostich's Roadcrafter) are warmer and very comfortable to wear as they eliminate the gap or compressed waistbands in the kidney area where core body heat is easily lost. The drawback comes when things warm up or nature rings the double bell, so that combination is best left for dedicated winter rides and is less practical for overlanding.

Your engine produces electrical power; capitalise on it with **heated grips** and **heated clothing**. As your body chills blood is drawn from the limbs to the core to sustain the vital organs. By heating your trunk, warm blood can be fed back to frigid limbs. My experience is that heated grips are brilliant, but even above freezing, heated jackets don't exactly replicate dozing in front of a roaring fire. They merely take the edge off – that's until you switch them off and notice how cold it really is.

New technologies using carbon fibre, woven heat pads or nano-ceramic infra-red microwire are leaving heated wire elements behind, and modern bikes now have **high-output alternators** to power such accessories. Check out the heated gear from Aerostich, exo2, Gerbing, Powerlet or Keis. Whichever you buy, get a **heat controller** (a rotating knob works best with gloves), choose a snug fit and wear it as close to your skin as possible. Disregard the urban myth that heated liners can reverse the effect of breathable jacket membranes to draw water in. As long as it's warmer inside than out, that won't happen, though it can occur with similar membrane gloves used with heated grips as the vapour flows from hotter (grips) into the cooler (gloves).

BIKE CHOICE & PREPARATION

LIFE ON THE
ROAD

3

The Big Day arrives and the Sky News chopper is buzzing the
neighbourhood while colourful street-bunting flutters in the
breeze. Or more likely, some friends and family are buzzing
around and the fluttering is in your stomach because one thing's
fairly certain, you'll be nervous. If you've had the time to prepare
thoroughly and get everything sorted and packed, pat yourself on
the back. Chances are though, like most mortals, you'll have overlooked something, or will be dealing with a last-minute cock-up.
This seems to be normal, another test thrown down from the gods
of the overland. Expect it.

One great way of avoiding a last-minute panic is to **pack the
bike days before you leave**, or gather everything you need in a safe
space like a garage. Assembling all the gear, at this stage you're not
yet chewing your lip over an imminent departure, but instead have
a few days to thoughtfully check the bike and tick off a checklist.
There'll still be eleventh-hour things to buy or do but, this way,
should the handlebars come away in your hands there'll be enough
time to bolt them back on and still stay on schedule.

SHAKEDOWN TRIP

Many of us will have travelled abroad in one way or another before setting off on our big motorcycle adventure. For the rest with less experience, the best way of reducing the shock of hitting the road on the big one is to hit the road on a small one. A **shakedown trip** of a week or two to somewhere as far as you dare will be an invaluable dress rehearsal. When the real thing comes along it won't feel so daunting, just another trip that's a little bit further this time.

On a test run you'll have a chance to refine your set up without unnecessary pressure. Some flaw may also manifest itself – a wobble or vibration, overheating, or that expensive jacket or helmet driving you nuts. Better to know this while there's plenty of time to do something about it.

... it's better to find all this out by wading out from the shallows rather than diving in at the deep end with a full backpack.

From western Europe, somewhere like Morocco, Turkey or even just eastern Europe can give an idea of what it's like to be in a significantly foreign country on the edge of the overland zone. From North America it's obviously going to be Mexico and Central America, while South Africans can roam far north into their continent, taking on progressively more challenging countries as they go. For those I've missed out, you get the picture.

A short test run or an **organised tour** (see p30) can be used to find out if you even *like* the idea of a long-haul trip of your own. You may acknowledge that a short trip is as much as you want to take on at this stage in your life. It's nice to go camping on your well set-up bike for a couple of weeks, but hauling it all the way to Vladivostok or Ushuaia might be too much of a commitment. Again, it's better to find all this out by wading out from the shallows rather than diving in at the deep end with a full backpack.

SETTING OFF

So here it is. You climb aboard, start the engine, heave the bike off the stand (don't forget to flick it up!), clunk into first and wobble off down the road, utterly appalled at the weight of your rig. Once out on the open road you wind it up and allow some faint optimism to creep in to your multiplying anxieties as passing motorists glance at you with what you hope is envy.

Finally on the move after months if not years of preparation, the urge is to keep moving, especially if you're heading out across a cold continent. Recognise this restlessness for what it is: an inability to relax for fear that something bad is going to happen. It's all part of the acclimatisation process as your life takes on a whole new direction.

Once abroad, try to resist covering excessive mileages in the early days. Racing through unfamiliar countries with perplexing road signs and 'wrong-side' driving can lead to misjudgements. If an estimated three-quarters of all overlanders achieve hospitalisation through accidents, rather than commonly-dreaded diseases, hyena attacks or banditry, you can imagine what that figure is for motorcyclists. In many cases it happens early in the trip.

Then again, it may be your head that's on the wrong side of the road, not your bike. It will be intensely galling, but if things don't feel right or get off to a bad start and you have a chance to correct them, turn back. If you didn't make a big splash no one need know. To help give yourself a good chance of not needing to do that, don't make any **crazy deadlines** to quit work and catch a ferry the next morning, or plan to pick up a visa three countries away in less than a week. Instead, after a couple of days on the road make a conscious effort to **park up somewhere** warm and sunny or visit friends to give you a chance to catch your breath. Spread out for a while, tinker with the bike and just get used to being away from home but not up to your neck in it just yet. If you're a bit shaky about the whole enterprise it can make a real difference to your mood. And especially when on your own, **managing your moods** is as important as keeping on the correct side of the road.

THE SHOCK OF THE NEW

Alone on your first big trip into foreign lands it's normal to feel self conscious, intimidated, if not a little paranoid. This is because you've just ejected yourself from your comfort zone and are entering the thrill of an adventure. 'Adventure travel' has become tourism marketing jargon to distinguish trekking holidays from lying on a towel by a pool. But as far as this book's concerned, an 'adventure' is what it always was: an activity with an uncertain and possibly dangerous outcome.

The less glamorous aspect of all this is the **stress** involved in dealing with strange people, languages, customs, places and food. Stress is

> ... setting off overland will be just about the most stressful and exciting thing you'll have done for a long time

usually what you're looking to get away from, but it's not necessarily a bad thing. Leaping into the air off the end of an elastic cord is stressful, so is standing up to give a speech or even taking a long-haul flight. To a certain extent it's an emotional response to losing control, and can also be classified as excitement. Your senses are sharpened and your imagination is stimulated, but with this comes irritability and, initially, an exaggerated wariness of strange situations.

Having probably lived and worked in a secure environment for years, for better or for worse, setting off overland can be just about the most stressful and exciting thing you'll have done for a long time. **Fears** of getting robbed, having a nasty accident, getting into trouble with the police or breaking down are all the more acute when everything you possess for the next few months is in arm's reach. This situation is not improved by the way overseas news is presented in the media: one atrocity or tragedy after another. Who'd want to go to places like these?

A crucial part of the acclimatisation to life on the road is learning to see the world for what it actually is: regular people getting on with their ordinary lives; just like back home. In the collection of over a thousand trip reports on the old AMH website the most common reply to the question: 'Biggest surprise?' was: 'Friendliness of the people'. Many experienced overlanders come to recognise that when all's said and done, it's the good people they meet on their travels who count for more than the number of countries they visited or the gnarly roads they rode.

STREETWISE MANIFESTO

- Don't ride yourself ragged; rest often.
- Don't ride at night unless unavoidable.
- Wild camp out of sight of the road or stay in the security of settlements.
- Keep a low profile in hostile areas or just avoid them altogether.
- In towns and cities park off the street overnight where possible. Many hotels will let you put the bike inside.

- Keep your valuables on you at all times, but have a back-up stash.
- Trust your instincts – if a situation or a place doesn't feel good, move on or be prepared to leave quickly.
- Avoid exposing cash or valuables in crowded places.
- Learn and use the local language – you'll be amazed at the positive response.

It's hard to think so when you've spent months setting-up the bike while keeping tabs on the latest international crisis, but without expecting to teach the world to sing in perfect harmony, this is perhaps the single biggest lesson to learn from travelling. One of the most frustrating scenarios is when you realise you've been rude to someone who was only trying to help or be friendly. This can be understandable when you've been pestered for days by hustlers urging 'Meester, psst. Hey Mister...'. Distinguishing genuine encounters from the others comes with experience, and very often the best encounters are found in rural areas where people are more 'normal'. Those with a proclivity for hustling having migrated to the richer pickings in the cities and resorts.

... when all's said and done, it's the good people they meet on their travels who count for more than the list of countries they visited or the gnarly roads they rode.

It's common to regard long motorcycle journeys as a series of hops from one congested, hassle-ridden city to another. Often it's a bureaucratic requirement to do with acquiring visas (city strategies are on p126 and p172). But out in the country pressures are less acute and locals indifferent to you.

So make the most of roadside cafés for tea breaks, meals and rests. They're great places to mix with local people without feeling like you're on stage. The owners and customers will be regulars used to passing travellers and may well treat you like any other customer. Very often, that's all you want.

Riding abroad

Experienced motorcyclists will be well versed in the need to ride defensively, position themselves conspicuously and to **anticipate the unexpected**. Chances are, out in the AMZ the local driving standards won't be what you're used to back home. In these places very often the **horn** replaces the steering wheel or brakes. What's missing is driver training and the respect we have for road rules and other road users (or the fear of the sanctions if we transgress).

Even if you're riding with all the due care and attention you can muster, the ante is upped further by a possible absence of licensing, roadworthiness testing and motor insurance. You'll be sharing roads with drunks, aggressive taxi drivers, amphetamine-fuelled truck drivers and ageing bangers which should have been melted down into cutlery years ago. Mixing with these unroadworthy crates are the imported, blacked-out limos of local criminals, businessmen and politicians (often all in the same car); stray domestic **this new uninhibited style of riding can be quite liberating...** and wild animals and dozy pedestrians who were never taught to 'look left, look right, and left again'. Throw in some more alcohol, a splash of Latino / Arabic / Indian machismo, donkey carts, bad roads, unlit vehicles, unsigned diversions and unfinished bridges, plus some grossly overloaded vehicles, and you've arrived in the crazy world of riding in the AMZ where anything goes. All this can require an acute period of adjustment as you shudder past another pile of impossibly mangled wreckage being hosed off the road.

What's needed is **alertness** mixed with a dose of **assertiveness** that doesn't extend to aggression. This can be difficult to judge when, because you're clearly a foreigner, you feel you're being singled out by local young men who regard being overtaken by you as an insult akin to looking at their sister. A good way of rationalising this is to acknowledge that among the hundreds of drivers you pass in a day, you might generally encounter only one dickhead. Don't always take tailgating personally: there's a different concept of personal space out in the world (both on the road and in daily life). In fact, after a while this new uninhibited style of riding can be quite liberating; what counts is that all road users are on the same wavelength, and this now includes you.

LOCAL DRIVING CUSTOMS

It's said that in Mexico, and certainly in many other places, a vehicle in front that you wish to pass will **signal** on the off side if it's safe to pass and to the near side (the kerb) if it's not safe. This is the opposite of what's done in Europe and North Africa, where a slow vehicle will indicate to the near side – 'pulling over' – that it's safe to go for it. Misunderstanding these signals could be grave so don't be rushed.

Use your own judgement and visibility when performing such manoeuvres.

Back home **flashing headlights** usually means go ahead; it can also mean 'watch out, speed trap / cops ahead' when done to oncoming vehicles. In parts of North Africa flashing seems to ask 'Have you seen me?', except that just about every oncoming vehicle seems to require this affirmation on a flat and perfectly clear road. If you don't flash back they'll flash again urgently.

It can also be a message indicating 'Hey dumbass, you've got your lights on in broad daylight!', but it's rarely pointing out something you don't know, such as a condor is making a nest on your panniers.

THE WRONG SIDE OF THE ROAD

Although it's less of a problem on a bike than a car, if you've never ridden in a country where they drive on the other side of the road it's natural to be anxious about dealing with things like roundabouts. Riding fresh out of a foreign port, or crossing a border where driving sides change (as when crossing the northern borders of Pakistan, Angola or Kenya), you're usually hyper-alert.

Roundabouts, or traffic circles to some, are a good example. They seem to be proliferating across the highways of the world as a traffic-signal free way of controlling traffic at a crossroads. In the UK you give way to traffic already on the roundabout, elsewhere you're supposed to give priority to those entering the roundabout, but I bet I'm not the only one to have ridden in countries where they do it both ways. The answer is to slow down, make eye contact and go for it when you feel it's safe.

In my experience you commonly get the side of the road wrong when either you've been on tracks with little traffic for days, or you pull off the highway in a rural area for a lazy lunch. On returning to the road, the lack of any roadside infrastructure or momentary passing traffic sees you instinctively do what you've done all your riding years: head off down what's now the wrong side of the road. Luckily, such mistakes are usually made on quiet roads.

The other time you might blow it is when you've been riding for 20 hours non-stop, chomping Nescafé straight out of the jar. In a moment of frazzled panic you don't know if right is wrong or left is right. This confusion can mess you up even if you're in a country where they drive on the side you're used to back home. As a Brit, for example, you assume anything 'abroad' must equate with driving on the right. Not if it's Kenya or Thailand or crazy India, where left is right, right is wrong and might is right anyway. One trick that can help is visualising a memorable street scene back home. To a Brit, Australasian or southern African, most of the world is on the other side; remember the homely scene and get on the correct side, quick.

CITY STRATEGIES

Cairo, Quito, Dakar, Delhi; it's a good thing they're all so far apart. Like it or not your ride will be punctuated by visits to cities like these where dealing with congestion, noise and pollution comes on top of security issues and the expense of staying there. You need to go to these places for spares or repairs, to check email, get visas and, who knows, maybe even to stroll around the national museum or admire the Old Town at dusk.

If you have the choice, try to arrange visits to big cities on your terms. Above all, in a big, unfamiliar city it helps to **know where you're heading**, as opposed to blundering around looking for a cheap hotel in the old quarter. If you're having trouble finding the place you fixed on, hire a taxi driver or a kid on a moped to lead you there.

Some places like Islamabad and cities in East Africa have centrally located camping parks which are great places to meet other travellers. Many cities have guarded parking compounds, but as they're usually a piece of waste ground so not necessarily good spots to leave a bike. Many small hotels have a courtyard or a storage lock-up where they'll be happy to stash your bike, while others allow you to ride it right into reception overnight. If you have to leave it outside, a **cheap bike cover** helps reduce passing interest in the bike.

Borders and checkpoints

No two ways about it, border crossings will be the most predictably intimidating episodes on your journey. Expect to encounter crowds of pushy locals, signs you can't read and instructions you can't understand, as well as helpers looking to make a tip and officials struck down with narcolepsy at the very sight of a starry-eyed foreigner waving a passport.

On top of all this is the worry that your papers aren't up to scratch or that a search will reveal something restricted such as a GPS or alcohol or even a proscribed guidebook. The learning curve can be steep as your passport disappears in one direction and your vehicle documents in the other.

Borders

Notorious crossings include entering western Russia, mostly due to the language and forms; Egypt; the Mauritania–Morocco border; any border into DRC, and some Central American crossings, where $5 handed out here and there oils the wheels. If you get through any of these in less than an hour and for free you've done well.

Elsewhere, where an alphabet or numerals are unfamiliar to you – notably Arabic – local 'helpers' in league with the officials may try and overcharge you on genuine mandatory expenses like insurance or other permits. The main Iran–Turkey border at Bazargan is known for this so learn your **Arabic numerals**, it's not hard – see p240.

Remember you're not the first person to put up with this and at the very worst your naivety or momentary weakness may cost a few dollars. As with the sullen staff you can encounter at consulates, look at these bottlenecks as the small price you pay for the freedom of being out on the road.

Border strategies

Over the weeks and months border procedures get easier to decipher as you learn the drill and the right levels of assertiveness required to slip through. Here are some guidelines; you'll soon develop your own strategies:

- Remain polite and smile a lot. They're stuck here day in, day out and don't get paid any more for being efficient.
- Impatience is usually counter-productive. Settle in for the long haul and have food and water on hand.
- Accept delays, queues and sudden 'lunch breaks' taken by the officials.
- Obey all the instructions for searches, however onerous.
- Resist confrontations; bite your lip in the face of provocation.
- But don't put up with people pushing in, outright theft, or 'This for me, yes?' attempts at petty extortion.

Stoicism and good humour can defuse a tense situation. Try to remember that the glamorous benefits of an ill-fitting uniform and an old machine gun soon pale when you're living in a tin shed far from your family and haven't been

LIFE ON THE ROAD

paid for six months. Recognise that if there's something wrong with your paperwork they have a legitimate excuse to follow their rules. Read the situation. If there's an opportunity to make a gift to cover a genuine transgression, pay up if you want to get moving.

The great thing about the comparatively slack attitude to rules and regulations in the AMZ is that it can work in your favour. An expired visa or other irregularity is not always the inflexible 'rules-are-rules' situation in Europe or North America that would see you locked up or on the next plane out. A small consideration and a promise to get it fixed is all that's needed to keep going.

Bribes

It's important to recognise that **bribes** aren't exclusively the unceasing daylight robbery of gullible foreigners, but a way of life in some of the countries you'll visit. You may resent this custom but that's just what it is, a custom that oils the wheels. A few dollars or euros can save hours, and these payments are usually tiny in the overall scheme of things. You'll know when you're expected to pay so accept it as part of travelling, but don't assume you must pay your way through every border or checkpoint just because your foreign number plate reads like a string of dollar signs.

Border procedures

Paperwork featuring impressive stamps is much admired out in the world and you'll amass a fair bit of locally issued documentation once you start crossing borders. One traveller described the paperwork collected at an Egyptian border as a 'folder that resembles a post-grad dissertation'.

To give you an idea of what to expect, the most common requirements are listed below. Apart from visas, unless otherwise stated all these **documents** are obtained at the relevant border or office. Some border officials may want to see vaccination certificates and in some countries there may be further procedures like the need to register with the police elsewhere within a given number of days. It may also help not to display any controversial or flashy gadgets like satnavs or sat phones too prominently. On arrival take a deep breath and proceed as follows:

- Track down and fill out an immigration card (example above)
- Take the card and get your passport stamped
- Complete a form to import your bike temporarily (your vehicle ownership document will be needed)
- ...or get your carnet stamped
- Fill out a currency declaration form, which may include 'valuables'
- Declare any restricted items or hide them well
- Show vaccination certificates
- Change money
- Rent local number plates (Egypt, China, among others)
- Buy motor insurance, if possible or necessary

Roadside checkpoints

Highway checkpoints are imposed by many countries to control or monitor the movement of the local population, very often on the main road into and out of a big town. They also crop up near borders to catch illegal immigrants and smugglers, and where you may also have to present your recently acquired papers if you've just entered the country. Very often you'll be recognised as a harmless tourist and waved through, but no matter how many times this has happened before, **always slow down** and make eye contact with the soldier – even if they happen to be quickly pulling up their pants – before riding on. In countries where assassins or suicide bombers use bikes, proper checkpoint etiquette is vital.

Some checkpoints alongside strategic installations or disputed areas will have elaborate arrangements of spikes, oil drums and single-lane barricades to slow you down. There'll be a 'Stop' sign set up a short distance from the actual checkpoint and possibly a guy up a tower with a gun too. At

> **In countries where assassins or suicide bombers use bikes, proper checkpoint etiquette is vital**

night these places may require you to turn off your lights. Wait at the 'Stop' sign until waved on, especially if there's already a vehicle up ahead.

As in the Moroccan-occupied part of Western Sahara, checkpoints may be required to take your personal and vehicle details, which is usually written by hand into a grubby exercise book. You can speed things up for both you and them by having this information pre-printed on a form to hand out. You can download and if necessary, adapt a French–English **checkpoint form** in Word at 🖳 www.sahara-overland.com/fiche. These forms can also be handed over to hotel receptionists at check in. At a checkpoint (or a hotel), resist giving your passport away to anyone other than men in hats, and even then be wary in suspicious situations.

Sometimes you'll be pulled over just because you're a foreigner on a flash bike and the cops are curious or bored. This curiosity can extend to hospitality, or it can go the other way and they can try it on, making up some bogus infringement, as they like to do in western Russia. As always, the old trick of turning into an imbecile and pretending not to understand any shared Earthly language can encourage them to lose interest. But, as with all such encounters it's best to flip up the visor, look them in the eye and kick off with a local greeting and a smile, as well as accede to all reasonable requests. A working knowledge of the current composition of the Manchester United football team can also help break the ice. In the 1970s many overlanders crossed Africa without delay by merely shouting 'Bobi Sharlton' at every official they met. 'Vaiyn Rouni' should do the trick these days, but unfortunately you're at their mercy and predatory types can read if you're nervous.

A lot depends on how you respond to each other, which is why **a greeting and a smile** is a good way to start, even if it's ignored. They may expect a condescending attitude from some cocky foreigner who's in need of taking down a peg or two. You may pull over for the nth time that day, thinking it's another shakedown and this time you're not going to stand for it, but learning how to slip through checkpoints like a well-lubed cable is all part of the game.

Changing money and bargaining

As mentioned early on, the best form of money is **cash drawn from ATMs**. The best hard currencies are euros in North and West Africa and parts of the Middle East, and US dollars everywhere else, best brought from home or withdrawn from an ATM.

Once you're on the road you'll find some borders have currency-changing kiosks with posted rates, while others will have a guy walking around with a satchel full of local cash and a calculator. Otherwise, the nearest town will have a bank, ideally with a cashpoint, which is the simplest way to obtain local currency without getting diddled. If there's a good network of them you need withdraw only a little cash at a time. This way you won't get stuck trying to change a weak local currency back into something useful.

If ATMs are unknown or they don't take your cards, it may be possible to buy the local currency in the preceding country. Otherwise, changing money officially can take hours in some banks, going from one counter to another. **Currency-exchange kiosks** in the centre of large towns won't necessarily be as dodgy as they look, can save hours and might even offer a slightly better rate than a bank. And in some countries you can simply pay your hotel bills or whatever in foreign currency.

'Sorry, no change' is something you're bound to hear when paying for a local service with a high-denomination note, so learn to hoard **low-denomination notes**: they're useful for tips or incentivisation.

Currency Declaration Forms

Some countries try and undermine currency black markets by using Currency Declaration Forms (CDF). On it you fill out all the foreign currency you're bringing into a country, and possibly other sellable valuables like cameras. Any further official exchange transactions you make in that country must match receipts or entries on the CDF, so that when you leave the cash you brought in equals what you're taking out, less what you officially exchanged.

Half the time these forms aren't even checked when you leave, but don't count on it. Any hard currency you don't declare on the form must obviously not be discovered on departure, but having a **stash of undeclared money** is a good way to cover unexpected costs or do a quick black-market deal.

BLACK MARKET

Using the black market to change foreign currency into local at an advantageous rate is an accepted, if these days less common, part of travel. It's also a popular way of fleecing naive travellers and by its very nature is illegal, leaving you liable to fines, confiscation of funds and even imprisonment.

Use the black market by all means (sometimes there is no choice and some banks will even encourage it to save work for themselves), but keep your eyes open and your wits about you. If you're a beginner, here are some guidelines:

- Establish exactly how many 'dogons' you're being offered for a dollar (for example). Repeat to them: 'So you are offering me 40 dogons for one dollar?' and if they agree then spell out the total amount you want to exchange: 'So you will give me 600 dogons for 15 dollars?'
- Ask to see the currency offered and check that the notes have the right number of zeros. It's helpful to learn to read the nine cardinal Arabic numerals if heading that way – see p240.
- If there's room for negotiation, go ahead. A wily black-marketeer is going to offer as little as he can for your valuable currency.
- Deal one-to-one and don't get rushed or drawn into any shady corners.

Watch out for **sleight of hand**. I was caught out with what I call the 'Romanian Hand Trick' near the Libyan border once. There's some ploy where they count out the money offered, then give it to you to count before taking your money. They then take it back to recount, and even though you're staring intently at their hands, something happens. They now take your money and hand over theirs which you've just counted. Only later do you realise you got done. If this 'you-count-then-hand-back' deal happens, switch to high alert.

The black market can represent a major boost to your funds in some places such as Venezuela, but don't stick your neck out for a measly 10%. While you should never take them for granted, you'll soon get the hang of these useful if illegal street deals. And if you're ever unsure, trust your instincts and walk away.

BARGAINING

Whether bargaining for souvenirs or negotiating for services, the first step is to appraise the object of your desire or your service needs and ask yourself **what you are prepared to pay**. Even if it's over the odds, once you've established this in your mind you should have no reason to feel cheated once you pay that amount.

When it comes to souvenirs, all the time-worn tricks will be tried to make you spend more: free shipping, two for the price of one plus a free pendant, but stick to your price for what you want unless you want the object at any cost. You may be asked to 'give me your best price', but remember that if you name a price, bargaining etiquette deems you're obliged to pay it, so don't let any figure pass your lips that you're not prepared to pay. Bide your time, because this – along with that wad in your pocket – is your greatest asset. If you have the chance, look around for a few days and get to know the vendors and what they have (often it's all from the same source). If you find it hard to simply walk away, say you might come back tomorrow. Try not to allow yourself to be intimidated, however persuasive the vendor. In Islamic lands be wary of being drawn in by a carpet seller to have tea unless you're confident you can handle the extreme pressure that may be put on you. In Morocco these vendors are notorious and can get aggressive to the point of virtually robbing you.

Negotiating a price for other services like mechanical repairs, guides or food is less customary. There's usually a **set price** for such commodities. Despite the market scene in *The Life of Brian*, locals don't go to the souk every day and engage in protracted negotiations for the same bag of onions they bought last week, unless it's a seasonal commodity or the quality has varied. But if you feel you're being overcharged, most likely because of your origins, give it a go or ask the price in advance. In some cases, not to barter is seen as weak and not playing the game. It's all part of the travel experience, with market encounters one of the few occasions you get to interact with locals as normal people, not men in hats with guns. Enjoy it.

Keeping in touch

NICK TAYLOR

Assuming you have a **GSM phone** (aka: 'mobile', 'cell' or 'handy'), you'll probably be aware that they're both expensive to use outside of your home country, and need to be less than 40km (23 miles) from the nearest GSM mast in line of sight. They can be ideal for short calls or text messages to co-ordinate a rendezvous with others, and are especially useful if you get split up. In remote rural or wilderness areas there probably won't be a signal, although in an emergency getting to high ground is always worth a go.

Per capita usage of mobiles in some African and Asian countries is much higher than in the West. The market is huge, especially as a courting aid among the young, with mobile phone boutiques and advertising everywhere. In some countries private investment has seen the network leapfrog a land line system that was never that good in the first place, and per-minute charges are much less than we're used to back home, especially for calls abroad.

Providing your own handset is **unlocked** to accept alternative providers (something easily done in any phone boutique), buying a **local SIM card** is a cheap way to stay in touch. If you can't unlock your phone, the cheapest Nokia 'dumbphone' does nothing but voice and texts and costs as little as $25. With your local SIM card just make sure you're joining a network that'll cover you on your intended travels; a little research online may help. India for example has several **regional providers** who might as well be in adjacent countries; what works in one state won't work elsewhere. Otherwise, to save you buying card after card, international roaming SIM cards are available from many providers, offering a good discount over your domestic provider when calling from abroad.

For a link back home there are a number of options. GSM phones are obviously the most convenient. Even without a local SIM card, the odd text message or a brief urgent call is usually cheap or important enough to be worthwhile. Failing that, if you want to have a good natter with those back home, **international phone cards** to use from a phone box or land line will be widely available.

Internet access

These days we're travelling with our own laptops, tablets or smartphones, picking up a **wi-fi** signal anywhere, either secure or unencrypted. While some parts of the world seem to be connected to the internet by a frayed washing line, in terms of price per bit, for getting a quick email out they can't be beaten. If you get a good connection, voice and even video calling is possible through Skype or one of the other voice over internet protocol (VoIP) services. All will be far cheaper than using your GSM phone. Using internet cafés is also an ideal way to upload larger amounts of data to a website, especially imagery.

The downside of **internet cafés** is their computers, complete with Fanta-stained mouse-mats, baffling keyboard layouts and who-knows-what sort of software installed – a key-logger recording your online banking password, perhaps? So it's best never to risk such activity on publicly used computers.

SATELLITE COMMUNICATIONS

Once the preserve of large corporations and government agencies, the cost of satellite communication including **GPS tracking** has dropped dramatically. As a phone, it's the only reliable back up if things go wrong while riding in remote areas. The case for GPS tracking is less clear cut.

Satellite phones

There are two principal **satellite phones**: Thuraya and Iridium. **Iridium** is the only company that offers truly global coverage (except North Korea), but if your travels exclude the Americas, currently Dubai-based **Thuraya** offers coverage from Norway to Australia and from Angola across to Mongolia. In other words, everywhere on land except far northern Russia, southern Africa and, as mentioned, the Americas. Charges per minute are around $1.50 with various prepaid packages giving free air time. You probably just want a scratch card for occasional use. In the UK, a used Thuraya handset goes for around £300 and is the size of a pre-smartphone mobile (see picture next page).

Both Iridium and Thuraya offer **data connections** of up to 60kbps (Iridium needs additional software otherwise it's a miserable 2.4 kbps). With an enabled handset, short **emails** can be sent using the telephone keypad. Some satellite phones like Thurayas can also accept your regular mobile's SIM card to work in ordinary GSM mode, should you be in range and the charges cheaper. This can be handy if your GSM phone packs up, but battery life is poor so in practical terms it's better to have a separate GSM phone as well as a satellite phone. Some handsets, notably Thuraya, can also pick up a GPS position after a few minutes, which can be easily forwarded as an SMS, although this feature can't really be used for anything but the most rudimentary navigation. Just like GPS or satnav, a satellite phone needs to be **out in the open** to get a signal. With Thuraya handsets, it helps to point the retractable antenna towards Somalia, above which their satellite is positioned.

Potential legal issues

Once outside the developed world, radios and other communications equipment including sat phones are generally **prohibited for civilian use**. In practice the question is rarely asked when crossing borders, and the worst thing likely to happen is the phone might be confiscated – though if you're current-

---

'I'M GOING BACK TO POSTCARDS AND POSTE RESTANTE'

That was a message I got from a guy who resurfaced in another country five days after his SPOT tracking disappeared in deeply inauspicious circumstances. In a single vehicle, he'd just crossed an unrecognised desert border where kidnappings and robberies had occurred. His last 'ping' was last thing at night, just when such events occur.

When his relatives contacted me I assumed the worst as his hitherto reliable pattern of messaging had stopped. Turns out it may have all been down to a sandstorm or the usual GPS tracking anomalies, but not before consular intervention deployed the French army to his last known position.

A similar thing happened to me trekking on a remote desert plateau while (unknown to us) jihadists attacked an oil base nearby. To block Thuraya comms the ensuing army operation scrambled the GPS signal across our area, just when those back home saw the news and wondered why our Spot map signals had stopped. Moral: a bit of tracking fun can also cause alarm when interrupted.

---

ly rotting in some awful, sub-Saharan prison, remember that the decision to take equipment like this into the country solely rests with you.

Such a situation befell AMH contributor Andy Pag in northern India one time. Being very popular with jihadis and smugglers throughout North Africa and west Asia, Thurayas were **banned in India** following the Mumbai attacks of 2008. Unfortunately, Andy – along with the other billion people in India – was the first to learn of this, which led to a short spell in prison followed by a few months of legal procrastination before he was let off with a 1000-rupee (£10) fine. Even more than GSM phones, satellite phones can be precisely tracked, so unless you know better, hide them well at borders, and in dodgy countries save their use for emergencies.

Spot 3 and Thuraya sat phone.

GPS trackers

The simplest automated way to let others know where you are is to use a **personal tracker**, like the well-known palm-sized Spot tracker, or a more discreet BikeTrac unit which is wired to your bike and designed primarily as an after-theft tracking device.

As well as sending 'All OK' or 'Help' messages to pre-determined contacts (and an all-out panic button of little use in the AMZ), a Spot can be used to pinpoint your position every ten minutes to a public or privately configured Google map page which currently drops locations older than two weeks. That's about as long as the recommended but less easily bought AAA lithium batteries last. BikeTrac works off the bike battery and will retain your full RTW track, but 'pings' with less frequency.

The problem with using these as trackers is the GPS signal is weak and your gadget's reception can be lost for days at a time without you knowing unless you check the online map or ask. It's essential to advise those who might worry not to rely on trackers as a live locator. If you're passing through a dodgy area and need to reassure someone, a voice call is best.

Maps and route finding

Although more than one rider has boasted of setting out with just an inflatable globe or no map at all, there's more than enough adventure awaiting you out there so you'll want a map of some kind to estimate distances, find towns with fuel, contemplate interesting looking diversions, and to help you navigate through or around a congested city.

Mapping these days comes in four forms: traditional inexpensive **paper** maps; the same map in **digital** form to download and display on a screen or print off – a raster map; scrollable and zoomable **vector maps** for satnavs like Garmin Zumos which can be expensive, or free from OSM (see p138), as well as **online** maps like Google Maps which of course require internet.

PAPER MAPS

The digital revolution may have mapped the world for us using online aerial imagery and routeable street-level satnavs, but some sort of **paper mapping** is still desirable. Light, portable, robust and battery-free, just like books, there's still no better way of easily displaying and accessing a large amount of information over a large area or subject in a simple, inexpensive medium. Like all printed media, a map soon gets out of date but, assuming it was accurate in the first place, if it's only a few years old it's still going to be useful.

Map scales

A paper map's scale is given as a ratio of how much smaller it is than the actual land surface: a 1:1,000,000 (1m) scale map is a million times smaller than the area it represents. This can cause some confusion: small-scale maps cover a larger area in less detail. Small scale = small [amount of] detail but big area; large scale = large [amount of] detail.

Small-scale maps with scales from 1:2m to 1:5m give you a big overall picture of an area, which makes them great for planning a trip, if not necessarily for following a precise route. A good example is the Michelin 700 series of maps covering Africa at 1:4 million. Riding in an unfamiliar country with anything above 1:5m scale becomes less detailed and so less useful, but it's handy to spread out on a table at the planning stage and get a feel for relative distances, or for a well-signed territory like Europe or North America.

LIFE ON THE ROAD

METRIC AND IMPERIAL MAP SCALES

Map scales are given in metric or imperial ratios. Most of the world except the US uses metric. With US mapping inches and miles prevail and so it's common for map scales produced there to have some abstruse ratio like 1:633,600 which happens to equal an intuitive 10 miles to 1 inch.

Providing they're accurate, maps with either scale are fine, but in the AMZ you want to **think metrically**. One km is 0.62 of a mile: a quick formula is **halve the kms + add a quarter to get miles**: 100km / 2 + 25% = 62.5 miles. Modern digital speedos can be reconfigured to display mph or kph.

Medium-scale maps between 1:500,000 and 1:2m are ideal for riding. On a 1:1m map, one millimetre represents one kilometre on the ground (1cm = 10km, 1 inch = 15.8 miles). If the cartographic design is good, the map will be easily interpreted and the millimetre/kilometre relationship makes distances on the map easy to visualise. A typical 1:1m map might cover between seven degrees of longitude and from five degrees of latitude, which is around 700km (440 miles) from east to west and 550km (340 miles) north to south.

LATITUDE AND LONGITUDE

If you expect to be using GPS to calculate your position on a paper map rather than just relying on a spot on your satnav, you'll need maps with a lat–long grid. This is a printed grid that actually criss-crosses the face of the map, and not just a lat–long scale shown around the edges; not all maps have this.

Latitude and longitude is a grid system used to pinpoint a location on the spherical Earth using horizontal (latitude) and vertical (longitude) measurements. (I find the expression "in southern latitudes" helps me remember which is which). The equator is the zero line of reference for latitude, dividing the globe into northern and southern hemispheres. The Greenwich or Prime Meridian is the zero line for longitude, dividing the world into western and eastern hemispheres.

Lines of latitude are parallel rings stacked up like cake layers. They divide the globe into bands at equal distance from each other so anywhere on the globe each degree of latitude is about 110km or 68 miles (or 60 nautical miles) apart. One minute of latitude (a 60th of a degree) equals one nautical mile or, more usefully on land, 1.85km or 1.15 miles. One second of latitude (a 60th of a minute) equals 30.8m or just over 101 feet.

Lines of longitude slice the earth into vertical segments like an orange. The width of these segments varies, being widest at the equator where, like lines of latitude, they're around 110km apart. Moving away from the equator lines of longitude converge towards the poles, where they meet.

The lat–long grid divides the globe into **360 degrees** (abbreviated as °). Each degree is divided into 60 minutes (abbreviated as ') and each minute has 60 seconds (or "); this is easily remembered as °, ', ", or zero, one, two. Positions are shown with latitude (N or S) followed by longitude (E or W).

With this system of co-ordinates it's possible to give a **grid reference** for anywhere on the planet to an accuracy of 15m using just six digits of latitude and seven digits of longitude. A grid reference in the traditional format looks like this: N35° 02' 45.44" W90° 01' 22.56" (Graceland in Memphis). However, these days seconds have been superseded by decimal fractions of minutes, so that the grid reference for the home of the undisputed King of Rock 'n' Roll would now be written as: N35° 02.757' W90° 01.376', although for navigation purposes rounding it up to N35° 02.8' W90° 01.4' is sufficient.

The default on Google Maps uses decimal degrees so Graceland is 35.045956, -90.022933. The first figure is called a northing and if it's preceded by a minus it's south of the equator. The second figure is an easting, but being preceded by a minus as in the case of Graceland means it's west of the Greenwich meridian. With this system the ° symbol is not used and the + symbol is considered redundant. You can set a high-end GPS and most satnav units to show a position in any of the above formats, and probably a few more besides.

Locating your position on a map

Locating your position on a paper map can only feasibly be done with a scale of 1:2m or less; a clear plastic ruler can help.

Putting a straight edge along a line of latitude will reveal that the seemingly horizontal line actually curves upwards in the northern hemisphere and downwards in the south. Meanwhile, measuring the distance between vertical lines of longitude will show them a little closer together at the top in the northern hemisphere and vice versa in the south. Only the equator can ever be depicted as a truly horizontal line. Depending on the map's projection, lines of latitude curve along a radius from the nearest pole, while longitudes diverge from the nearest pole. This means that **trying to draw your own grid** on a map with any degree of accuracy is not as easy as it sounds.

Anything **large scale** below 1:500,000 (1cm = 5km, 1 inch = 7.9 miles) is where terrain and landforms as much as any tracks will govern where you can ride. In other words, when things get gnarly you'll need knobblies and a large-scale map to work out a way through.

As you can potentially cross a 1m-scale map in a couple of easy days that can add up to a lot of maps which is why a small scale map or **driving atlas** is handy, backed up with maps in a GPS or satnav.

Know your maps

There's a lot to be said for taking an interest in your paper maps. Inspect your route or area closely before you go there, study the key and see what every-thing means and how **relief and road hierarchies** are depicted.

You'll occasionally find what's shown as a track on a map is now a two-lane highway, but most frustrating is when what's depicted on a map as a good road turns out to be a track. Assuming a perfectly good road was not dug up in some barmy prisoner rehabilitation scheme, this is incompe-tent map-making and, like a travel guidebook making up information, you rightly lose confidence in the information.

Along with accuracy, the best car-tography offers a balanced combina-tion of **clarity and detail** that enables you to read the terrain like a book. If

You can't beat a paper map to give you the big picture.

you're lucky enough to live near a good map shop you can inspect over half a dozen maps of the same country. Compare scales, clarity and the quality of the paper and see which suits you best; not everyone likes the same look.

A new edition of a paper map can sometimes mean the same map with a redesigned cover. Although satnavs were made by driving every road, it's just too expensive to update paper maps on the ground. All that effort and expense just gets copied (including mistakes) by other mapmakers.

In countries where the Latin alphabet is rarely used on road signs – including China, some Arab-speaking countries and Russia (see p199) – hav-ing a map with the **local alphabet** can be more useful than you think. Even if you can't read it, a local will, and you can also compare the illegible (to you) squiggle on a road sign with the matching squiggle on the map, to work out where you're going.

SATNAVS AND MAPPING

After centuries of paper mapping we're now accustomed to using routeable satnavs to get around. We key in a destination and an on-screen map guides us all the way there, while if you can hear it, a soothing but authoritative voice tells us which turns and junctions to take along the way. It's a graphic, map-based version of what you might get in the 'Destination' menu on Google Maps.

LIFE ON THE ROAD

In a foreign country that has satnav mapping coverage it also saves struggling with paper maps and illegible road signs when you want to be concentrating on dodging the mayhem around you. The problem is that this wonder of technology has yet to cover the world adequately and it'll be many years before it reaches the levels of street-by-street mapping we're used to in Europe and North America.

But some countries are already giving it a go. Right now you can buy downloadable maps for a Garmin or TomTom satnav for South Africa and East Africa, Turkey, Chile, Brazil and Argentina, western Russia, India, Malaysia and Thailand – the total cost: several hundred pounds. Very often the detail is patchy and many interesting places – some Andean countries, Central America, much of Africa and Asia – are yet to be mapped like this.

As with computer software, certain advocates of **open sourcing** like www.openstreetmap.org have taken it on themselves to try and map the world and then offer their versions for free, or for a minimal price; in places these have better detail than what Garmin and the others sell.

Just remember, it can be a mistake to rely solely on satnavs as you may do back home. Above all they lack the **big picture** around you, currently something that can only be achieved with a paper map.

Maps for your satnav

For a GPS or satnav unit to be useful in a navigation sense, they're best combined with imported mapping onto a GPS unit with a **usefully sized screen**. Aim for a 5-inch diagonal screen as found on some TomToms and Garmins.

Cars can use a laptop running GPS software plugged into a regular GPS receiver to display their position; on a bike this isn't practical although now with Garmin CustomMaps it's possible to eliminate the laptop and scan, calibrate then import a digital image of a decent paper map (a raster map) into a Garmin GPS unit, providing it has enough chip power to display it. You could even scan in a satellite image which is the next level in satnav display options; photographic 'streetview' type imagery is already available.

Whether you can be bothered to do any of this is another matter, though it would work well in remote areas where proprietary satnav maps have not caught up and probably never will. Even then, you can just whip out a paper map down to 200,000 scale and transpose your lat and long off the GPS.

 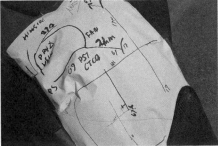

Left: A used Garmin Nuvi car satnav, £50; waterproof case off ebay, a tenner.
Right: old school nav – not waterproof.

Digital maps

Raster maps can be bought (see above), but now any map in digital form, even a scanned paper map, can be used as long as it's been **calibrated**, something that's easily done with software like OziExplorer, Fugawi, TTQV, or MacGPS Pro, or as an image layer imported onto Google Earth and manipulated. The accuracy of your position on such a map will depend on how accurate the map was in the first place (a matter of distortion or 'projection' – the perennial cartographic quandary of displaying a spherical object like a planet in a two-dimensional plane like a sheet of paper or screen) and how well it was scanned. Scanning a map is a time-consuming task and can be an infringement of copyright. Of course it's only the former that puts people off, so have a dig around to see what's online.

Among others, the German mapping house Reise Know-How covers the whole world except far eastern Russia with over 180 maps, all of which are available as **digital pre-calibrated raster maps** for all the above-listed software except MacGPS Pro; they cost around €15 – ironically about twice the price of the identical plastic paper map. Other far-sighted mapmakers may be following suit, but hopefully with the price the right way round.

Also from Germany, Touratech (🖳 www.ttqv.com) sells all sorts of digital mapping for GPS units (as opposed to satnavs). In places the detail matches or exceeds mapping sold by TomTom and Garmin, but then so do the prices. Although I've not used their maps, knowing Touratech's background I suspect their mapping catalogue is bound to be more practical in the AMZ than the more urban or domestic offerings available for satnavs, but be warned, you need to get right into digital mapping to get the best out of TTQV. Unless you're a techie you may find yourself pulling your hair out trying to get an expensive new map to display on your satnav.

Online maps

As long as you have internet you have access to the vast range of global mapping available online from Google or Microsoft's Bing, to name the two main players. Both offer WYSIWYG **aerial imagery** with a quick random check showing that ever evolving Google is still far superior.

As mentioned already, aerial images are very useful, especially in cities, but the plain map graphic screens can be a less cluttered way of getting a good city-centre map. Using a screen-grab feature or software like Google Map Buddy to make a bigger-than-screen-sized map, you can then calibrate it by layering it over Google Earth (as explained earlier), download it to view as an image or print it off. Doing this you then have **a paper** or **GPS raster map** of just about anywhere in the world, with Google Map back-up to help identify actual buildings from a waypoint so you know what you're looking for when you get there.

With a wi-fi or GSM signal it's possible to cut out the paper element and

view such a map on a smartphone or iPad, except that with a phone you'll be paying heavily for the privilege anywhere abroad, unless you use a local SIM card. Some can be bought for internet-only use, costing just a euro a day.

Don't forget that in most cases, unless you're engaged in some black op, entirely adequate paper maps exist individually or can be found in guidebooks. Also be aware that out in the world, paper, digital and online maps will never be able to keep up with what you might actually encounter in any given place or season. At this point you'll be no better off than Lewis and Clark, Marco Polo or Bilbo Baggins and will have to pull up and ask a local.

FINDING YOUR WAY AROUND

Stepping back a bit from the mind-boggling possibilities of digital mapping, successful navigation anywhere basically requires keeping track of two things: where you are now and which way you want to go. To do this you can deploy any number of the navigation aids listed here.

Orientation and trip meter

Even when travelling in unfamiliar territories it's always useful to know your orientation (N, S, E or W), not least when trying to get out of a city. As long as you can see it, **the sun** can help. Using an analogue watch, point the hour hand at the sun; halfway between that point and 12 on your watch is south in the northern hemisphere (or north when south of the equator). This technique only works between 6am and 6pm but anyway, after some practice a quick glance at the sun and the time will do the trick. A **magnetic compass** is easier to use but on- or close to a bike can become unreliable due to interference. I keep one in a clear sleeve pocket where it's vibration free and easy to read.

Get into the habit of resetting the **trip odometer** each time you fill up with fuel. It can help establish your position and is the most reliable way of gauging how far you can ride on a tank of fuel.

Not getting lost

Blindly following roads or tracks without giving a thought to landmarks, orientation or maps is the most common way of getting lost. If in doubt, stop and think or settle on ending up somewhere unexpected – it's all part of the adventure. Otherwise look around you, consult your map or ask a local. If none of this is possible and you haven't a clue, **turning back** is the most sensible action. At some point along the way you just came you were not lost.

Lost near towns

Between towns there's usually only one main road heading in one direction, but getting confused near settlements is a universal experience, especially settlements that are inland or lacking in some other helpful geographical landmark to narrow your options, be it Bogotá or a Turkish village.

The bigger the settlement the more roads converge, offering a baffling choice of routes as well as more distractions than you can handle while trying not to run over a street vendor. In the countryside, routes might connect a village to all sorts of places: the river, another village, a rubbish tip; or it might start off in your intended direction only to turn away or peter out. To-ing and fro-ing across town is more frustrating than unnerving, though it's something that, where available, good satnav mapping can minimise.

Ask the audience

Asking someone can be hit-or-miss which is why we cling so dearly to our nav gadgets. A lot depends on who and how you ask. Don't make Tony Christie's elementary error of **pre-suggestion** by asking 'Is this the way to Amarillo?' Instead, take a tip from master navigator Dionne Warwick and enquire politely 'Do you know the way to San José?' It won't guarantee a correct answer but hopefully won't elicit the **automatic affirmative** nod just to please or get rid of a stranger. Although you may be steaming from the ears by this point, remember to be polite and, as with all exchanges, start with greetings and handshakes.

> **Don't make Tony Christie's error of pre-suggestion by asking 'Is this the way to Amarillo?' Instead, take a tip from Dionne Warwick and enquire 'Do you know the way to San José?' There's a big difference.**

Unless you're in a place where people might be literate, avoid suggesting that locals look at your map. In the remote corners of the AMZ it's generally only tourists who use and understand maps. However, drawing a mud map in the dirt, or in the dust on your tank top can be useful.

It also helps to **ask the right person**. In the AMZ I've found policemen, soldiers and older men to be the most reliable, knowledgeable and straight. Women and young girls might rarely travel out of the village, will seldom be drivers, and are less likely to speak English. In some remote places they may also be embarrassed by your attention; elsewhere they'll enjoy teasing you. Groups of kids or young boys may mislead you for a laugh, to get a tip or cadge a free ride to impress their friends. Sometimes it's less hassle to just try and work it out for yourself, which eventually you always do.

LIFE ON THE ROAD

Lost in the wilderness

Getting completely lost is rare, but even when you're just temporarily disorientated you can become anxious, especially if there are other worries pressing on your mind or it's getting dark. At times like this use your logic to work out where you went wrong. It's almost always your navigational mistake and not the commonly blamed map or the Pentagon messing with the GPS signal. Good navigators always recognise their own fallibility.

The most common reason for getting lost is not paying attention to your orientation, then jumping to conclusions and trying to make your situation fit what you think are the facts. Very often this is down to **pre-empting** or over-anticipating a landmark or turning – a natural consequence of your mild anxiety in not wanting to miss it. You feel that something doesn't add up until you can't deny it. It takes some experience, but in the city or the bush you'll soon gain a feel for whether a road or track is the one you want to be on.

Stop and have a good look around. If you're out in the wilds, **get on to high ground** and scan around. Assess the 'quality' or feel of the track you're on; does it appear well travelled? Are there telephone or other power wires that'll lead to a village for sure? Is a track corrugated or showing other signs of frequent vehicular use, or just littered with the bones of your predecessors? Check your position and bearing from the GPS if you have one. Look at all the facts objectively, not just the ones that confirm your preferences. Above all, rest assured there was a point, not too long ago when you weren't lost. If you can't correct your mistake, **go back**, waiting till daylight if need be.

With a set of knobblies you may think you can go anywhere, but unless you can clearly see where you're trying to get to, taking **cross-country short-cuts** as a way of getting back to where you were can often get you in more trouble. Play it safe and go back the easiest and safest way, however galling it seems, or be prepared to face the consequences.

Riding together

Getting completely lost is rare, but on or off the highway or in a busy city, losing sight of your riding companions isn't so hard to do as you battle with the traffic. This will happen for sure so right at the outset, establish some clear rules and signals. The simplest **signal** should be flashing headlights: 'I am slowing down or stopping'. On seeing this the leader should stop and wait or turn back if necessary. For this reason it's worth having a **rear view mirror** and using it regularly.

On the dirt or in town, a common way to lose each other is when the leader stops to wait for the follower to catch up. After a while of waiting and wondering, the leader retraces his route to look for the other rider who, in the meantime, has raced ahead to catch up with the leader who's now nowhere in sight. It's the responsibility of all riders to look out for each other – this should stop any arguments about whose fault it was. The leader should slow down or stop if he gets too far ahead of the group, who in turn should keep together.

If you do lose sight of each other in town, get the mobiles out or continue to the previously agreed location. Out in the wilds, ride to some high ground, turn off your engine, look around and listen. In this position you're also more likely to be seen by the others too. Failing this, **an agreed procedure** should be adhered to. For example, after a certain time out of contact, you should all return to the point where you last stopped or spoke together, or get on the phones if they work. If fuel is critical you should stop ahead at a clear landmark, such as a village or junction. The whole point of riding together is to give each other much-needed support so resist any individualistic tendencies while traversing remote tracks.

GOING COMMANDO

Besides breakdowns (see p180) or an accident (p171), a more serious situation might occur when you find yourself trapped in the wilds under or alongside an irretrievable bike. Once you're sure you're in trouble follow the '3 Ps' below:

Protection (shelter)
Arranging shelter from the elements will greatly extend your ability to survive. In the case of an injured partner, shelter will be essential while you go for help. Depending on where you are, this means erecting shade or a windbreak if you're not carrying a tent. Get in the habit of wearing some kind of head covering to minimise heat loss or sunstroke; a crash helmet or a scarf will do if you've no hat. With protection secured you can now turn your attention to either recovering your bike, rescuing your partner, or preparing to walk out.

Position
If you've been keeping track, your position shouldn't be hard to pinpoint. It may be just a short walk back to the last village, where someone can help you drag your bike out of a ravine, or it may be miles to a minor road. If you're sure no one will come this way you must be prepared to walk back to the last sign of human presence.

Look on the map to see if there's some place to get help which you'd overlooked. Consider torching your bike, or just a smoky component like a spare tyre or a seat, but *don't waste smoke and signals on the off chance they may be spotted.*

Provisions
Establish how much food and water you have and how many days it will last. **Water** is by far the most critical aid to survival. Wherever you are you can survive a lot longer without food – which you should consume frugally anyway, as digestion uses up water. Staying where you are obviously uses less energy but might not be an option offering much hope. If there's a river, stick close to it, settlements or human activity usually accompany them.

Dos and dont's
- **Don't go alone** into remote areas in bad weather.
- **Know your limits.** There's no rescue service.
- **Avoid known danger areas** where there are bandits, terrorists, wars or landmines.
- **Don't travel in desert regions in summer or high mountains in winter.** Summer is when most desert travellers die because survival margins shrink drastically.
- **Know where you're going.** Keep on the track and avoid cross-country short-cuts. Carry adequate route information, navigational tools and communication devices.
- **Never carry on when lost.** Stop before you go too far, accept that you've made a mistake, and if necessary retrace your steps.
- **Carry enough fuel and water** for your entire planned stage, including a reserve. Difficult terrain and physical activity will greatly increase consumption of fuel and water.
- Even before things go wrong, **avoid wasting water**. Get into the habit of being frugal with your washing and cleaning.
- **Carry essential spares and tools and know how to use them.** You should at least be familiar with tyre removal and repair, and fault diagnosis (see p180).
- If travelling in a group **keep your companions close** or tell them what you're doing and where you're going, both when riding and when going for something like an evening stroll.
- **Avoid riding at night.** Even on the tarmac roads there's a danger of unlit vehicles and stray animals.

LIFE ON THE ROAD

Wild camping

On the road it's surprising how rarely you actually need to camp, and not taking camping gear should mean you carry less stuff, though it rarely works out like that. The truth is, disregarding the savings in paying for accommodation, camping wild is part of the big adventure. There'll come a day when you either have to, or want to park up in a nice spot and enjoy a night out. Sure it means a whole lot of extra gear, but that should really add up to no more than 6–7kg extra, plus food. In return you get the autonomy not only to ride where you like but also stay where you like.

I can guarantee you it'll be the nights spent wild camping out in the mountains or deserts ... that'll make up the best memories of your moto adventure ...

Sleeping, cooking, eating and drinking are the basic elements of camping (washing too, I suppose). The greater the comfort and efficiency of these elements, the better the quality of your camping experience, and on a long ride it needs to be. As with all biking gear, it all depends how committed you are to saving space and weight.

I can guarantee you it'll be the nights spent wild camping out in the mountains or deserts, or the occasions when you're invited in by the rural locals that'll make up the best memories of your moto adventure, not a night in a crummy hotel listening to scuttling cockroaches, dripping taps and barking dogs.

Dealing with onlookers

Even before you settle down for the night, for lunch stops and the like, do yourself a favour by **parking well off the road or track**. Besides the safety factor of not getting run over or choked by dust from passing trucks, this avoids giving too much of an open invitation to chancers or the inquisitive – particularly relevant when you're too close to a settlement.

It's amazing how in certain countries, even if you think you're miles from anyone, an audience will emerge, seemingly from thin air. Initially you may think this is all part of the travel experience, but being stared at by 22 kids as you eat your lunch is not a normal situation.

In many poorer countries concepts of privacy and personal space are not so valued and the idea of sleeping alone and away from others out in the bush is regarded as suspect or deviant. Don't be surprised if, just when you've pitched the tent and donned your slippers, a local or even an army patrol rocks up to see what you're about. Out of concern they may even advise you this is not such a good place to spend the night on account of bandits or wild animals, and that there's a perfectly fine hotel half an hour down the road. It can work both ways of course; as often as not you'll be invited for a meal, when it'll be your turn to watch exotic people enacting mundane tasks.

Choosing a spot for the night

All this underlines why it's a good idea to try and not be seen heading for your night's camp and once there, **not to be visible to passing traffic**, or at least be at a point where you're far enough away to discourage casual visitors. This can be easier said than done but will make for a more relaxing night. The first night or two wild camping alone can be frightening, and over the months you're bound to have a couple of unnerving encounters.

As the sun sinks it's common to keep on riding 'just over that rise' to find somewhere that feels just right, until it's too dark to see anything and you end up sleeping in a ditch alongside what daylight reveals to be a dead dog, as I did once. Try and pin down a good spot well **before dark**, especially if you may have trouble getting far enough off road.

If you're confident you won't disturb someone or cause a commotion – the usual problem with wild camping, rather than issues of security – the answer can be to go right up to some isolated dwelling and **ask** if you can camp near-by even if that won't be so wild. If the road or track you're following is sur-rounded by fields and you decide to camp among them, you can be pretty sure that in a developing country you won't get the hostile reception from a farmer that you might back home. Nevertheless, on arable land make the effort not to ride over or trample crops, or upset carefully dug irrigation ditches.

Be careful about how far and how hard you roam in your search for noc-turnal seclusion; you don't want to make any manoeuvres or river crossings that may be difficult to reverse the following morning. It can also a good idea to **switch off your lights**, to avoid attracting attention, even if on a modern bike with 24/7 lights this requires adding a switch.

Once you find a spot, give yourself a few minutes to adjust and absorb your new locale. You may have been so intent on finding a place that you haven't noticed someone's nearby shack, the awful reek of undefined roadkill, clouds of mosquitoes stirring from a stagnant pool, or a slavering pack of rabid dogs zeroing in on your camp from all directions. And almost perfectly **level ground** is also more important than you think.

Trees of course make ideal cover. It's also worth noting that sand loses the day's heat quicker than rocky places. Altitude above 1000m (3280ft) will also have a noticeable effect on overnight temperatures, though as below, that may be something you want in the tropics.

It can be quite unnerving when you're settled in and then someone looms up out of the dark to 'say hello'. Depending on their behaviour, you never know if they're just being friendly while emboldened by drink, are on the scrounge, or have other ideas. In this situation you may prefer to **move on** to avoid the nagging fear of theft. As said earlier, it's the main reason why camping far from a road and, at least initially, being discreet with your lighting are good ideas.

A grassy knoll in the Karakoram.
© Margus Sootla

MOTO CAMPING GEAR

Many motorcyclists are into activity sports like rock climbing, mountain bikes or kayaking and will have their own well formed ideas on what follows; for the rest here are some basic guidelines. Carrying camping gear on a bike rather than on foot, I'd suggest **lack of bulk** is more important than lightness. An extra 5kg is a lot when you're hauling a backpack over the moors, on a bike it's a gallon of fuel, so don't get too hung up on the scales. Aim instead for compactness.

If you don't own and use good gear already, the £500+ you might spend on a quality set up may be a bit galling for the nights you actually use it. In much of the AMZ you don't need to camp and in Asia accommodation can be cheap, but would you rather spend the night in a €3 roach hotel or out in the wilds? As said, wild camping is part of the adventure.

Tents

On my early Sahara trips I just unrolled my sleeping bag on my jacket, slept badly, woke up aching and one day will doubtless be crippled by arthritis. Now I carry either just the inner tent against insects or the outer against rain. In still conditions a tent adds about 5°C or 9°F to the ambient temperature, though as importantly it's a comforting shelter – or an annoying cocoon. I err towards the latter so for this reason prefer a tent on the large side. If you're planning on spending several days in one place you'll also appreciate a **bigger tent**, and on a warm, windless night you can always just lie on it like a groundsheet.

Resist splashing out on an expensive shelter built to withstand a Himalayan blizzard, or at the other extreme, an ultralight tarp. And there's no real need to faff about with guy lines unless it's a gale, though you may want to uprate to solid pegs like MSR Groundhogs. For occasional use, a simple two-pole crossover design stands up by itself and can cost as little as £10/$15 for a single skin job as below left.

For me the best sort of tent erects intuitively and allows inner-only pitching for an airy insect dome (handy as a mossie net in a basic tropical hotel, too). Three-poles minimise unsupported slabby sides to reduce maddening flapping which two-pole tents (including Hilleberg tunnels) are prone to, but they need at least two pegs to stand. Well-positioned guys enhance stability when needed, and a large annexe with a high enough entrance makes for easy access, and a place to sit upright in. Add good ventilation and, depending on how you sleep, a floor at least a foot longer than you are tall.

Left: Single skin cheapie; compact and OK for occasional use. **Right**: about £200 buys you a proper 3-kilo, three-pole tent. A roomy and stable shelter, though external pole sleeves catch the wind.

MY KINGDOM FOR A CHAIR

Not all may agree but for camping I think a light camp chair is no extravagance, especially for those at an age when joints don't bend like they used to. Let others scoff, then wait for them to ask: 'ooh, can I have a sit?'. Perching on your Touratech Zega is not the same thing.

Some sleeping mats come with accessory frames to fold the mat into a plush, lean back chair. At ground height it's great for dozing or reading, but it needs elevating for say, cooking or whittling. On the right, a $70 Monarch from Alite in the US pivots on its back legs (like you were told not to in school)

but weighs just 600g (21oz) and assembles in a minute. Best of all it's tougher than it looks.

Sleeping mats and bags

Old style closed cell foam sleeping mats are bulky for the comfort they offer but won't puncture. Nowadays, though expensive for a piece of open-cell foam in a bag with a plug, your Therma-Rest-type sleeping mat works much better. I managed for years with a three-quarter-length Ultralight model but now use a full-length Exped Synmat Ultralight of about a litre volume with basic, sand-proof plugs rather than twist valves (inset below).

As for **sleeping bags**, look for compactness and warmth within your budget while recognising a good mat makes a big difference. Get the best bag you can afford which can mean spending over £150/$250. Aim for a three-season bag rated as comfortable down to freezing point. A boxed foot and a 'mummy' head cowling alone are worth an extra 'season's' rating.

Pure goose **down** still can't be beaten as a filler and shouldn't be confused with inferior feathers which are sometimes in the mix. Not only does down fluff out to fill a large volume (the key to insulation), it still compresses better than any man-made fabric and will do so for many years so takes up less room – the weight saving is negligible these days. The drawback is that down clumps up when **wet** and takes a long time to dry.

In my experience **synthetic bags** lose their loft after what might effectively be only a few weeks use; and warmth for warmth they're bulkier than down too. A hiker might use their synthetic bag every night; on a bike it may be left compressed for weeks – bad for recovery but no problem for down which feels nicer too.

Whatever you use, **air** your bag every morning by turning it inside out and letting it hang in the breeze. And decompress it every chance you get. Especially with down you want to stretch the washing cycles out as long as possible as it reduces loft in the long run; use a liner or wear something.

Five-kilo hotel to go: Vaude Odyssey tent, ME Kilo bag and Exped UL mat (also inset).

Cooking

Running a motorcycle it makes sense to use a small **petrol (gasoline) stove**. You have a tank full of the stuff so if you ever run out, not being able to make a brew will be the least of your problems. Getting into camping takes some adjustment and clumsy accidents are common when you're tired or still getting the hang of it. A reliable, uncomplicated and stable stove goes a long way to minimising this.

The problem with petrol stoves is modern ones are designed to run on '**white fuel**', a cleaner fuel than that which comes out of most outback bowsers. Lead-free gasoline is better as prolonged use of low octane leaded fuel may eventually clog your stove's pre-heater pipe (aka: generator; not all have them) or do the same to the jet. I'd guess this process takes a couple of months of daily use, so consider a spare generator or carry the jet-cleaning needle. Top your stove up with unleaded when you can or before you get out bush where ordinary leaded fuel may be all you'll find.

Using local leaded fuel your stove may spurt and smoke a bit before it fully warms up, but once hot and being under pressure, petrol stoves go like the clappers and put out much more heat than propane. Bulky Jetboils apart, the windshields which come with most stoves are ineffective. Get, make or use a proper wind break – it greatly increases efficiency and saves fuel.

Anything that claims to run on **multi-** or **dual-fuel** is either a play on words (ie: it runs on leaded *and* unleaded – big deal), a compromise in the jet size, or requires fiddly changing of jets. On the road you want a simple petrol stove, not something that claims to run on diesel, white fuel and Heineken.

A Coleman 533 I used for years (renamed a 'Sportster' in some markets) needed white fuel or unleaded, but ran fine off African gas pumps with an occasional 'unleaded burn-through' back home. It was still on the original generator when it finally fell apart. To start it, simply pump, turn fuel tap, stand back and light. This kind of ease of use is the key for all sorts of overlanding equipment. I replaced it with a more compact Coleman Featherlite.

Which brings us to what I call 'red bottle jobs' or RBJs, a stove with the fuel bottle (usually red) attached by a hose or pipe to a compact burner. I tried an early Optimus Nova which squirted fuel from the clip-on connection, watched new Primus and MSR stoves spluttering and then permanently blocking after a couple of hours' use, despite cleaning and replacing parts. Others have reported reliable results from RBJs whose variable reliability

Left: Primus RBJ. Note windshield. **Right**: Coleman Featherlite drinks like a YZ but keeps on trucking.

could be down to excessively lean running so it doesn't run out halfway up the Matterhorn. But they cost twice as much as a gas-guzzling Coleman, require fiddly assembly which can lead to leaks or blockages, plus regular cleaning or maintenance, the last thing you want to do when you're ravenous. Another drawback many also mention is the **noise** of some RBJs and the poor heat control: all or nothing.

Whatever you get, consider a stove's **stability**, both on the ground and for holding pots; there's nothing more frustrating than watching your half-cooked spaghetti vongole tip into the dirt. Unlike some already mentioned, in my experience the Coleman models are ideal in this respect: the squat compact shape of the one-piece unit sits securely on the ground, and the wide burner gives off plenty of heat and support for a pot.

If you're only having an occasional roadside brew you might get by with a butane gas can and a compact Pocket Rocket-style burner. But even if you find a refill, will it fit your burner? As a last resort there's always firewood.

One-pan cooking

It may sound extreme but a half-litre **mug** and a one-litre **pan** with a lid will do. A plate is unnecessary and a spoon and a penknife are all the cutlery you'll ever use. You can cook your rice/pasta, put it in the mug with a lid on top to keep it warm, and then if you're not simply throwing it in with the pasta, cook whatever else you have, chuck the pasta back in and eat with just a pan and a cup to wash. Avoid pouring hot water away: use it for soup or washing up.

Resist trick titanium cookware from camping shops. A sturdier stainless saucepan with a spot-welded rather than rivetted handle will take rough use and sand-scour cleaning without getting grubby or bent.

Water containers

In hot lands sip water on the move from a two-litre plus **hydrator** in your back-pack or a jacket pocket designed for it. I've found Camelbak bladders more pliable than Platypus which can acquire pinprick leaks in the folds.

You'll need more water than you think for an overnight 'half-board' camp, especially if there's no source nearby. A sturdy MSR **water bag** of **10 litres** takes little space when empty, though caps can leak so take a spare. Bags give you capacity but are awkward to actually use; some sort of bottle is easier to avoid spillage. A pouch for a 1.5L plastic water bottle attached to the bike or an external pocket or mount on your pannier gives easy access at all times.

Left: Waterbags for capacity; bottles for utility. **Right:** if using wells, bring cord or risk dying horribly.

LIFE ON THE ROAD

Off-highway riding

I bet it's possible to traverse the entire AMZ: South America, Asia and now even Africa without leaving the tarmac. But where's the fun in that? Wherever you go in the world, mastering the techniques of riding off sealed highways will be one of the major elements of your adventure. When there's a trail of dust billowing off your back wheel you can't help thinking you really are far from home and heading into the unknown. It's out here that adventures are ripe for the plucking, from uninterrupted wilderness to unexpected encounters with the sort of people you'll only meet in the back of beyond.

The key difference on dirt is that **traction** is unpredictable so a constant reading of the terrain is vital. Like skiing and all that stuff, it's this engagement that brings rewards. Ever since Kenny Roberts rewrote the book on GP racing, it's well known that today's top racers developed their rear-wheel steering and sharp reactions from sliding around on dirt bikes. And besides sharpening your road-riding skills, off-roading provides the exhilaration of road racing at a fraction of the speed. By the end of the day you'll be parked up in some scenic and remote location, shagged-out, filthy, but satisfied. Unless I'm very much mistaken, this is largely what adventure motorcycling is all about.

Gently does it
Riding off-road is fun, but until you get the hang of handling your loaded bike on various surfaces, take it easy. As a rule you'll find **50mph/80kph** is a maximum cruising speed on any dirt surface. On a heavy bike at speeds greater than this it's not possible to react quickly enough to the ever-changing surface. Riding on dirt is never predictable – part of the fun but also a danger.

Adventure motorcycling is not about smouldering kneepads; it's about surviving the long ride so never take risks, resist the impulse to show off and always ride within the limitations of:

- Your vision
- The terrain
- Your experience
- Your bike's handling abilities

Ready for a beating
Be in no doubt about the hammering your bike is going to get on dirt roads, or the just-as-frequent mashed tarmac roads you'll encounter. Much of the advice on bike preparation given in earlier chapters is concerned with limiting damage when riding over rough terrain. Lightly-framed dual sport bikes with heavy loads, or cast-wheeled road tourers were not built for a beating on corrugated tracks, and frame, rack or tank fractures are common problems. Besides offering agility in the dirt, a lightly-loaded bike will put less stress on the already hard-working wheels, suspension, transmission and luggage rack. Make sure they're all up to it.

DIRT ROADS

Most of your off-highway riding will be on rural dirt roads rather than cross country. At their best these tracks are straight and flat, with a smooth and consistent surface requiring only slightly reduced speeds. But dirt being what it is, this won't last for long and most tracks will have been rutted by passing traffic, washed-out by rains, blown over with sand, littered with rocks and, likely as not, corrugated.

Corrugations

Corrugations are a name for the washboard surface which an unconsolidated track develops as a result of regular, heavy traffic. The accepted explanations for these infuriatingly regular ripples of dirt are the braking and acceleration forces of passing traffic or the 'tramping' shock absorbers of heavy trucks.

In a car you grit your teeth and pray that the shocks won't explode; the best solution is to accelerate up to about 50mph/80kph and skim across the top of each ripple, so reducing vibration dramatically. On a bike, the same practice gives a smoother ride too, but at this speed your wheels are barely touching the ground and your traction is negligible. In a straight line this isn't too dangerous, but on a bend it's possible to skim right off the track.

Wealthier countries grade their corrugated dirt roads once in a while but the honeymoon only lasts a few weeks. In the developing world, the passing of a grader is most likely an annual event just after a rainy season.

The good thing is that on a bike you only need a tyre's width to get by and you'll often find corrugations shallowest or non-existent on either edge of the track, though rarely for more than a few metres at a time. You'll find yourself forever weaving around trying to find the smoothest path. On a plain it might be easier to avoid a corrugated track altogether and ride in far greater comfort and freedom alongside the track, but realistically this option is rare.

Corrugations do have one small saving grace. If ever you're lost or wondering which way to go, the most corrugated track is the one most frequently used and probably the one you want to follow. But overall, corrugations are just a miserable fact of dirt-roading and a good place to have knobbly tyres with slightly reduced pressures, a well-supported subframe and a comfy seat.

When the going gets rough, stand up

Standing on the footrests over rough ground is probably the most important technique beginners should master because when you're standing up:

- Suspension shocks are taken through your bent legs not your back.
- Your bucking, sliding bike is easier to control.
- Your forward vision is improved.

Contrary to the impression that standing up makes your bike less stable, in fact it has the opposite effect. It transfers your weight low, through the footrests, rather than through the saddle when you're seated. This is why trials riders and motocrossers always tackle tricky sections standing on the pegs. Back home test

LIFE ON THE ROAD

Weight forward, elbows bent to absorb the impacts, knees ready to do the same.

your standing stance with knees locked out: if you're stooping uncomfortably fit **higher bars and/or bar risers** (or maybe lower footrests) so you feel you could ride like this all day.

When standing up, **grip the tank** lightly between your knees to give your body added support. As you get the hang of things, standing becomes instinctive. You'll find it's not always necessary to stand right up; sometimes just leaning forward, pulling on the bars while momentarily lifting your backside is enough to lessen a jolt. Strive to be **relaxed** in this stance by not overgripping your handlebar grips – a common response – or squatting which will soon tire your thighs. It's not about running at the dirt and attacking it, it's about responding with fluidity to the bike's movements. In a nutshell: **sit down when you can, stand up when you must.**

RIDING IN SAND

Riding on compacted trackless sand is one of the joys of off-roading. For most of us though, sand riding means being stuck on a track in one of two **ruts** carved by passing vehicles. Short of ice, this is one of the most difficult riding surfaces because you're effectively riding a channel about a foot wide. If you can avoid ruts, do so.

Sandy ruts

If it's a soft stretch of sand like say, crossing a sandy creek, don't be afraid to stand up and accelerate firmly at the right time. Momentum and acceleration are key so stand up and with snap of the throttle, blast assuredly across, lightening the front wheel to stop it getting buried. Keep the power on and keep on the pegs for as long as it takes, no matter how much your back wheel weaves and bucks around. So long as the front wheel remains on course you're largely in control. Keep off the brakes, especially the front. If you need to slow down use the gears and be ready for the bike to become violently unstable. The reason it does so is important to understand: as you slow down loose sand builds up in front of the front wheel and erases the steering's 'self-straightening' caster effect. With caster lost, the front wheel wants to flip to either side and down you go. Luckily, speeds are slow and landings are soft. Keeping the power on helps skim over loose sand, minimising build up.

In prolonged sandy ruts about 20mph/30kph in second is the best speed, the low gear allowing a quick response. Avoid crossing deep ruts or riding out unless absolutely necessary. If you must, hurl your weight in the preferred direction while standing up and gassing it – and hope for the best.

Low tyre pressures

Dropping tyre pressures to as little as 10psi (0.7 bar), flattens a tyre out and its 'footprint' on the sand lengthens significantly (rather than widens, though it does that a little, too). Doing this changes your normally round tyre into more of a caterpillar track, increasing your contact patch and dramatically improving your traction, even with a trail or a road tyre. It can mean the difference between riding confidently across a sandy section or slithering around barely in control,

Reduced tyre pressures: actually a longer more than a wider footprint.

footing constantly, losing momentum and finally getting stuck or falling over – every few minutes.

The trouble is, as mentioned way back on p86, in this severely under-inflated state a tyre gets much **hotter** due to the internal friction created by the flexing carcass (just as you get hot doing exercise). Softened by the heat, a tyre becomes more prone to punctures. Keep speeds down on soft tyres and be sure your security bolts (if present) are done up tight as this is just the sort of low-pressure/high-traction situation which brings on tyre creep (see p89).

RIDING OVER ROCKS

Rocks are going to be just about the last sort of surface you want to tackle on your overlander. Most commonly it'll be a short stretch over a creekbed where the bridge or roadway has been washed away. This'll be a real test of your bike's suspension damping as well as your ability to respond dynamically to its feedback. And it's one place where **light bikes** shine.

Every time your suspension rebounds, it's pushing away the mass of the bike, most likely a few degrees

Stand up and let the suspension do the work.

off vertical. As your bike lurches that way, you compensate with your body in the other, but if the momentum of that rebounded mass belongs to a XT1200Z or Triumph Explorer rather than a KTM690, a CCM 450 (or any 250 you care to mention) it's going to take a lot more skill, brawn or luck to control.

Falls can be bone- or engine-cracking here, so often the safest path is just to **paddle** inelegantly, feathering the clutch as you lurch between rocks while the bashplate earns its keep. Otherwise stand up and, holding your weight as light as a cat, edge forward at little more than walking pace, responding to compression with bent limbs, and to the rebound with all the balance and finesse you can muster, while steering along the least gnarly path and, if necessary, slipping the clutch to soften the torque of an over-powerful bike.

LIFE ON THE ROAD

Stuck firm, and it's only the Urals.
© Mikhail Sorotkin

RIDING IN MUD

Even on a 120kg competition bike with fresh knobblies, mud and especially bogs or swamps can present the dual challenge of negligible traction and treacherous suction, let alone the staggering laundry bill. No two ways about it, riding a portly overlander with road tyres through mud is plain exhausting. While sand responds to certain acquired techniques, the occluded mush of water-logged terrain has no cut and dried rules, but if it's a **rutted trench**, pick one rut and stick to it, either attacking it standing up or paddling, walking or, as above, being helped across. Whatever it takes.

Some tracks crossing the Congo and Amazon basins and in far eastern Russia are notorious wet riding challenges. Puddles stretch away before you with vehicles sometimes backed up behind a bogged-down truck.

On a bike, tyres are critical: aggressive treads at low pressures make all the difference, but blasting blindly into a huge puddle is a recipe for a muddy face plant. If you can't find a way around the side, recognise it's going to be a slow and tiring paddle, and be ready to stop if the trough deepens. You're usually forced to ride through the trenches dug by the last truck's spinning wheels, but depending on the period since the rains ended, these pits can drown an entire car. If you're not sure, **wade through first**.

Ironically the fallen tree offered the best traction for miles. © Mikhail Sorotkin

Bogs and swamps

The large expanses of water-logged wilderness found in temperate zones can be harder still to deal with, as any tracks through this sort of terrain tend to be few and irregularly maintained. Perhaps the best known examples are found in far eastern Russia such as the original Old Summer Route of the Kolyma Highway between Yakutsk and Magadan (see p205), only rideable in summer by which time the tundra melts into a quagmire.

This is a tough place to ride alone: in a desert you can extricate a bike from sand with a little digging, and along the flooded channels of central Africa there are usually enough other travellers or villagers around to help out. A bike ridden up to its bars into a Siberian bog could take days to extract so avoid big trackless mires where possible; you may well lose your bike.

Learn to recognise what sort of vegetation inhabits water-logged ground, be it reeds or moss; keeping to high ground is not always the answer. Even with help, in terrain like this your mileages may drop to single daily figures while your ability to deal with this exhausting pace can be numbered in hours.

RIVER CROSSINGS

Who can resist the thrill of cutting a big V-shaped shower of spray as you blast across a shallow river? The other side of this photogenic scenario is a bent crankshaft inside an engine ruined by hydraulic lock: the consequences of a piston sucking in and compressing uncompressible water.

The first thing to do at a substantial and unfamiliar water crossing, be it a wild river or a flooded ford – is to **stop and have a good look**. Just because tracks lead down one river bank and up the other doesn't mean the crossing is rideable today. At a flooded ford wait for other traffic to drive through to give you a chance to gauge the conditions. Resist 'spectator pressure' to have a go. This is how people drown.

Walk first

Crossing a river is like the rock riding described a page back except you can't see the rocks. Better then to **walk first**: a pair of wet trousers dry quicker than a drowned engine. Walking establishes the strength of the current, the nature of the river bed and, of course, the maximum depth. If the current, river bed and depth add up, ride your foot route slowly, and once you're committed, don't stop.

Generally, **if you can walk it unaided, you can ride it**, but on a smooth concrete ford, the power of a rushing current not even a foot deep can push your wheels to the downstream edge before you reach the other side. Anticipate this by keeping- or steering to the upstream side.

Generally the 'plimsoll line' on most conventional engines is halfway up the barrel and below the air filter intake, but wet electrics can snuff out an engine blasting through a two-inch puddle, so before you take the dive, spray in and around the plug cap and other vital ignition components with a water dispersing agent like WD40 or GT85. Remember that the consequences of falling over can be as bad as riding in too deep; keep your thumb over the **kill switch** and hit it the moment you lose control. Once on the far side expect a bit of spluttering as the engine steams itself dry.

Top: Foot recce can save a drowned bike. © Walter Colebatch. **Middle**: Even a ford this shallow can push you off the edge. **Bottom**: If it gets deep engine off is less risky, but needs at least three people. © Mikhail Sorotkin

Experienced riders take no chances when crossing rivers. © Mikhail Sorotkin

Power walking the bike

If riding is too risky, walk your bike across on a running engine with yourself on the **upstream** side so there's less chance of getting trapped under the bike should it fall. Keep the revs high in first gear. This helps purge any electrical spluttering, avoids stalling and keeps pressure on the exhaust blowing out of the silencer. And be ready on that kill switch.

Truly, madly, deeply

Very rarely you might come to a river crossing which is way too deep to ride through but which, for whatever reason, you simply must cross. It's possible to totally submerge a bike providing the fuel, induction and exhaust systems are completely sealed off.

Doing this is no small job and you risk ruining your bike, so make sure there's no alternative. Naturally the maximum depth you can walk through is limited by your height, but realistically don't attempt anything deeper than the height of the seat and don't try this radical procedure alone. This is what to do:

- Remove as much weight from the bike as possible, including the tank
- Set the engine on compression so the valves are closed
- Plug the exhaust, seal the air filter in a bag and disconnect the battery
- Fold and tie all oil tank, battery, engine and carb breather hoses
- If you have some rope, set up a line from bank to bank

Once the bike's as good as submerged there's no need to rush. Don't be distracted by rising bubbles, it's too late to do anything about it now. With at least two of you pushing and pulling, inch across and on the far bank let the bike drip dry – don't attempt to start it until you're sure it's fully drained.

Pull out the exhaust bung and stand the bike on its back wheel draining any water which may have leaked in. Release the hoses and drain the carb. Drain the airbox and reinstall the filter. Remove the spark plug and turn over the engine, hoping that no water spurts out of the plug hole; if it does, see below. Once all these procedures have been completed check for a spark and if all's well, fire the bike up and hope there's not another deep river a few miles further down the road.

LIFE ON THE ROAD

DROWNED ENGINE: WHAT TO DO

The worst has happened and your bike has taken a lung-full while running, or has fallen over and filled up. It's not the end of the world; this is what to do:
- Stand the bike up and drain the exhaust.
- Drain the petrol tank.
- Take out the spark plug and kick or tip out water.

- Drain the carb (if present) and squeeze out the air filter.
- Remove the stator cover, drain and dry.
- If the engine oil has a milky colour, it's contaminated with water and needs changing.
- Once everything has dried out, test for a spark first and, if the bike runs, give it a full re-lube at the earliest opportunity.

Health and medical emergencies*

DR PAUL ROWE

The key principle to avoiding illness and injury on your trip is that prevention is far better than cure. However, with some prior planning and a small first-aid kit you will be able to deal with most ailments which arise, to keep you and your group riding.

First-aid kit

A small plastic box is ideal and should include the following:
- Paracetamol
- Strong painkillers (analgesics)
- Anti-malarials
- Antacids
- Anti-diarrhoea tablets (Loperamide 2mg)
- Laxatives
- Antihistamines
- Rehydration powders
- Broad spectrum antibiotics (eg amoxicillin 500mg)
- Multi-vitamins

Equipment
- Latex gloves (good for oily repairs too)
- Tweezers (for tick removal)
- Sterile syringe set with two hypodermic needles per person
- Sterile dressings, plasters, bandage
- Alcohol wipes ('Sterets'); can also be used to start fires
- Superglue
- Antiseptic cream
- Durapore tape
- Safety pins
- Thermometer
- Savlon antiseptic concentrate
- Steristrips

Good **painkillers** could make the difference in being able to carry on riding in an emergency, so see your doctor prior to departure and request a supply of Codeine Phosphate 30mg or Tramadol 50mg tablets. Also ask for some amoxicillin or similar antibiotic (beware of any group member with penicillin allergy) as wound infections, dental abscesses, ear and urinary infections are all more common during remote travel.

Although contrary to the manufacturers' advice, a lot of space can be saved by removing tablets from their blister packaging and putting them into small zip lock plastic bags. Just remember to label them clearly.

* This section is also on the website under 'Resources'.

LIFE ON THE ROAD

Obtaining supplies

Between a friendly doctor and your local pharmacy you should be able to obtain most of the kit for your trip. For anything else, try these sites:

UK	BCB Ltd ▣ www.bcbin.com
	Lifesystems ▣ www.lifesystems.co.uk
	SP Services ▣ www.spservices.co.uk
	St John Ambulance Supplies ▣ www.stjohnsupplies.co.uk
US	Safety Central ▣ safetycentral.com
Canada	Mountain Equipment Co-op ▣ www.mec.ca
Australia	First Aid Kits Australia ▣ www.firstaidkitsaustralia.com.au

Minor injuries

Minor cuts and grazes are common ailments. Apply the following general principles:

- Stop the bleeding.
- Clean thoroughly to reduce risk of infection.
- Keep it dressed to maintain cleanliness.

Bleeding is stopped by simply applying **direct pressure**, elevating the limb and bandaging firmly to hold the dressing in place. Dilute some Savlon concentrate in clean water and clean wounds thoroughly, picking out any gravel or other foreign material. If the wound is gaping you can close it with either Steristrips or ordinary household superglue (Loctite). Hold the wound edges together and smear the glue along the surface, maintaining that position for one minute. It will flake off after a few days once it has done its job. Steristrips are sticky paper strips which are very good at holding wound edges together but are less effective in humid environments.

Foreign bodies should be removed whenever possible but otherwise can be left in place for removal by a surgeon once you return home. The exceptions are any organic material (wood, splinters, thorns, fangs) which are likely to become infected or anything embedded in your palm or sole which will become too painful for you to function normally. For these you will have to venture to a local medical centre for removal. Any spills which leave gravel in your face need to be cleaned meticulously or may leave permanent scarring.

Planning for serious injury, illness and evacuation

Most riders give little forethought about what would happen if they were to become incapacitated during their trip. Thankfully these events are rare, but some pre-trip planning will help things run a lot smoother if things go wrong.

A worst-case scenario can be broken down into the following stages:

Casualty event → First aid → Stabilisation → Summon/move to help → Casualty evacuation → Repatriation.

Consider what you would do at each stage after initial stabilisation, which is dealt with later in this chapter. Go through some scenarios in your mind asking yourself questions about how you would cope with an emergency at different parts along your proposed route.

HELMET REMOVAL

It cannot be emphasised enough that **at the scene of a motorcycle accident, leave the casualty's helmet on until professional help arrives**. Attempts to remove a helmet by untrained persons can worsen a fractured neck and cause permanent total paralysis or even death. Even if you have had a little training or read the description that follows, the attending paramedics will have performed this manoeuvre many times, so leave it to them. This is the case in all developed countries but where trained help is in short supply you will be glad you practised amongst your group beforehand.

However, a description of the correct technique for helmet removal is included here on the premise that in a remote motorcycling emergency where the casualty's airway is compromised, some knowledge is better than none at all. If you're heading on a long, remote trip, go on a first-aid course which covers helmet removal and practise at home until you can get the helmet off without moving the neck at all. **Two rescuers** are required. Some of the latest helmets feature removable padding to make this task easier.

● **Step 1** Rescuer 1 kneels above the patient's head. Grasp the helmet as shown with fingertips curled around its lower margin touching the jawbone. Hold firmly to immobilise the head in line with the body.

● **Step 2** Rescuer 2 kneels alongside the patient's torso, opens the visor and checks the airway and breathing, then undoes or cuts the chin strap.

Rescuer 2 then places one hand so that the jawbone is grasped between the thumb on one side and the index and middle fingers on the other side. The other hand is placed at the back of the neck with the finger tips reaching up under the back of the helmet.

The rescuer now clamps the patient between their forearm (front) and (wrist) (back) bracing the head, taking over in-line immobilisation.

● **Step 3** Rescuer 1 now pulls the sides of the helmet apart and rotates the helmet up and backwards by pulling the mouthguard over the patient's nose.

● **Step 4** Next the helmet is rotated the opposite way so that the back of the helmet slides up around the curve of the back of the head.

● **Step 5** Now Rescuer 1 can gently pull the helmet off. After helmet removal, maintain in-line immobilisation at all times.

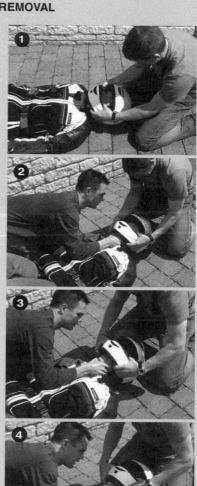

How will you raise help? Will there be a mobile phone signal or do you need to carry a satellite phone? Are there any dwellings or bases with VHF radio? **Who will you call?** Is there an ambulance service and if so will you have to pay cash? Can you leave your travel plans with someone who will come looking for you? How can you signal an aircraft? How long might it take to get rescued?

If you're spending a significant amount of time in an area it may be worth identifying where the local hospitals are, roughly the level of care they provide and whether there are likely to be any English-speaking staff there.

In the event of a **serious accident** the involvement of an established international recovery agency can be a godsend. These 24/7 organisations are dedicated to the evacuation and, if necessary, repatriation of those injured or taken ill overseas. However, aeromedical transfer can get extremely expensive so be sure that your travel insurance includes cover for this. Your insurance company will want to be involved from the earliest stages and can be a useful ally at this stressful time so should be contacted at the first opportunity.

First-aid training

Ideally, all members of a group should have some first-aid training. If you travel alone you take an accepted risk, but prior first-aid training could still save your own life. In the UK conventional first aid is taught by St John's Ambulance Service (🖳 www.sja.org.uk), the British Red Cross (🖳 www.red cross.org.uk) or look for 'first aid training' in your region.

However, practising first aid in a remote environment with poor communications, adverse conditions and sub-optimal transport can all get challenging. Add to this that the responsibility may fall on you to straighten broken limbs, stem haemorrhaging and all the rest, it would be wise for at least one in a group to undertake one of the more advanced first-aid courses aimed specifically at expedition first aid.

Aeromedical emergency transfer agencies

IPRS Aeromed (UK) 🖳 www.iprs-aeromed.com
Air Ambulance Network (USA) 🖳 www.airambulancenetwork.com
Swiss Air Ambulance 🖳 www.swiss-air-ambulance.ch

It is a good idea to keep all your **important information** and phone numbers together for use in an emergency. Write all of the following onto a piece of card, laminate it and keep it with your passport:
- Information about any medical conditions you have, prescribed medications and known allergies.
- Blood group if known.
- Next of kin with contact details.
- Contact numbers of insurance company, travel agency and some international medical evacuation agencies.
- One fallback number at home who can be contacted in any emergency to help you summon assistance.

First aid and basic trauma management

Significant injuries are rare amongst motorcycle travellers, despite the perception that it is a 'dangerous' form of transport. The key factor to improving survival in the event of a serious accident is prompt access to definitive care, i.e: a hospital with surgery and intensive care facilities. As soon as you have made the scene safe and performed a brief Airway, Breathing and Circulation assessment ('ABC', see below) your priority is to get help to the scene or, depending on experience, location and vehicles available, perform a rapid stabilisation and transport to hospital.

ABC

Although there follows a brief description of the ABC approach to trauma, it must be emphasised that a book is no place to learn such skills. Any group embarking on a serious motorcycle journey needs at least one person who is trained in first aid, for whom this should be an *aide memoire*.

A   Airway and Cervical Spine

The airway extends from the mouth down to the larynx and ends where the trachea (windpipe) divides into the left and right lungs. After trauma the airway may be obstructed by dislodged teeth, blood, facial bone fractures or, most commonly, the tongue falling back into the pharynx (back of the mouth) because the patient has been knocked unconscious. The signs of an obstructed airway include noisy breathing, gurgling and distress. A patient who can talk has a clear airway.

If you suspect airway obstruction you must carefully remove any obvious blockage from the mouth and then perform a **jaw thrust** which will lift the tongue clear of the back of the mouth thus opening the airway. To do this, approach the casualty from their head end, place your thumbs on their cheekbones either side with your middle fingers tucked in behind their jawbone (mandible) in the groove just below the earlobe. Now push the jawbone vertically up towards the sky and hold it there, checking again to see if air is now moving in and out of the patient's lungs. This manoeuvre is safe even in the presence of a possible spinal injury because the head is not tilted – only the jawbone is moved. Basic airway management of this type is the most important skill for any casualty carer. Without a clear airway the casualty will die in minutes.

Cervical spine protection is included with Airway in ABC because of its fundamental importance. What is meant by this is that the force of impact may have fractured neck bones (cervical vertebrae) or disrupted the ligaments which hold the vertebrae together. Any further movement such as turning the head or moving the casualty without proper stabilisation could push the broken bone fragment into the spinal cord thus permanently paralysing the patient from the neck down.

However, a patient who is confused, has the distracting pain of a broken limb, or is buzzing from an adrenaline surge may not perceive the pain of a fractured vertebrae, so it is prudent to **assume that every trauma victim has a spinal injury**. Keep the patient still and their head supported in line with their body until professional help arrives.

B   Breathing

Management of specific chest injuries is beyond the scope of this book. However, you can help inbound medical personnel to guide you by exposing the casualty's chest and relaying to them the following information:

- Respiratory rate, i.e: number of breaths per minute.
- Whether there are any open or gurgling chest wounds.
- Whether one side of the chest is moving more than the other.
- Respiratory distress: is the patient talking normally or short of breath?

Repeat your observations every few minutes.

C   Circulation

Bleeding from open wounds may be easy to identify and stop but not from broken bones or internal organs. As an adult begins to lose some of their five litres of circulating blood, the body compensates by going into shock. This medical application of the word shock refers to significant blood loss not psychological fright.

Signs of shock

- Fast heart rate.
- Fast breathing rate.
- Paleness.

Signs of severe shock include:

- Reduced consciousness level.
- Weak pulse; may be too weak to feel.

At an **accident scene** there are several things you can do to reduce bleeding:

- Always remember scene safety; airway and spinal injury first, no matter how spectacular a wound initially appears.
- Apply firm pressure to wounds. If blood soaks through, apply more padding, always keeping the original directly pressed on the wound.
- Elevate injured limbs.
- Lay the casualty down and raise legs.
- Realign and splint broken bones.
- Internal bleeding into the chest, abdomen or pelvis can only be fixed by surgery. The best way to help here is to summon medical help as quickly as possible.

Fractures and splints

Broken bones are extremely painful, with most of the pain coming from the broken bones grating against each other and the jagged ends sticking into the surrounding muscles and skin at unnatural angles.

It follows that the pain can be greatly reduced by repositioning the broken limb into its normal realignment and holding it in that position. A comfortably splinted arm could make it tolerable to ride pillion on a bumpy track.

In addition to pain relief, the other major benefit of splinting fractured limbs is to reduce blood loss from the ends of the broken bones. To improvise a splint you will need something soft around the limb to provide padding, such as clothing or a sleeping mat, followed by something stiff to fasten to the outside to provide rigidity eg sticks or tent poles. Straighten whilst providing traction (pulling along the length of the limb) and have the splint ready to apply by testing it on the good side beforehand. For the patient this will be extremely painful but you will rarely do any more damage and the end result will be worth it.

Once a limb is immobilised it must be elevated, either in a sling for an arm or onto a padded pannier for a leg.

Other points regarding bone and joint injuries

Dislocations occur when a joint comes out of its socket, typically the shoulder, elbow, fingers or kneecap. The joint will be very painful, immobile and appear deformed compared to the other side. It needs to be located back into the socket by a medically-trained person as soon as possible.

Fractures where the overlying skin is broken are called open fractures. These are serious injuries and need urgent medical attention. Spinal, pelvis, and leg fractures require a stretcher and proper immobilisation so are impossible to transport by motorcycle.

A fractured **collar bone** (clavicle) is relatively common following a fall from a motorcycle. The treatment here is to hang the affected arm in a sling for four weeks. Although intensely painful, there are reports of people continuing to ride with this injury.

Immunisations

Vaccinations need to be sorted out at least **six weeks** prior to departure as some may require several doses and also to allow time for your sore arm and mild flu-like symptoms to subside.

They're available from your doctor or travel clinic. Depending on where you're going and your prior immunisation status, your doctor will select vaccinations based on current state Health Department and WHO guidelines Owing to these variables your vaccination list might not exactly match that of your travelling companions – a source of anxiety for some but nothing to worry about. Online you will find a useful vaccine recommendations generator at ▣ **www.fleetstreetclinic.com**.

Apart from Yellow Fever, which remains the only disease for which you must hold a WHO-approved certificate for entry into some two-dozen countries, mostly in **Latin America** and **Central Africa**, there is no legal obligation to have any of these jabs prior to travel.

Vaccination course notes

Hepatitis A	Single dose.
Hepatitis B	Three doses at 0, 1 and 6 months. Transmitted by sexual intercourse and blood. Advisable for a prolonged trip.
Japanese B Encephalitis	Three doses at 0, 7 and 28 days. Recommended for Southeast Asia. Rare but fatal in 30% cases.
Meningitis	Single dose. Africa's 'Meningitis Belt' runs from Senegal to Ethiopia.
Rabies	Three doses at 0, 7 and 28 days. Rare but 100% fatal. Prior vaccination only buys time and medical attention must be sought in the event of contact with source.
Tetanus	Single dose. Get up to date before any trip.
Typhoid	Oral or injection. Common in all developing countries.
Yellow Fever	Single dose.

Diphtheria, Polio & Tuberculosis	(BCG) Vaccinations are routinely given in childhood in developed countries. If you think you may not have had them, ask your doctor about a booster dose.

With all these conditions it is worth remembering that having a vaccination does not make you immune and it is always best to avoid coming into contact with the source of the disease in the first place. Having said that it is important to keep in perspective that all these conditions are incredibly rare and it would be a shame to let paranoia about contracting some exotic condition dissuade you.

There are many sources of information about travel vaccinations and other health issues on the internet:

Medical Advisory Service for Travellers Abroad 💻 www.masta-travel-health.com

World Health Organisation 💻 www.who.int

Travel Health Online 💻 www.tripprep.com

Travel Doctor 💻 www.traveldoctor.co.uk

Diarrhoea

Loose bowel movements occurs in up to 80% of travellers, usually simply from an altered diet or the stresses of an upset body clock, while infective diarrhoea is caused by contaminated food or water. It follows that the latter may be avoided by taking food handling and preparation precautions:

- Prepare your own food.
- Wash hands frequently.
- Protect food from insects and rodents.
- Keep food preparation surfaces spotless.
- Cook food thoroughly and eat immediately.

In addition be particularly cautious with:

- **Shellfish and crustaceans** As filter feeders they tend to concentrate whatever organisms may be in the local sewage outfall which may also contain poisonous biotoxins.
- **Raw fruit and vegetables** Although 'healthy', the locals may well use human faeces as fertiliser. Clean thoroughly or peel.
- **Dairy products** Boil milk before consumption.

Infective diarrhoea may be caused by viruses (which will not be helped by antibiotics), bacteria (E. Coli) or other parasitic micro-organisms (eg Giardia, Campylobacter, Shigella). Whatever the cause, the symptoms will be loose stools, abdominal cramps and loss of appetite with or without vomiting and high temperature. There may be bloody diarrhoea. These illnesses are usually self-limiting and will settle in a few days without treatment. One exception is amoebic dysentery (caused by an organism called Entamoeba) which is distinguished by a slower onset and bloody diarrhoea without fever. Medical attention with a full course of medicines for around two weeks is always needed.

Treatment

The most important aspect when treating diarrhoea of any cause is **adequate rehydration**. Powder sachets (eg Dioralyte) should be made up with clean water or you can make your own by adding **four teaspoons of sugar plus one teaspoon of salt and a little lemon juice to a litre of water.** Water which has been used to boil rice makes a good alternative.

Antidiarrhoea tablets (Imodium, Arret, etc) temporarily mask the symptoms but prevent the body from flushing the harmful bacteria from the intestines. As such they are best avoided unless you absolutely have to keep riding. The antibiotic Ciprofloxacin (500mg taken twice a day) is effective against most infective causes of diarrhoea but it is only worth considering obtaining a supply from your doctor if you're heading somewhere very remote or tropical.

Medical assistance needs to be sought if you have:

- Diarrhoea for more than four days.
- Diarrhoea with blood.
- Fever (temperature greater than 39°C/102°F) for over 24 hours.
- If confusion develops.

Spiders, snakes, and scorpions

Films like *Arachnophobia, Anaconda* and *The Mummy* have much to answer for. Apart from some non-venomous blood-sucking/flesh-eating spider species, none of the above has much to gain by running up and biting you; you're just too big to eat. They will only resort to doing so as a self-defence measure if they feel threatened.

Of the many **spider species** throughout the world that will give a painful bite, only **four** are actually dangerous to humans. The Sydney Funnel Web is the most poisonous, although no fatalities have occurred since the introduction of antivenom in 1980. First aid for a bite by this spider is similar to that for a snake bite (see below) The other notorious species include Latrodectus (Black Widow, Redback), Loxosceles (Recluse spider of North and South America) and Phoneutria (Brazilian Wandering spider), all of which caused fatalities in the days before the introduction of antivenom. Treatment of these bites consists of cleaning the site, applying a cold pack, giving a pain killer and getting the victim to a hospital.

Snake bites

Fear of snakebites is common among travellers despite the fact that they're exceedingly rare and, with correct management, **rarely fatal**. The most sensible precaution with snakes is simply to avoid the places where they are likely to be. This means wearing covered footwear in long grass or deep sand, stepping well clear of fallen trees and avoiding hollows. Never approach or provoke a snake.

When camping, keep your tent zipped up at all times, shake out your boots, helmet and jacket each morning if left outside, and be extra careful when collecting firewood. Snakes are attracted to your campsite for warmth (your cooling engine or warm body) and food, such as rodents feeding on your scraps. If any of your group is unlucky enough to get bitten by a snake, you will need to take the following action:

- Reassure the victim. They will be terrified and as such their heart will be pumping harder, accelerating the venom through the system.
- Calmly explain that only a small minority of snakes are lethal to

humans and of these, only 25% of bites inject enough venom to be harmful to an adult. You can also add that death from snakebite is not immediate, as depicted by Hollywood, but with correct first aid there is time to get to medical help.

- Cover the bite with a clean dressing. Never suck or wash a wound as it does not help and the hospital will need to swab the site to identify the venom.
- Bandage **the entire limb**, about as tightly as you would strap a sprained ankle, so it should be difficult to insert a finger under the edge of the bandage. This slows the spread of venom into the body (by occluding the lymphatic vessels). This is the **Pressure Immobilisation Technique**.
- **Splint the limb** by strapping alongside something rigid like a stick or tent pole. This stops muscle movements squeezing venom from the limb into the rest of the body.
- Give paracetamol or codeine painkillers, **not aspirin**.
- Transport to hospital, keeping the patient as still as possible.

If you're alone follow the same protocol but leave out the splint – you will still be able to ride. Move quickly but do not run. Never attempt to kill or capture the snake. Ignore local snake-bite remedies – it's the **antivenom** available from a hospital which will save your life should envenomisation have occurred.

Scorpion stings

Although dangerous scorpions do exist in Africa, North and South America and the Middle East, the chances of a sting being life threatening are almost zero. The most common effects are severe localised pain, swelling and numbness which begin to subside after one hour, similar to an intense wasp sting. Signs of a more severe sting include sweating, shortness of breath, abdominal pain, high temperatures, progressing very rarely to death. Antivenom exists for these cases. Debate exists as to whether it is necessary to visit hospital after a scorpion sting at all. I would say almost certainly not unless the symptoms are progressive. First aid is as for spider bites.

Back pain

Long days spent hunched over the 'bars (as opposed to *at* bars) makes back pain common amongst motorcycle travellers, even in young people and those who have never had any previous problems. Poor posture and relative inactivity cause the muscles of the lower back to go into painful spasm and can irritate the nerves where they run through the muscle causing pain down the back of the leg. This is **sciatica** and symptoms can be very debilitating.

The muscles in question do not work in isolation but rather in an important balance with other muscle groups, namely the deep abdominal muscles (Transversus Abdominis), deep back muscle (Multifidus), pelvic floor muscles and the diaphragm. The key to alleviating low back pain is to redress the balance by exercising these other muscles – something which can be done with a few simple exercises as you ride:

- Regularly tense your pelvic floor muscles gently and hold for 10 seconds whilst breathing normally. These are the same muscles you use to stop yourself passing urine. If you feel your abdominal wall muscles tighten you are clenching too hard.

● Tilt your pelvis by pushing your hips forward so that your back is straight from top to bottom. Hold for 15 seconds.

These principles and exercises are the fundamental basis of **Pilates**, a system of exercise which can be of great benefit to back pain sufferers. If you are prone to back pain when you ride you would be well advised to go to some Pilates classes prior to embarking on a long trip. The numerous subtleties are best taught by an instructor and you will learn a number of exercises which you can do while riding.

Exercise

Although motorcycling undoubtedly uses up more calories than driving a car or sitting at home channel surfing, it's important for your general wellbeing to do some **regular aerobic exercise** at the end of a day's riding. Anything which gets your limbs moving and heart pumping will make you feel healthier, sleep better and have more energy to cope with whatever the trip throws at you. Playing keepie up with a hacky sack or running after a frisbee are good sociable activities using items which take up little room in your panniers. Skipping with your tie-down rope is another good one.

Dentistry

The phrase 'prevention is better than cure' has never been more applicable when it comes to teeth problems on the road. A visit to the dentist several months in advance is an essential part of your pre-trip preparation for the following reasons:

● Almost all dental problems are predictable.
● Any small, previously unnoticed dental cavity can turn into a painful infection under the conditions of poor oral hygiene associated with overland travel.
● Acute toothache can become one of the worst types of pain and can be incapacitating.
● Dentists are few and far between in the developing world.
● Hygiene standards are not assured in such places. Transmission of HIV, Hepatitis B and C are possibilities.

Should a gum infection occur the symptoms can be subdued with painkillers, frequent teeth cleaning, hot saltwater mouthwashes and the antibiotics from your first-aid kit. **Oil of cloves** is a well-known remedy to numb toothache.

Altitude sickness

Humans can start to feel the effects of lack of oxygen over about 2600m/8500 feet, a height at which a bike engine will still be functioning without a problem.

Most people will feel unwell if they ascend above 3000m (9850ft), with much variation in individual symptoms and their speed of onset. Headache, fatigue, shortness of breath, dizziness and difficulty sleeping are the common complaints which develop within 36 hours and settle within a few days as acclimatisation occurs. They occur simply due to lack of oxygen and are nothing to do with your level of physical fitness or smoking. Acclimatisation is the process by which the body adjusts to the lack of oxygen with increased heart rate, faster breathing rate and more frequent urination. Vivid dreams are normal during this time.

LIFE ON THE ROAD

MALARIA

Malaria is endemic throughout the tropical world as far north as southern Turkey, down to the northern part of South Africa. It kills 1–2 million people every year, with travellers being more susceptible than those indigenous to malarial areas.

Since the disease can only be transmitted to humans by the mosquito, the simplest measure is to **avoid being bitten**.

Mosquito avoidance

● Wear long sleeves and long trousers between dusk and dawn when mosquitoes are active.

● Use insect repellent containing DEET (50% is enough) applied to all exposed skin.

● Use individual lightweight mosquito nets. Soak in Permethrin every six months to increase insect repellence.

● Use vaporising insecticides or slow-burning mosquito coils in sleeping areas.

Antimalarial medication

There are two vitally important points here which cannot be stressed enough.

● Taking these medicines alone **will not prevent you from catching malaria**; they must be combined with the anti-mosquito measures listed above.

● The course of tablets must be **completed as directed** (ie. four weeks after returning) even if you are symptom-free, as the organism can lie dormant in your liver.

The choice of anti-malarial drugs which your doctor will prescribe depends on geographical area, time of year and emergence of resistant strains in that area. The tablets will be either daily or weekly. Most of the drugs available will have some side effects, the only one worthy of mention here being Mefloquine (**Lariam**). The side effects of this have been well publicised and include stomach ache, diarrhoea, insomnia, loss of co-ordination and psychological changes, albeit in a minority of people.

However, it is effective against the most dangerous form of malaria (multi-resistant Plasmodium Falciparum strains) and currently recommended for high-risk areas in Africa, the Amazon and South East Asia. Due to the possibility of intolerable side effects occurring, it's advisable to start taking Mefloquine up to a month prior to departure to allow time to change drugs if necessary.

Useful malaria info websites

⌨ malaria.lshtm.ac.uk
⌨ www.malaria-reference.co.uk

Acute mountain sickness is the most severe form of altitude sickness experienced by mountaineers who climb too rapidly. It can be fatal and must be treated by immediate descent, although ordinarily would not occur at altitudes normally attainable by a motorcycle.

Heat-related illness

Heat-related illness describes a range of symptoms which occur as the body temperature rises; from heat cramps through to heat stroke which can be fatal. Humans need to maintain the core temperature very close to 36.5°C/97.7°F. Heat acclimatisation occurs mainly during the first ten days after entering a hot climate and is aided by exercising at cool times of day for an hour. The body adapts by gradually lowering its core temperature and making the sweat less salty, meaning you actually have to **drink more** once acclimatised.

The important factors leading to the development of overheating are:

● High ambient temperature.
● Humidity: cooling by sweating is less efficient in high humidity.
● Heat production: exercise, feverish illness.
● Reduced heat dispersal: heavy protective clothing.
● Dehydration.
● Bodily factors: obesity, lack of acclimatisation.
● Alcohol: exacerbates dehydration, reduces perception to overheating.

Symptoms of heat illness include headaches, muscle cramps, nausea and fainting. Swelling hands and feet are common after travel to a hot climate but settle in a few weeks. Any reduced consciousness or confusion in a person with body temperature over 40°C means that **heat stroke** is setting in, requiring urgent cooling treatment and transfer to hospital.

Treatment consists of **cooling and rehydration**. Stop all activity and find shade. Evaporation is an efficient cooling technique: undressing the patient, keep the skin moist while fanning. Bathing in water, application of ice packs or transfer to an air-conditioned environment also help.

WATER PURIFICATION

Water is lost through sweating, urination and vomiting so in hot climates must be drunk frequently. A life lived off tap water can make you forget that this is a natural resource which falls from the sky. Along with **wells**, rivers in wilderness areas and shady rockpools are all safe sources of clean water.

Polluted water is most commonly found near human activity but **bottled water** is now commonly available throughout the world. Use it but check the cap seals as refilling empties is a well-known scam in poorer countries. Eliminating bugs from water can be done in three ways:

- Boiling for four minutes (but see below).
- Sterilising with chemicals like chlorine, iodine or silver.
- Filtration.

Boiling uses up fuel and, along with tablets, does not remove impurities in dirty water. Furthermore, water boils below 100°C as altitude increases, so add a minute to your boil for every 1000 feet/300m above sea level.

Sterilising tablets (or liquids) are a less fiddly way of getting pure drinking water. Cheap and effective, their drawbacks include giving water an unpleasant taste (especially chlorine-based tablets), the need to wait from ten minutes to two hours to take effect, and the fact that they can't remove impurities. Iodine can be poisonous if overdosed and silver compounds are slow. For visibly dirty water pouring through a rag helps as it may remove cysts in which bugs like giardia or amoebic dysentery lie dormant.

Manually-operated **filter pumps**, like the well-known Katadyns or MSRs, are fast but expensive and if a ceramic core cracks as it gets thinner, it's had it. These types of pumps are slow and may require cleaning every litre in silty conditions so do your best to pre-filter water.

LIFE ON THE ROAD

TRAVEL HEALTH TIPS

- **Get immunised** against commonly-known diseases.
- **Avoid getting bitten** by insects, snakes, rodents and, of course, larger predators.
- **Take malaria pills** – better still use a mosquito net and repellent.
- **Take a first-aid kit** containing at least the items listed on p157.
- **Drink frequently**, particularly at altitude, and if necessary rehydrate (see above).

- Be sure that your **water source** is clean.
- **Eat nutritious** freshly-cooked food and avoid re-heated meals.
- **Travel insurance** is useful but in the end medical cover is more important than property insurance.
- **Back home**, if you don't feel well (readjustment often produces some ailments), consult your doctor and tell them where you've been.

When things go wrong

Not every day on the road will go as you'd wish and if you're very unlucky you might find yourself in a nightmare-like situation, made all the more stressful because you're abroad. The most common misfortunes on the overland trail are serious illness or injury, road accidents, trouble with the law, and theft. Much less common dangers include rape and assault, armed robbery, kidnapping, the total loss of your bike and being imprisoned.

Travelling in foreign cultures has its perils, and if you find yourself in one of the above scenarios it's as well to remember that the rules, laws and customs of your home country won't apply. Getting out of a legal tangle could be as simple as paying off the right person. With any other show-stopping catastrophe, your best option may be to get back home with the help of travel insurance and your government's representative abroad.

Before you leave it's worth apprising yourself of exactly **what your government can do for you** when things go wrong abroad; this should be set out on their foreign office or travel advice website. It may not be as much as you'd hope, because they're bound by the laws of the nation that hosts their diplomatic mission. One further caveat: if an insurance provider can find a reason for not paying out on a claim, expect them to try their utmost to do so. See p20 for more on buying the most **appropriate travel insurance**.

SERIOUS ILLNESS OR INJURY

When you or one of your party is afflicted by a serious illness or major injury, or has been in a road accident (more opposite), it's time to make use of your travel insurance. This is what you're paying for and the person on the end of the all-important helpline will be practiced in dealing with your predicament even, in my experience, up to the point of offering basic medical advice to keep a person alive. It's worth locating this **helpline number** on the policy document and storing it in a few other places, including on your mobile phone. There's advice on **trauma first aid** in the preceding section

However, don't expect travel insurance costing a pound or two a day to get you the sort of emergency support that expensive sporting events or rallies can muster. Once you make the call they won't mobilise International Rescue and despatch a Chinook full of nurses to pluck you from your predicament by nightfall. Instead, in most cases the patient must be brought to a town or city with a hospital, a journey which, depending on the condition of the patient and access to painkillers, can become very uncomfortable.

... don't expect travel insurance costing a pound or two a day to ... mobilise International Rescue and despatch a Chinook full of nurses to pluck you from your predicament by nightfall.

Getting to a hospital will be the priority, and better still, to a hospital in a city with an international airport. You may want to contact your embassy at this time, especially if you've been injured in a criminal attack. If nothing else, embassy staff should be able to recommend local medical facilities as well as legal help, money transfers and so on. If you find yourself needing medical help then consider the following issues:

- How far do you need to travel to reach a decent medical facility? If your condition is serious think about initiating some standby treatment.
- Public hospitals in developing countries can be poorly maintained. Mission hospitals or private facilities can be a better bet.
- Healthcare workers can be demoralised and underpaid. Be polite and don't make criticisms openly. Clarify issues with payment up front.
- Check the expiry date on any medicines prescribed and what the ingredients are.
- If you're seriously ill and in need of hospitalisation, contact your insurance company straight away. This is exactly what it's for and not to do so may invalidate future compensation. If necessary they may organise evacuation by air.

Once a seriously ill patient is stable, the travel insurance provider will almost certainly organise **repatriation**, but this is unlikely to be a Lear jet loaned out by *Médecins Sans Frontières*. If the patient is able to go on a scheduled flight, even in a wheelchair with a drip, that's what they'll use, although transportation to and from the airport and any stopovers should be covered. If any payments for medical services have to be made, make sure you get receipts or guidance from the insurers on how to proceed.

If you don't have travel insurance you'll be on your own of course, though this need not mean financial ruin. Getting out of a fix can cost no more than the price of a visit to a hospital and then, if necessary, the next flight home.

ROAD ACCIDENTS

A 2010 report by the FIA Foundation (⌨ www.fiafoundation.org) titled 'Bad Trips' estimated that of a global total of about 1.5 million, 25,000 tourists die annually abroad as a result of road accidents. As a tourist, this is by far your most likely cause of death, but one over which you have some control. When others are involved, be they drivers, pedestrians or even livestock, the situation can become extremely intimidating. The familiar procedure of the speedy arrival of police, ambulances and the exchanging of insurance details could be muddied by the formation of a curious and possibly hostile crowd.

Small inter-vehicle shunts with minimal damage usually don't need to result in the police being called, and can either be shrugged off or **settled on the spot**. If all are in agreement, it's the best way to resolve the situation. A local in the wrong might well offer to get your bike repaired; you may want to do the same if you feel you were at fault.

If you've seriously **hurt or killed someone**, most likely a pedestrian, then you're just going to have to ride out the events and hope for the best. This must be understood though: in the poor countries through which you'll be riding it's a mistake to think a pedestrian shouldn't be wandering along the road in the first place. Even on a motorway of some kind, in most AMZ countries the road is also the **pedestrian's right of way**; in countries like India, it's the right of way of a good few animals too, many of them extremely valuable or even sacred.

Following an accident, it's best not to admit any liability, even though you may get locked up for a short while until things are sorted out. This is the time to get in touch with **your government's representative**, if there is one. If the details are not to hand (check the city listings in a guidebook), it may be simpler to call someone at home and ask them to track down the contact details for you online.

Motor insurance bought locally ought to cover you for such events, but it's not uncommon to see it as having little actual value save being something to present at checkpoints. While having it may not magically solve the situation, not having it will certainly make it worse.

If you're thought to be in the wrong, local mobs can gang up on you and, in some places, victims who are probably desperately poor can see the chance to make a quick buck. I read of travellers in Ethiopia being charged several hundred dollars for running down a cow. On a bike that would take some doing, but in similar situations travellers have been advised by well-meaning policemen to **swiftly leave the scene** and not come back. At other times the policeman or other authority figure may insist or suggest some sort of **on-the-spot compensation**. It's up to you to judge whether it's required, fair, or extortionate, but as a foreigner on a flashy bike, you won't have too many cards in your hand. Many travellers are so freaked out and indeed outnumbered that they'll happily pay anything to get out of there fast.

THEFT AND ROBBERY

As long as wayfarers have travelled, brigands, swindlers and associated rat-bags have preyed on them. You may not think it but the perils are much reduced compared to 500 or 2000 years ago, although the need for vigilance both on the road and in foreign settlements remains the same.

Accept that on the road it's possible that you may lose something or even everything, through carelessness, bad luck, **theft** or outright robbery. Much has been said about the need to keep your valuables safe, but in the end it's all just stuff that can be replaced, albeit at a price and great inconvenience. This is just a simple fact, the not-so-glamorous side of travel.

Theft is just a pain, from your person or your bike; the perpetrator is long gone before you noticed anything is missing. **Robbery or mugging** is another matter. During the months preceding your departure, it's likely at least one person – an individual who reads tabloids and doesn't get out much – will have expressed alarm at your adventurous itinerary. 'Africa/ Iran/Colombia, are you crazy?' You might knock back some bluff reply, but underneath you can't help thinking they might have a point.

More city strategies

Cities anywhere are the lairs of thieves who prey on conspicuous and gullible tourists. Markets and crowded travel termini are favourite haunts for pickpockets. If you find yourself wandering into these places, check that everything is zipped up and be alert. Try to keep the evidence of your wealth or your confusion under wraps. **Wallets** should always be zipped into inside jacket pockets or kept in money belts, not bulging from a back trouser pocket.

If you're walking around with a day pack on your back, don't put valuables in there. I find a **shoulder bag** that swings round to the front where you can see it is better.

Avoid gazing cross-eyed at town plans on street corners with your mouth half open. In dodgy cities like some African and Latin American capitals, **plan your route** before you walk out of your lodgings and when you do walk, imitate the advice given to women walking alone at night: march with a single-minded purpose that emits the signal loud and clear: 'Don't even think about it, punk!'. Beware of pats on the shoulder, newspapers, flowers or babies being shoved in your face, people claiming to be wiping bird droppings off your jacket, and any other number of distractions which are time-worn **set-ups** for snatches or pickpockets. If you expect to be coming back drunk from a bar in the early hours, carry only things you can afford to lose.

Guidebooks advise leaving your valuables in the hotel's safe or at reception, but not all **hotels** you'll stay in will inspire a feeling of security, so some travellers prefer to keep valuables on their person at all times. It's best never to leave valuables in your hotel room.

Getting robbed

While theft is usually an urban problem, robbery, or what's quaintly known as banditry, usually occurs in rural or remote regions, and is as likely in the US or the Ukraine as anywhere else. Again, be wary of set-ups like a **feigned breakdown**. Generally, a family group sat at the roadside by a steaming car will be what it seems, but a couple of shifty-looking sleazebags may have other plans. If you're unsure of the situation, **keep moving;** someone else will help them soon enough if they really need it.

If the game is up the important thing to remember is that, assuming they're not severely intoxicated, they've little to gain by harming you as that could result in a whole lot more trouble. Acting as a submissive tourist is the best strategy. Valuables are what the robbers are usually after, not your bike. Galling though it may be, let them have it all.

Carrying weapons for self defence

Many bikers wonder whether they should carry a weapon as a means of self defence and, if so, what kind. You might imagine situations where it could be reassuring to have some mace or **pepper spray** which is recommended in some ursine habitats and sold elsewhere as an urban self-protection agent. But ask yourself how often are you likely to come up against a witless sole assailant who can be taken out with a quick squirt?

The fact is, you'll almost certainly never need to act like this, and possibly won't even have the aggressive instinct to do so when you should. Your best weapon is the common sense to not put yourself in such situations or avoid them if you see them coming, although you never know what you might manage on the day. One mild-mannered overlander I know managed to relieve a drunk, threatening soldier of his AK-47 and later bent the AK's barrel sideways in a tree in his bid for world peace.

Most of us have never seen a **handgun** and would consider the idea of carrying one abroad absurd, but for overlanders from societies where gun ownership is widespread, the prospect of travelling without a gun may be

LIFE ON THE ROAD

unnerving, even if they know it's bound to be illegal. Using a handgun or even a knife to protect yourself might be advisable if you're prepared to face the consequences, including getting it wrong. When you're feeling a bit insecure it can be fun to fantasise about wasting the dirtbag who tried to rob you, but most people appreciate that real-life armed struggles and fights aren't the beautifully choreographed hip-kicking balletics from *The Matrix*, but clumsy affairs.

The reality is if you're indeed under attack and unable to flee, you'll be either petrified or just very frustrated that it's happening. Either that or you'll have a shit-hot story to impress people with down the road.

POLICE TROUBLE

It pays to be on your best behaviour abroad, if for no other reason than you can land yourself in trouble for any number of unknown and unexpected transgressions. These can include immigration or visa infractions, a road-traffic offence or accident, entering or 'spying' in a restricted area (including some border areas), possessing illegal drugs or bootleg DVDs, smuggling (including prehistoric artefacts or fossils), not fully declaring something (including certain foods and gadgets), talking with the wrong people or just being in the wrong place at the wrong time, political or religious insensitivity including insulting behaviour, or being disrespectful about the head of state. The list goes on.

Once they have you they'll be in no rush to admit a possible mistake and release you. You don't have to be in a North Korean-style police state to recognise that **human rights** in many of the countries you plan to visit are woeful. Falling foul of the system and having to undergo even a short spell in prison could be traumatising. Whatever you think of the quality of policing back home, it'll be heavenly compared to the pitiless contempt for citizens' rights you're likely to encounter abroad. You can also be **set up** for any of the above offences by corrupt police or vengeful locals who you may have annoyed.

If arrested for something serious, the first step is to get in touch with a friend or family member and then your embassy or consulate

If you're **arrested for something serious**, the first step is to try and get in touch with a friend or family member and then your embassy, high commission or consulate, or an embassy or honorary consul that might represent your country. This is vital if you're not to disappear, because you'll be helpless and need people on the outside to fight your case.

Drugs

Drugs offences probably get more young overseas travellers in trouble with the law than anything else. Not a few of them have been set up by dealers or guest-house owners working with the police. The best advice must be to just say no while you're on the road, unless you're clearly in a comfortable situation. Otherwise, along with any number of other traps you can fall into, there's too much at stake.

Adventure motorcycling – the bird's eye view

Lois Pryce advises on the pleasures and pitfalls of women riding solo.

I'm pleased to say that the last few years have seen an increase in the number of women entering the wonderful world of adventure motorcycling, either solo or as part of a couple. But outside the Western world, a woman on a motorcycle remains an unusual sight and you'll still be regarded as something of a novelty once you venture into the AMZ: Africa, Asia or Latin America.

A mud-splattered woman astride a loaded up bike, rumbling into a remote village, is not something those villagers will forget in a hurry. Although your status as a travelling circus act can sometimes feel overwhelming, all well-travelled women riders report countless incidents of immense kindness, generosity and encouragement from men and women alike (if you exclude officers of the law, of course). There is definitely a hearty dose of goodwill out there for female adventure motards.

It's a man's world
The feminist revolution didn't make much of a dent outside the West so in the developing world as a general rule men do the drinking, smoking and driving (sometimes all at the same time) and women look after the home and have babies. This is of course normal life for the majority of the world, but it can be a bit of a culture shock to the independent Western woman arriving fresh out of emancipated Europe or North America. Bear in mind though that in their world you yourself are a one-woman, two-wheeled, travelling culture shock. You'll be a novelty item everywhere you go, so expect to be stared at, pointed at, quizzed and (hey, if you're lucky) even poked and mauled. There's nothing quite like being surrounded by a crowd of shouting, sleeve-tugging men yelling 'where is husband?' to make you want to roar off into the distance. While this can be intimidating at times, it's generally borne out of genuine curiosity, so if you can grin and bear it with a friendly smile, and brush off unwanted overtures without bruising anyone's ego, you should manage to ease your way out of most situations leaving everyone's pride intact.

Different strokes for different folks
Although there are some generalisations that can be made about the experience of being a woman on the road, situations differ depending on where you are. Culture and religious beliefs will determine a large part of your experience and how you're viewed as a female, especially if travelling solo.

Latin America is a popular destination for women riders as it's certainly one of the safest and most comfortable places in which to travel, once you understand that the Latin male ego is as fragile as his country's economy. When you enter Mexico from the US there's no sign saying 'Welcome to Machoworld – you are entering the land of the Latin Lover' but it's obvious that you're now playing by a different set of rules. Masculinity reigns supreme

LIFE ON THE ROAD

... any feminist principles are best left at the Mexican border in the receptacle provided.

and the division of the sexes is abundantly clear. Machismo is as much a part of the Latin American culture as dictatorships and civil war, a fact one simply has to accept. On the whole this macho approach manifests itself as chivalry rather than lechery but nonetheless, travelling solo in this part of the world can require some re-adjustment of your behaviour and at times, severe gritting of the teeth. But there's no use in allowing it to wind you up as this only provides extra entertainment for your 'admirers' while spoiling your day. It's hard, but any feminist principles are best left at the Mexican border in the receptacle provided.

Africa is a tougher proposition. The Muslim countries can be an isolating experience for women who often find themselves facing what appears to be male hostility. It takes a reformatting of one's cultural hard-drive to understand that when someone refuses to speak to or look at you, they're in fact being respectful rather than rude. Often you'll encounter complete incredulity that a woman is capable of riding a motorcycle 'like a man'. In the Algerian Sahara I was once detained at a checkpoint, just because I was a woman, even though I was with a tour agency escort in a car (the rule for all tourists in Algeria). Even then, the rewards to be gained from travelling by motorcycle through this beautiful and fascinating part of the world far outweigh any negatives, and for a less intense version, Morocco and Tunisia provide a more tourist-friendly, Westernised experience.

South of the Sahara being ignored will be the least of your problems. The attention you will garner as a girl on a motorcycle is usually completely harmless but it can be intimidating when each time you stop you're surrounded by a clamouring group who think nothing of touching you and your belongings. You do eventually get used to it and realise that your sense of 'personal space' should have been sent home with your feminist principles. Like most places on this earth, the further away you get from heavily populated areas, the more pleasant your African experience will be. But as opposed to Latin America where women are revered, albeit in a sexist fashion, life is tougher in Africa for women. This is apparent everywhere and is mirrored in the way they're treated in a society which operates on a 'survival of the fittest' basis.

Many women riders report favourable experiences in **Asia**, especially in what are thought to be challenging countries like Iran and Pakistan, where they tell tales of lavish hospitality and genuine friendliness. My own experiences in Iran were the most generous and heart-warming of any country I have visited, particularly the interactions with the younger generation who are keen, verging on desperate to connect with anyone from the 'outside world'. The older guys have a more traditional view of a woman's place in society but this rarely translates as a hostile reception (unless they happen to be an Ayatollah or a member of the Revolutionary Guard, in which case, tuck your hair into your helmet and pin the throttle). Although initially wary about venturing into what is considered an unwelcoming country for Western women, it soon became apparent that Iran was going to be one of the highlights of my AM antics and I felt safer there than in certain areas of London! It was disconcerting at first when passing motorists would drive up close, blast-

LIFE ON THE ROAD

ing their horns and yelling out their windows at me but they were usually just waving with hysterical excitement at seeing a foreign motorcycle on the road, inviting me to their house for tea or filming me on their smartphones.

Any lascivious behaviour you encounter in Islamic countries is usually the result of a guy conflating his internet porn with re-runs of Friends, and can be handled with a firm brush-off, or just a firm brush. As a woman you're rarely viewed as a threat and if you're travelling solo you'll often find that the locals will feel sorry for you. In these more family-centred cultures it's inconceivable that a woman would want to put herself in such a supposedly dangerous situation! So rather than the predictable horrors that the folks back home will warn you about, you may find it's the excessive hospitality that gets you in the end. It's a good idea to carry photos of your family, invent a 'respectable' profession like a teacher, and talk about your father a lot.

Travelling in Muslim countries does bring its own set of rules for women travellers; simple things like shaking hands or walking alone with a man can be misread and in places the dress code required is not exactly conducive to motorcycling. It can be a frustrating business to have to constantly cover up, especially in hot weather, and it's hard to avoid getting oil stains on your hijab while you're doing your routine checks each morning but the best approach is to think of the photo opportunities – you can't beat that bike 'n' burka shot!

> **It's hard to avoid getting oil stains on your hijab ... but think of the photo opportunities – you can't beat that bike 'n' burka shot!**

Ahead of the pack

As a motorcyclist you already have a huge advantage over the average gap-year student trudging her sorry way along the backpacker trail. This is alarmingly apparent as soon as you get off the bike and change into your flip-flops for a wander around town, only to find yourself accompanied by the hissing and catcalling of over-attentive local men. Although you're not totally exempt from harassment while riding – filtering through grid-locked, sweltering Lima while being barraged with lewd suggestions from the stationary cars was one particularly memorable day for me – the bike will almost always help in gaining you respect. Arriving in a town on a motorcycle invariably raises you to near-male status from some men's viewpoint, while promoting you to a Wonder Woman figure in the eyes of the women who, never having even contemplated leaving their village, let alone on a motorcycle, will proclaim you to be very brave. Just don't tell 'em how easy it is or the world will fall apart!

Him indoors

Out in the AMZ family life features more prominently than in Western society and you'll frequently find yourself being quizzed about your personal situation. As well as discussing your family and carrying photos of them, it can be useful to invent a husband who's just nipped off to buy some bike parts (or another suitably manly pursuit). Throughout Latin America I wore a fake wedding ring, giving me instant respectability and helping me out of all sorts of tricky situations, including negotiating my way through a Mexican roadblock with a hastily concocted tale of my devoted spouse urgently awaiting my arrival in the next town. But where my imaginary husband really came into his own was at police and military checkpoints where I was regularly met with the two standard questions: 'Are you married?' 'YES!' and 'Do you have any drugs?' 'NO!' Get these answers the wrong way round and you could find yourself on the receiving end of a marriage proposal from a prison warder.

WOMAN, KNOW YOUR PLACE

While the Benny Hill-style pestering is undoubtedly annoying, it's usually harmless and often tempered with a gentlemanly regard for old-fashioned chivalry. God forbid that a woman should adjust her chain tension or even check her oil unaided! So when Jose (who was pinching your arse in the super-market a few hours previously) spies you by the roadside miserably watching oil pouring out of your crankcase, any unsavoury thoughts are banished by the gleaming opportunity that has presented itself: to be a knight-mechanic in shining armour! Tools, pick-up trucks, friends, brothers are all rounded up and an unholy cacophony of banging and clanking ensues until you're up and running again, with not a pinched bottom in sight. There is only one rule in this situation which must be heeded: Do not offer any advice. Even if you absolutely know they're doing something wrong, or they've picked up the wrong size socket, or haven't replaced the washer or whatever. Don't try telling them. As far as they're concerned, you wouldn't know a 12-mil ring from a loaf of bread. And more importantly, they don't want you to know any-thing – it'll only offend their sensibilities. So just sit there, let them over-tight-en the bolts and make precise adjustments by hitting things, because y'know what? They'll fix it a whole lot quicker than you will. Once again, a feminist stance has about as much currency here as the Argentinean peso in Alaska.

Trust your instincts

Of course you don't want to go around shunning contact with every swag-gering moustachioed man you see (er, actually maybe you do). But there's that fine line to be trod between using your common sense and turning into a para-noid wreck. The communicating and mingling with the locals is all part of the experience, and travelling by motorcycle makes this a much more viable prospect than it is for the backpackers who are bussing it from one tourist attraction to the next. Your common sense will naturally find that correct level of wariness while still satisfying your urge for adventure. Just remember to be patient and genial while retaining an air of confidence, even if you don't feel it at the time. Some of the people you meet may not see things the way you do, but for the short time that your paths cross, it doesn't really matter.

And finally...

In the run up to your departure you'll be inundated with horror stories from well-meaning friends, colleagues and family members. 'You'll get raped!' I remember one panic-stricken acquaintance declaring hysterically as I set off for Mexico. These people must be ignored. Of course, one can't deny that bad things can happen and that there are nasty people out there. But this is as applicable to Tunbridge Wells as it is to Tehran. Doom merchants need to know that good things also happen and there are nice people out there. Alternatively, save your breath and start packing. Sure, you'll have some tough or miserable days, and days when you wish you hadn't got up; it's the same for all independent travellers. But you'll never wish you hadn't set off.

FILMING WITH AUSTIN VINCE

Anybody can film their adventure. The billions of hours of unwatchable bike-mounted Go-Pro footage on YouTube prove that.

However, making an **engaging** film of your adventure is a totally different thing. You cannot wing it. If you want a 4-minute mash-up of cool shots with what you think is great music then there are almost no rules. All you have to do is have everything in focus. But if you want to make an actual documentary that strangers can enjoy then sadly, there is a code.

You must

● **Keep the camera still**. This includes pissing about panning and zooming. This single fact gets you 50% to being like a pro.
● **Have a story**, however simple and include yourself in it. Add 10% pro to cart.
● Follow a **set structure** which reduces to:
Opening sequence/mission statement
Then Transition shots
Sequence 1
Transition shots
Sequence 2
Transition shots
Then Sequence 3 and so on, right up to Closing sequence /wrap up and The End.

What is a sequence?

When you get an interesting place, person, experience shoot a proper sequence. Sequences are the meat of your finished show. This means say, twenty separate shots at a given location that tell the story visually. If the story isn't interesting then put the camera away until you are somewhere memorable. A sequence really can be shot 'silently', ie: without you telling us what's happening. However, the film is better if you're in it so shoot a piece to camera (PTC) where you tell us what's happening. Nevertheless, shoot the shots so that in the edit you can still tell the story without using your PTC.

What is a transition shot?

Intersperse your sequences with transitional shots that get you from one location to the next. A film is a wall, most of the wall is bricks. The sequences are the bricks whilst the mortar is the transitions. Simple, eh? Drive-bys, maps, roadsigns, day counters and local colour all make great transitional shots. You cannot shoot enough local colour! Cover this with commentary and music to suit your taste. This augments you by 7%.

Keep production values high. Being an amateur doesn't mean that focus, exposure and sound issues are beyond you. This is the 'grammar' of television and every modern human subconsciously acknowledges it as a result of zillions of hours of watching TV. You have to serve it up this way because the public aren't capable of digesting your blurred, wobbly, wind-noise-drenched masterpiece. Collect 12% pro credits.

You must not

● Move the camera around.
● Ever give a running commentary from behind the camera unless you are Ben Dover. That's another 7%.
● Confuse your amazing trip with the idea that your film will also be amazing. These two ideas are unconnected. Earn 4%.
● Confuse fancy HD cameras with the solid principles outlined above. Notice how none of the principles are related to what camera you own. Give yourself 2%.
● Underestimate how much time and effort it takes to make even a 20 minute watchable film. However, be encouraged. Like motorcycling around the world, anyone can do it, you just have to try.

Random tips

● Make the film about where you are and what you see, not a 'me, me, me' video diary. Another 8% for reading this far
● Show don't tell. People find this tough. For example, don't tell us 'phew, it's hot', show us pictures that demonstrate this.
● Shoot things in different sizes and cut from the wide to the tight in your edit. Yup, it means shooting the same thing twice! Concrete is strong because of the different sizes of the aggregate. Similarly, your film is enriched by many different shot sizes being used in one sequence. Watch the graveyard shootout at the end of *The Good, The Bad and The Ugly* to see how this is done.
● Every time you shoot something you must answer the question: 'Where will this be used in the final edit?' If you cannot answer that then put the camera away.
Congratulations *AMH* reader, you're a 100% Pro film-maker. Go get 'em, cowboy!

AUSTIN VINCE'S most recent film is *Mondo Sahara*. He curates the **Adventure Travel Film Festival** with Lois Pryce.
🖳 adventuretravelfilmfestival.com

LIFE ON THE ROAD

Bike maintenance and troubleshooting

Even today a motorcycle is a fairly simple machine on which it's easy to see or feel if something is wrong and to track it down quickly. As a result of that you can pretty much coincide a service and check over with your oil changing intervals of every few thousand miles. Due to superior oil filtration technology modern machines now have service intervals of up to 10,000 miles, but out in the AMZ halving your oil change intervals is one of the best things you can do to ensure engine longevity, especially if you're running on ordinary local oils. This is where older, cooler running machines in a lower state of tune have benefits, being less sensitive to sub-optimal fuel and oil.

Unless you've run your bike for a while, or took a thorough test trip, there are sure to be tweaks you make in the early days of your big trip as you settle into the machine: suspension, tyre pressures, ergonomics, adjusting loads. Otherwise, do a checkover at the end of rough stages of several days, be it dirt tracks or bad roads. **Home-made fittings** are especially prone to failure.

IMPROVISED REPAIRS

Making your own repairs is something that worries inexperienced riders, and there can be unease about getting what might be a bad job done by a local metal basher. Often all you need is to **bodge** something to keep moving. It's actually very rare for a bike to be completely stranded and unrepairable, and it's worth recognising that, though you may not think so now, the more irresolvable the problem, the greater the ingenuity of you or the people around you in fixing it.

Even if it's not your nature, try and develop a systematic and logical approach to **fault diagnosis** balanced with a lateral approach to problem solving. That should give the two halves of your brain something to think about. **Improvisation** is at the heart of many roadside remedies and how many of the developing world's vehicles keep running. The advice that follows is generalised, but with just about all the remedies listed here, it pays to initially ride slowly and to check a repair frequently. Very often a first repair isn't effective; you may have to get more lateral. These ideas cover only vital items that must be addressed to maintain mobility. Usually, as long as you can get the engine running, however badly, you can get to somewhere to fix it properly.

If not using disposable latex gloves (from car shops or chemists), wet your hands with soap, let them dry then get to work. You'll find they rinse clean much more easily afterwards. If you forget, a paste made up of washing-up liquid or soap with **sand or sugar** cuts as effectively through oily grime.

FAULT DIAGNOSIS AND FIXES

If you don't know exactly how engines work approach it this way: will it start; will it run; will it go, steer and stop? Engines **won't start** for two main reasons: no electrical power or no fuel. More rarely some mechanical issue like a broken starter motor may be the problem, or more commonly these days, a relatively insignificant electronic malfunction may disable your engine by default.

Should a **warning light** or **fault code** appear somewhere on the dash, get on the internet to find out what it means (or secure this data beforehand). It's not uncommon for engine operation warning lights to light up even though the bike runs fine. I had just this on a Versys and thanks to the owners' forum was a little amazed to learn my bike had a DIY **diagnostics port** under the seat. Simply earthing that port with a bit of wire and the ignition on ran a sequence of Morse-like flashes on the dash which could be decoded from a list of faults (in my case something about warming an O_2 sensor. Emissions are a common cause of warning lights). The light went out but came back occasionally. I ignored it. The lesson here: establish if your bike runs a similar easy-to-use system because knowing the problem is a big step towards fixing it.

Assuming not all bikes have the simple Kawasaki DIY system, you can now get error code readers or emergency diagnostic code tools like the GS911 gadget for just about all GS BMWs. They work with a PC or smartphone and can read and then clear an errant fault code. Quite possibly it's something you'd never have known about in the old days until that component or system failed. Loose, worn or dirty connections will still probably be the physical cause of such an electronic malfunction, but that now includes an array of **sensors** and other electronic components (probably as on my Versys), all of which can complicate matters.

Once running, if an **engine** runs badly or intermittently, it's usually due to a poor air/fuel mixture or the spark, though again on electronically-managed fuel injected engines, besides a loose connection or faulty battery, some electronic sensor may be playing up. Despite the fact it needs clean fuel at high pressure, **electronic fuel injection** hasn't proved to be a weak spot on modern bikes. If anything EFI bikes run better over a wider range of conditions.

If the engine runs then only the **transmission** can stop you but **gearboxes** make noises for thousands of miles before they pack up entirely at which point it's a major repair. A **clutch** shouldn't go unless it's been ragged, such as slipping it through deep mud or sand or a climb on a hot day. When it's gone it can happen fairly fast and it won't come back though you can fix it in an hour by the roadside. On a bike it's usually the friction plate(s) that go – a single 'dry' plate like on pre-watercooled GS boxers (like a car), or wet plates in oil as on most other bikes. Some hyper-slippery synthetic oils don't suit wet clutches. On an old machine or something like a KTM690 it's worth taking a spare. **If needed, gaskets** can be made from cereal packet cardboard, or just use gasket sealant.

Steering head and wheel **bearings** also give warnings before they collapse completely, but are consumable parts whose life will be shortened in dusty or wet conditions. Certainly on a old bike, new bearings all round are a good idea before departure. They're easy enough to buy on the road from any engineering workshop, especially if you can supply the worn item to measure up.

LIFE ON THE ROAD

Fault	Possible cause	Suggested fix
Engine won't turn over; dim or no lights.	Flat battery, faulty alternator (see p185).	Get another battery or jump start; in freezing conditions pre-warm engine and battery.
Lights are fine, but starter won't engage.	Some sort of starter safety cut-out in operation.	Is sidestand up, box in neutral and clutch in? If not, a switch may think it is.
Starter motor spins but won't engage.	Can still be a weak battery or a worn starter. More likely a dodgy solenoid switch or a jammed Bendix gear.	Sharply tap the starter housing with rock to release jammed Bendix. Or remove to check and clean the solenoid.
Engine turns over but won't start.	No spark at the plug. No fuel.	Check for spark by removing a plug and turning engine over with plug against cylinder head; check fuel level.
Engine running badly or misfiring.	Inadequate battery charge. Poor fuel mixture. Blocked fuel filters. Faulty EFI; dirty plugs. Very high altitude (see p184).	Charge or replace battery. Check for air leaks in the fuel system. Check plugs. Check fuel pump. Check/replace fuel filters.
Oil pressure light won't go out, even above 2000rpm.	Faulty oil-pressure switch (unlikely). Engine-oil level low or oil very old (thin). Badly worn engine, (usually associated with knocking noises).	Check oil level and oil switch. Change oil. Rebuild engine following a cylinder-compression check (the latter easily done with a gauge).
Overheating.	Engine rpm too high or ground speed too slow for ambient temperatures and load; broken or jammed fan; loose or worn radiator cap or leaking hoses; insufficient coolant or oil level. Radiator fins blocked or mashed; old, worn engine.	Check oil and coolant levels, radiator and cap (squeeze hoses; leaks evaporate almost instantly). Check fan switch or wire to horn button. Slow down if it's 45°C in the shade. You're ragging it and need a new or bigger engine.
Flat battery.	Discharged overnight; faulty alternator. Low fluid level in unsealed battery.	Jump start; recharge battery. Top up with distilled water, though any water will do in an emergency.
Spokes loose or broken.	Lack of maintenance; crash or heavy impacts with too soft tyre pressures.	Retension, making small changes. Pull sideways rim deflection into alignment, by tighten spoke on opposite side. Zip tie spoke crossings.
Fuel consumption increases dramatically.	Unnoticed headwind or heavy going; low tyre pressures; dragging brakes; blocked air filter; very high altitude; fuel leak; poor fuel; worn engine.	Slow down, accept the causes or deal with them systematically.
Clutch drags (clunky or stiff gearchange).	Cable needs adjusting or is breaking.	Adjust and check for fraying, usually at the lever end.

Fault	Possible cause	Suggested fix
Ruptured brake line.	Damage, rust or perishing.	Slow down and replace when possible.
Leaking radiator.	Rust, damage.	Without radiator sealant, use curry powder, egg white, or ground cork to seal leak; remove radiator and repair with solder.
Split radiator hoses.	Old age, wear or poor fitting.	Bind tightly with duct tape and zip ties, though replacement is better.
Broken or leaking exhaust.	Vibration, old age, rust.	A fracture mid-pipe can be splinted with a cut-open tin can and a pair of hose clips or lockwire. Leaky joins can be filled with a JB Weld. Up to a point bikes run without much of a silencer.
Cracked metal fuel tank or engine/gearbox casing.	Rock or accident damage, weak mounts, vibration.	A bar of soap rubbed into a cracked tank is an old bodge though 'chemical metal' epoxy pastes like JB Weld are better. Plastic tanks can be repaired with epoxy glue.
Engine cuts out in hot and slow conditions.	Vapour lock (carb engines only). See also p62.	Let engine cool or drape fuel pump with a wet rag to cool it and condense the fuel vapour. Only a short-term solution.
Engine management warning light appears on dash.	ECU has registered a fault (there may not be one).	Establish fault or clear error code (see previous page).
Exhaust pops and bangs on hard deceleration.	Unburned fuel is leaking into the exhaust system and exploding there.	Exhaust valve needs adjusting (not closing fully) or is burned out and needs regrinding.
Brakes mushy and lack power.	Air in the brake fluid.	Bleed system (see last page).
Chain slips on rear sprocket.	Chain loose; sprocket worn.	Adjust chain; accelerate gently and replace sprocket asap.
Persistent punctures.	Tyre finished; thorn(s) or nail still in tyre, pressure too low.	Replace or inflate tyre; closely inspect tyre inside and out.
Handling anomalies (wobbling, weaving, shaking).	Bad weight distribution; worn bearings (wheels; steering head; swing arm); something loose or misaligned following repair/crash/transportation; tyres worn, low or inappropriate for speed/weight of bike.	Readjust loads; check bearing for play and tighten (head) or replace (others); sort the tyres out; slow down.
Clutch slips (engine revs but bike goes nowhere in gear)	Clutch overheating; cable too tight; clutch plates wearing out.	Slow down; allow bike to cool down; replace plates or try boiling in detergent.

LIFE ON THE ROAD

GETTING PARTS

Messrs Honda, Suzuki and Yamaha may sell motorbikes in every corner of the world but that doesn't mean that parts for your Euro/US model, not to mention KTM, BMW or Triumph will be available or even obtainable in far flung places.

Having witnessed a Thai parts supplier stuff my piston in his pocket, hop on his scooter and disappear off into the Bangkok traffic in a trial-and-error search for some piston rings that 'might' fit, convinced me to forget the expense and have parts couriered from home. The resulting series of catastrophes remains the most frustrating part of my trip. How can it take *two months* to get a gudgeon pin for a Honda XR400?

Should you need parts from home, to minimise the tedium of waiting weeks or months for them to arrive, try the following:

● Before you leave, locate one, or two parts suppliers who specialise in your bike. Big multi-franchise dealerships often carry plenty of parts for the latest models but very little for trusty old overlanders.
● Contact them and explain where you're going. Ask them can they ship parts abroad and if they have done so before. If they look promising get a contact name.
● Check how much stock they actually carry. Some places which claim to have every part available often don't.
● If they don't have a part in stock, ask where they'd get it from. Some UK dealers, for instance, get their parts from Europe which takes longer. If it's Japan or elsewhere in Asia you could be in for a long wait.
● Do a little research on your bike. Are any parts notorious for failing and/or being difficult to obtain? Are some identical to those found on more common machines? Dependent on cost, you might want to pre-order or maybe leave it with a reliable friend.

● See if it's available used on ebay.
● If you order from abroad, use a courier like DHL or FedEx. Regular postal services may offer a 48-hour international parcel service, and your package might reach the destination country in that time, but once in customs it may stop dead.
● Couriers usually offer a customs clearance service, and although more expensive, if you consider the cost in time, money and sheer frustration of hanging around for weeks, they represent good value.
● Expect the worst. Sadly, someone along the line may mess up. Think about what could go wrong and plan accordingly. Always give detailed instructions and keep track of all involved.
● Get the parcel's online tracking number. As soon as your package has landed get in touch with the nearest courier office, preferably in person and bringing all your documentation.
● If second-hand parts are being sent, make sure they are completely free of oil, uranium, anthrax or any other substance that could be deemed 'hazardous'. Airlines can get funny about what's in a package. If in doubt, check with the courier or airline first.
● Ask your supplier to reduce the value of each item on the invoice and therefore the amount of duty you have to pay. But don't get too carried away; customs aren't stupid.

If it all goes wrong, don't get stressed. Ranting and raving may make you feel better, but will make your situation worse.

The above may seem excessive, but it's all based on real life incidences which have left people tearing their hair out. A few hours' pre-departure preparation could save a lot of time on your trip.

RICHARD VIRR

With **disc brakes** the usual problem is mushiness which means air has got into the brake fluid, again usually due to ageing brake lines (steel braided are better than rubber). To bleed a brake get 100-200ml of brake fluid, a clear hose and an 8 or 10mm ring spanner to undo the bleed nipple down on the caliper. Fit the hose to the nipple and dip the other end below it into a jar with a bit of brake fluid in it. Then with the brake fluid reservoir cap open, pump the brake. As you feel resistance quickly open and close the bleed nipple to eject hopefully aerated fluid. Keep doing that, remembering to top up the reservoir as you go, until what squirts down the hose has no bubbles in it.

ENGINES AT HIGH-ALTITUDE

Carbs work best when mixing consistent levels of fuel and air. Above 3000m/10,000' the air density drops and your bike (especially smaller ones) will run 'rich', which actually means 'run very poorly indeed'.

Fitting smaller jets in the carb is a fiddly roadside job; lowering the carb needle is a bit easier. Both tricks reduce fuel flow to lean out the mixture and balance it with the reduced oxygen levels. To get over a high pass 'adding' air to briefly rebalance the mixture is easier, for example temporarily removing the air box lid or even the air filter.

All these steps must be reversed once you lose height. EFI bikes also lose power at altitude, but the mixture adjusts itself.

Common battery problems

When you run into electrical problems – the vehicle is dead or won't fire up – before testing the alternator as described below, check all **fuses** and for secure battery terminals. It's possible to have low-wattage items like small lights working, but not have enough power to turn the starter motor. A quick wiggle of the **battery terminals** may be all that's needed. Even if the cables aren't loose from shaking, oxidisation can make a poor contact (which is why terminals are greased with Vaseline). If this looks like the cause, file the clamps and lead battery terminals. Don't forget to check where the battery's negative lead is earthed, usually at the bike's chassis. Regular steel rust can develop here too, degrading the contact. After unbolting, this is easily remedied with a file as above, or by rubbing the removed lead on a gritty rock until it's shiny bare metal again.

Next, if the battery isn't a maintenance-free sealed item, check the **electrolyte fluid**. With the battery level (in the horizontal sense), electrolyte acid should cover the plates of all six chambers. If it doesn't (it's common for levels to be uneven), top them up with **distilled water**. The battery may well recover, but you ought to wonder why the levels suddenly dropped unless you've not checked them for months. At worst, the battery is being overcharged by a faulty voltage regulator.

To top up, any water will do if you're desperate, but don't confuse boiled water (sterilised) with distilled water. Boiled water may well be *more* mineral-rich (less distilled) than normal water; it's the evaporated steam that, once condensed might be called mineral-free or distilled and so won't cake the plates. You can make your own with a still, but as Ray Mears has shown, it's slow.

Charging system – the alternator

When due to age, wear or possibly overuse (too much drain on the electrical system), an **alternator** starts malfunctioning (it can become only partially efficient), your bike may continue running as normal, but the battery won't be charging fully. After a few hours, or if you suddenly increase the electrical consumption by plugging in heated clothing for example, the **red charge warning light** (usually a 'battery' icon) will light up on the dash. Lights will soon dim and the engine may misfire or stop altogether.

On seeing this warning light **don't stop the engine**: chances are the battery won't have enough power to restart it. Instead turn off what electrical ancillaries you can. Modern engines rely on precise levels of electrical power and engines will shut down quickly if the system voltage drops minimally.

LIFE ON THE ROAD

RECHARGING ELECTRONICS

Never mind the bike, these days you need a full array of cables, adapters and chargers to keep your show on the road.

Above all, make sure it all works *before* you leave, make use of the bike's 12-volt charging capacity (the USB 12-volt cig charger centre right is very useful, for example) and if possible, have back-up methods of charging gadgets (wall, bike, solar, storage battery) as well as importing data from SD cards.

Before you stop the engine, get a **voltmeter** or multimeter (a device for testing electrical circuits and levels), set it to 'DC' and check the voltage across the battery terminals with all lights and so on turned off. With the engine running at about 2000rpm it should read between 13.5 and 14.5 volts – normal for a 12-volt battery. If the voltmeter reads much less than 12 volts, the alternator is not functioning fully. You can make further checks by turning on lights and revving the engine. The reading across the battery terminals should still show around 14 volts as the alternator adapts to the added load on the battery. If it reads less than 12 volts or worse still, starts dropping before your eyes, the alternator is kaput. If it rises way over 14 volts as you rev the engine the **regulator** isn't regulating and may have already cooked your battery. Even these days, faulty or badly wired **regulator-rectifiers** are a common fault on bikes. It may be another easy-to-replace spare worth carrying.

Alternators can only be repaired by a specialist so replacement is the simplest route. It's not always possible to see the break in the alternator's windings, but if on removal and disassembly they appear black rather than coppery, it could be a bad sign. And the bad news is you're unlikely to find an alternator exchange service for your bike in the AMZ.

A carved up tyre returns some compression damping to this cooked GS11 shock.
© Margus Sootla

Rear shock

Exacerbated by force-multiplying leverages, the modern single rear shock on a loaded overlander running over rough terrain can have a hard time. Bathed in waste engine heat, it creates heat itself as internal valving tries to dampen the coil spring's in-built tendency to rebound.

On a bike coil springs rarely break, and if they do, the way they're wrapped around the damper's body means they just drop by one coil. More commonly seals in the pressurised insides wear out or burst, something which again requires a professional rebuild. BMW GSs running two-up, especially the 1150s, were prone to this problem which can be temporarily fixed with tyre rubber, as shown left.

Jump leads and push starts

It's said that modern bikes aren't suited to jump starting and some leads come with built-in 'surge protection' gizmos to stop the ECU from getting a jolt. Be that as it may, a pair of bike jump leads (thinner than car ones) at least a metre long are well worth carrying. Without them, any bit of thick wire will do, even a coathanger.

Push starts are hard work without a helpful gradient, especially on big singles. If the engine's cold, pull in the clutch and roll the bike to free the plates. Then, click up into second and pull the bike backwards onto compression. This way, when propelled forward, the piston(s) will have a bit of momentum before hitting compression and the spark. Start off in neutral and once moving at running pace or more, pull in the clutch, click up into second and dump the clutch as you jump heavily onto the saddle. Your weight helps load the back tyre to make it grip and so, turn the engine, rather than skid. The key is to synchronise dumping the clutch with landing on the seat – easier if you're already astride and whizzing downhill, rather than huffing and puffing alongside. **Towing** is another more awkward way of doing it, and it's said bikes can also be started parked **back to back** with wheels touching, like a rolling road. You'll need centrestands but it's worth a try.

Worrying noises

Diagnosing errant sounds from your engine takes experience and is another good reason to take the bike on a test run for a few days as the added weight can reconfigure the harmonics, not something covered in the owners' manual. Obviously noises you need to react to swiftly include scraping or an ever-louder knocking from the engine. Low-octane petrol or high temperatures can also make an engine sound noisier. After riding off road it's not uncommon for a stone to get caught in the brake disc cowling or under a bash plate where it rattles annoyingly. Don't beat yourself up about over-reacting to noises; it's a common neurosis when in remote locales. But it's actually quite easy to isolate and so diagnose a noise while riding along by following these actions:

Noise	Possible cause
Only at a certain speed or increases with speed?	It could be something loose on the bodywork/exterior or speed-related resonating.
Only in a certain gear?	Probably a faulty gearbox. While riding along, pull in the clutch and let the revs drop. If the noise is still present it's not the engine and is coming from the gearbox, wheels or bodywork.
Noise drops off as the revs drop, with the clutch in.	It's the engine or clutch. Stop soon and investigate.
Rev engine in neutral	If the noise increases with revs it's coming from the engine.
Engage neutral and coast	Does noise match the vehicle's speed as it slows down? It could be the shaft drive/chain or wheels/bearings.
Sirens	Pull over.

LIFE ON THE ROAD

Shipping overseas

Horizons' **Grant Johnson** *on crossing the parts you cannot ride.*

If you're going to ride the world eventually you'll encounter either a large body of water or a no-go area. Either will require transporting the bike. There are two main options and a number of creative alternatives.

Sea shipping should be less expensive than air, but port charges at both ends can actually add considerable amounts to the cost. I know of cases where shipping relatively short distances was more expensive than flying. Then there's the question of risk – ports are much more prone to theft or damage than airports. Finally, how much will you spend during the three to ten weeks before you actually ride out of the port? Many people underestimate the time and cost in **waiting for your bike** to arrive or be released, although it can work at either end of a big trip when you're back home while your bike's at sea.

Creative alternatives to shipping include leaving your bike overseas. Many more riders are doing this now. One thing to consider is that some countries (such as Malaysia) accept the Carnet de Passage, and others (such as Thailand) stamp the vehicle information into your passport on entry, so you can't leave without the bike. One rider had to ride from Thailand into Malaysia in order to fly back to England temporarily without his bike.

Sea freight

The decision whether to use air or sea is often made when you first check the price – an airfreight company may quote say US$1500, and by sea freight it's only US$800. Sounds like an easy choice until you factor in the port charges at the destination. To unload the container from the ship is US$50, to move the container to the other end of the dock is US$75, to unload the container and get your crate out is US$100, to move your crate to the shipping company is US$50, and paperwork costs for customs and fumigation add up to several hundred more. All of a sudden it's not such a good deal anymore.

Apart from short **'banana boat'** crossings as pictured left, sea freight is best suited to low-value/high bulk commodities like crude oil, ore or livestock. A motorcycle is a small, high-value item of little volume, yet is a single consignment liable to the same series of charges as a quarter million tons of Russian coal.

In our experience the cost is the minor aggravation. What's worse is when the bike doesn't arrive as promised. One traveller shipped out of the UK to Ecuador, planning on

'Banana boating'. © Margus Sootla

three months travelling around South America. As a former RTW traveller she was experienced so left lots of time but on arrival, no moto. A quick call to the shipper in the UK revealed that the bike was still on the dock, waiting for a ship. Sea freight for another couple ended up taking over six weeks from the UK to Mombasa. This story illustrates the risk of dealing with small companies and agents versus larger shipping companies who have their own staff at both ends. I've heard of loads more horror stories like this, but the lesson here is that sea shippers don't give you the full costs. No matter what they promise, it's not a guarantee.

If the bike isn't there when you are, you can spend a lot of time on foot or in taxis, and generate a lot of frustration dealing with shippers, forwarders, backwarders and customs. As mentioned above, it's safest to ship the bike home *after the trip*, when it doesn't matter so much how long it takes. Ports in Europe and North America aren't usually as expensive as most of the rest of the world, but whatever port you choose, you're much better off choosing a **busy, high-volume port**, even if it's not the nearest to your destination. For more on single-vehicle shipping check out the detailed, 20-page article by Doug Hackney in Chris Scott's *Overlanders' Handbook*.

Air freight

Transporting your bike by air is **much more reliable** even if some countries' airlines are increasingly reluctant to put these 'dangerous goods' inside their passenger planes. You might have to look for an air cargo company. It has become especially difficult to ship a bike into and out of the **USA**. Many travellers find it's much easier to ship via **Canada** when travelling to North America, and in fact one of the major shippers to and from the USA, *Motorcycle Express*, is based in the USA but primarily ships via Canada. You'll find a directory of air freighting agents at ▣ www.azfreight.com. In the UK James Cargo and Motofreight have made a good name for themselves.

Most other countries aren't a big problem, but you'll often find that the airline doesn't want to deal directly with you; they prefer you to use an agent, but very often the agent's fee is money well spent.

Crated versus uncrated

Whether you ship crated or uncrated, you'll usually only be required to drain the tank, disconnect the battery or even leave it behind. Some will require the bike to be crated, which involves either building a crate or finding a friendly bike shop with crates to throw out. These days new bikes come in metal frames (as right) which are harder to customise. Wood is easier to DIY.

Air freighting uncrated is a lot less hassle of course and common on some routes like Panama to Colombia or Ecuador with Girag, though they suggest you film-wrap your gear for security. Lufthansa may well still ship uncrated to anywhere they fly; Frankfurt is their European hub.

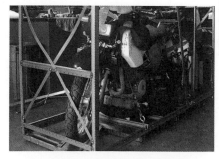

Metal frame crate. © Sean Flanagan

Air freighting tips

Even sealed batteries may be forbidden cargo so you'll have to buy a new one at your destination. To dodge this hassle some carefully pack the battery in an inert box and attached it to the crate floor, with other gear covering it. Or just stash a sealed battery in your baggage, after thoroughly insulating the terminals with melted wax or tape. At least it looks like you tried to be safe if discovered.

We usually left the front wheel on when shipping – it can be an advantage to be able to just wheel the bike out of the crate and ride away. All I do is take off the mirrors and windshield, but it does cost a little more. Sometimes the warehouse where you pick up the bike will insist you take the crate away.

Weight versus volume

If the weight is over a certain level you pay by weight, if under you pay based on volume. Bikes are bulky, and you have to work hard to get the volume down in order to pay the weight price. But you can also sometimes find that there's a big **price break** over 300kg, enough to make sure you save money by getting the weight over 300kg, not under. Ask about price breaks, and what happens if the weight is more or less, as well as the breaks on volume, if any.

Other packing tips

Don't fully compress the forks; use a block, if possible. The bike should be tied down on its blocked suspension, about halfway down. It should not be resting on the stands, only on its wheels, and vertical. Use up to six good tie downs and don't skimp on the crate.

To really squeeze the volume down, take the front wheel off, rest the bike on the sump and tie it down securely. You can also take the rear wheel off, front fender, panniers, and the handlebars. Just unbolt the handlebar clamp(s), leave the cables and wiring attached, and turn the bars sideways, wrap up and secure. Always remember that the goal is to make the crate smaller.

There's more on HU database at ▣ www.horizonsunlimited.com/tripplan/transport/shipping

ASIA
ROUTE OUTLINES

4

From Istanbul or the Urals to a stone's throw from Alaska – and from above the Arctic Circle to below the equator close to Australia, **Asia**, the world's biggest landmass, just about has it all. And for an overland motorcyclist it's all getting easier, with new overland routes and visa-free regimes. Asia offers sealed highways from the Bosphorus to Singapore and right across Russia to Vladivostok.

Part of the appeal of riding in Asia is its rich and diverse historical and architectural heritage, a range of fabulous cuisines as well as the **low cost of living** in the south of the continent (potentially much less than Africa or Latin America). In places fuel prices can be among the lowest in the world too, though they're finding ways of making you pay.

HOT SPOTS
Apart from North Korea which won't be opening to overlanders any time soon, hot spots remain **Syria** as well as all but the Kurdish north of **Iraq**. **Yemen** and **Afghanistan** away from the Wakhan Corridor are very risky, as are parts of the **Russian Caucasus**.

Saudi, China and **Vietnam** severely restrict or complicate independent travel with motor vehicles, and importing a bike into Japan gets difficult and expensive, too. **Iran** requires an escort for Brits and North Americans but that may be history in the face of a diplomatic thaw. **Pakistan** has laid on transit escorts for years but that is more down to security. The great news is that **Myanmar** is now open between India and Thailand and maybe China, too.

VISAS FOR ASIA
Visas will have a major impact on your route because getting them for Russia, Iran, Pakistan, India and some of the Central Asian 'stans can't always be done in an adjacent country in a day or two, let alone at a border. Assuming things have eased up, Iran will still take weeks to acquire, something that's best done before you leave. In Turkmenistan you might find yourself racing across, simply because a short transit visa means you don't have to pay out for the 'escorted tour' that's required with the longer tourist visa. Russia offers an easy solution: one long duration visa. More detail follows.

CARNET COUNTRIES IN ASIA

Bahrain, Bangladesh, Cambodia, India, Indonesia, Iran, Japan, Kuwait, Malaysia* Nepal, Pakistan, Qatar, Singapore, Sri Lanka.

* If arriving by ship as opposed to visiting from Thailand overland.

THE ASIAN CLIMATE

For trouble-free bike travel across Asia there are two things you want to avoid: the tropical **monsoon** on western coasts from June to October, and, more importantly, **winter** anywhere north of the Himalayas.

For Asia-bound riders starting from either Europe or the east, if you're heading towards India, leave in summer and ride into the autumn. If Central Asia or even just eastern Turkey is your destination, plan to arrive in the spring or early autumn – winters in the Asian interior are extreme. Further north, eastern Siberia will only be rideable in the late summer (see p203).

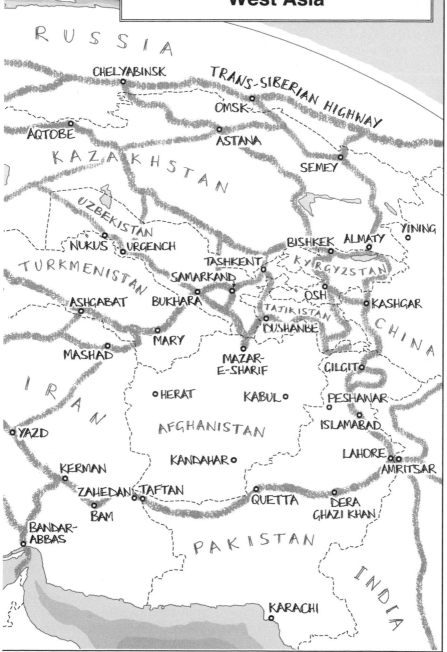

Main overland routes across West Asia

PRINCIPAL ROUTES: TAÏGA, HIGH ASIA OR TROPICS

Unless you're a family of Yakut herders bound for a snorkelling holiday in Sri Lanka, Asia overland is primarily a lateral transit and broadly speaking there are **three principal routes** between east and west:

- The Trans-Siberian route and its adventuresome offshoots run across Russia to Vladivostok from where ferries sail to South Korea.
- The 'Silk Route' links the Caucasus with the mountains of Central Asia, to join eastern Russia with Mongolia, or western China for India.
- Finally, the 'Road to Singapore' runs through Turkey and Iran to India then across Myanmar for the rest of Southeast Asia.

Coming from Europe, around Turkey and Iran the high and low routes interweave with the middle route, but as you move east the mass of China divides your options. On this eastern side the mainland termini of all routes are more specific: possibly Magadan but more likely the conurbation of freighting sea terminals around Vladivostok in Far Eastern Russia with ferry links to South Korea and on to the port of **Busan**, or **Singapore/Kuala Lumpur** (Port Klang) on the equatorial tip of Southeast Asia. These are the key ports you'll want to ship to if you're approaching Asia from the east.

Mile for mile, culturally, historically and scenically **Central Asia** offers the diversity that Russia lacks while also being **carnet-free**. It was through this region that the fabled Silk Roads developed two millennia ago; a network of trade routes along which not only silk, but paper and gunpowder and, of course, ideas shuttled west to Europe via places like Samarkand, before trade passed into the hands of western Europe's 17th-century seafaring empires.

For the time being **China** sticks to its historic isolationism, at least for motorcycling – on a bicycle you can go pretty much where you like. Otherwise you'll need to organise the expensive escort and permits months in advance.

Borders in the far west and east of **Mongolia** means this distinctive and undeveloped country can be transited in full via Ulaanbaatar any way you dare, or you can use the route to the north from Ulan Ude in Russia. The only entry point into China is south of UB on a track that becomes a road to Beijing.

Turkey

Traditionally, coming from the Balkans, **Asia** begins once you cross the Bosphorus from Istanbul into Asia Minor. As a taste of what lies ahead, rather like Morocco, **Turkey** offers just enough challenges to curb complacence. Although a long way from western Europe to be treated as a test run for the big trip, it's a destination in its own right, full of fascinating sites that you wouldn't want to rush, even if you could. The east and north-east regularly feature as highlights among overlanders, although in the ethnically Kurdish areas along the Syrian, Iranian and Iraqi borders, watchtowers and checkpoints are a common sight and tensions have recently escalated.

Most travellers get an e-**visa** at ⌨ www.evisa.gov.tr/en – border visas are being phased out. Buy **motor insurance** for up to three months and that's it. The downside is the high price of **fuel** which may well dictate how many miles you cover here. But whichever way you go, it's hard to choose a bad route. At the far end of Turkey the party could be about to end so brace yourself. Excluding going back home, you have five options:

- Ferry Trabzon to Sochi (Ru). Irregular and anyway crossing Georgia is easy
- Into the north Caucasus and over into Russia for Kazakhstan
- Cross the Caspian Sea to Turkmenistan or Kazakhstan
- Southeast into Iran, either direct or via Kurdish northern Iraq
- A ferry to Israel for Jordan, Egypt and the rest of Africa

NEGOTIATING THE MIDDLE EAST

At the time of writing (you'll be hearing this phrase often ...) the war in **Syria** shows little sign of ending. The conflict has greatly disrupted overland traffic from Turkey to Africa, but Asia remains relatively immune. Currently the options are the **ferry** to Israel, then overland to Jordan. With northern Sinai at present off limits, the daily ferry between Aqaba, Jordan, down the eastern arm of the Red Sea to Nuweiba in the Egyptian Sinai (🖳 www.abmari time.com.jo) has become the only way of getting into Egypt. Coming north, don't even think about crossing Yemen, even if there are boats from Djibouti. And if you wake up in Dubai after a particularly heavy night, don't worry – there's a ferry to Bandar Abbas in Iran. No one need ever know.

Be aware that even though **Israel** can stamp you in and out on a piece of loose paper rather than in your passport, countries like Sudan and definitely Iran, have been known to closely check the dates and places on passport entry and exit stamps. If they find the point of entry was at an Israeli border, they may well turn you away, especially if they're having a bad day or don't like the look of you. In fact, you rarely hear of such problems in Sudan.

THROUGH THE CAUCASUS AND ACROSS THE CASPIAN

For many the Caucasus represents the jumping off point – the sudden transition from the home comforts of Europe to the rigours of Asia – although over the past few years **Azerbaijan** and **Armenia** have become more tourist-friendly and overlanders may feel that they're still in eastern Europe.

Entry points from Turkey are at **Batumi** and **Vale** and once in Georgia there's no rush as you **won't need a visa** and can stay for up to a year. Make the most of it because the next two countries eastwards aren't so accommodating. Be sure to hang out in the capital Tbilisi, as well as Kakheti, Georgia's wine region and home to a number of beautifully situated monasteries. In Azerbaijan the unspoilt and mountainous northern regions are also worth a look – Kifl and Lahıc being two of the area's highlights.

Most find the *Lonely Planet* guide for Georgia, Armenia and Azerbaijan a decent travel companion and for Azerbaijan, Trailblazer's guide is hard to beat. As these are all former Soviet republics, **Russian** will be the most useful **language** here, though English will be understood too. It's unlikely you'll get your head around Georgia's ancient, curly Kartvelian script.

Fuel, money and internet

Petrol is around two thirds cheaper than Europe. **ATMs** are widely found in all major cities and many regional towns. Some fuel stations in Georgia and Azerbaijan take credit cards, as do many hotels in major towns, but as always, it's safer to pay in cash.

You'll find plenty of inexpensive **internet cafés** in all major cities as well as free wi-fi in hotels, smarter cafés and restaurants, especially in the capitals.

Riding in the Caucasus

As for local driving standards, the Georgians are the most aggressive and impatient, although outside the major cities there's little traffic. Road manners in Armenia are good, whilst Azeri truck drivers should be passed with caution. For some reason driving standards in **Baku** are far more chaotic than the rest of Azerbaijan, so sharpen your mirrors and be prepared.

Apart from Azerbaijan, **traffic police corruption** is better than it used to be, so if you're stopped for speeding and have picked up bad habits in either Russia or Central Asia, offering to pay your way out may not be the right thing to do.

Motor insurance is only compulsory in Azerbaijan where it should be issued to you at the border for around $15. You'll be unlikely to obtain motor insurance at any Georgian or Armenian borders, although it's possible to buy it in the major cities, if you can be bothered. In Georgia, **Imedi** provide local and Green Card insurance (useful if you're transiting Georgia on the way home). They have offices in Tbilisi (20 Chavchavadze Ave) and in Batumi on the Black Sea. Note, if you are entering Turkey from Georgia it'll cost you far less to obtain your Green Card in Georgia than it will from a European company or at the Turkish border.

North Caucasus and the road to Russia

Once you've explored Georgia you have three options: **north to Russia** direct from Georgia, or via Abkhazia or Azerbaijan, **south to Armenia** or **east to Azerbaijan**. Versions of the first option have become preferable as Azerbaijan's transit visa and uncertain ferry schedules put overlanders in a pickle. All this has come to pass as the brutal secessionist war in Chechnya seems to have run its course, although in 2008 Russia was provoked to complete its 'annexation' of the contested Georgian province of **Abkhazia** in the northwest. With a transit visa from $5 for 12 hours you can enter Russia this way but it can get a little edgy here, and coming from Russia via Abkhazia into Georgian can't be done as you'll have insulted Georgian territorial integrity.

A much less contentious border into North Ossetia (Russian) exists at **Kazbegi/Verkhny Lars** on the road from Tbilisi to Vladikavkaz ('Kavkaz'; 200km). Buy **Russian insurance** at the border; it's about €20 for three months.

Turkey and Armenia's borders remain firmly closed, whilst crossing from Turkey to the Azeri enclave of Naxçivan limits you to exiting either into Iran via Culfa-Jolfa or returning to Turkey. Note that you also can't cross from Armenia to Azerbaijan and if coming from Georgia, Azeri officials may quibble over an Armenian visa stamp if you've come direct rather than hanging out in Georgia for a bit. Conversely, there's no problem entering Armenia with an Azeri visa stamp. Read all this while looking at a map and it makes sense.

Whichever way you do it, crossing into **Armenia** is relatively expensive: visas are available online and at the border they may offer to skip the stamp if you ask, but you'll have to pay various taxes to bring your bike in for up to 15 days; a 30-day vehicle permit is available. Have photocopies of everything.

It's only possible to exit Armenia via Georgia or Iran – you can't get back into Turkey from here. If crossing to Iran be sure you have your visa otherwise you'll have to pay another spurious departure tax.

Azerbaijan and the Caspian

Coming from Georgia with your Azeri visa, crossing into **Azerbaijan** is straightforward. The northern crossing at **Lagodekhi** is more foreigner-friendly than Krasny Most. Visas can be arranged in Batumi on the Black Sea or in Tbilisi; a 30-day **tourist visa** takes three days to process and costs around $100 but with a vehicle Azerbaijan insists on a temporary importation deposit up to the full value of the bike which of course is a non-starter unless you're related to the president. Most go for the a **5-day transit visa** for $20, or $40 double-entry and valid for 30 days from date of issue.

The problem is that the welcome from the men in hats in Azerbaijan is not always so warm and the associated motorcycle permit is usually valid for only 72 hours. Assuming the ferry game will take longer than that to unravel, you'll be stuck. You can leave the bike in the port's customs area at Baku or Alat and hope it'll be secure there, and if you need to ride the 70km from one port to the other the customs guy should stamp and sign off your bike permit. It's said that fines for overstaying the bike permit a few days aren't huge, though don't try that with the visa.

Exiting from Azerbaijan to **Iran** at Astara on the coast is possible, but not many travellers go this way and of course Iranian visas don't grow on trees. You can also cross from Baku up into Dagestan, **Russia**. It's an 800km ride to the Kazakh border near Astrakhan via the ancient Silk Road city of Derbent on the Caspian. These may be good escape routes if your plans to catch either ferry go awry, but depending on your experience, few overlanders willingly throw themselves through Azerbaijan's burning hoops just to ride out the easy way overland. Most are intent on ferrying over the Caspian Sea.

Across the Caspian Sea for Turkmenistan or Kazakhstan

The idea of crossing the Caspian Sea on a boat from **Baku** to **Turkmenbashi** in Turkmenistan – or now from **Alat** south of Baku to **Aktau** in Kazakhstan – has a romantic ring about it, especially to any CS Lewis readers. But with no fixed schedules and baffling delays once at sea, the frustration and run-around in getting you and your bike onto and then off either boat puts travellers off, especially now the Russian north Caucasus is safe.

The hassle adds up to grumpy and corrupt officials, the uncertainty in securing a place, and more bribes, especially at the Turkmenistan end where you're faced with another five-day rat run. The vessels are primarily rail freighters with a few spare cabins, a long way from a P&O pleasure cruise with a karaoke happy hour. Once heading for either Turkmenbashi or Aktau, the boats seem to float motionless for days on the 200- or 400-km crossing.

If leaving from Baku enquire at the ticket office at the port (N40° 22.47' E49° 51.94'; the Lonely Planet Baku map marks the ticket office, customs and the loading point) about the next departure and get on a list. Tickets aren't sold until the departure is imminent and once that's decided, loading can happen very quickly so don't stray too far. Passenger tickets for both crossings are still around $110 per person for a basic en-suite cabin with a window, and about the same again for your bike, plus another $20 for clean sheets and toilet paper. There's a café on board but that can run out on longer crossings so bring extra food and water for up to two days.

For Turmenistan see p207, for Kazakhstan see p209.

Russia

Unless you detach yourself from the trans-Siberian tramline, scenically, mile for mile Russia can lack diversity, but it sure is a great way of sweeping across the continent on one fat visa. At 17 million square kilometres (6.6m square miles) the half of this land mass above 60°N probably has the lowest population density on earth and geographically, 'Europe' ends rather too neatly at the **Ural mountain** chain, running from the Arctic Ocean down through the Kazakh border and into the Caspian.

Away from the southerly network of the **Trans-Siberian** railway and highway, land-based travel can be arduous. In winter major rivers such as the Ob, Yenisey, Lena and Kolyma become navigable ice roads or *zimniks*. In the short northern summer melted snow saturates the top soil and any attempt at building and maintaining a highway becomes literally undermined as an annual temperature swings 40°C either side of freezing point. Roads expand, crumble, freeze and then get washed away by floods.

Above all, do yourself a favour and learn the **Cyrillic alphabet** (see opposite) so you don't end up in Xandyga when you wanted to get to Huevos Rancheros; it's not totally alien to the Roman alphabet and numbers are the same. English or German may get you by in the West, but not east of Irkutsk. Learning a few phrases greatly enhances your trip so get on it.

BORDERS

Borders will be one of the prime places to demonstrate your fine mastery of Russian. They'll appreciate it and the arduous processes should take less time and be more fun. Forms are normally in Russian so try and find a female officer – they're ever more frequent at border posts these days – as they'll always be the first to help you and may even write out your forms for you.

Assuming all your paperwork is in order there's no need to pay out any bribes. You'll get there just as others have done before you. Without help, expect it all to take several hours. Consider yourself lucky that you're not a truck driver at the wrong end of a 50-kilometre queue and a three-day wait. Unfortunately, the need to **re-register** and renew permits continues once you're in Russia.

VISAS AND REGISTRATION

There was talk of easing regulations with the EU and allowing a reciprocal 30-day visa to be issued at a border, but then the war in Ukraine kicked off, Crimea was annexed, sanctions were imposed by the EU and relationships soured. As an innocent traveller you're caught in the middle.

As with Iran and the Central Asian 'stans, a felicitous alliance with certain visa agencies has developed. You have to use them and apply in your home country – they do all the work for you, including obtaining the so-called letters of introduction ('LOIs'). You'll be hearing a lot about them from now on.

CYRILLIC ALPHABET

Cyrillic letter	Roman equivalent	Pronunciation*	Cyrillic letter	Roman equivalent	Pronunciation*
А а	a	father	П п	p	Peter
Б б	b	bet	Р р	r	Russia
В в	v	vodka	С с	s	Samarkand
Г г	g	get	Т т	t	time
Д д	d	dog	У у	u, oo	fool
Е е	ye	yet (unstressed: year)	Ф ф	f, ph	fast
			Х х	kh	loch
Ё ё	yo	yoghurt	Ц ц	ts	lots
Ж ж	zh	treasure	Ч ч	ch	chilly
З з	z	zebra	Ш ш	sh	show
И и	i, ee	seek, year	Щ щ	shch	fresh chips
Й й	y	boy	Ы ы	y, i	did
К к	k	kit	ь		(softens preceding letter)
Л л	l	last	Э э	e	let
М м	m	Moscow	Ю ю	yu	union
Н н	n	never	Я я	ya	yard (unstressed: yearn)
О о	o	tore (unstressed: top)			

* pronunciation shown by underlined letter/s

The most basic is a **single-entry tourist visa** which lasts 30 days and costs around £130 through an agency in the UK, less for other EU nationals and from $250 in the US. A **double-entry** visa allowing a second 30-day visit within a year costs about 20% more, and both take about a week to issue. You must have confirmed accommodation or transit information for every night of your stay in the country, but the small fee for a visa support letter can get round this requirement. Brits (as well as Danes) now have to submit to a full fingerprint scan which will require a visit to the visa agency. A month-long double-entry visa will easily be enough to get you across the country with a drop down into central Kazakhstan or Mongolia.

Anything of longer duration or with multiple entries is classified as a **business visa**, although you don't have to wear a bowler hat or be involved in any sort of commerce. Costs for a double-entry 90-day business visa start at over £200 for Brits (15% less for most EU citizens) and take at least two weeks to issue; to get it within a week costs half as much again. Prices and delivery times **for multiple-entry business** visas lasting six months are nearly double for Brits (a lot less for others) and take two weeks. Visas need to be used within a year, which is longer than most.

With a visa like this you could just about fill up the riding season to-ing and fro-ing between the Baltic and the Pacific, while visiting Central Asia, Ukraine, Mongolia and, if you're quick, the North Pole. However, technically the consulate can refuse to issue a multiple-entry visa if you don't have a previous Russian visa in your passport, although as with all things Russian, this law is not enforced consistently. Unless you're sure you'll be in Russia for only a couple of weeks, get the **longer lasting business visa**; Russia is a big country and your plans may change.

This is the former USSR so getting a visa is just the start. Within **seven days** of entering the country (excluding weekends and holidays) you must **register** your visa with the Office of Visas and Registration (OVIR, aka UFMS, Federal Migration Service Organisation). Your passport or the immigration card you filled out at the border is stamped, and you obtain a **registration slip** showing the period you're registered to stay in any one place. In addition to the dates, it'll also include details of where you're staying. Very often the **hotel** you're staying in immediately after crossing the border will do this for you for a minimal charge. However, this applies more to the popular tourist cities of Moscow and St Petersburg in the west. In many provincial cities some hotels will register your visa for a fee, even if you're not lodging there.

If you're not passing through the west or are camping, a **Registration Support Letter** will help you register yourself at the nearest OVIR. You'll be asked to complete a **Notification of Arrival** form; it's in Russian so you may need some help; see the image on ⌨ www.realrussia.co.uk. Give the top part back and possibly get another stamp on your migration card or passport.

It's not over yet. In theory once on the road you need to register in any sizable town within three working days but, if you're not staying there for three working days or more, then technically there's no need to register. However, on the road it's worth doing so once in a while and getting another **registration slip** to avoid any potential problems with 'gaps' in your registration. And don't forget to de-register your visa back with the OVIR every time you leave Russia if you're on a multiple-entry visa.

There are obviously plenty to choose from, but the realrussia.co.uk website is well designed, up to date and shows graphics (including translations) of immigration documents. It also has a useful list of **restricted provincial cities** with details of where and how to register if not staying in a hotel. They include Barnaul or Novosibirsk if coming out of north-eastern Kazakhstan, Gorno-Altaysk if coming out of north-western Mongolia, Irkutsk north of Ulaanbaatar, plus Vladivostok and Khabarovsk. They even run a forum to discuss Russian topics. Pay it a visit because this could all change.

Vehicle documents

A translation of your vehicle ownership document will be useful if stopped, although the temporary importation permit (see below) issued at the border ought to suffice. Get an IDP too (see p22). **Motor insurance** (*strahavanie*) you buy at the border and pay in roubles at around €20 for three months.

No carnet is required; instead you get a three-month **temporary importation permit**. It can be extended for up to a year if your visa is that long but if you leave Russia for the 'stans or wherever, the permit expires and if you come back you have to start again. Get the triplicate barcoded **customs declaration form** (sometimes available in several European languages) and indicate on it that you're temporarily importing a bike. Insist on a stamped copy that includes a description, otherwise there'll be problems getting out of Russia, Belarus and Kazakhstan which are all joined in a customs union.

As you ride away from a border after what may have been several hours bouncing around chasing documents and stamps and doing that leg-kicking Cossack dance, resist the urge to gun it; just down the road radar speed traps or more document checks are quite likely.

ON THE ROAD

Petrol prices in Russia start at around 30 roubles a litre (about $0.55). Generally fuel costs more in the far east and in western cities. If you're visiting Kazakhstan, petrol costs about 30% more; in Mongolia and Ukraine it's about 35% more. To stop runaways, at most fuel stations you pay first, then they turn it on. As some have found, if the nozzle has no trigger you can get splashed in the eye looking to see if your tank's full. Medic! On the trans-Sib east of Chita there are **roadhouses** every 150km or so, but in the sticks you know the drill: fill up or run out.

For **mobile internet**, you'll need to show your passport to buy a SIM card. Buy the **countrywide** tariffs from the country's three main operators: Beeline, Megafon or MTS because by European standards they're amazingly cheap for the masses of monthly data you get. You can top up at ATM-like terminals in most shops. Don't bother looking for **free wifi** out in the sticks; get a dongle or SIM and rely on the cheap mobile internet.

Driving standards in Russia are poor; a combination of uncarworthy roads, unroadworthy cars, **drunkenness** and a healthy dose of machismo, evoking Putin in one of his raunchy vids. Once you factor in dealing with the *militizia*, in big cities it may be easier to park up and get around by taxi or even on foot. **Radar traps** and checkpoints are found on the edge of every town as well as places in between, and you'll almost certainly be stopped for speeding or crossing solid white lines whether you did so or not. **Speed limits** are 60kph in town, 110kph on motorways or as signposted. Maximum fines for moderate speeding are only around 300 roubles; but just 5kph over the limit will get you a ticket unless you settle on the spot and negotiate the fine.

They'll want your passport, immigration documents, registration slip, IDP, TIP and anything else you got ending with P, to copy into their ledgers. If they don't ask for these immediately it's probably a prompt for a bribe (*straf*) of 300 roubles or less, or maybe just a friendly chat about your cool bike. Carry photocopies of everything as losing one item to them puts you in a fix and can mean having to cough up a bribe or a spell in the salt mines.

There are a couple of Russian road atlases or, as they call them, auto-atlases. They cover just about all of the ridable parts of the country at scales from 1:200,000 in the west to 1:3 million in the east, and are occasionally available from specialist map shops in Europe or North America, but at three times the price. Once in Russia these atlases may take some tracking down outside the big cities. However, unless you're roaming off the beaten track, a regular folding road map, either European or Russian produced, will do you. You'll find Russian editions for sale in fuel stations.

Of the proprietary digital maps to import into your GPS from the likes of Garmin, their current Russia download is hopeless in the east, just where things begin to get interesting. The best available will be on OSM 💻 www.openstreetmap.org. And although it's all in Russian, web browsers can translate 💻 www.roads.ru/forum to get up-to-date news of the state of roads.

Dodging the police – the other 'Great Game'

Thanks to a combination of post-Soviet poverty and the devalued rouble, **bribery and corruption** are a way of life in Russia and the 'stans of Central Asia. The first handy thing to know is it's easier for them not to stop you if you don't make eye contact, so remember: sunvisors down, tunnel vision on whenever you see the cops. Learn the rules of the road, though admittedly this is trial and error. Here are some pointers to get you started:

- Speed limits are 90kph (56mph) on highways and 60kph (37mph) in towns. As in Europe, town limits start at a sign and end at the same sign with a red line through it. Except that in Russia these signs can be miles after the last house to give the radar cops a chance.
- Never cross a solid white central line. Cross on dashed lines only, or use designated U-turn areas. After speeding, this is a common trap.
- Signs often tend to tell you what you can do, rather than what you can't. In most cities like St Petersburg, Moscow as well as Almaty, Bishkek, Tashkent or Ashgabat, if there's no turn left sign then you can't.
- Slow down if you see a police car, even if you're under the speed limit.
- If an oncoming car flashes you, it's probably because there's a police radar check up ahead. Alternatively, you're in the way and he's coming on through regardless.

At checkpoints make sure you closely observe the painfully slow speed limits. If there's a 'Stop' sign, wait there until you're waved on, even if it's just 10m to another one. This 'double stop' combination is a nice little earner for the rozzers; don't give them the satisfaction!

When you're **stopped**, first find out why. They may just be interested in where you're from, especially on a moto like those Langvei Rount chappies. If they request your documents, again, politely ask: *'prabliem?'* ('Is there a problem?') and add that you're a simple tourist. Be reluctant to hand over essential documents if you suspect the policeman may be difficult and will need inducement to give them back, but definitely don't refuse to hand them over.

If you're stopped for **speeding** ask to check their radar read-out if they don't show it. For a minor offence that's 10–30kph over the limit, a smile, a chat and a postcard of Kate Middleton at Ascot may be enough; if not then pay a 'fine' or *straf* of no more than a few hundred roubles. For that amount don't push your luck and ask for a receipt, and bear in mind they'll often initially ask for something like $50. Negotiate down by showing them the sorry contents of your wallet, which at all times contains no more than 300–400 roubles. It's even worth having a special 'cop' wallet for such encounters.

If, however, they're claiming you were doing 140kph when you were actually doing 57, then ask to see the radar, the speed sign and argue for as long as it takes. When they ask to see your passport, show them a copy of the photo page; same with your visa and other documents.

It's illegal to pay traffic fines in dollars so if they ask for dollars deny that you have any (*U menya nyet; 'I have none'*). It's a form of bargaining though don't treat it as such. Usually they'll then ask for a hefty sum in local currency which will be more than is in your pull wallet. You should end up paying no more than $8 unless you were more than 40kph over the limit, or have jumped a red light, both of which are much bigger fines. You may find yourself in their sweaty, nicotine-tinged Lada whilst negotiating the *straf*. Don't let this put you off, it's all part of the experience and who knows, you may have never seen the inside of a Lada up close before.

If you speak Russian then above all don't waste this god-given talent on the cops. Make their job as tedious as possible by smiling a lot, repeating 'tourist' and feigning subterranean IQ. If you're lucky, they might give up on you as a bad job; their next victim will be along shortly.

WESTERN RUSSIA

Western Russia feels like Eastern Europe, and if you're from Europe and are no stranger to centuries-old buildings, aggressive driving or a bored cop with a radar gun, you may not be so impressed with heartland Russia compared to what lies ahead – or indeed to the south via Turkey and the Caucasus. Many people find a **much warmer welcome** along with a more adventurous frontier ambience in the distant outposts, even in the huge cities of Far Eastern Russia. If you're Pacific-bound, you may want to dodge west Russia via the Caucasus to Kazakhstan as it's another country out east.

Heading east of the Urals the adventure approaches, but not until you've traversed the thousand-mile basin of the Siberian Plain and reached Novosibirsk. The principal overlanding route now closely parallels the Trans-Siberian Railway, the only route that traverses the entire country. Even then, it only goes as far as Vladivostok, 10,000km from Moscow but still 2500km short of the easternmost extreme at Cape Deshneva on the Bering Strait.

To the south-east of Novosibirsk lie the **Altai mountains** and a sealed road right up to the western entry into Mongolia at Tsagannuur (see p231). Even if you're not heading for Mongolia, the wild Altai region and the border track to Tuva to the east are well worth exploring (permits required; check the HUBB). You now leave the Siberian plain and ascend imperceptibly onto the like-named plateau towards Krasnoyarsk on the Yenisey River, the natural boundary which separates western Siberia from the more interesting eastern side.

NORTH OF THE TRANS SIBERIAN

Looking at a map you'd think there's only one major highway to Far Eastern Russia, and you'd be right. That road parallels the Trans-Siberian Railway and is now sealed right through to Vladivostok. While the surface lasts, it's easy riding in most weathers. But there's another, less well-known railway reaching to Far Eastern Russian's Pacific ports; the 4400km 'Baikal-Amur Mainline' or **BAM** which runs around the north side of Lake Baikal to meet the Pacific at the port of **Vanino**, opposite Sakhalin Island. Where there is a railway there's a service road. Or so you'd hope.

Now as well known as the Kolyma Highway among hardcore adv-ers, the BAM was a failed Stalin-era project similarly built over the bones of tens of thousands of Russians or WWII prisoners of war. Work was suspended on Stalin's death, but revived in the 1970s in the face of cooling Soviet-Sino relations because the vulnerable Trans-Sib ran too close to the Chinese border.

Completed at huge cost, the line recovered from being a Cold War white elephant and now, instead of supplying secret bases and gulags, trains run along it day and night, transporting goods from the Pacific ports, serving mines and sustaining the depressed communities strung out alongside it.

The BAM track traverses just a fraction of Russia's vast eastern wilderness, buried in turn by winter snows then flushed by the thaw before a brief, hot, insect-ridden summer – the only time to consider riding the BAM.

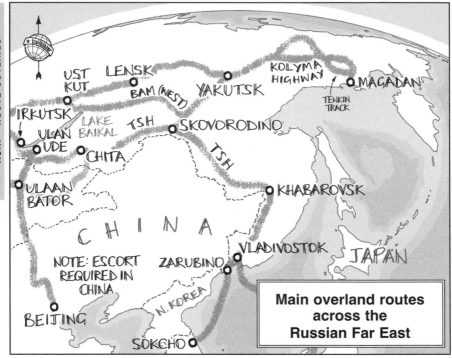

Main overland routes
across the
Russian Far East

So if you're finding the Trans-Siberian Highway a bit of a yawn and think the Kolyma (see opposite) is too obvious, take off along the BAM and see how far you get. **Tynda** on the north-south Amur-Yakutsk Highway divides the western and eastern BAM. In 2009 Walter Colebatch (🖳 www.sibirskyex treme.com) and his chums managed most of the BAM in a westerly direction, and in 2014 five riders set out from Vanino to finish the job (🖳 www.bam riders.com). Only half got to Tynda, occasionally resorting to log rafts, Kamaz 6WDs and the train. One bike even ended up under a train.

Nearly ten per cent of the line is made up of **rail bridges**, well over 4000 span hundreds of rivers and swamps. You may think that as long as the locos keep running, these rail bridges could be used. Sadly that'll be a *nyet*. Armed guards control major rail bridges and even just walking across to ask permission to ride across can earn a hostile: *zapresheni!* (forbidden). Where guards are present, tread gently.

EAST OF IRKUTSK

A thousand kilometres from Krasnoyarsk, **Irkutsk** is a city with a distinctive European feel. Founded in the mid-17th century a few years after Yakutsk, unlike the former it retains a largely Russian rather than native Yakutian population. A beautiful road leads around the edge of Lake Baikal to Ulan Ude and the start of the Wild East.

Ulan Ude is the capital of the vodka-loving (though it makes some aggressive) Buryat Siberians and where you can turn south for the main route into **Mongolia** (more on p231). From **Chita**, another old Russian outpost, the **Amur**

Highway runs all the way to Vladivostok. A short distance after Skovorodino the **Amur-Yakutsk Highway** leads up to the city of that name and the Kolyma Highway to Magadan, the easternmost point on the Russian mainland accessible in summer.

North to Yakutsk

Soon after Skovorodino, depending on recent weather the promisingly named **Amur-Yakutsk Highway** can be 1150km of either recently graded fast dirt, or all-out mud wrestling carnage. It crosses the BAM route at **Tynda** and is interspersed with sections of asphalt, crossing two mountain ranges before dropping into the Lena basin. With a northbound railway ending about halfway at Aldan, there's more traffic than you'd expect and along the way there are plenty of roadhouses and towns. Getting into Yakutsk itself requires ferrying across the Lena River, now 4km wide, from Khachykat to Bestyakh on the west bank, about 80km upstream from Yakutsk.

YAKUTSK AND THE KOLYMA HIGHWAY TO MAGADAN

On a slightly lower parallel than Fairbanks in Alaska, **Yakutsk** is just 400km south of the Arctic Circle (accessible along the Lena or by plane to Zhigansk). If the road is in good shape Yakutsk could be worth the return 2300km ride from Skovo', even if you're not planning to continue to Magadan. As various private interests tear their way into the region's mineral deposits, the city is one of the few in Siberia that seems to be prospering and possesses a notable proportion of native Yakut (aka: Sakha) and Evenk inhabitants.

Most likely though, you'll only find yourself in sunny Yakutsk if you're heading to, or have come from Magadan. And for the eastbound, Magadan really is the end of the road in Russia.

'The Road of Bones'

The Old Summer Route (**OSR**) part of the Kolyma Highway has became an adventure bikers' rite of passage, rather like crossing the Sahara. And like the Sahara, it can be over before you know it, or it can turn into an epic.

Mondo Enduro were the first overland bikers to do it in 1995, accessing this once restricted region of the former USSR. The pioneering traverse barely featured in their film because the much tougher Zilov Gap on the then non-existent Amur Highway had already ruined all their cameras. Now there are organised Road of Bones tours and since 2009, an easy way round to Magadan.

Built in the 1930s at great human cost to enable access to the region's rich mineral resources, like the BAM track, the section between Kyubeme and the ghost town of Kadykchan was falling into disuse before its rediscovery. Countless bridges had collapsed, the track subsided and maintenance fallen to the last party to pass by, these days mostly local hunters in AWD trucks or 4x4- and moto-adventurists.

From Yakutsk via Khandyga to the turn off (fuel) for **Kyubeme** and the OSR is 700km of good or dusty gravel involving summer-only **ferries** across the Lena and then the Aldan rivers. At this point the official way arcs 650km north via the mining outposts surrounding **Ust Nera**, before bending south to meet the original route at Kadykchan.

The gnarly bit lies in the **240-km section** of the OSR between the outpost of **Tomtor-Oymyakon** (155km east of Kyubeme and hitting a record -70°C in winter) and the end at **Kadykchan**. This can take a day and a bit on a pair of slick 690s – or over a fortnight, having abandoned your Ural outfits and walking out, starving, out of fuel and beaten by the river crossings. Besides the obvious suitability of your ride, much depends on the **weather** in July, the optimal month. Hit the OSR in a dry spell and it's only dust you're eating. Hit it wet and the OSR kicks back.

Some 60km south of Kadykchan is the settlement of **Susuman**. At the junction here you can follow the more scenic and less truck-clogged alternative route – the so-called **Tenkinskaya Track** – via Ust Omchug (food, fuel) to rejoin the main road at Palatka, just 80km from Magadan where you either turn back or ship out – usually to Vladivostok or thereabouts.

THE AMUR HIGHWAY TO VLADIVOSTOK

Beyond Skovorodino is the Amur Highway to Khabarovsk and how this highway will survive the road-wrecking 80°C temperature variations of the Siberian seasons remains to be seen. They say sometime around 2012 the length of the new highway was intact, before frost heave, pounding trucks and floods begin to break it up, along with the money to do anything about it.

Roadhouses with **food and fuel** are plentiful, although secluded wild camping isn't so easy as the road is built up over the swamps and Armco may stop you getting off the road to good spots. **Khabarovsk** is a relative late developer, but along with Vladivostok is now among the biggest cities in Far Eastern Russia, with up to three quarters of a million inhabitants. You'll see many Japanese and South Koreans establishing businesses here, and with a **Chinese consulate** at the Lenin Stadium (N48° 28.8' E135° 02.8') on the west side of town just north of the city beach, there's a chance to nip over the Amur for a day trip to China (without the moto, of course).

Vladivostok and the end of this particular road are just 850km away, through the wooded hills where the huge Amur tiger once harried the railroad builders of the late 19th century before its private parts got ground down into aphrodisiacs. Perennially miserable weather doesn't make Vladi the most inspiring place to end your trans-continental trek. But you're here.

GETTING OUT OF VLADIVOSTOK

Arriving at Vladivostok most will put their bike on a ferry to Japan or South Korea. Conventional cargo shipping out of Vladivostok is possible, but costs and bureaucracy issues make it a less than attractive option. DBS Cruise Ferry (🖳 www.dbsferry.com/eng) operates between Vladivostok, Donghae (South Korea), and Sakaiminato (Japan). Offices are in room 239 of Vladivostok ferry terminal, right behind the Trans-Siberian Railway terminal. If going on to Japan after visiting South Korea, you can take DBS again or the less expensive Korea Ferry (🖳 en.koreaferry.kr) from Busan to Hakata. Even leaving the country, customs procedures in Vladivostok can be difficult; it may help to get in contact with Yuri Melnikov at Links, Ltd. (🖳 links-ltd.com). You'll almost certainly need help with customs getting into the country.

A new ferry service is scheduled to run between Vladivostok, Zarubino (200km south of Vladivostok), and Niigata (Japan), but details have not been finalised as of the end of 2015. The operator of the ferry to Wakkanai (Japan) from Korsakov on Sakhalin Island cancelled its service at the end of the 2015 season, but a new service is scheduled to start in 2016.

Korea doesn't accept **carnets**, but you may be required to make a refundable deposit. Japan does require a carnet in most cases. If you do your research into the laws and procedures, and have the time and patience to work with the bureaucrats, you may get into Japan without one. If you decide to take the less stressful route and use a carnet, you still need to have it validated by Japan Automobile Federation (JAF). Information is available in English on the JAF website (🖳 www.jaf.or.jp/e). Procedures will go faster if you fax a copy of your document in advance. There are JAF offices near Sakaiminato and Hakata ports, and the ferry company personnel should be able to direct you to them (or even give you a lift if you ask nicely). My website 🖳 www2.gol.com/users /chrisl/japan has plenty of details on the bike temporary import scene.

From Korea or Japan, most of the major shipping companies provide services to help you get on to your next destination. Shipping agent Wendy Choi in Korea (wendy choi2@gmail.com) may be able to help you get your bike on a boat or plane someplace.

CHRIS LOCKWOOD

Central Asia

Assuming you're wanting to get round the north side of Afghanistan, the four smaller 'stans of Central Asia offer a much more satisfying alternative to hauling along the Trans-Siberian Highway or the interminable steppe of Kazakhstan away from its eastern corner. The highlights here are the yurt-dappled pastures of **Kyrgyzstan** and the stunning Pamirs of **Tajikistan**. The fiery deserts of **Turkmenistan** and Silk Route cities of **Uzbekistan** cap off a rich cultural experience. As in much of this part of the world, central Asian people – be they Kazakh or Kyrgyz, Turkmen, Uzbek or Tajik – are amongst the most hospitable you'll meet, making the irritations just about worth the effort.

Language, maps and money
Although **Uzbekistan** and **Turkmenistan** are slowly moving to modified Roman alphabets, learn the **Cyrillic alphabet** (see p199) so you can read the road signs. **Russian** is still the lingua franca throughout the 'stans although the universal 'Salaam aleikum' of Islamic lands goes down well.

Gizi Central Asia and Kazakhstan **maps** (1:3,000,000) cover the entire region effectively and the German *Reise Know-How* (1:1.7m) provides better detail and information on smaller routes. As for **guidebooks**, Lonely Planet is the major player for Central Asia.

ATMs are found in all cities but very rarely anywhere in between. Fuel stations will generally only accept **cash** – although in an emergency you'll probably be able to pay in US dollars at a terrible rate. After US dollars, euros will be the most useful **hard currency**. Uzbekistan is the only 'stan where a currency black market of at least half as much again prevails. Changing dollars is not difficult here. **Credit cards** are really accepted only in expensive hotels in large cities, and the occasional Western supermarket aimed at ex-pats in places like Astana and Bishkek.

BORDERS
Most Central Asian borders are open daily in daylight hours. Chinese road borders with Kyrgyzstan are at the 3672-metre **Torugurt Pass** 180km north of Kashgar and the 3005-metre **Irkeshtam Pass** 240km east of Osh, 80km from Sary Tash and about 250km west of Kashgar. It has a slightly better reputation for formalities but it's a long, rough track up from Sary Tash. Expect both to be closed at weekends and on public holidays on either side.

Turkmenistan's borders require mind-boggling paperwork. Here, a pre-arranged **guide** is mandatory to ride through the country on anything other than a five-day transit visa and despite the exorbitant expense – about $100 a day or about half of what you'll pay for the whole crossing – a guide certainly helps at the border. Caravanistan (🖥 www.caravanistan.com) or DN Tours (🖥 www.dntours.com) are experts in arranging self-drive logistics and guides. Getting into **Kyrgyzstan, Uzbekistan** and **Tajikistan** is much less complicated. The general rule with border paperwork is, if you need it, someone will ensure you have it before you're allowed to leave the border area. Your carnet is not recognised here; keep it stashed.

Customs declaration form

As in Russia, a **customs declaration form** must be completed in duplicate, sometimes triplicate. The form is normally in Russian (sometimes you might get an English one) and it's essential it's filled in correctly, so if in doubt get an official to help you. Both copies are signed and stamped and one or more is retained by you until you leave the country.

Due to the currency black market, Uzbekistan is the only country where you must accurately declare the amount of dollars you're officially importing. What you don't declare can of course be used on the black market, just make sure that stash isn't found on departure.

Vehicle importation or transit certificate

This varies from country to country and some charge a fee, for example $20 in Tajikistan or 500 som in Kyrgyzstan (they may ask for more). Most countries will give you fifteen days on your certificate, or as long as you ask for, though **Uzbekistan** may insist you can have only three days to transit the country; make sure you ask for more; there's a lot to see there.

Vehicle tax or transit fee and motor insurance

A transit fee is seemingly only necessary for Tajikistan and Turkmenistan, and costs $20 in the former, with another dose on the way out. A dollar amount is calculated on your pre-approved route mileage in Turkmenistan. Turkmen fees are complex and expensive: expect to pay around $150–250 in transit fees, comprising the mileage-based fuel price differential, mandatory third party liability and numerous documentation fees.

Insurance is required in Kyrgyzstan, and theoretically a legal requirement elsewhere, but only Tajikistan and Turkmenistan demand you get it at the border. Elsewhere it's sometimes available at the borders and buying it is up to you.

Vehicle documents

Throughout the 'stans a multi-lingual translation of your vehicle ownership documents (in the UK known as an International Certificate for Motor Vehicles) may be useful if stopped, if for no other reason than to add to the 'document surge' with which you can bore and confuse your tormentor.

Obviously, you'll need your domestic driving licence; an International Driving Permit (IDP) to back it up helps. Theoretically, none of the CIS countries now require your bike to be declared in LOIs, visas or passports so you're not 'attached' to your machine and may be able to nip home for a break.

VISAS AND REGISTRATION

The entire visa system throughout the 'stans is in a constant state of flux and the degree of time, paperwork, difficulty and cost involved varies considerably. Use what follows as a guide only and see what's new at the excellent ▬ www.caravanistan.com, an invaluable resource for cutting your way through the Gordian complexities of the 'stans. Note that LOI (or letter of introduction) is getting rebranded as 'visa support', but amounts to the same thing.

(Cont'd after Trip Reports section)

Istanbul to Vladivostok – Suzuki DL1000

Name, Year of birth, Job Jamie Duncan, 1975, travel journo
Trip and date Istanbul to Vladivostok, 2014
Duration, distance, cost 4 months, 20,000km, £5000
Bike model and year Suzuki DL1000 V-Strom, 2014
Modifications Touratech sump-guard
Bike's strong point Great chassis, easy to ride and
  surprisingly capable
Bike problems Fuel pump and rear shock in KZ
Biggest headache Many, from Russian vodka
Biggest surprise Not crashing in Mongolia; Chechnya and Dagestan
Favourite places Pamir Highway, Mongolia, Georgia
Next trip West Africa   **Photo** Khiva, Uzbekistan © Jamie Duncan

* * * * T R I P R E P O R T * * * *

Australia to London – Suzuki DR650

Name, Year of birth, Job David Smith, 1985, Government
Trip and date Australia to London, 2014-15
Duration, distance, cost 10 months, 45,000km, $15,000
Bike model and year Suzuki DR650, 2012
Modifications Tank, fairing, suspension, panniers
Bike's strong point Rugged and simple
Bike problems Flat tyres and loose wires
Biggest headache Stuck in No-Man's-Land between Uzbekistan
and Turkmenistan
Biggest surprise Crossing paths with so many other overlanders
Favourite places Ladakh, Kyrgyzstan
Next trip Alaska to Patagonia

Photo Attabad Lake, northern Pakistan © David Smith

```
*  *  *  *  T R I P    R E P O R T  *  *  *  *
```

India – Royal Enfield

Name, Year of birth, Job Sathyaprakash Dhanabal, 1983, IT
Trip and date Sivakasi, Himalaya, India
Duration, distance, cost 20 days, 2000 km, £600
Bike model and year Royal Enfield Thunderbird 350cc, 2009
Modifications Petrol racks, handlebar
Bike's strong point Solid, easy to fix & ride at altitude in comfort
Bike problems Fuses blow in heavy rain, weak front disk
Biggest headache Extra fuel made bike heavy in rain or off road
Biggest surprise Taking time to acclimatise works but oxygen didn't
Favourite places Khardungla, Rohtang, Leh, more plains
Next trip Nordic countries on my Versys

Photo Himalayan foothills © Sathyaprakash Dhanabal

Russia – KTM 690R

Name, Year of birth, Job Mikhail Sorokin, 1974,
Bike parts dealer
Trip and date Russia, Nizhny Novgorod, May 2015
Duration, distance, cost Two weeks, 3000km, $350
Bike model and year KTM690R, 2011
Modifications EVO1 Adventure Fairing Kit
Bike's strong point Suspension and powerful engine
Bike problems Rocker arm intake
Biggest headache/surprise Flood destroyed bridge
Favourite places Mongolia, Pamir
Next trip Polar Urals

Photo Nameless Russian swamp © Mikhail Sorokin

```
*  *  *  *  T R I P   R E P O R T  *  *  *  *
```

Iran – Yamaha TTR250

Name, Year of birth, Job Lois Pryce, 1973, writer
Trip and date Iran 2013/14
Duration, distance, cost Two months, 3000 miles, £2000
Bike model and year Yamaha TTR250, 2006
Modifications 22-litre tank, remodelled seat, lowering link
Bike's strong points Indestructible, super reliable, 80mpg
Bike problems Comfortable max speed 60mph
Biggest headache Patchy road signs and headscarf aggro
Biggest surprise Iran not overtly religious; unconditional hospitality
Favourite places Alborz Mountains, Yadz, Dasht e Lut
Next trip Back to Iran… ad infinitum

Photo Hotel staff, Shiraz © Lois Pryce

Kazakhstan leads the way with **no visa** required for many nationalities if you spend less than fifteen days in the country – an experiment that at the time of writing was to run until the end of 2017. Anyone would think there's a World Cup or Olympics up for grabs. Even given that it's about 3000 kilometres wide, with that sort of inducement you'd be encouraged to get your skates on and anyway, you can nip into a neighbouring country and re-enter Kazakhstan (ideally next day) at which point the no-visa meter is reset.

If for some reason you take a fancy to the place, one- or two-month single- or double-entry visas are obtainable in Kazakh embassies in Bishkek, Tashkent and Dushanbe and take a week to process. No LOI needed. The only gnat in the ointment is that all overland arrivals must register with the OVIR within five days of entering, unless they get a second stamp on their white entry card. It seems that most overland entry points now give you this second stamp. Without it you face a $130 fine when you leave the country. See the caravanistan website for recommended OVIR addresses.

No visa is needed for **Kyrgyzstan** for nationals of 44 countries for stays of up to sixty days and no requirement to register once in the country. **Tajikistan** nearly followed the above example but for the moment sticks with visas in advance; no LOI needed. You'll also need a permit for **GBAO** (Gorno-Badakhshan Autonomous Oblast – essentially eastern Tajikistan) to ride the **Pamir Highway**, obtainable from numerous travel agencies or embassies when you apply for your visa for around $75. Gorno-Badakhshan is Tajikistan in the raw, Central Asia's adventure biking filet mignon.

The Tajik embassy in London issues same-day 30 or 45 day, entry/exit date specific single- or double entry visas for £140; about as high as it gets. It's said not to bother in Washington, so currently recommended places to get Tajik visas in the region include Istanbul ($50 while you wait or $25 in a couple of days); Bishkek (same day $75 plus GBAO too; Ashgabat (while you wait if they're in the mood) and Almaty (two days, $110 with GBAO).

For **Uzbekistan** an LOI is not required with visa applications for most Western Europeans and Americans, although applications take at least a week. You'll need an LOI if getting a visa from a consulate in a neighbouring country, obtainable from numerous travel agencies, but with it your visa application is processed more quickly, therefore many choose the regional LOI route. The visa cost varies from $70–110 depending on where you're from and where you obtain it as well as the sun's electro-magnetic field. The Uzbek consulate in Bishkek is said to be one to avoid, while Ashgabat again gets good reports.

And finally there is the police state of **Turkmenistan**, the most difficult 'stan for visas. A tourist visa requires booking an expensive 'tour' at around $200 a day all inclusive. Most don't want to do that so go for a **transit visa** costing around $85 allowing three to seven days (usually five) to typically cover the 1200 kilometres between Turkmenbashi and Turkmenabat.

Among the many permutations, applying in say, Ankara, and collecting in Baku works (don't apply in Baku), or from the other end, apply and collect in Dushanbe a week later. Others report the refusal of transit visas from various other regional consulates. As much as in any other country, securing a Turkmen visa is prone to violent consular mood swings but at least with a five-day transit you don't have to get involved with OVIR registration.

If you're transiting **Turkmenistan** westwards for the Caspian ferry, you'll probably need a tourist visa with all that comes with the deal. The authorities are fully aware of the ferry delays so won't issue transit visas.

If you're entering Turkmenistan on a pre-arranged transit visa, your visa dates are fixed. Should you be delayed for four days getting into the country, you'll only have one day to leave Turkmenistan. As it's over 1200 kilometres along the rough M37 main road to the Uzbekistan border post, this isn't a realistic prospect which is why visa-free Kazakhstan looks so much better.

ON THE ROAD IN CENTRAL ASIA

Coming off the Caspian ferry at Turkmenbashi, there's a raft of entry fees, taxes and fuel taxes to pay before you can clear customs. A fixer will help. You should get a **receipt** (*polichenie*) for everything – ask for one before you hand over any money. Unless you're on a transit visa your most important document will be a green A4 sized 'map' certificate, detailing your approved route through Turkmenistan. Without a guide, the customs process can take up to eight hours so note the parking charges in the port.

Heading westwards, aim for the customs office at Turkmenbashi port (N40° 00.37′ E53° 00.89′) and put yourself on a list for the next sailing. There will be a $20 departure tax and other small fees, but you pay the passenger cost to the crew and for the bike once you disembark at Baku.

In Kazakhstan, Kyrgyzstan and Tajikistan, away from the principal cities there's a lack of traffic, though like Russia, beware of **drunk drivers**, especially in Kyrgyzstan. As in most Asian countries, drivers pull out of side roads without paying too much attention and in rural areas goats, sheep and cattle are a common sight on the roads. Big cities tend to be more aggressive – drivers in Almaty can be pushy towards bikers.

By far and away your biggest headache whilst riding in the 'stans will be the *militzia*'s dedication to self-enrichment – or could that be topping up an inadequate wage. **Checkpoints** entering and leaving major towns are a favourite cash-cow as are cunningly hidden radar speed traps. Always play the imbecile, as explained earlier.

Speed limits tend not to be clearly demarcated. Work on 90–100kph on rural highways (though in many places the road condition will make these speeds unachievable) and 50–60kph in towns. Many towns have signposted 40kph and even 20kph zones around schools. Police tend to congregate round these areas (for the fines, that is).

In Tajikistan routes between Khorog and Dushanbe are prone to landslides, floods, earthquakes plus civil unrest around Khorog. It's all part of the adventure, not least the 400-km **Bartang valley** between Khorog and Murghab. There will be rivers. For an excursion into **Afghanistan's Wakhan Corridor** get a visa and permit in Khorog, (about $100 each) and cross at Eshkashim; it'll be hard yakka on big bikes. A geopolitical relic of the 19th-century Great Game, forget crossing into Pakistan without yaks and a disguise worthy of Younghusband.

Petrol prices average around 50% less than Western Europe, with prices a bit higher than that in Tajikistan and Uzbekistan, and a bit lower in Kyrgyzstan, Kazakhstan and Azerbaijan. If your bike can hack it, the 80-octane leaded yak piss is widely available and cheaper.

Parts of southern Kyrgyzstan and the Pamir region of Tajikistan experience regular **fuel shortages** which lead to dramatic price spikes at which time beware of water and other contaminants. It's the same story or worse in **Uzbekistan** where fuel shortages seem endemic the further you get from Tashkent, so fill up whenever you can and consider added fuel capacity for the odd chance you get the good stuff. It'll help in desolate western Kazakhstan too. Otherwise you can easily buy over-priced watered-down stuff by the roadside, so having a water-separating **fuel filter**, such as the smallest Mr Funnel or similar, is a good idea out here. Petrol in **Turkmenistan** is among the cheapest in the world but as a foreigner they get you with a **fuel tax** or some such at the border. If you need help with tyres or bike work in Osh, Kyrgyzstan, look up 🖥 www.muztoo.ch.

ACCOMMODATION

Expect to pay between $50 and $70 for **guesthouses** in the capitals and other major cities where you want to get your bike off the road. Outside the cities, roadside *gostinitzias* or *chai-khanas* (teahouses) are good, inexpensive alternatives. It should be possible to avoid the decaying and overpriced Soviet bunker-hotels, although for the experience you should consider staying in at least one.

If **wild camping** try to attach yourself to a local roadside café, yurt or farmhouse to legitimise your presence and provide some extra security for the night. If this isn't possible, make sure you're well out of sight of the road (see p145) though you're only ever likely to get hassle from a passing drunk or the cops. As it is, camping with a local family will doubtless provide memorable hospitality for which many of the Central Asian peoples are famed.

Elsewhere, Kyrgyzstan and the Pamir region of Tajikistan have extensive **homestay** networks which are cheap, convenient and delightful experiences. They cost around $25 per person half board. The flat deserts of Uzbekistan and Turkmenistan don't lend themselves so well to wild camping. There are many **B&Bs** in the touristy cities of Bukhara, Khiva and Samarkand.

Iran

For many overlanders Iran is an unexpected highlight of their journey across southern Asia, with some of the most cultured and welcoming people you'll meet. Iran is more developed than many expect, except they've taken their own route. Absent here are all the familiar brands of Western consumer culture – Pepsi, iPod, Burger King – that pervade the rest of the planet, although many exist under local names.

The roads are in great shape and the range of landscapes from mountain, lakesides, coasts and desert are especially striking. Human rights for Iranians may not be so rosy, but regionally Iran is far from unique in this regard. Providing you behave respectfully – which off the bike includes women wearing a head covering and an enveloping *chador* – you'll not be harassed by officials for your nationality, despite the high profile posturing of politicians on the international stage. Foreigners' movements within the country aren't tracked too closely, though Iranian friends might be checked up on, so as in many countries like this, beware of putting locals in compromising situations and avoid **political discussions** unless you know better.

VISAS AND GUIDES

These have been the main stumbling blocks but it may be about to get a whole lot easier. Getting a visa depends on your nationality and the diplomatic ambience at the time. That's got rather turbulent in relation to the economic sanctions imposed due to Iran's nuclear programme. As a result Brits and Canadians joined the Americans in requiring an **escort**, not a great incentive even if it's said no one checks at the border. Americans are still unlikely to get in overland, but for Brits a thaw occurred with the reopening of their Tehran embassy in 2015. It's quite possible that before this edition is pulped, the escort requirement for Brits will be dropped and there's even talk of a visa-free regime for many countries, which will really open the tourist floodgates on Iran. For the moment you still have to dance the visa dance, and for that to succeed you don't want any evidence of having visited Israel in your passport.

As with Russia, using an approved **travel agency** is the only way to go. This can cost up to £200 for Brits or more like €50 for many Europeans. What you actually get is a **visa authorisation number** from Tehran. When applying don't mention travelling by moto (or pushbike/motorhome for that matter); that's officially 'not allowed' but you'll cross the border fine. With the number, visit the consulate you nominated to get the actual visa. In Turkey they're in Istanbul, Ankara, Trabzon and Erzurum, or quite possibly by now **on arrival** at the border. Iranian visas are valid for **three months** with the usual 30 days which can be easily extended twice. Women: cover your hair for passport photos. Lots more up to date tips can be found at ▨ caravanistan.com.

TRANSIT OF IRAQI KURDISTAN

Depending on the ISIS situation, you can cross into **Iraqi Kurdistan**, an autonomous territory which reaches 150km from the Turkish and Iranian borders.

Fifteen kilometres south of the Turkish town of **Silopi** is the frontier post which leads to **Zakho** in Iraqi Kurdistan. Here a regional **visa** is issued for fifteen days. With a TVIP, costs add up to about $20.

Bring **dollars**; nothing else will get you Iraqi dinars, or just pay in dollars for most things. **Petrol** is low octane but works out about 20% less than Turkey, and other commodities and services are cheaper.

Most will be coming here either to tick off a quick visit to boast 'I've been to Iraq', or are going to or from Iran. From Turkey head southeast via Dohuk to the capital Erbil,

Mosul and, skirting Kirkuk, continue to Al Sulemanyah for the Iranian border at **Beshmaq** near Marivan – all up about 450km. There's another crossing to the north at Rawandiz for Piranshar in Iran. The roads leading into Iran from either of these obscure frontiers are not the greatest testaments to civil engineering.

Entering Turkey from Dohuk can lead to an interrogation and search. It's worth appreciating that Turkey is hostile to Kurds and 'Northern Iraq', while the PKK have waged a guerrilla war against Turkey since 1984.

Many riders report a warm welcome in Iraqi Kurdistan (and in the Kurdish areas of neighbouring countries too), although it's said the place isn't that interesting or scenic by regional standards.

LANGUAGE, MONEY AND INTERNET

Farsi is the language, but the alphabet is Arabic (for numerals see p252) and many young people speak English. The currency is the rial, currently about 33,000 to the euro. Iranians commonly quote prices in **toman**: one toman equals ten rials so that's 3300 toman to a euro. You can get by on about 80,000 toman (€25) a day. Bring euros or dollars in cash – foreign credit cards won't work in Iran and getting extra money officially is difficult.

Don't be too irked if you discover you're paying ten times what locals do to get into museums and the like. It's official policy, the same in many neighbouring countries and anyway, it's still pennies. Less officially sanctioned overcharging goes on in some hotels so be prepared to bargain (although hotels do pay higher taxes for foreign guests).

Internet and **mobile phone** access gets restricted by the state at times, but **cyber cafés** with slow connections are everywhere. Reception for foreign mobile phone service providers is patchy; local SIM cards are easily bought and much cheaper, but even they can be hit and miss.

MAIN BORDER CROSSINGS

Iran has borders with seven countries, but most overlanders are transiting between Turkey and Pakistan, or possibly to or from those two countries via Turkmenistan. A **carnet** is needed, though it's said that a local version is available at the border for a few hundred euros, including incentives. As you'll need one for Pakistan and definitely India, you may as well include Iran.

There are two border crossings with Turkey. **Dogubajazit – Bazargan** is used by most, a busy commercial border that's open all year but can be slow and a little corrupt. Southeast of Van in the midst of a similarly militarised zone of Turkish Kurdistan, is the **Esendere – Sero** crossing. Less used by travellers, forcigners can be treated like VIPs on both sides of the border, though in midwinter this crossing may be snowed in.

Show your passport to any official that makes eye contact and they'll either wave you in the right direction or stamp it and fling it back at you. On the Iranian side expect a cup of tea and officials speaking good English. They'll guide you through the entrance process which involves a thorough search and triple check of your documents and chassis (VIN) number. There is no fuel tax in Iran (despite what some might try on) and the fuel card rationing system – Iran's way of trying to curb smuggling – has been dropped.

ON THE ROAD IN IRAN

It's at least 2400km from Turkey to Taftan just inside Pakistan, but as always and visa duration notwithstanding, if you can get off the direct trans-national highways so much the better. Along with the wide open desert and distant ranges, the **architecture and bazaars** in cities like **Esfahan**, **Yazd** and **Shiraz** as well as the ruins of **Persepolis** and what's left of Bam are what you've come here to see. As a guest in Iran, you'll be waved through toll booths and, as with fuel, attempts to pay will be met with a confusing look to the sky and tut, the Iranian equivalent of shaking your head.

Petrol used to be among the most subsidised in the world, but the impact of western sanctions and soaring inflation forced Iran to raise the price to around 1000 toman (or $0.36 at the time) a litre, still the cheapest around.

Highway madness

Iranian drivers are demented and so riding through cities can become a contact sport until you get a feel for the rules. To save you some time: there aren't any. A motorway may have three marked lanes following the Western convention; actual lane capacity depends on how many vehicles can fit abreast without the outside ones falling off the edge or having a head-on. In Tehran it's often less stressful to arrive or leave in the dead of night.

Steady, predictable riding is the key to avoid being shunted. Keep an eye out for cars reversing fast or driving in the wrong direction on the motorways. Usually they're thoughtful enough to confine themselves to the hard shoulder, but it's not uncommon to find traffic coming straight at you in the fast lane.

A lull in the madness © Lois Pryce

Roadside recoveries

When you need a break the better roadside fuel stations will often have restaurants and resthouses, as well as mechanics. As for **food**, the only complaint might be that the ubiquitous **kebab and rice** gets pretty repetitive in Iran, but try *dizzy*, lamb stew and pitta, but you'll need to ask the waiter to show you how to eat it and so provide some all-round entertainment. Eating out isn't cheap in Iran, so to save funds be prepared to cook. At the same time the generous Iranians make it hard to pay for anything out of your own pocket, part of a social custom called *tarof*, but make sure to put up a fight to pay if your host is clearly being generous beyond their means.

To Pakistan

On the east side of the country, the Iranian police will probably escort you the 400km from the city of Bam via Zahedan to the **Pakistani border** at Taftan. As with so many of these escorts, it's a largely futile exercise intended to protect you from the bandit hordes and means progress will be slow as you'll have to stop at check points along the way for escort changeovers. As things stand, there's little chance of making it from Bam to Taftan in a day.

Fill your tank with cheap Iranian fuel well before the border as Pakistani truck drivers and Baluchi smugglers can run the final filling stations dry. As a last resort you can get cheap smuggled fuel in Pakistan.

Entering Pakistan you'll be competing with local lorry drivers for the attentions of those little rubber stamps and their uniformed keepers. The Iranian side involves visiting an unfathomably high number of counters with hand-written ledgers, something that must be tackled in a specific order which you'll eventually divine.

Once you've patiently endured watching Iranian officials valiantly trying to make sense of your unfamiliar documents, there's a tough initiative test to find the actual exit for Pakistan.

Pakistan

Perhaps because, coming overland from the west, it's the first place **English** has been widely spoken for a while, that many overlanders find Pakistan an unexpected highlight on the ride to India. This despite the fact that the security situation has deteriorated to the point where convoys of siren-wailing **police escorts** herd overlanders swiftly the 1500km between Taftan and Lahore, close to the Indian border near Amritsar. Unless you manage to evade these escorts, before you know it Pakistan has slipped by which will be a great shame.

From Lahore you're allowed to continue unescorted to the border, which also means you can slip off and head north to Islamabad, continue up the fabled Karakoram Highway right through to China.

VISAS
Get them in your home country (several regional consulates in the UK) as they can be valid for up to six months. In adjacent countries it's harder. You'll need an LOI from an agency like 💻 snowland.com.pk, along with a basic itinerary. Long extensions are easily obtainable. If coming from China on the KKH, they won't let you leave Tashkurgan without a visa.

BORDERS, FUEL AND RISKY AREAS
Coming from Iran, if you clear formalities at Taftan after 2pm, expect to be told to spend the night there before joining a free and compulsory armed escort across the badlands of Baluchistan to Quetta, and then right across Pakistan to Lahore. The customs compound is a safe haven for overnight camping.

Pakistani frontier officials are friendly, straightforward and fast by Asian standards. A **carnet** is necessary, though bikes have been allowed in without them in the past (an apocryphal story you'll hear from many carnet lands). There's one official border crossing to Iran, at Taftan, one to India at Lahore and the seasonal one with China at the 4693-metre Khunjerab Pass, the highest border crossing in the world. As for the Khyber Pass crossing into Afghanistan, it's unlikely you'll want to go there just yet, and forget about nipping over the Wakhan in Tajikistan too. Elsewhere it's sealed roads and the usual mayhem between Iran and India, with **petrol** going for around the regional average of $0.70 a litre.

The 630km between the border and the first big town of **Quetta** can all seem a bit close to Afghanistan's Helmand province for some people's liking. Expect a rough, hot, dusty ride as the road is in bad shape east of Dalbandin, with sand tongues and even steel ropes or chains hung across the road near checkpoints which can be difficult to spot at low sun angles.

Depending on checkpoints and escorts, you can ride between the border and Quetta in about ten hours, but two days is considered normal. There's a rest house at Dalbandin halfway; in Quetta you'll be confined to your hotel.

Travellers have long been warned of bandits in **Baluchistan** and in Sind Province (Karachi and Hyderabad), as well as to avoid travelling at night or in remote areas, a precaution that's become more widespread in recent years. Certainly the south-west corner of Baluchistan, south of the Quetta road down to the coast, is an area few overlanders visit.

What's known as **Waziristan**, the region bordering Afghanistan, more or less between Quetta and Peshawar was never under state control and is now the main front line with the Taliban. Even in the good times overlanders had difficulty visiting this region, and these days it's unlikely you'll get anywhere near it. Peshawar has also become too dangerous to be visited for too long by conspicuous foreigners.

NORTHERN PAKISTAN AND THE KARAKORAM HIGHWAY

The way things are at the moment, Pakistan can be a hard nut to crack, but one highlight that many riders agree is worth the effort is following the **Karakoram Highway** (KKH) and its offshoots up towards the Chinese, Indian and Afghan Wakhan borders.

All of northern Pakistan is designated tribal territory that never really came under state control, although that can be said for much of the country. However, it's the significant cultural difference between what used to be called the Northern Areas, now Gilgit-Baltistan through which the upper KKH passes – and the legendarily notorious region once known as the North West Frontier Province alongside Afghanistan, which will impact on your experience. It could be summed up on the one hand by the proud, xenophobic and ethnically Afghani Pashtun who occupy the former NWFP (and who make up the core of the Taliban) – and the much more tolerant and approachable Balti followers of the Ismaili Muslim sect living in the north of Gilgit-Baltistan. Here women and girls are more conspicuous and unveiled, social attitudes are more progressive and even Ramadan is not so strictly observed. 'For us, every month is holy' a guy once told me in Karimabad with a grin.

With mountaineers still drawn to several of the world's highest peaks, and the less driven attracted to the 'Shangri-La' reputation of the Hunza valley, tourism in the area collapsed following 9/11, then slipped further following the Taliban killing of ten foreign climbers at Nanga Parbat base camp in 2013 in response to US drone strikes. And yet the few who make the effort to get up here admit it's one of the continent's highlights.

The free **map** of the KKH, still available at 🖳 www.johnthemap.co.uk, gives you a feel for the area. Otherwise, we found the two-sided Nelles 1.5m map of Pakistan was the best, as was the better-than-average Lonely Planet **guidebook**. I also used Trailblazer's *Himalaya by Bike* with a detailed and well-mapped account of the KKH, along with 10,000 kilometres of other high mountain routes in this part of the world, including the Indian Himalaya (see p222).

The Karakoram Highway

The Karakoram Highway runs for 1300km (800 miles) from Islamabad over the 4693m Khunjerab Pass on the Chinese border and on to Kashgar in Xinjiang. Built in the 1970s and regarded as one of the engineering wonders of the world, it's become one of the world's great rides, tracing a former arm of the Silk Route along the Indus valley which in places is lined with thousands of petroglyphs dating back 5000 years. It also passes through the densest concentration of 7000-metre peaks in the world, and it is this dramatic contrast with the surrounding peaks towering over the Indus and later, Hunza valleys far below which makes the KKH so special, especially compared to the higher roads of Ladakh and Spiti in India (see p223).

Part of the reason for all this mountain drama is that the Karakoram is one of the most **seismically active** areas in the world, where the Indian continental plate pushes under the Asian plate, lifting the Himalaya and the adjacent ranges as it goes. Because of the steep, loose slopes, at any point along the mountainous stages of the KKH **landslides** frequently block the road after a downpour or one of the frequent tremors. Diggers move in fast to clear the blockage and rebuild a road, but as you'll read below, bigger landslides can disrupt travel on the KKH for years.

Altitude and lodgings

Sat on a bike, the effects of high altitude can easily be overlooked as you climb a series of impressive and daunting switchbacks. Until that is, you need to do something like stand up. Acclimatising takes time: **drink lots of water** and once above 3500 metres or so, aim not to sleep more than a couple of hundred metres higher each night. If you feel bad **descend immediately**; even a few hundred metres helps (there's more on p167).

Lodgings along the way are plentiful and a **fuel range** of 250–300km will cover you. Hotels can get pretty grotty in the villages. If you want a change from camping, look out for the PTDC motels (🖳 www.tourism.gov.pk) dotted around the north. They cost around $30 half board and are often set in great locations. The *Madina Guest House* in Gilgit is a travellers' favourite.

The lower KKH

Leaving Islamabad, an **alternative summer route** to the KKH towards Chilas runs up into the hills at Murree, on towards Muzaffarabad and over the 4170m Babusar Pass. In doing so it avoids the lower reaches of the KKH in Indus Kohistan where the welcome from the Pashtun villagers is not always so warm; wild camping is a bad idea on the KKH between Abbotabad and Chilas. Even before the Taliban came on the scene, police periodically escorted travellers to beyond Chilas – not a town to linger in. After Chilas, you pass the bulk of Nanga Parbat mountain whose 8126m summit is just 40km away, but towers nearly four and a half miles above you.

From Chilas towards the Chinese border, and even before the 2010 floods, there's a lot of **road-widening** construction going on, with frequent detours and long sections of gravel. Pakistan is trying to make sure the port of Karachi gets its share of China's 'New Silk Road' programme.

Excursion to Skardu

Even if you're not planning to cross into China, northern Pakistan still has a lot to offer, with two or three obvious excursions off the KKH. Late spring and early autumn are the best times to travel, but the KKH itself is open all year as far as **Gilgit**, situated at only 1500m and some 600km (370 miles) from Islamabad.

A short distance before Gilgit, the Indus river barrels off eastwards towards **Skardu**, at times a precipitous and narrow road you'd not want to attempt with your Vario panniers on full extension. Over the churning Indus far below, the occasional, quake-proof suspension bridge straddles the tectonic front line, leading to isolated villages and their surrounding terraced plots.

Skardu (2500m, 8203′) is set in a vast desert-like basin with roads leading to the area's famous peaks and the disputed Line of Control with Indian Kashmir. The route to Askole and K2 is constantly being rebuilt with some very rough sections and daunting hairpins high above the river. East from Skardu to Khapalu is sealed, beyond to Hushe is rough or blocked, but offers astonishing scenery below the 7800m peak of Masherbrum.

Gilgit and the high road to Chitral

Gilgit is a sprawling administrative centre set in a basin and hosting occasionally violent altercations between the Shia and Sunni. In the bazaar you'll wonder just how many mobile phone boutiques a town needs. From here there's an easy route west that lacks the exposure of the Skardu road, around 360km to **Chitral** over the 3720m **Shandur Pass**, of polo field fame, and with a couple of fuel stops on the way. Ask first if Chitral is safe to visit. It's a spectacular ride up to the broad, yak-dotted plateau where the Pass is situated; a great place to camp or even spend a day or two.

Continuing west, you pass into the Hindu Kush and the NWFP, or Khyber Pakhtunkhwa as the province is now known. The road deteriorates as you drop down past Mastuj and Buni, leading to Chitral, just 30km from the Afghan border. Over the domes of the town's mogul mosque the distant peak of Tirich Mir is visible to the north. Chitral is a congested, one-street town lined with bazaars. Continuing over the 3118m Lowari Pass towards Peshawar is thought to be too risky, so the only way out is to return to Gilgit.

Hunza and the road to Kashgar

Continuing on up the KKH beyond Gilgit, the ascent begins in earnest and soon you arrive at the fabled **Hunza Valley** where people were thought to live to over a hundred on a diet of apricots, sunshine and wacky backy. With the 7788-metre mass of Rakaposhi to the southwest, most hotels are based in the town of **Karimabad** (Hunza), although Altit is friendly and cheap.

In January 2010 a huge landslide blocked the entire Hunza valley at the village of Attabad 14km up the road. Very soon a **lake** backed up, submerging four villages and over 30km of the highway. In the intervening years the KKH has been re-aligned and new tunnels dug so that by the time you read this you won't have to perch your bike on a skiff to cross the lake. A good place to catch up with the latest news is the 💻 www.pamirtimes.net website.

Passu is a small village where the Batura glacier nearly reaches the highway and where a famously photogenic cluster of spire-like peaks rise above the valley. Some 84km short of the Khunjerab Pass, **Sost** (2790m) is a rough and ready trading post where the Pakistani border formalities are done. Without a **Chinese visa** and all the escort arrangements (which take weeks to organise; see p229), Sost is where you'll need to deposit your passports if you wish to make the two-hour excursion up to the Pass as the valley tightens in around the frost-mangled KKH. Jammed in an ever-narrowing cleft, one-in-one scree slopes teeter just a tremor or a downpour away from the next tumultuous landslide. When it rains, the stones start rattling down ominously.

Into Xinjiang, western China

As you top out at **Khunjerab**, the land opens right out into broad valleys dotted with grazing Bactrian camels. Just below the pass is the Chinese immigration post at **Pirali** – expect a chilly reception and heavy searches (more on p230). Smooth asphalt rolls down 125km to the ethnically Tajik town of **Tashkurgan** (3115m).

It's another 275km along newly elevated sections of the KKH to **Kashgar**, over the 3995m **Ulugrabat Pass** where Karakul Lake spreads out beneath the snowy mass of Mustagh Ata peak. From the lake you drop down through the Ghez river canyon, pass a checkpoint and head on through Tajik farming villages and past the hazy Pamirs to **Kashgar** from where you'll probably be heading for the Kyrgyzstan border posts via the Torugurt or Irkeshtam passes.

The cost of this short transit isn't wasted because, as a way of linking the 'stans of Central Asia with the Indian sub-continent, the Xinjiang transit allows a journey among some of the world's greatest mountain ranges and is well worth the weeks and thousand-odd dollars it may cost to organise. Coming from Europe and Russia via Central Asia, picking up the KKH to Pakistan, visiting India and then heading back via Iran and Turkey is one of the greatest overland journeys around.

India

I have to say that after over ten years on the road and well over 70 countries, India was the most difficult place to ride a motorcycle. You're left totally drained at the end of each day to the point that I was unable to enjoy the riding. Your concentration and awareness has to be full-on and 360° every second you're on the road. It's exhausting.

Lisa Thomas ☐ www.2ridetheworld.com

You'd think if you've ridden all the way overland across Iran and Pakistan, India would be just another crazy south Asian country. But within a short distance of the border you'll see that yes, there is an 'eleven' on the scale after all. This land of over a billion, the world's biggest democracy (for what that's worth) can still take your breath away: the pollution and filth alongside beauty and ancient splendour, the anarchic road manners and the scoffing at safety or even common sense despite a suffocating bureaucracy, and of course the emerging wealthy elite amid a mass of the world's poorest people. Over 3000km from tip to toe and almost as wide, you can't expect to see it all, but if you give it a try you'll come back with some tales to tell.

Riding here you'll be fighting for your place on the road with every mode of land transport since they invented the wheel or slung a noose around an ox. Horn-steered Tata trucks and buses trail a wake of carcinogenic soot past Victorian three-wheeled contraptions, slick Bajaj scooters and blacked-out Range Rovers, while among them all a humble farmer leads a cow to market with a tree trunk on its back.

It's not for everyone and sounds daunting, but once you catch on and recognise that the Highway Code is just a prequel Dan Brown failed to get published, riding a bike in India becomes 'adventure motorcycling' alright. By turn terrifying, exhausting and frustrating, above all it's an unforgettable sensory feast to which it's hard to feign indifference. All you have to do is learn fast and then keep up. Heading west, many riders get on their knees in thanks on crossing into Pakistan, knowing that India is behind them. And Pakistan is thought to be so dangerous that, if you give them a chance, the police will escort you right across at high speed.

VISAS AND BORDERS

Visas are available in Islamabad in three days with a Letter of Introduction (LOI). Try to get the longer, **six-month** visa, even though it starts on the date of issue. An LOI is not required for a visa issued in your home country. In the UK the job is now outsourced and costs £82 for a single-entry three-month tourist visa, with six months on discretion. Otherwise go for the 30-day online visa for half that cost; you'll need to upload documents.

The only land border with **Pakistan** is at **Wagah–Atari**, 20km from Lahore and 40km from Amritsar, open daily 10am-4pm. Arrive early and bring lunch as the immigration process on the Indian side can take hours (the Pakistani side, by contrast, is relatively efficient). Bikes are often searched. You must have a **carnet** and you should try to buy **third party motor insurance** at the border, although you might have to wait until Amritsar for this.

There are several crossings into **Nepal** (see p228) which include Sunauli in Uttar Pradesh to Bhairawa (south of Pokhara) and Raxaul in Bihar to Birganj (south of Kathmandu). For **Bangladesh** the most straightforward is **Benapole**, 75km north-east of Calcutta. The Indian side is shabby, but the Bangladeshi side is highly efficient, especially for foreigners. They'll want a carnet, but bear in mind that even after India you may find the Dhaka–Chittagong Highway a recurring finale of *Scrapheap Challenge* on crack. The only overland route into **China** is via Nepal, and for **Myanmar** it's Moreh in Manipur, more on p232.

PRACTICALITIES

Part of the fun is that **English** is widely spoken, even to a limited extent in the smallest villages. **ATMs** can be found in major cities and tourist areas. Otherwise the black market or licensed **money changers** might offer a slightly better exchange rate and will be much less tedious than major banks. Bureaucracy for anything from buying a train ticket to extending a visa is truly mind-boggling. It's often easier for a travel agent to organise tickets for you. If you're heading away from big towns, have a stash of pounds, dollars or euros and make sure you hoard small denomination rupees.

There's something to be said for not using the ubiquitous Lonely Planet **guidebook** if you want to avoid the tourist tramlines and ghettos; break out and try the *Footprint India Handbook* in conjunction with Nelles or LP maps. The *Rough Guide to India* is also very comprehensive.

A great Indian road trip website with a lot of knowledgeable local content, as well as routes to places you've never heard of is 🖳 www.indiamike.com. Local SIM or phone cards or even phones are easily bought and much cheaper than your own and **internet cafés** are widespread.

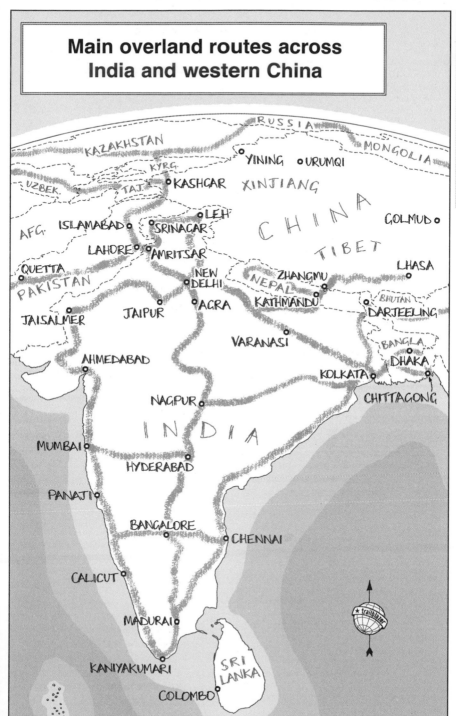

Main overland routes across India and western China

ASIA – ROUTE OUTLINES

EXPLORING THE INDIAN HIMALAYA

I haven't ridden all of this route or been to 'mainland' India for any longer than necessary, but a great fortnight's riding is to be had up in Indian Kashmir. All the things that can get to you down on the plains: traffic, congestion, heat, filth, are less frequent up here where a laid back Buddhist culture and its ancient monasteries (gompas) have survived for centuries. The fact that you'll be riding over some of the world's highest roads is almost a side issue. Providing you have a head for heights and good weather, in the 2-3000 kilometres between Amritsar and Shimla you can't fail to have a fabulous ride.

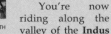

© DAVID SMITH

For a fuller picture check out the lively Indian forum: 🖳www.bcmtouring.com/forums/forums/l adakh-and-zanskar.24. You may also want to read the box on riding at altitude on p185 as well as the information on p167; a breakdown at over 4500m while unacclimatised could get nasty.

Srinagar to Shimla
If coming from Pakistan, swing north at Amritsar for the city of Jammu and on to **Srinagar** at just 1600m. This conservative Muslim corner of India is not without its sectarian troubles and has a heavy army presence. Renting a houseboat out on Nagin Lake is the done thing here; the guidebooks can tell you all about that. With that ticked off you're ready to ride east some 440km to Ladakh's capital, Leh. Following the alpine Sindh valley, 110km from Srinagar is your first pass, Zoji La at 3545m after which you coast down to Drass which one day in 1995 awarded itself the accolade of 'second coldest village in the world' at minus 60°C (for the coldest see p205).

You might try and shoot through militarised **Kargil** (fuel) just a couple of miles from the disputed Line of Control with Pakistan and only 90 kilometres from Skardu, just off the KKH. All along this section you'll encounter army convoys who expect you to get out of the way, pronto.

On the way up to Namika La at the village of Mulbekh (fuel), you'll pass your first **Buddhist stupa** (shrine) and the pass itself (3700m, 12,140') is decorated with colourful prayer flags, something you'll be seeing a lot of in the coming days. After a brief dip, you reach Fotu La (4105m, 13,469') the **high point** on this ride to Leh and where you're actually crossing to the north side of the Great Himalaya Range. Some 15km down the road is **Lamayuru** with its clifftop gompa. If you develop a taste for them, another hour down the road are a couple more at the peaceful villages of Alchi and Likkir.

You're now riding along the valley of the **Indus** river which flows 3000km from Mt Kailash in Tibet to Karachi in Pakistan. About 30km from Leh is a viewpoint where the clear turquoise-green Indus mixes with the sediment-heavy Zanskar river coming up from the south (or so it looked to us).

If you arrive mid-season **Leh** can be a throng of backpackers and other tourists in search of Shangri-La (that's not another pass, by the way), but unlike most of them you have your own wheels and if your head's up to it, set off the 40km up to **Khardung La** – at 5359m (pictured) one of the world's highest drivable passes, although there's a higher one on this ride.

If you just want to ride the pass you can probably get by without the Inner Line permit and leave your passports at a checkpoint on the way up. If however, you want to head over and down to the remote **Shyok and Nubra** valleys, get the permit and extra fuel (Deskit might have fuel). You'll get as far as they let you up here, as the Nubra Valley leads north to the Saichen glacier where even the Line of Control gets blurred. One night in 2012 the 'two bald men fighting over a comb' stand-off between the Indian and Pakistani armies was again questioned when 138 soldiers stationed at one of the highest and coldest outposts on Earth were buried by an avalanche.

EXPLORING THE INDIAN HIMALAYA

If you're ready for more it's possible to continue south-east from Khalsar junction along the Shyok valley to Aghyam and turn south here over the 5200-metre Wari La to **Taktok**, close to a junction with the road that leads to the **Pangong Tso lake**, a popular day trip from Leh via Karu. That involves crossing the **Chang la** pass while over the lake there are views east to Tibet. It's said foreigners can't ride beyond Pangong towards Chushul, but Guarav Jani's film *Riding Solo To The Top Of The World* describes the ride along the very border of China to the isolated gompa at Hanle.

Leaving Leh to take the popular ride to Manali you'll need a range of 350km assuming you top up at **Karu** (the turn off for Wari La and the Nubra loop, or Pangong Tso lake). Locally, two-litre Coke bottles are used as fuel containers, the reasoning being that if they can survive transportation from the bottling plants down on the plains to Ladakh without exploding, they'll manage a couple of days with petrol in them.

At **Upshi** you turn south for Rumtse and the **Tanglang La** (5300m) with an optional diversion to Tso Kar lake on the far side. Alternatively, with a bit of off-roading ability, carry on another 100km up the Indus valley to Mahe Bridge and turn west for Puga and Polo Kongka La (4970m) which leads down to the other side of Tso Kar (Tso Moriri lake may not be worth the effort) and to the Manali road near the road camp at Dibring, some 25km south of Tanglang La. This will add some 100km to the range you need between Leh and Thandi. Whichever way you got here, you're now on the Morei plains, an arid 4500m-high basin between more high passes. At the southern end the road drops into a canyon and **Pang**, a string of seasonal tents and cafés, followed by an impressive climb up to Lachulung La (5077m) and another pass before dropping down the heaped hairpins known as the **Gata Loops** from the base of which it's a short ride to **Sarchu**, offering more rudimentary lodgings and food.

Beyond here you cross back to the south side of the Great Himalaya Range at **Baralacha La** (4918m) where the long descent brings you out of the barren heights down into more vegetated, inhabited and finally forested lands for fuel at **Thandi**, some 385km from Leh.

Most will now scoot up the Chandra river valley to the hamlet of Gramphoo and turn off for the 3988-metre **Rohtang La**, the most treacherous of all of the Manali–Leh passes. Set against the south-facing flank of the Himalaya, it catches all the north-bound monsoonal rains and is usually the first to get either drenched or snowed up, while the northern passes you've just crossed remain cold but dry. At any time the road can become a muddy causeway of mired trucks heading up to re-supply the army camps.

The **Leh–Manali Highway** is officially open from around June until September 15th, but this is the cut-off date the BRO (Border Roads Organisation) are obliged to clear passes in the event of early snow. Roads can be rideable way beyond that date.

Manali is covered by the guidebooks, but if you're not ready for banana-pancake Babylon just yet, at Gramphoo take the rough track along the Chandra valley up to Kunzum La (4501m) and cross the watershed into the fabulous **Spiti valley**.

Soon after Kato village the road bridges the Spiti river. Although it's a dead end for anything other than a moped, riding up towards Chicham reveals some spectacular Bryce-Canyon-like hoodoos (rock spires) along the Spiti's eroded banks. Chicham, along with touristy Kibber on the far side of a chasm covered by a span (cradle on a cable), are among the world's highest villages.

Back in the Spiti valley you pass the gompas at Kei (and the track back to Kibber) to arrive at the town of Kaza (fuel, restos, guest houses) where you'll need an **Inner Line permit** to ease below the Chinese frontier at the bridge checkpoint at Sumdo. Beyond here the famously unstable slope at Malling used to cause headaches and require a span, as at Kibber. Now they've built a road around the top to Nako village, though it still won't take much of a tremor or downpour to set off the tethering rubble slopes.

Mile by mile you now lose height until you've passed the new dam and at **Rampur** are at barely over 1000 metres and probably experiencing an oxygen high.

Now back down among distinctive **Lahaul**'s pine forests, it's half-a-day's bend-swinging up again through the trees to the busy hill resort of **Shimla** where you can pull up and look back at your photos of what has been a mind-blowing ride.

Accommodation in India is cheap and plentiful but you get what you pay for. A budget of around £10-15 per night will usually find you in a decent mid-range hotel, outside of Delhi and Mumbai. Excepting the Himalaya, **wild camping** in a country of over a billion is not so easy. Expect visitors.

As for the **best seasons** for riding, the hyper-humid build-up (late March and April) as well as the subsequent **monsoon** (May–late September) are well worth avoiding. Riding into the cool post-monsoon season makes more sense, unless you're heading up to Kashmir and Ladakh where the cool Himalayan season runs from the clearing of the high passes in June until September. After mid-September it's said the road crews of the Border Roads Organisation (BRO) stop clearing the bigger landslides or early snowfall until the following summer, although it's possible to keep riding up there well into October; there's more on p223.

ON THE ROAD IN INDIA

Driving in India is about as chaotic and unpredictable as it gets and the driving rule 'Might is Right' is the only law both here and in Bangladesh. Bus drivers are particularly deranged and seem to be chasing impossible schedules. Exploit your bike's agility and ABS if you have it, but don't get carried away; **keeping pace with the local flow** works out best so a small bike does fine here. Even on a 140-horsepower catapult with titanium hard parts you're still at lower-foodchain levels on the road. Some riders have suggested viewing other road users as having only blinkered forward vision; nothing else exists which is why a **loud horn** is vital. Rear view mirrors are merely for hanging tassels or judging squeeze-through width.

Locals have no faith in the traffic police (who are virtually non-existent anyway) or the judicial system, so if you're involved in an **accident** the usual advice is to disappear as quickly as possible, irrespective of whose fault it is. With the countless hazards that Indian roads throw at you (see opposite page for a partial list), **avoid riding at night** if you can help it. Potholes, cows and the homeless all roam the roads at this time, so if you must do so, ride with full beam on (everyone else does), cover the brakes and take it easy.

Aside from the ceaseless widescreen chaos and carnage, there are few other tricks to master in India. The **police**, whilst certainly corrupt, are generally insipid and if you're ever stopped and asked for 'baksheesh' then hold your ground, be firm and rude if necessary, and don't give in. Hard and fast traffic laws are unheard of in India

Petrol works out around $1 a litre. **Motor insurance** takes a bit of effort. Try to get it at the Pakistani border or the first big town.

Where to go

India is a vast country, packed with geographical, cultural and ethnic diversity. From the snowbound Himalayan expanses of Ladakh to the deserts of Rajasthan; the lush alpine valleys of Kashmir and Himachal Pradesh to the steamy tropics of Kerala; the cosmopolitan frenzy of Mumbai to the mist-clad plantations of Assam and the far northeast. There is **too much to take in**, even with a few months and your own wheels.

Your entry point and ultimate destination beyond India might dictate your itinerary. If **shipping** onwards from India, chances are you'll finish up in

INDIA – YOU'RE STANDING IN IT

Bovids

General Purpose House Cow (GPHC). Varying in colour from brown to black and white, they wander aimlessly through traffic. Dangerously limited ability to reason.

Buffalo. Black with laid back horns. Used for working the fields, pulling carts and obstructing traffic. Walks slowly and once moving keeps going in that direction no matter what. Make sure you're not coming the other way.

Brahmans or 'Sacred Mobile Roundabouts' (SMR). Grey to white, smaller in the south, up to 1.8m tall in the north. Cocky, will not budge under any pressure. Creates its own roundabout with other Brahmans. Has eyes with 180-degree vision. Objectionable 'Holier than a GPHC' attitude. Immune to all intimidation; scoffs at warp-factor air horns.

Goats

Commonplace and also contemptuous of traffic. Whole families cohabit in permanent squalor on median strips. The young ones are dangerous as they make sudden moves and lack respect.

Pigs

Have the tendency to cross the road in gangs and change course midway. Often seen stranded across median strips where they are able to disrupt both directions of travel. Nevertheless, said to be highly intelligent, verging on conspiratorial.

Dogs

Less intelligent than a GPHC with learning difficulties. Minor hazard.

Monkeys

Very dangerous and unpredictable – jump out of the bush screaming and race along the road baring their teeth. Avoid braking hard on any Fresh Flat Monkey Formations (FFMFs), which otherwise have passed their most dangerous phase and are on the path to reincarnation.

Old men on pushbikes

There are two varieties. First is the 'I can't afford a hearing aid. Pardon?' type. Prone to making sudden right turns with perfectly bad timing. The second variety usually wears glasses fashioned from sawn-down coke bottles polished with coarse sandpaper and held on by copper wire. These guys steer straight towards you with an 'I can't believe my eyes' attitude and change course just prior to impact.

Truck/bus drivers

The biggest threat to road users on a daily basis. Drip-fed on amphetamines and have adapted the Nietzschean axiom 'That which does not kill me and is not an SMR can be run at/run over/run off the road.'

Government vehicles and army jeeps

Attitude: 'We own the road so we drive in the middle – what are you going to do about it/ I am too important/have a big gun'. Yield or face the consequences, including several forms requiring stamping and countersigning by India's speciality: a Permanently Unobtainable Person (PUP).

Grain crops in need of thrashing

Can appear on the road in all arable areas up to a foot deep. Apply the same caution as with FFMFs. Dry stalks can block your radiator or wedge against your exhaust and set you ablaze.

Everything else I forgot to mention

Whatever it is, it's out there on the road and heading for you!

RICHARD WOLTERS

Mumbai, Chennai or Calcutta but as a rule, clued-up riders try to avoid getting involved with shipping in or out of India. Life is just too short for that. Flying your bike out of Nepal was the preferred method with plenty of agencies in Kathmandu specialising in that service, until transiting Myanmar (see p232) came onstream for about the same cost.

Head for the hills

Aside from some of the classic high mountain road trips (see box on p222), there are a handful of must-sees down on the plains, if you can put up with the fellow tourists. A ride encompassing **Delhi, Agra, Varanasi** and not least

INDIA ON A CLASSIC ENFIELD

Once built in Chennai (Madras) using the original casts from the parent company in Redditch, Royal Enfield India is still on a roll. The beloved vintage-style cast-iron models are no more; the current lineup now features Unit Construction Engine (UCE) models, a move necessitated by emission regulations. Royal Enfield India has been dragged into the 21st century still clutching its pushrod single engines.

The company continues to make all the right moves with unprecedented popularity in India and overseas. With the Continental GT and new, all-terrain Himalayan, designs have departed from the original's inimitable character. But it's not all sunshine and roses.

Today, there are **three** types of classic Enfields, each available as a 350- or 500cc. The cast-iron (CI) models based on the original British dies, the aluminium-engined models developed with AVL in Austria, and the current (UCE) models with the gearbox in the crankcase like all modern bikes.

Though each of these models has a different heart, most retain the look and character of the original classic and the 'Export model' Enfields sold abroad continue to be superior to the ones you buy in India.

Bullets have been described as 'always sick but never terminal': if you're expecting modern Japanese reliability, a Bullet isn't for you. But a tune-up (plug, points, tappets) every 500km will go a long way to keeping the show on the road.

The challenging nature of Indian roads keeps things interesting and will mean a top speed of around 50mph/80kph on any machine. If you're planning on a lot of highway riding, it's safe to assume a daily average speed of 40kph. In this sort of environment the Enfield is perfectly suitable and will give you a journey to remember as well as plenty of roadside encounters. The bike's poor reputation for reliability is exaggerated: treat it right and it'll last.

For a Himalayan adventure a 500cc bike is best; this motor will chug steadily over the world's highest roads. Down on the plains and in the south the 350 is fine.

Model differences

All AVL and UCE models and some of the later CI models have the gear lever on the left, a five-speed gearbox and more reliable electronic ignition. Older Bullets have the shifter on the right as in the British Royal Enfield era. A popular crash scenario for nascent Bulleteers involves stamping on the gearlever thinking it's the brake.

New Enfields

Modern India is in the midst of a love affair with the Royal Enfield. As a result there's a waiting list for some models. If you're unwilling to wait, many dealers will sell you a brand-new bike at a premium.

Bullet 350 Twinspark (350) Rs104,900
Bullet Electra Twinspark (350) Rs117,700
Classic 350 Rs125,500
Thunderbird Twinspark (350) Rs136,600
Bullet 500 Rs150,500
Classic 500 Rs160,400
Desert Storm (500) Rs162,900
Continental GT Rs192,000
Himalayan 400 TBA

Reliability

Though the new UCE models have made great strides in reliability compared to the older CI models, it's the AVLs that are most reliable. They enjoy the advantage of being built on a decades-old platform, with better mechanicals where it matters most. The first-generation UCE still have some kinks.

Spares

The diversity of models and the new-found popularity has resulted in a spares shortage, especially for the newer models. Spares for the 350cc CI are most readily available, even in small towns. The rarer 500cc models have a perennial spares availability issue. Karol Bagh district in Delhi remains the best place to get spares at the cheapest rates in India, though check the origin.

Buying used off travellers

Departing foreigners advertise in travellers' hotels in areas like Paharganj or the New Delhi Tourist Camp. Standard price for a CI 350, regardless of age, is around Rs40,000; you'll rarely pay more than Rs60,000. Right now Rs100 equals £1, $1.50 or €1.35.

Used dealers and rentals

The main Delhi bike market in **Karol Bagh** district has several dealers, the best known being Lalli Singh (🖳 www.lallisingh.com). I had a good experience with SoniMotors who rented me a 500cc Bullet with toolkit and sale-or-return spares (very few needed) for just Rs300/day, but current prices are

INDIA ON A CLASSIC ENFIELD

around Rs1000/day. Tony Bullet Center (💻 www.tonybulletcentre.com) also has rentals. Rentals in Manali or Leh cost much more and the bikes are substandard.

All the above offer no time limit repurchase at about 30% less than you paid. Depending on your bargaining skills, used dealer prices are around a third higher than buying privately. If you're planning on using a bike for more than six weeks, it works out cheaper to buy and sell than to rent. The owner of Nanna Motors, near New Delhi Tourist Camp, is a good mechanic (recommended by owners of foreign machines) and can sometimes help with bike purchase (including new bikes). In the summer season his son also runs a garage in Manali.

Modifications

After crash bars, the most popular modification is an after-market exhaust. A short pea-shooter silencer gives the best look and sound, but you'll find many others in Karol Bagh, with varying levels of loudness.

A common issue when touring is fouling of the air filter due to oil overflowing from the catch can. This happens if the catch can is not drained or when the bike falls to the right. A simple fix is to remove the air filter and fit an old style one that sits outside the right-side tool box instead.

Useful extras for Indian touring include: petrol filter, fueltap lock, battery isolation switch, different handlebars and a reshaped seat to improve handling and comfort, as well as crash bars, racks and super-loud horns. None of these add up to more than a few thousand rupees.

Running an Enfield

Get used to the fact that you'll spend a lot of time nurturing your machine. Apart from regular carb cleaning, check nuts and bolts frequently – Enfields shake themselves to pieces on pot-holed Indian roads. As said before, a plug, points and tappets check every 500km will be time well spent.

Passing about one per hour, getting to know your nearest Enfield-wallah isn't difficult. These roadside 'mechanics' who over many decades became intimate with the CI models, haven't spent similar time with the AVL and UCE models so if you have one it would be better to visit an authorised company workshop. Spares are available in all but the smallest towns. Besides the usual items, carry cables, spare tubes, a chain link, rectifier and a coil. Always try to buy original Enfield spares, cheaper imitations have an even shorter service life. If you're heading up to Ladakh and Zanskar, it's best to carry all necessary spares with you.

Be prepared for roadside repairs everywhere and anytime, although most towns have a dedicated Enfield 'metal-basher'. Note that it's worth supervising all work to check it's actually being done and that no old parts are being substituted. You have been warned.

Prices for common repairs are: puncture Rs50; carb' clean Rs50; oil change Rs600; rebore and new piston from Rs3000 to Rs13000 depending on the model; fitting new clutch plates Rs450. In India **petrol** costs around Rs70 a litre and a 350 Enfield will return around 80mpg or 25-35kpl.

Documents/regulations

Ownership papers: it's not strictly necessary to get these in your name as long as the owner on the documents has signed the transfer. That said, a sale letter from the seller stating you to be the buyer will help. If planning to sell the bike in a state other than the one it's registered in, you must obtain a 'no objections' certificate. Most dealers will organise a name transfer for a fee although being India, this can take a few weeks.

Third-party **insurance** is mandatory, if worthless. It costs around Rs850 (£10) a year, and is obtainable at any insurance office. Any driver's licence will do. In practice almost every foreign rider can get by in India with their own driving licence as the average policeman doesn't know an IDP from AC-DC. However, if entering overland it would be sensible to be armed with an IDP. Helmets are required in India.

Taking a Bullet out of the country

Since about 2000, it's only possible to ride your Indian-registered Bullet to Nepal. Under new regulations, riding one back to Europe or wherever is virtually impossible. The only realistic way to do it now is to try and buy a Nepal-registered 'export model' in Nepal, have your carnet issued in your home country and ride it out of India to the rest of the world.

GAURAV JANI

Rajasthan would leave few people disappointed and includes many of India's cultural highlights, although you're very much on the beaten track.

Possibilities for exploring India's vast centre will give you a memorable taste of more remote, local life. Consider setting out across the **Deccan Plateau** and visiting the beautiful hill station of **Pachmarhi**, the caves at **Ellora** and **Ajanta**, the erotic 10th-century temples at **Khajuraho**, and then ending up in either **Mumbai, Goa** or if time permits, tropical **Kerala** in the deep south.

Riding east of **Calcutta** will be rewarding – the remote and intriguing states of **Sikkim, Nagaland, Manipur** and **Arunachal Pradesh** all require permits. This area is far removed from the rest of India, both culturally and geographically. Far-east India isn't without its problems and ongoing insurgencies, but it's now the way to Myanmar (see p232), so make sure you have a good look around.

In the end does it really matter where you go or what you see? Much of the fun of India is simply the day-to-day riding, observing and surviving – hair-raising and exhausting, though it is. Get used to it and it becomes an unforgettable experience that you actually might miss one day.

NEPAL AND EXCURSION INTO TIBET

For once getting a **visa** for Nepal couldn't be easier, and after India some travellers experience a kind of reversed PTSD which can lead to dizziness and euphoria. Simply rock up at the border and pay for 15, 30 or 90 days at around $10 a week. You can stay for up to five months per calendar year on a tourist visa, and it takes no time to renew the visa once inside the country.

Coming from India you'll be pleasantly surprised: lodging, meals and **petrol** are as cheap. What's missing is the sound of truck horns and oncoming vehicles trying to rush you on the path to reincarnation.

As an **overlanders' hangout** Kathmandu with a vehicle doesn't have a lot going for it. **Pokhara** is nicer and there's a free campsite in the tourist Lakeside part of town, as well as a more secluded spot at Palme, five kilometres up the lake track.

The Tibetan capital of **Lhasa** is just 1000km from Kathmandu along the **Friendship Highway**. With a Chinese visa and Tibetan travel permit, a bus tour via Everest Base Camp (Tibetan side) is fairly easy to arrange at the cost of around $100 per day. Riding up there on your own bike is not something you can organise on the hoof in Kathmandu. Special group visas as well as permits must be applied for months in advance – see next page.

Note that the G219 road across the **Tibetan plateau** to Kashgar stays well above 4000m and frequently crosses 5000-metre-plus passes between Lhasa and the G315 Khotan road southeast of Kashgar. Whichever direction you do this, it may be better to grab a week's acclimatisation at around 4000m in a neighbouring country rather than suffering in China at over $100 a day. Once on the plateau there's no quick way down if altitude sickness strikes, bar an emergency flight out of Shiquanhe (aka: Ngari or Gar) airport, near the Indian Kashmiri border.

China

Under current policy, it is very complicated to have a self-driving trip for international tourists, including going through public securities and customs. The complex procedure makes foreigners' self-driving hardly possible in China. Secretary-General Wei Xiao'an, China Tourism Leisure Association; Aug 2015

For years riding your own vehicle in China has been restricted to being escorted on expensive 'tours' that took months and months to set up with approved local agents, some of whom exhibited divergent levels of professionalism and avarice, with eye-watering costs of several thousand dollars depending on the size of the group, the nature and number of provinces you visited.

As always, tales flitted around the web of the odd rogue traveller who waltzed through or hoodwinked officials, very often on either a discreet local bike, an 'extra-full' Chinese driving license or some other inscrutable combination. As the penalty was getting your bike confiscated, most gave China a miss or limited it to the transit between Pakistan and Kyrgyzstan (see p230).

As things stood at the time, to ride in China you needed:

- Customs, national and regional permits for every province to be visited
- Chinese driving licence
- Temporary Chinese registration plates
- Motor insurance
- Government approved escort; their food and lodging paid for by you

Then it emerged that China had changed a law in 2013 to permit unescorted transits, but for obvious reasons tour agencies had been slow to pass this

CHINESE BORDERS

China has land borders with 14 countries, some open to all ('multilateral' is the word), some closed to foreigners (bilateral) and others closed, vacuum-sealed and razor-wired.

Others may be added but the following borders are open to foreigners with their own transport, albeit with varying degrees of difficulty.

Bordering country	Chinese province	Border town/post	Comments
Nepal	Tibet	Zhangmu	
Pakistan	Xinjiang	Khunjerab	
Kyrgyzstan	Xinjiang	Irkshstan	The easier Kyrgyz crossing
Kyrgyzstan	Xinjiang	Torugurt	
Kazakhstan	Xinjiang	Horgos	
Mongolia	Inner Mongolia	Erenhot	Only border for foreigners
Russia	Inner Mongolia	Manzhouli	
Vietnam	Guangxi	Youyiguan/ Pingxiang	Can close suddenly and difficult to enter anyway
Vietnam	Yunnan	Hekou	
Laos	Yunnan	Mohan	
Myanmar	Yunnan	Ruili	Myanmar permit required
Hong Kong	Guangdong	Shenzhen	

on, or less cynically, didn't want to risk being the first to put it to the test. A couple of enterprising German riders persevered for a year-and-a-half and in 2014 paid about €2500 to *legitimately* ride from Kyrgyzstan to Laos over two months. They spread the news and others followed their lead, getting staggeringly variable quotes from the same agencies (it's all on the HUBB) until it seems, one party deviated from their strictly prescribed itinerary, had their vehicles confiscated and set the whole process back for all who followed.

This unescorted option didn't claim to be necessarily cheaper than joining a big organised tour group, but at least a precedent had been set. Then, in 2015 an edict was issued: 'China's tourism is going global and becoming more open, aiming to link to the world'. Effective October 2015 all the complex, time consuming paperwork was being ditched to encourage self-driving foreign tourists – but the escort requirement remained.

If that's the case then in a year it flipped from 32 pages of protractedly acquired paperwork but a reasonable fee and no escort along a set route that avoided Tibet and Xingjiang – to much less paperwork and so presumably speedier and less costly organisation, but with the expense and drag of an escort. Being China, this later option sounds more plausible: an easing of pedantic bureaucracy to encourage independent tourism in the face of a waning economic boom, while still constraining their freedom to wander. Part of the problem may be that overland tourists typically arrive from the west via the vast, little populated and remote autonomous provinces of Xinjiang and Tibet where China's been battling civil unrest for years. If it's like other autocratic countries, you can imagine that adversaries within the ruling elite – military versus tourism, for example – are trying to protect their hegemony.

For the moment you imagine the escort rule will remain, at least in the autonomous and contentious western provinces where for most of us the lure of adventure motorcycling is greatest.

XINJIANG TRANSIT

Coming from Myanmar and heading for Europe, we wanted to explore Central Asia before getting to Iran. That meant doing a quick China transit organised through www.kashgarsilkroad.com who were OK. You have to negotiate thoroughly and lock in details about the price and inclusions. NAVO are better known but quoted much higher.

We were a group of four bikes and a couple in a Land Rover; price per bike was $900 for four days to save costs. Most quotes are for five with a day in Kashgar. For two bikes it'd be more like $1600 each and solo about $2100, but negotiation is very possible.

Both the Khunjerab (from Pakistan) and Torugurt (to Kyrgyzstan) passes are **closed on weekends**, plus we had to be in Kashgar on a weekday to get our temporary Chinese licences and number plates from our escorts (not that we ever used them).

We were delayed a week by a landslide on the KKH, but to their credit the agency rescheduled it all, so perhaps a rush service is possible. **Chinese visas** were straightforward in Kathmandu and Islamabad, not so in Delhi (for our group, anyway).

Coming north across the Khunjerab Pass, the checkpoint on the Chinese side was the worst I've ever experienced. Ridiculously over-the-top security and faceless bureaucracy. We spent around six hours up there at 4500 metres even having all our SD cards scrutinised; it's a wonder we didn't pass out.
DAVID SMITH

MONGOLIA: YOU ARE THE ROAD

Mongolia is one of Asia's great AM destinations; your 'golf course' fantasy made real and on an epic scale too. Food can be rough and accommodation grotty or overpriced in the few tourist areas, so a **tent** is a must – it's how most countryfolk live. **ATMs** work in modern Ulaan-baatar (UB), elsewhere they're rare so carry dollars or local tugriks.

Besides English, Russian is useful and the ring-bound 1:1m *Monsudar Mongolian Road Atlas* has the best **map** detail, though don't assume a bold red line adds up to any sort of a road as you understand it. Otherwise US TPCs can work well with a GPS and a good sense of direction. **Petrol** works out around $0.86 a litre, but quality drops right off in the sticks. The same goes for **drinking water** so fill up regularly or plan to filter.

Visas and borders

Four land borders are open to foreigners at present: **Altanbulag–Kyakhta** south of Ulan Ude; **Tsaagannuur–Tashanta** in the far west, 600km south-east of Barnaul in Russia, and **Ereentsav-Solovyesk** 900km east of UB and some 250km south of the Trans Sib – handy for Vladivostok or if coming from there, visa in hand. Turning up at the **Zamyn Uud–Eren Hot** for China requires months of preparation (see p229).

Considering where you are, formalities are simple; allow a couple of hours and a couple of dollars to maybe get your tyres disinfected plus $30 for motor vehicle insurance. Carnets out here are nothing more than a type of Cornish ice cream. Americans get a three-month visa at any border, most others get it in advance and it's valid for 90 days.

Mongolian consulates in Siberia

Irkutsk
11 Lapina ul.
N52° 16.8′ E104° 17.1′

Ulan Ude
Near corner of Prostsoyuzaya and Lenina ul; look for a large domed roof.
N51° 49.9′ E107° 35.0′

Both do a 30-day tourist visa for $100 same day, or $55 next day (pay in roubles)

Planned stays longer than a month require registering within a week of arrival at the Aliens and Naturalisation Office at the Ministry of Transport off Genghis Khan Ave, in UB (N47° 54.6′ E106° 54.8′). Get thoroughly deregistered there before departure.

If not riding there, consider putting your bike on the **Trans-Siberian railway** in Moscow. Direct trains to UB leave weekly, take five days but cost at least $800.

Riding and running a bike

'Extreme continental' is how they classify the Mongolian **climate**, which means two out of three days are sunny and rain is rare. UB's average annual temperature is actually a couple of degrees *below* freezing so don't expect to break out in a sweat, even in midsummer in the Gobi, while elsewhere or at other times, be ready for snowy sub-zero episodes even if the aridity makes deep snowfall rare. Up in the Mongolian Altai it can be freezing at any time.

There are about three paved roads in Mongolia, all emanating from UB: up to Altanbulag; west to the touristy Kubla Khan capital at Arvaiheer and east 550km to Baruun-Urt, with another 350km to the Russian border. Elsewhere is common land with no fences, few signs and indistinct tracks. Once you get your head around the fact that you are the road, it's an easy country to get around compared to the bug-ridden waterlogged taïga to the north. Pick a spot on the map and as long as the steppes are dry and mountains, deep rivers and lakes permit, you can ride straight there.

Therefore, unless you have the migratory instincts of an Alaskan salmon, a GPS and a good map (like the TPCs mentioned) is useful. As in Russia watch out for **drunks** and drunk drivers at all times of day, and avoid riding at night.

Checkpoints are rarely troublesome and Mongolians are generally honest and friendly, but it's not unknown for things to disappear overnight so if camping, sleep out or with everything inside.

Cheeky Mongol © Tom Bierma

Southeast Asia

Cheap living, good roads in places, a great climate in season, **food** and scenery and amazing beaches and islands all combine to make Southeast Asia one of the world's **most popular tourist destinations**. And now, after nearly sixty years, you can ride there again overland on a new road built from northeast India to Myanmar. It's all here, from the isolated Angkorean temples deep in Cambodia's jungle; the western and northern ranges of Thailand and Laos, Malaysia's rugged and unspoilt east coast and the gilded shrines of Myanmar.

Some countries have been well and truly discovered, and on a bike the thought of slugging it out with hordes of frizzy-haired backpackers and package tourists might not sound too appealing. But having your own wheels opens up the beaten track in Southeast Asia. You'll have no difficulty avoiding Thailand's heaving beaches and the tourist tramlines of Chiang Mai, or skirting the tourist trails of Cambodia as well as picking and choosing your remote jungle destinations in Laos. Only Myanmar requires an escorted tour.

Southeast Asia comprises six mainland countries and three island nations. **Vietnam** still forbids entry to foreign bikes, unless they're from Cambodia, Laos or China (buying one in all but the latter is easy enough). **Singapore** can get complicated and expensive with a bike too. Of the island nations, **Indonesia** is the easiest to reach, although the numerous ferry rides can become tiresome (see box on next page). Consequently this section focuses primarily on the five easy overlanding countries: **Thailand**, **Cambodia**, **Malaysia** and **Laos**, plus Myanmar in the box below. Like Japan, you may find Singapore and the other countries more easily visited without the bike.

MYANMAR: THE ROAD TO MANDALAY REOPENS

Another hue to Asia's diverse cultural palate awaits riders in Myanmar which, as predicted, now allows **escorted rides** between India and Thailand.

You can get in from Thailand without a tour, but due to the sensitive border area alongside India's Manipur province, an escorted transit (with a bit of sight-seeing) is required to secure the border permit. It's up to you to contact agencies like 💻 www.bur masenses.com and find others crossing at the same time so as to reduce costs.

Border crossings are **Mae Sot** (Myawaddy) in Thailand and Tamu/**Moreh** on the Indian side, about 1400km apart, via a direct route. As this was written the above agency quoted $1200-1400 per bike for a group of six or three riders for the 12-day

crossing, including B&B accommodation and all other fees except other meals, your visa and fuel. Petrol goes for about $0.90 a litre.

E-visas for Myanmar are only valid for fly-ins, not transiting overlanders, so you'll need to apply for a visa (around $25) at an embassy. Validity is one to three months with 28 days in the country. Nearby consulates include Dhaka, Bangkok, Kunming, New Delhi, Kuala Lumpur, Kathmandu and Bangkok where they can do it in a day for 810 bhat.

It's said there's no overland crossing to Bangladesh for foreigners, and a border crossing with Laos was due to open in early 2016. No one's tried Kunming either, but that'll happen soon enough.

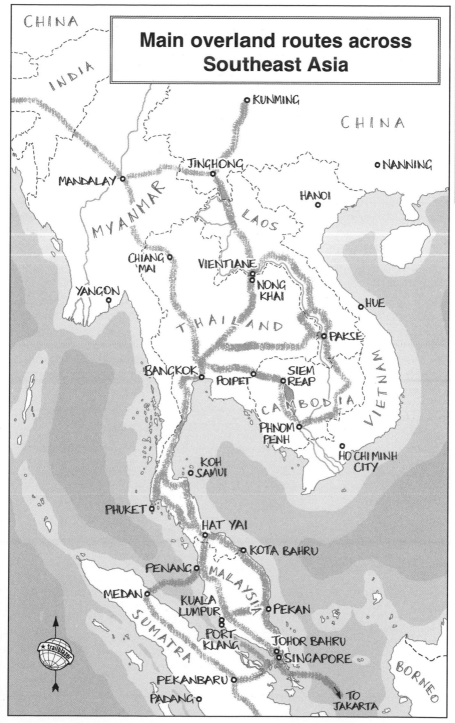

Main overland routes across Southeast Asia

ASIA – ROUTE OUTLINES

PRACTICALITIES

Visiting this region can be a bit of a holiday if you've come from India, Indonesia or even China. **English** is widely spoken, as is French in much of Indochina. **ATMs** are everywhere in Singapore, Malaysia and Thailand, and **credit cards** are widely accepted at major fuel stations. In Laos and Cambodia ATMs can only be found in cities and tourist destinations and fuel stations take cash. In these two countries it's usually possible to pay for all your fuel in US dollars which will save endless trips to ATMs which often don't dish out large amounts. There are no currency black markets save for a slight discrepancy in Cambodia.

Maps and online info

Besides **OSM** options for your sat-nav, *GeoCenter* have several **maps** covering the entirety of Southeast Asia (1:2m). In Laos and Cambodia, *Gecko Maps* (1:750,000) have excellent local detail and the *GT Rider Touring Map of Laos* (1:1m) is waterproof, and GT also has smaller maps covering parts of Chiang Mai in northern Thailand. The associated website, 💻 www.gt-rider.com, is an online goldmine of information for riding in northern Thailand and Laos.

BORDERS

Throughout Southeast Asia you'll need your vehicle ownership documents, your domestic driving licence and an IDP. Your bike isn't stamped into your passport in any Southeast Asian country but some issue TVIPs. Crossing from **Singapore** to **Malaysia** and vice versa is straightforward; most don't need a visa, although both will want a **carnet**. With a bike, **Singapore** is often considered more hassle than it's worth; for more information on riding there visit 💻 www.lta.gov.sg. You need an **International Circulation Permit** (ICP, S$10

DARWIN TO KL – RIDING THROUGH INDONESIA

You can ship between **Kuala Lumpur and Australia** for around $800 over three weeks, with rigorous inspections at both ends, or you can do the same with no crating between **Darwin and Dili** in Timor Leste. It's all handled by ANL Logistics for around $580 while you fly. Schedules change and ships get cancelled or re-routed, so make sure you have some flexibility. If heading to Australia beware: the bike must be *forensically* clean.

Indonesia issues 30-day visas on arrival; extensions are easy in major cities. The Timor border is relaxed, but expect a detailed search by the Indonesians. In **Kupang**, West Timor the usually packed and often cancelled ASDP car ferry runs twice a week (18 hours) to Larantaka or Ende on Flores.

Here you'll find world-class scenery, crazy driving and komodo dragons. Ferry to Sumbawa at 9am sharp (8 hours) – further west ferries linking Sumbawa to Lombok, Bali, Java and Sumatra run hourly. Try to avoid west Java – anywhere within 200km of Jakarta is in near constant gridlock.

Indonesia is inexpensive: ferry prices are halved for under 400cc bikes and hotels, food and fuel are all very cheap – you can survive on **$25 a day**. The people are supremely friendly too, and if you can fall in with a local biker club you'll be escorted like royalty across the archipelago.

To get between Indonesia and Malaysia, contact the well-known Mr Lim (cakraship ping@gmail.com) who'll lash your bike to an onion boat between **Medan and Penang**, and handle the eye-watering logistics at both ends. Expect to pay around 600RM and 1.3 million IDR, but watch out for Indonesian agents demanding more.

DAVID SMITH

in Singapore) in both Malaysia and Singapore – a blue tax disc without which you can't buy insurance.

Crossing into **Thailand** from any neighbouring country is easy, if a little slow and grumpy. No carnet, instead you'll be issued with a 30-day TVIP which you hand back on departure or extend for up to six months. Buy motor insurance at, or very near, the border.

Crossing to **Cambodia** from any of its neighbours is refreshingly efficient and corruption free (Thai customs officials aren't averse to conning tourists out of a few dollars for 'form fees', have lots of $1 bills to spare). A **carnet** is optional (there's no TVIP here) and so is motor insurance. Hunt around for a Lao-Viet Insurance Company kiosk or get it when you can – no one seems too strict on this.

Shipping from Singapore to **Indonesia** can be easy with companies such as Samudera (💻 www.samudera.com) who regularly ship containers from Singapore to Batam, Palembang and Jakarta in addition to numerous other smaller Indonesian destinations. You'll need an IDP and motor insurance to ride in Indonesia. Driving standards here are amongst the worst in Southeast Asia. **Ro-Ro** ferries operate between Bandar Lampung and Jakarta (crossing about one hour) and between almost all of Indonesia's islands.

VISAS

With the region being so open to tourists, many countries don't require visas, or issue them at land borders. Those who need them generally pay in US dollars. For **Malaysia** no visa is required for British, US, Australian or EU nationals for stays of 1-3 months; same with **Singapore** which issues 'Social visit passes'. For **Thailand** a free 15-day visa waiver is issued on arrival. This can be extended by 30 days at the Thai Immigration Department in Bangkok, or by exiting and re-entering the country at any land border. **Cambodia** issues e-visas online, otherwise get a 30-day tourist visa on arrival from $30, depending on nationality. **Laos** also does a 30-day visa at land borders from $35. Most foreign visitors can visit **Indonesia** visa-free for 30 days.

POLICE AND FUEL

Outside of Singapore and Malaysia, police in all Southeast Asian countries are not averse to a bit of petty bribery. If you're stopped by the police, don't attempt to speak the language, be polite and firm. Spurious accusations of petty offences should be strongly denied; if it's speeding then ask to see the radar reading (Thai police are especially fond of estimating your speed). Continued harassment is unlikely and with a little patience the police will usually let you carry on because it's far easier for them to pick on the poor locals.

Unless you're in a restricted area (in Long Chen in Laos, for example, or near some sensitive parts of the northeastern Thai–Cambodia border) checkpoints are unlikely to give you any hassle.

You'll find **petrol** cheapest in Indonesia at around $0.64 a litre, followed by Vietnam and Thailand from $0.85 to $0.90. Laos is about $1.10, Cambodia $1.30 and Malaysia $1.48. Fill up in larger towns and on highways to avoid the risks in buying out of bottles from roadside sellers.

5 AFRICA ROUTE OUTLINES

Africa presents the biggest challenge of the three continents covered in this book, or at least that's how some perceive it. Many accomplished riders have travelled the world and the seven seas, but have never set a sidestand foot down in Africa. As always, it's not as bad as you hear and the hotspots are easily avoided. Moreover, the Chinese bitumen party has sealed the gaps on the main routes through Congo, north Sudan and northern Kenya, so a heavy- or road-oriented bike becomes less of a liability. Of course it remains to be seen how these rapidly built roads will themselves handle a few monsoons or Saharan summers under the wheels of the typically overloaded local transportation.

The headaches of riding across Africa include regional conflicts, road conditions, the climate (in the wrong season) and petty corruption, but most often getting a **visa**. Some countries only issue visas easily in your home country; on the road consulates will present hurdles, delays and eye-watering tariffs while former border visas are becoming e-visas applied for online. This all varies with your nationality, where you apply and where you cross a border, and not least, the cut of your jib or their mood on the day (things often change when consular staff move on). What works for one rider with a Colgate smile gets you nowhere and all your advance planning may unravel in your hands. It's part of the adventure, but what can't be sorted can lead to unplanned expenses in freighting your bike around. Having a **second passport** can definitely help when making visa applications, as well as having enough **paperwork** (relevant, kosher or otherwise) to choke a full-grown hippo.

And yet behind all this is the lure of the imagery and landscapes we're all so familiar with and, less expected by overlanders, the generosity and warmth of the ordinary people you'll encounter who struggle to survive under some of the most mismanaged kleptocracies on earth.

Whichever route you take, you'll cross the equator somewhere. © Rob & Ally Ford

REGIONAL EXPLORATIONS

As much as any other continent, overlanders feel compelled to take on a **trans-African crossing** from Casablanca or Cairo down to Cape Town, not least because it's one of the great overland routes. When starting from Europe, once you're south of the Sahara you may as well keep going, although crossing the Sahara these days is just a two-day road ride. Even then, getting to Senegal from Morocco and especially Sudan from Egypt is quite a trek, and once in these countries your regional roaming options are still limited by topography, climate and politics. So, unless you're an old hand, initially most will see Africa as somewhere to cross rather than a place to explore.

One exception is **Morocco** (see p240). With just enough of an edge to keep you on your toes, it offers the perfect introduction to Africa and makes a great place for a shake down for longer travels in Africa or elsewhere. Another is **southern Africa**. Relatively stable, sharing the time zone with Europe, and with winter – their best riding season – coinciding with the northern summer vacation, many tour operators offer **fly-in and rent tours** here. From South Africa itself, visits to half a dozen nearby countries can be ticked off as far north as Kenya, and on tour you can have the ride of your life, even if – or perhaps because – it's all organised for you.

In between lie the feral republics of **central Africa**; principally the Democratic Republic of Congo (DRC). No one heads here for kicks as they do in the places mentioned above, not least because issues with Angolan visas can mean an onerous 2400km run through southern DRC to or from Zambia (see p250). Probably more than anywhere else in Africa this is a place to test yourself and as such, along with the former central Saharan crossing (see p239) it's the bit you dread most but remember best.

MAPS AND GUIDEBOOKS

The three 1:4m scale **Michelin maps** (Nos 741, 745 and 746) are regarded as the best paper maps for crossing Africa, though in central Africa they're not keeping up – no paper map is. A road may be where it says on a map, but whether it's a still-steaming blacktop with a crisp white line down the middle, or a motocross course, you'll just have to ask locally or find out for yourself.

Lonely Planet, Rough Guide and Bradt produce regional guidebooks in paper or e-book form with useful titles for parts of North, southern and East Africa, but don't keep up with the less visited countries. For that you have the internet: LP's **Thorn Tree** (▢ www.lonelyplanet.com/thorntree) or of course the **HUBB** (▢ www.horizonsunlimited.com/hubb).

FUEL PRICES AND MOTOR INSURANCE

While in some North African countries petrol costs about $0.22 a litre, and in Nigeria it's only twice that, in Egypt, Sudan and Ethiopia, as well as Botswana and South Africa you pay around $0.80 a litre. In Kenya and Tanzania it's about $1, and over $1.20 in Mozambique, Malawi and Zambia. With Zimbabwe at around $1.55, petrol costs more than in Europe.

On the west side it jumps from $1 in Morocco to around $1.30 in Mauritania, Senegal, Mali and Burkina and DRC, dropping steeply through Benin or Ghana to Nigeria. Gabon, Congo and Angola are at around $0.90 and Namibia is under $0.75. Prices will change but the relativity won't.

AFRICA – ROUTE OUTLINES

For non-UK EU nationals your domestic **bike insurance** can cover Mediterranean countries. Elsewhere, buy as you go. Countries in a given region often band together in common markets (sometimes sharing a currency too) with one policy covering all participating countries. In West Africa the ECOWAS agreement (🖥 www.ecowas.int) covers just about all of the region, while on the east side COMESA (see p258) does the same from Sudan to Zimbabwe, and ECCAS supposedly covers Central African states from Chad to Angola. Certainly in the ECOWAS zone motor insurance bought there – known as a *carte brune* (🖥 www.brown-card.ecowas.int or 🖥 www.cima-afrique.org) will be valid in all the countries as far as Chad, so it's safe to buy motor insurance for the several weeks you may expect to spend in that region.

Trans-African routes

Typically a ride across Africa will clock up at least **11,000km/7500 miles** and take two months. Today, North Africa and the Middle East are still reeling from the 'Arab Spring' of 2011 and the consequences of this have had a major effect on overland access. As a rule, political instability develops quickly and subsides slowly, while lawless regions in an ostensibly stable country are another hazard to overlanders who blunder in. Once in a while a brave individual manages to cross a country or region long thought off limits. The word gets around and others follow as such a route tries to circumvent the already-mentioned logistical and bureaucratic visa contortions. At least these days news spreads quickly online. All you have to divine is whether the new route is here to stay, an abberation and not least, whether they've even heard the news at the border posts you'll pass through. The key things is once you're in a country, you're in and ought to be able to stay there for the duration of your visa.

EAST OR WEST SIDE?

Negotiating Africa overland is like a game of snakes and ladders and right now there are only two ladders across the Sahara: the **Nile Route** down to Khartoum then east into Ethiopia for Kenya where the riding eases through Tanzania and southwards via Zambia, Malawi or Mozambique to South Africa. Or the **Atlantic Route** for Senegal or Mali which converges on Nigeria before slipping down the equatorial west coast for Namibia or Zambia.

East is easier and offers more classic African icons: pyramids; Nile; Kilimanjaro; Serengeti and Victoria Falls. The **western route** (from Cameroon and the Congos) needs a cunning visa strategy and an appetite for adventure.

The way things have been in recent years, once you start down one ladder it's fairly dangerous, unpredictable or expensive to ride across to the other until you get down to Zambia where the neck of the 'Y' joins up. The enduringly ungoverned mass of eastern DRC as well as the Central Africa Republic (CAR) and south-western Sudan see to that. If you're thinking of riding **there and back**, visas and other challenges fall into place better if you go down the west side and up the east.

North Africa and across the Sahara

North Africa can provide a taste of the continent which is distinctly different from sub-Saharan Africa and it was desert biking and Dakar Rally clones like the GS, XT-Z and Africa twin which kicked off the popularity of adventure motorcycling. The problem is the best countries for deep desert travel: Libya, Algeria and parts of Niger and Egypt, all now require a private security outfit or an expensive **escort** – and riding with a 4WD isn't exactly adventure biking.

The **Sahara** has for centuries been an ungoverned barrier separating what lay to the south from the Arab-influenced Mediterranean. In the 1980s the classic crossing ran from Morocco through Algeria down to Mali or Niger. Then in the 1990s political troubles beset northern Algeria and an unconnected desert-wide rebellion in the south cut off northern Mali and Niger. The region closed as the **Atlantic Route** opened up with the waning Polisario war. Around the same time Libya inched open too, though transitwise it was always limited to Tunisia and Egypt. Then in the Noughties desert tourists became targets for kidnappings by Islamist groups and now post-Arab Spring the central Sahara has reverted back to its lawless roots.

AFRICA – ROUTE OUTLINES

WHERE CAN I SEE THE REAL SAHARA?

The Sahara stretches from the Atlantic to the Red Sea, but rolling along a highway past either you don't exactly feel like Lawrence of Arabia. To feel the full exhilaration of desert biking you have to get onto the sands and pistes but in recent years the security implications brought about by groups like AQIM and now of ISIS make this risky.

Libya is clearly a basket case and will remain so for a while. It's the same with the adjacent Ténéré of northern **Niger** and even in the Western Desert of **Egypt** where, in 2015, a dozen tourists were mistakenly shot up by Egyptian gunships hunting smugglers.

Algeria (pictured) is the greatest desert biking destination of all, and actually safe enough away from borders, but escorts and an oil-based economy which puts little value in tourism has suspended the party time.

The Tubu of northern **Chad** never had any truck with AQIM-types and the spectacle there equals anything in the Sahara. The problem is getting there through West Africa, let alone expensive escorts. **Tunisia** may have a corner of the Grand Erg sand sea, but has also proved to have weak security

and is a pricey ferry crossing just to ride some dunes. In northern **Sudan** you might try to traverse the Nubian desert east of the Nile, but most here are intent on simple overlanding. The **Mallan** Sahara has long been off limits and even in the good days didn't add up to more than a north-south transit.

And that leaves **Morocco** (see p240) including their part of Western Sahara, and the southern and western quarter of **Mauritania**. Here, as Austin Vince's 2013 DVD *Mondo Sahara* showed, you can have a desert adventure out in the sands. Or see what's new at ⌨ www.sahara-overland.com.

MOROCCO TO MAURITANIA

Coming from Europe, **Morocco** offers ancient Moorish cities on a par with western Asia, as well as tracks over the High Atlas to the fringes of the Sahara.

Ferries leave the Spanish ports round the clock and take as little as 30 minutes. There's no need for a carnet or, in most cases, a **visa**, making entry and paperwork relatively undemanding. Even then, if it's your first time out of Europe, Morocco can be intimidating: cross to Tangier Med, a modern port with few hassles. Elsewhere, stick with someone who knows the ropes.

Imperial cities excepted, northern Morocco isn't so interesting. The fun begins in the **Atlas** which along with the desert beyond, is best in the **intermediate seasons** when it's neither baking at over 40°C or freezing on the High Atlas. At any time after summer you can get massive disruption from floods.

Petrol costs about 40% less than Europe, while food and lodging can be less than half, especially away from the tourist traps and resorts. All these qualities make Morocco an ideal place for a test run, but also add up to a great short-range overland destination in its own right. For the long version, along with 10,000km of GPS routes and all the rest, see my *Morocco Overland* book with updates at ⌨ **www.sahara-overland.com/morocco**.

To Mauritania

Even before they sealed the Mauritanian section, the **Atlantic Route** to Mauritania was a rather dull way of crossing the Sahara. Inland routes to Moroccan-controlled parts of Western Sahara aren't so interesting so most bomb down the coastal highway to the Mauritanian border where a few kilometres of sandy piste lead across No Man's Land. Stick to the obvious and well used tracks here as people have been needlessly blown up by landmines following their own routes. A visa at the border now costs a hefty €120; small bribes and fixers' fees from €40 and even parking fees are recent developments.

Many travellers don't take to Mauritanians and are encouraged by the checkpoints to speed south to the grubby capital of Nouakchott for a Mali visa (N18° 06.5' W15° 58.7'; about 6500UM) or mostly visa-free Senegal. The country's reputation took a hit when the Dakar Rally left, followed by a handful of attacks and kidnappings of western tourists. But security wise Mauritania is on the case as much as it can be, while as yet not insisting on border-to-border escorts which means you can roam the southwestern corner of the country – anywhere to the north or east is largely trackless and less safe.

With the right bike and company, for a taste of the Sahara take the sandy, 520km run east along the railway towards **Atar** (rest up there at *Bab Sahara*, on the west edge of town at N20° 31.2' W13° 03.7'). Then explore the Adrar as far as Chinguetti or Ouadane and take the more demanding crossing south to Tidjikja, possibly with a guide. From Tidjikja head for Kiffa and Mali. All up this'll add a memorable fortnight and an under-rated African highlight.

ARABIC NUMERALS										
0	1	2	3	4	5	6	7	8	9	10
.	١	٢	٣	٤	٥	٦	٧	٨	٩	١.

RTW – BMW R1100GS

Name, Year of birth, Job Simon Thomas, 1969, on the road
Trip and date RTW, 2003 to date
Duration, distance, cost 12 years, 423,000km so far, dare not calculate cost
Bike model and year BMW R1100GS (later 1150 motor), 1999
Modifications Tank, 21" wheel, subframe, suspension, etc
Bike's strong points Reliability, strength, character
Bike problems Weak rear subframe
Biggest headache Wiring loom repair after Amazon crash
Biggest surprise We're still on the road and loving it
Favourite places Sahara, Gobi, Bolivia/Argentina, Thailand, Botswana
Next trip Today's ride to somewhere new

Photo Senegal River, Mali border © Simon Thomas

* * * * T R I P   R E P O R T * * * *
UK to Cameroon – Kawasaki KLR 650

Name, Year of birth, Job   Jamie Duncan, 1975, travel journo
Trip and date   UK to Cameroon, 2015
Duration, distance, cost   4 months, 11,000km, £5000
Bike model and year   Kawasaki KLR 650 Tengai, 1989
Modifications   New shock and springs
Bike's strong point   Paint job
Bike problems   Everything else
Biggest headache   Visas and documents
Biggest surprise   Bike made it as far as it did
Favourite places   Morocco, Ghana, Togo, Benin
Next trip   North America or Iceland or back to Africa

Photo Aba, south-east Nigeria © Patrick Davey

* * * * T R I P R E P O R T * * * *

Sahara – Honda XR650L

Name, Year of birth, Job Chris S, 1960, books and tours
Trip and date Sahara, 2003
Duration, distance, cost A month, 6000km, £2000
Bike model and year Honda XR650L, 2002
Modifications Giant tank, fat spokes, heavy racks
Bike's strong points Honda reliable, suspension
Bike problems Just too heavy at times
Biggest headache Fuel, water and brigands
Biggest surprise The thrill of pure off-piste riding
Favourite places Southeast Alg; it's all there
Next trip A bit more Mauritania

Photo Changing tyres, Grand Erg Oriental, Algeria

Morocco Tour – BMW F800GS

Name, Year of birth, Job Eric Bissonnier, 1966, Finance

Trip and date Morocco, 2015

Duration, distance, cost One week, 1000km, £1100

Bike model and year BMW F800GS, 2009

Modifications Wunderlich seat + Air Hawk II, Jesse luggage rack + back plate, Touratech Desertio windshield

Bike's strong point Comfort on road + fast pistes, mpg, robust

Bike problems Power delivery on tracks

Biggest headache Edgy throttle a challenge on narrow Atlas piste

Biggest surprise Scenic beauty of the Atlas, friendly people

Favourite places Anywhere S of the Atlas; and Switzerland

Next trip Morocco again: W + S of Zagora; Iran

Photo Jebel Sarhro

West Africa

West Africa covers the sub-Saharan region from Senegal as far east as Cameroon and Chad. Much of it was once under French colonial rule and today **French**, and to a lesser extent English (in the Gambia, Sierra Leone, Liberia, Ghana and Nigeria) will be the **languages** you'll use the most. A romantic notion is to ride right along the **Atlantic coast**; the problem is that between Dakar and the Ivory Coast border, there is no road and some countries in this corner of West Africa can be hard work. Coming from the north and still wet behind the sidepanels, most riders choose to make it easy on themselves by reducing the borders and visas so as to save their energy for central Africa where there'll be less choice. As it is, since the Arab Spring, right across West Africa anti-government protests and coups (or coup plots) have become more numerous, and with key countries like Mali and Nigeria under attack and with the ebola epidemic of 2014, overland travel dwindled on this side. Southern Mali and Burkina remain safe to cross, despite a bloodless coup in the latter, and as this is written the scourge of Boko Haram is either in retreat in northeast Nigeria, or there are more newsworthy atrocities elsewhere.

Local currencies in West and Central Africa

Travel in this region is eased by the **CFA currency** which is shared by Senegal, Guinea Bissau, Mali, Ivory Coast, Burkina Faso, Benin and Niger. It's abbreviated on currency websites as CFA XOF. The other CFA currency zone (CFA XAF) covers six Central African countries: Chad, CAR, Cameroon, Congo, Gabon and Equatorial Guinea.

You can't use one in the other zone, except possibly near borders between the zones. The international rate of exchange is the same for both and pretty stable at about 655 to a euro.

WEATHER IN AFRICA

Two climactic factors govern your departure and route: summer in the Sahara and the equatorial monsoon. The Sahara crossing in Mauritania and Sudan is a road, but when things go wrong you need to act decisively as your margin for survival shortens quickly when it's 45°C (113°F) in the shade.

More commonly though, the **Saharan summer** is a time of sandstorms when the night time temperature stays over 30°C for weeks. This round-the-clock heat drains your body and stresses the engine, travel becomes endurance rather than enjoyment. It's not a time to be riding pistes alone.

In central Africa the **rains** fall for up to ten months a year, certainly from June to September alongside the equator, and to a lesser extent from February to April. South of the equator the sealed road network makes the rains in eastern and southern Africa from November to April less of an issue, although your ability to explore off the beaten track will be greatly reduced.

If heading across the continent from Europe and wanting an easy time of it, **set off around October or November**, riding into the Saharan winter and the central African dry season.

SENEGAL, MALI AND BURKINA FASO

Leaving Mauritania, the border on the Senegal River at **Rosso** has long had a reputation for intimidation on both sides but in 2015 things appeared to lighten up. As it was, many avoided the ferry and headed 50km downstream to the **Diama** dam bridge (via a 'national park' fee). That's all the simpler now the track has been improved. In Mauritania buy ferry ticket (or pay bridge gate fee), pay communal tax, and pay to export your bike. On the Senegal side where **visas have been ditched** for most, pay about €10 for a laissez-passer, pay communal tax and go to the police. Previously they made this all more complicated and costly so be warned: this border may return to rogue status.

Once on the way, several **checkpoints** on the road to St Louis might also be angling to dish out fines for minor or invented transgressions. Regional **Carte Brune insurance** is sold at the border for up to six months.

Like many African capitals, **Dakar** can be a grind (Mali visa, 25,000 CFA, from one day; Burkina 48,000CFA, next day) but the old colonial capital of **St Louis** just down from the border is well worth a stop;. The ever helpful *Zebrabar*, 18km south of St Louis (N15° 51.9' W16° 30.7') is a popular hangout for overlanders.

From Mauritania you can head directly into Mali. The road is sealed from Kiffa to Nioro and on to **Bamako**, and there's a sealed route coming in from Tambacounda in Senegal via Kayes too. Stay clear of Nema for the moment.

Better to get a visa in advance but if entering Mali without one, you might get a two-day pass to continue to Bamako. Bamako can be a little crazy and even risky after dark, but it's a useful place for visas, especially for Nigeria (see below) which is getting harder and may be an e-visa by now. South of the main bridge *The Sleeping Camel* (N12° 37.5' W07° 59.2') is a good place to meet travellers.

Located a thousand kilometres northeast of Bamako, **Timbuktu** was briefly over-run by jihadists and became subject to strict Sharia law. The last tourists in 2011 ended up kidnapped or shot, but since then it may be just within the limits of state control and therefore safe for a quick visit. Travel in southern Mali is fine except for the pricey fuel.

WEST AFRICAN VISAS

Burkina Faso visa in Bamako
Off rue de Guinee, just east of the US embassy. N12° 37.9' W08° 00.9'
Three photos and 24,000CFA for a 3-day, transit visa issued same day, or 94,000CFA at the border.

Nigerian visa in Bamako
South of the bridge, close to the *Sleeping Camel* on the RN7 to the airport. N12° 37.0' W07° 58.6'. Displays a visa price list for each country. 40,000CFA. Recommended.

Ghana visa in Ouagadougou, Burkina Faso
Ave d'Oubritenga. N12° 22.7' W01° 30.6'
Four photos and 15,000CFA. 1-3 days.

Nigerian visa in Accra, Ghana
Onyasia Crescent. N05° 36.4' W00° 12.0'
Currently they only issue Nigerian visas to Ghana residents, and diplomats. Same story in Togo. (I eventually got my Nigerian visa in Cotonou. Very easy, 84,000CFA, absolutely no interest in my paperwork but had to explain why I didn't get it at home. Issued on the spot. It's on Rue 230, at N06° 21.0' E02° 23.9').

Benin visa in Accra, Ghana
Airport West Rd. N05° 37.0' W00° 11.2'
Very easy, next day. Need hotel reservation. Also in **Ouagadougou** somewhere on Ave Prof. Joseph Ki-Zerbo. Cost 40,000CFA and issued on the same day.

EAST TOWARDS CHAD OR NIGERIA

From Bamako, sealed roads run via Burkina Faso to English-speaking Ghana, or Benin. From Niger there's not much chance of getting into Algeria, and beyond Zinder the bitumen breaks up and disappears altogether around Lake Chad. This was always a tough, sandy bush track of at least two days riding to **Chad**'s expensive capital, N'Djamena, but these days it passes through uncomfortably close to Boko Haram territory, so no one's done it for years. As it is, Chad's only viable exit is south into Cameroon. On the east side around Abeche they get jumpy and if you do get into Sudan, you'll need to fly your bike from Al Junaynah over the Darfur to Khartoum for about £150 – as done by a fluent Arabic rider in 2014 – or try and join the escorted convoys.

Nigeria

Despite **cheap fuel** (often sold watered down just over adjacent borders) and a chance to commune in English after a few Francophone countries, **Nigeria** didn't have a great reputation even before the wave of atrocities carried out by Boko Haram. Remember though, this is a country of 100 million people so as long as you keep your wits about you, a swift transit ought to pass without incident. The situation isn't helped by the fact that local motorcycle taxis or 'okadas' have been banned in some cities, following their use by criminal gangs, assassins and suicide bombers, though overseas riders aren't affected. Unless you know better, make life easier on the nerves by taking a low transit across the country, perhaps swooping past Abuja for some key visas.

Abuja to Cameroon

In Abuja many camp free round the back of the Sheraton Hotel (N09° 03.8' E7° 29.1'). Pull up to reception, ask nicely to camp and they'll show you where to go and where to shower by the squash courts. They may refer to you as a 'tourist', as virtually none of the other foreigners in the hotel will be. Down on the southeast coast, **Calabar** remains your best option for an easy Cameroon visa, then head up to Ikom and across into Cameroon at **Ekok**. The once notorious track heading east is now sealed, with white lines and shiny armco.

GETTING SOUTHBOUND VISAS IN ACCRA, ABUJA AND CALABAR

Angola in Accra, Ghana
Liberation Road, just west of airport.
N05° 36.60' W00° 10.62'
Bank statements plus copies of everything; 30-day tourist visa for $150. Takes up to two weeks. To be certain, **get it back home**.

Cameroon in Abuja, Nigeria
469/470 Lobito Crescent, Wuse 11 (near Hilton Hotel). N09° 04.24' E07° 29.4'
90-day validity, 30-day visa single-entry. Normally two days, 50,000CFA or N17,500. Or try friendlier Calabar.

Congo-Brazzaville
On same road as Cameroon embassy, above.

Same day N13–18,000, next day N10–12,000. Price varies depending on how you look. Valid 90 days from issue for a single entry 30-day visa. Or take a chance at the Doussala border with Gabon: 15 days for 20,000 CFA.

DRC
Azores St. N09° 04.9' E07° 28.1'
N17,000, similar documents to Angola, with visas required for onward country, but may insist you **apply in your home country**.

Cameroon visa in Calabar
Off Spring Road. N04°59.8' E08°19.44'
Two photos, two forms.
While you wait and from 51,000CFA.

Western Route via DRC

You'd hope that once you've made it into Cameroon you're fully getting into the swing of things. On the forecast are days of churned up mud tracks, heat, humidity, over-friendly insects, opportunistic cops and obnoxious consular staff until, slightly stunned, you pop out of Angola's or DRC's southern frontier into Disneyland southern Africa. Enjoy any new tarmac roads while they last. Chances are the climate, pounding cargo and lack of maintenance will see them only last a few years. This western route could be entering a golden age of all-weather accessibility before the jungle reclaims it all.

With the various **visa hassles** on this route, it's often a case of simply getting to the next country rather than cruising around like the Fonz, as you can on the east coast. Many will be out of their comfort zone, locked in the charm offensive to get visas while riding a dawn-to-dusk race before others expire. All this can sour the rhythm of your trip and even on the easiest routes this'll be the toughest stage of your trip, so it's common to **team up** with others.

It's also worth noting that paper or digital, **maps** are hit and miss in this part of Africa. Place names won't match up and you'll pass through villages that don't exist or miss villages that do. It's all part of the fun, but having Tracks4Africa (tracks4africa.co.za) and other pre-researched **waypoints** comes into its own here, allowing you to explore with some vague idea of where you are some of the time. Along with that, knowing some **French** (though not always letting on) and having a good stash of cash is a big advantage. It's a jungle for sure, but ATMs don't grow on trees.

GABON TO ANGOLA

On the new road from the Nigerian border, most have an easy time in Cameroon, despite having to hang out for days in Yaounde getting what may be the final batch of visas. And despite the extra visa, most head for **Gabon** on their way to Congo-Brazzaville because, as you'll read in the box on p245, it's a little easier. Forget **Equatorial Guinea** – for some reason they make overland access virtually impossible.

GETTING SOUTHBOUND VISAS IN YAOUNDE, CAMEROON

Most of the embassies you want are in the Quartier Bastos at the north end of town.

Gabon
Rue 1816, Bastos. N03° 53.7′ E11° 31.2′
A photo and form, 35,000CFA. Pick up next day if express fee paid, otherwise three days. Smarten up and learn some French or don't expect a warm welcome. Also said to be available at the border.

DRC
Blvd de l'URSS, Bastos. N03° 53.7′ E11° 30.8′
Photos, form, copy of passport, 100,000CFA. Very easy and helpful people; next day.

Congo
Rue 1815, Bastos. N03° 53.3′ E11° 30.8′
Photos, hotel reservations, vaccinations and 60,000CFA which must be paid into bank across town. 9.30pm–noon. Four days.

CAMEROON TO CONGO DIRECT

If a Gabon visa proves to be a pain in Yaounde fear not, it's possible to ride directly into the Republic of Congo (or 'Congo-Brazzaville' as it's known to distinguish it from the river or the DRC). What you save on acquiring one less visa you may pay back schlepping along overgrown, waterlogged tracks until you get to Ouesso.

Ouesso via Socambo

Opposite the southeast corner of Cameroon, the key town to aim for is **Ouesso** on the Sangha river in Congo-Brazza, and about 800 clicks from Brazzaville.

The feral option runs east from Yaounde along the N1 via Bertoua to Yokadouma then south another 300km to **Socambo** (N01° 41.6' E16° 07.8'), a few kilometres – but over the river and border – from Ouesso. Bush meat poaching, gun-running and border disputes abound in this forgotten corner of Cameroon where the heart of darkness is lit by a 15-watt bulb. Last heard, the tarmac ends some 350km east of Yaounde, at Mandjou.

From Socambo logging ferries come and go from the mills at **Pokola**, about 60km downstream, but on the wrong side of the Sangha for Ouesso. Better to load the bike on a *pinasse* (dug-out canoe) or a smaller *pirogue* and cross directly to Ouesso. It's been done, but this is still pretty out there.

Ouesso via Mbalam

An hour south of Yaounde, turn east at Mbalmayo onto the N9 and follow logging tracks 430km southeast to the border at **Mbalam**. Before Mbalam, the tar runs out at Sangemlima but the piste has been improved and is now maintained (slippery in the wet, though).

On the Congolese side little used muddy tracks lead through Mpé and Souanké to Sembe. It's now sealed pretty much all the way from Sembe to Brazza (and the road building crews are pushing on for the border).

Next stop, Brazzaville on the Congo river, opposite the border with DRC.

After Cameroon, Gabon is expensive, the fuel isn't but the roads feel empty. Along the equator there are **no seasons** to speak of; it rains pretty much all year so it's a matter of luck whether you hit a bad road during a wet spell. Rain is a mixed blessing though, it cools everything off for a while and allows a decent night's sleep. Around here you'll appreciate a tent which can be pitched with the inner only like a mossie net, but under a shelter.

It's only about 270km from Yaounde via Ebolowa to the border with Gabon. Immigration is done at the police station in Bitam opposite the *Shell*, but expect the Gabonese side to be unhelpful, even though some travellers have reported getting visas on arrival here. At least it's a tarmac road from the border for 400km as far as the **junction** just after the equator at S00° 04.6' E10° 57.5', and just before Alembé, where a road leads east to Lope National Park.

Here you have **three options** to get yourself into DRC and lined up for Zambia or Angola. Neither add up to a precise itinerary and there are other routes; instead it's merely a trio of possibilities which between them juggle bad roads, awkward visas and tricky borders. Whatever weather you get on the way, that comes free.

- Head east on the N3 for Franceville (470km) then follow a new road to Oyo in Congo (another 350km) and down to Brazzaville (450km). This should become the main all-weather road to Brazza once the Chinese have finished with Congo.
- Head south through Gabon any way you like and once you get to Dolisie in Congo, turn east for Brazzaville (360km) initially along a very rough road and adjacent rail road.
- With a double-entry Angolan visa, at Dolisie head west on for Pointe-Noire on the coast, then enter the Angolan enclave of **Cabinda** (220km). Once in DRC, head inland from Muanda (60km from Cabinda) to Boma – a tough ride in the rains. Cross the Congo river bridge into Matadi (220km) right on the Angolan border.

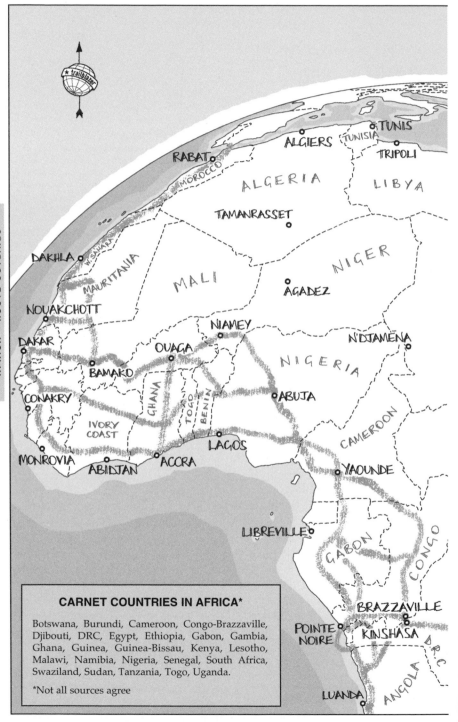

AFRICA – ROUTE OUTLINES

CARNET COUNTRIES IN AFRICA*

Botswana, Burundi, Cameroon, Congo-Brazzaville, Djibouti, DRC, Egypt, Ethiopia, Gabon, Gambia, Ghana, Guinea, Guinea-Bissau, Kenya, Lesotho, Malawi, Namibia, Nigeria, Senegal, South Africa, Swaziland, Sudan, Tanzania, Togo, Uganda.

*Not all sources agree

Main overland routes across Northern and West Africa

AFRICA – ROUTE OUTLINES

ASKING DIRECTIONS IN AFRICA

On stopping to buy water, a snack or to confirm directions, at times young men were 'in my face' and the attention could be intimidating. One time a local farmer among the group seemed especially aggressive. I didn't take it personally and it was interesting to note that when I addressed him directly, answering his questions genuinely and asking some myself, he seemed to come around – indeed warning off a couple of other young smart asses who were suggesting exacting a 'toll' from me.

I had a similar experience in Cameroon. Stopping for directions at a fork, I chose someone whose appearance suggested some 'worldliness'. He was a teacher who instantly took responsibility for the situation but as the inevitable crowd gathered the usual argument broke out and things became quite heated. I was to experience this further into central Africa and knew it was a cultural trait that didn't necessarily mean what it would back home in Ireland.

Remaining unperturbed was the best strategy. My defender had a stand off with one chap, accusing him of saying 'silly things' about me. The other guy backed off, things calmed down and the teacher would not let me go before I knew exactly where I was, the name of every village and even the hills all the way to Bamenda, my destination.

HUGH BERGIN
🖳 www.kilkennytocapetown.com

Southeast for Oyo (Congo)

Roadwise, the rot may well set in south from Mevang in Gabon, and as far as Lambarene and the Congo border at Doussala is the usual central African scenario. So take the newly sealed route east out via Lopé National Park to Lastourville (probably sealed by now), after which it's tar to **Franceville** all the way to the border at Lekoni. **Border formalities** are said to be easy enough; maybe a little trickier is heading west into Gabon from Congo. Few maps show this yet, but once in Congo it's 200 kilometres of newly sealed road over grass-covered high plains via Okoyo to Oyo, 450km from Brazzaville.

In **Congo** the people are friendly again and, for a central African capital, **Brazzaville** manages to be quite a safe city – until you get too close to the ferry port, that is. Many overlanders camp for free at the recommended *Hippocampe Hotel* (S04° 16.4' E15° 16.7') where great Vietnamese food is served. If heading north and in need of Gabonese or Cameroonian visas, see the box on p252.

Southwest for Pointe-Noire and Cabinda

Backing up to Mevang in Gabon, most pass on expensive Libreville (despite a Yamaha dealer there) and once over the bridge at Lambarene, 160km down the road, head southwest 700 clicks to Pointe-Noire on the coast of Congo-Brazza. From here you'll be crossing the Angolan enclave of Cabinda for DRC so make sure you have an Angolan visa sorted. Once in Congo immigration is done 50km after the border at Nyanga, where there's also a Catholic mission.

An alternative route to Congo turns off at Moanda before Franceville, and takes a little-used route south via Bakoumbe to the border and Mbinda for immigration. **Mila Mila** (S03° 42.9' E12° 27.1') is a junction that doesn't appear on most maps and where a corner-cutting track leads through the hills to Pointe-Noire, 150km away. Otherwise continue south to Dolisie junction where the railway runs from Pointe-Noire to Brazzaville, and turn west. Even in the rain it's a beautiful ride on a great road. At Pointe-Noire, camp with the bon viveurs at the Yacht Club (S04° 47.3' E11° 50.9').

Cabinda (Angola) and southwest DRC

Like a lot of the cities on this coast, **Cabinda** isn't cheap. Oil, imports and ex-pats see to that, and for many travellers the place doesn't encourage extended stays, especially with visa fuses burning. If you've had enough you might try and find out about a ship or even a military Antonov transporter to Luanda, or just a ferry with bike space to **Soyo**, 70km away on the south side of the Congo estuary. Otherwise, cross into DRC and head inland on a graded dirt towards Boma and Matadi. This track can be perfect or a mire when the heavens open; one Lithuanian rider rode his KLR into a puddle so deep both he and the bike disappeared. Hours later passers-by helped fish them out.

Once at Boma you rejoin tarmac and head north through the hills to come back down to the Congo River for the **toll bridge** into scenic Matadi, 120km from Boma. In dry conditions riders with fraying Angolan visas have done Cabinda to the Matadi bridge in a day. Among other places there are **missions** to stay at in Muanda (S05° 55.9' E12° 20.5'), Boma (S05° 51.2' E13° 03.4') and Matadi (S05° 49.9' E13° 27.7'). If heading for Angola, at Matadi there could be a crossing to Noqui and a new road – or it's 80km to **Songololo**, see next page.

Dolisie to Brazzaville, or slipping quietly over the Congo

On and off **Dolisie** is one of the few places to get an **Angolan visa** en route. Even then, it can depend on your nationality and any number of other less tangible factors. With prices from $200, it seems like a private enterprise but in 2015 10-day single-entry transits were issued so look around for the red-over-black Angolan flag – and a florist. Faint heart never won fair visa.

East from Dolisie, the 360km to Brazzaville was once plagued by Ninja separatists until they disbanded to pursue solo careers. Today the road remains well and truly rooted to Mindouli, 140km from the capital. When dry and dusty it can take two days to cover those 220km; when waterlogged and blocked by trucks it's polite not to ask. Expect roadblocks with set tolls or try the **train.**

South of this road there are **alternative crossings** to the main Congo ferry that runs between Brazzaville and Kinshasa. Both involve following little used tracks on either side of the river. At **Mindouli** turn right and cross into DRC then follow a gnarly track south a 100km to **Luozi** where a pontoon drops you on the far bank at **Banza Sanda**. The track continues south to the main road near **Kimpese** not far from the Angolan border at Songololo.

Or, coming from Brazzaville, turn southwest at Kinkala for Boko where the tarmac ends. A track leads to Manyanga and DRC border where the track deteriorates to Luozi. In off-road miles the distance is about the same for both approaches to Luozi, but **if it's wet** you're better off throwing yourself at the mercy of the Brazza-Kinshasa ferry. Think twice about the ferry at Pioka, 25km directly east of Luozi. It's said the track on the south side to Gombe Matadi has holes deeper than you are tall. Allow two days for either route.

DRC: THE CONGO FERRY TO KINSHASA

Brazzaville might be an easy-going place by regional standards, but it's time to stiffen the sinews and board the **ferry** to Kinshasa in the Democratic Republic of Congo (DRC). Start by scouting out the costs and timings, because the regular vehicle ferry is frequently out of action, although with a bike you can make a deal for a smaller passenger boat. The Brazzaville side is easy enough with a semi-fixed tariff of inflated prices of around 20,000CFA; the crossing takes 20 minutes to an hour. Arriving on the Kinshasa side they're on you and the costly whipping can take several hours. Lately they've been **denying entry** on visas not issued in your country of residency. All negotiable no doubt, but also more reason to slip in via Luozi (see previous page) or get your DRC visa at home.

Kinshasa

After all that, is it any surprise not everyone finds **Kinshasa** a relaxing place to spend time? The situation fluctuates, but this is one country where hanging around too long can get costly or unpleasant. Kinshasa hotels are expensive so most end up camping for free at the *Procure Sainte Anne Catholic* **mission** (S04° 18.0′ E15° 18.9′) next to the cathedral, a short distance from the ferry terminal, and opposite the US embassy (with others close by).

The track to Lubumbashi and Zambia

Even with its visa difficulties, most travellers would still choose to continue to Angola and so Namibia for the Cape, but to do that you need a visa and as things stand you won't be getting it here unless it flies in courtesy of DHL.

The alternative means heading east some 2400km to Zambia via Kikwit and Tshikapa, then Kananga, Mbuji-Mayi, Kamina and Kolwezi for Lubumbashi and on to the Zambian frontier at **Kasumbalesa**. In the 1960s this was the N1 highway with an adjacent railway and trams running in the towns. Fast forward half a century and the neglect and wars have seen the sort of dehumanising collapse of society for which DRC is infamous.

It's good tar for the 530km to Kikwit, and at the other end from Kolwezi to Lubumbashi and Kasumbalesa, but that still leaves well over 1500km along the atrophied remains of the former N1. Whatever geniality you've experienced so far dries up as incessant and aggressive demands for hand-outs, as well as village 'registration' fees and other bogus taxes add to the sustained effort on what has undoubtedly become the toughest 'main' overland route in Africa. Some days in the rain you'll barely manage to cover 50km.

If you, your bike and its tyres are up for it, allow up to **two weeks** to get across without help from a truck, or investigate the Kinshasa–Lubumbashi **cargo plane**. For a preview of what lies ahead, look up the Al Jezeera documentary on YouTube ('Risking it all – DRC') as well as a Belgian couple's 2011 account of travelling on XT660Zs (💻 www.roamingafrica.be).

Or, until the day the Chinese hose it all down with bitumen and bridges, consider what's emerged as a **less difficult option** (including fewer venal cops). About 145km after Tshikapa, in Mutombo turn south onto the **N29** and follow it south via Kazumba, Luiza and Musumba Kekese. About 30km before Musumba, at S08° 16.2′ E22° 35.7′, get pirogued across the 100-metre wide Lulua river. Then at Sanduwa on the same river, cut east and south on the R607 to rejoin the N29 and later the tarmac (and N1 route) at Kolwezi.

ANGOLA

It's 270km of good tar from Kinshasa to the most used **Songololo-Luvo** crossing which leads to initially good roads in Angola. Even then it can still take half a day to get it all done and on the road to Luanda, and at the mercy of a five- or maybe a seven-day **transit visa**, every hour counts. Coming north you might

AFRICA – ROUTE OUTLINES

KINSHASA TO BRAZZAVILLE FERRY

At Kinshasa port it was the usual mob scene with stupid ferry prices being thrown about. I ended up using a guy just so the others would leave me alone. He wouldn't give a price in advance for his services but got me through customs and immigration very quickly. But then he tried to change the cost on my 'ticket' (a scrap of paper from the ticket counter) from 38,000CFA to 138,000. When I caught him and questioned the cashier she screamed at him. I paid 38,000CFA.

I rode onto the ferry, though people were yelling at me and each other the whole time. One would get in the way to try to block me, another would pull him away and the fixer kept trying to discuss his fee, but I just rode aboard.

On the ferry fixerman then asked for stupid amounts of money. I gave him my remaining CFA and kwanza and suggested he'd do much better next time by being honest. The ferry was beginning to move so he cursed at me and hopped back ashore.

On the Brazzaville side there were a few steps to negotiate before I could ride up the ramp so I needed help to get the GS off. I'd been talking to some decent guys on the boat (the joys of speaking French!) and we worked out a deal: two to lift the bike at $2 each, then $5 each to the two who arranged it, helped lift the bike, and did the whole immigration dance for me, including getting the visa! Everything worked fine and they never tried to ask for more cash.

So, for me and the GS it was: ticket $42; Kinshasa fixer $10; Brazzaville help $14 and Congo-Brazzaville visa $50.

DAVID RADFORD
🖳 www.gsguy.wordpress.com

have got a 30-day tourist visa from the Angolans in Cape Town (S33° 55.2' E18° 25.4'), but that requires some luck and persistence. All of which is a great shame as, despite the ruined roads and very high prices, like Nigeria or Sudan, the ordinary people of Angola make it a favourite amongst overland riders. Encountering delays on a five-day pass adds to the pressure, but **over-staying** by a few days need not mean transportation to the local equivalent of Devil's Island. If it's just a couple of days they may let you go, or argue over the fine, but it's best not to get caught living it large in Luanda with an expired visa.

Make sure you have enough fuel when you enter from the north to get 300km to N'zeto where the first reliable fuel supplies start. **Land mines** are still a problem in Angola – don't leave the road unless you're following a recently used track and crap on the road if you have to. Because of this, **bush camping** takes some effort or risk, but as always there's a network of missions.

Trans Angola

If not trying Matadi–Noqui, at Songololo turn south to **Luvo**. Change your dollars on the Angolan side. No carnet needed, the TIP lasts up to a year and it should be cheaper fuel and 50km of new road to M'banza-Kongo and another 250km to **N'zeto** on the coast. From here the 200km down the coast to Caxito is 'under construction' or brand spanking new.

From Caxito it's tar to **Luanda** where the few have benefited greatly from Angola's long overdue boom until oil prices dropped. A Via Expresso **ring road** can speed up your transit: as you come in from the north stay on the good sealed road that descends into a potholed mess within the city limits, until you see a motorway overpass (S08° 46.2' E13° 23.2') and roundabout. This is your ticket around Luanda so if that's what you want, get on it. Otherwise, if you want to stay see if they still let you **camp for free** in the secure car park at the *Clube Nautico* (Yacht Club) down in the marina (S08° 48.1' E13° 13.4').

NORTHBOUND VISAS IN LUANDA AND BRAZZAVILLE

LUANDA

DRC
Largo de Joao Seca, just south of the South African embassy and near the hospital.
S08° 49.52' E13° 13.74'

Congo
Rua de Joao de Barros, by Meridian Hotel.
S08° 48.22' E13° 14.55'

Gabon
Near the Miramar Park and just east of the Congo embassy. S08° 48.51' E13° 15.0'

BRAZZAVILLE
Both just south of the Meridian hotel and a ten minute walk north of the Hippocampe Hotel.

Gabon
Boulevard du Maréchal Lyautey
S04° 16.12' E15° 16.65'
Possibly same day and 45,000CFA

Cameroon
Rue Gouverneur Général Bayardelle
S04° 16.17' E15° 16.54'
Two days and from 51,000CFA

Leaving Luanda

South of Luanda follow the coast 540km to **Benguela** on mainly good tar. Watch out for police with radar guns and the few road tolls. The humidity finally begins to drop, the land turns to savannah and at night you can enjoy the cool again. The checkpoints, desperate scams and general aggro of the equatorial countries drops off too; maybe it is the climate after all.

From Benguela you can head inland towards Quilengues and Lubango, another 130km on, rising up to a cool 1500m. Otherwise continue along the coast to Lubango via the impressive **Leba Pass**. Lubango to the border can be done in a day if you leave early. Expect new tar, torturous dirt roads or ruined tar. The main border crossing is at **Oshikango** (Namibian side), but if it's not too wet try the track from Xangongo down to Ruacana in Namibia.

Crossing the border you may find yourself wincing like Steve McQueen being let out of the Cooler in *The Great Escape*. The strain of the previous weeks lifts – hanging around for visas, then dashing cross country against the clock. Some find the adjustment quite a shock and in a perverse way, may even miss the struggle that, when not waiting for visas, gave each day a purpose. Ahead lie the fabulous desert landscapes of **Namibia**, as rich as any you've seen so don't be in a rush as the pressure's off now. Just make sure you **ride on the left**. The finale down to Cape Town is a piece of cake, as long as you keep vigilant in Namibian cities. For Southern Africa see p258.

ON A MISSION

Christian missions make great overnight havens and on this western route represent the only secure and fully functional accommodation plus a great source of information.

The most you should expect is a place to camp and the way to the washroom. Sometimes there's a fee structure, otherwise make a cash donation. Don't let the dog collar put you off haggling if you're staying for a few days.

Should you be faced with a choice, go for the nuns rather than priests as their missions tend to be cleaner and better organised.

ANDY PAG

The Nile route

Much less of a challenge in terms of terrain and visas, the long-established 'Cairo to Cape' run down the east side of Africa is the classic route. Composed largely of former British colonies, **English** is widely spoken and as few as **seven** English-speaking borders separate Cairo from Cape Town, though tempting lodges and fees at some borders all add up. On this side a Visa card and the **US dollar** is the hard currency of choice; further south the **South African rand** is acceptable in the countries which border RSA.

South of the equator those with Commonwealth nationalities can usually get **visas** at the border, although Brits pay much higher prices. Coming north from Kenya, your Ethiopia and Sudan visas don't fall into place anywhere near as well. And now with the main routes in northern Sudan and northern Kenya **sealed**, for the moment you can ride all the way on tarmac; make the most of it as the good surface may not last. It does mean the right **season** is less critical, though as you near the equator the increase in **elevation** creates a more equable climate, with a lushness to the scenery that makes places like Uganda well worth the diversion. Away from expensive game parks, mile-for-mile the lowland plains or *veldt* of Tanzania and Botswana can get dull.

Highlights and hotspots

Highlights include the monuments of pharaonic Egypt, the desert of northern Sudan, Ethiopia's highlands and Coptic culture, Uganda and the White Nile, the game parks or chilling on the Indian Ocean coast. As you get to Zambia or Botswana, Namibia's worth the detour before wrapping it all up.

If it's **wildlife spotting** you're after, be aware that bikes aren't allowed in most of East Africa's **game parks**. You need a rental car or to join a tour – both less expensive in South Africa or Namibia than Kenya or Tanzania. Even then, chances are you'll see plenty of animals by just riding around on back roads.

Places to **avoid** (or where they won't let you go) include northern Sinai and the Western Desert in Egypt, the easily avoided border regions with South Sudan as well as western Sudan, eastern Ethiopia and Somalia. No one's ventured into the Central African Republic or far into eastern DRC for a while, either. The South African AA has a good website; of particular value on the more commonly travelled east side: Crossborder Information 💻 www.aa.co .za/services/travel-services/into-africa/cross-border-information.html.

EGYPT

Egypt's in a bit of a state following the 2011 revolution and subsequent democratic elections which didn't agree with the military powerbase who re-established control in 2013. Along with the western spread of ISIS, this has seen a collapse in mainstream tourism on which the country is heavily reliant.

What hasn't changed is the still mind-numbingly protracted **paperwork** required when entering with a vehicle – you'd think they might connect the two, but cross-border security has been ramped up. There's some confusion

SOUTHBOUND VISAS IN CAIRO	
Sudanese embassy in Cairo 3 Ibrahim St., Garden City (just behind a petrol station) N29° 59.7′ E31° 14.6	**Ethiopian embassy in Cairo** 21 Mohammed El Ghazali St. Dokki (near Dokki metro station) N30° 02.5′ E31° 12.3′

whether visas on arrival are no longer issued for overlanders and an **e-visa** system may be in place by now. Although some claim to manage without one, you'll need a **carnet** (as do most countries on this eastern route) even if they pedantically issue you with their own TIP. Add to that a temporary driving licence, rented Arabic number plates (for which your deposit is supposedly refunded on departure, though some end up *paying* to return them), plus vehicle registrations (which might only be valid for a month, unlike your visa or TIP), x-rays, permits and on-the-spot fees which you'll lose track of. **Insurance** is LE52 a month bought in monthly segments. With costs being arbitrary (even when posted blatantly on a wall), it all feels like a well-oiled system of informalised taxation; there's rarely an outright demand for *baksheesh*. In or out, it will all run to some $200 or more and take half a day. Just remember, it's not only you who pays and it's really only pocket money. The latest details will be on the HUBB's North Africa Forum.

The bigger difficulty is **getting to Egypt overland**. The situations in Libya and Syria won't improve soon and flying a bike in will really throw you in the bureaucratic deep end – expect it to take days and days. At the time of you-know-what a **Ro-Ro** service between Lavrio near Piraeus in Greece to Haifa, **Israel** (weekly, 60 hours) is the only way. Or pick up the same service in Cyprus, having ferried to Girne, North Cyprus from Tasucu in Turkey (7 hours). The Israeli-Egypt land border at Eilat-Taba on the Gulf of Aqaba may be off limits depending on who's got the upper hand in north Sinai, so proceed to Jordan for the regular **ferry from Aqaba to Nuweiba** (allow half a day at each port) in the Sinai and skirt round the southern edge and up to Suez.

Once in Egypt **fuel** is cheap, so are the half-empty lodgings and the monumental splendours are well known and not to be rushed. You're likely to need to stop in **Cairo** for onward visas – brace yourself for your first immersion in the madness that is urban African **traffic mayhem**.

The **Western Oases** of Bahariya, Farafra and Dakhka make a rewarding excursion, but right now you need an escort and can't camp out in the desert safely. And even before the current troubles you couldn't roam west of that road towards the Great Sand Sea and the fabulous Gilf Kebir without a guide, all sorts of permits and armed guards, all of which took months to organise.

Crossing to Sudan

For years crossing into Sudan required negotiating a place on a disorganised ferry from **Aswan** across the world's biggest artificial lake, even though perfectly good overland routes existed. Then in 2014 a land border finally opened with Sudan on the 22nd parallel on the east side of the lake. Getting there still supposedly requires joining a costly **convoy to Abu Simbel** on the west side, where a ferry (50LE) crosses Lake Nasser 10km to Qustul on the Egyptian east bank and 55km north of Wadi Halfa in Sudan, with the border post halfway.

There's also a less well known road on the west side, running down from Abu Simbel to Argeen on the border and on to Dongola. There's talk that one day this may become the main crossing, avoiding ferries and Wadi Halfa altogether. Some have negotiated to use it, but the charges paid to the Egyptian army who seem to run the whole deal down here are huge.

So for the moment Abu Simbel to Wadi Halfa it is. You might think that's an improvement but this is Egypt so the costs manage to match the old Aswan ferry. Only the time is reduced, so that's something. Taking the pre-dawn convoy out of Aswan, you can be in Wadi Halfa by nightfall. Here, an entrepreneurial guy called Mazar Mahir has long been the fixer or 'clearance facilitator', charging ten dollars to stamp his stamp. Some pedantic types resent this; others find his services very helpful and his fee is really quite negligible in the scheme of things. 'This...', as you'd better learn soon '... is Africa'.

Northbound from Wadi you can take a ferry direct to Abu Simbel or reverse the land border; the direct ferry must be quicker and the total to get out of Sudan and into Egypt will run to about $250, most of that for Egypt, even though the Wadi–Abu Simbel ferry ticket is officially less than a dollar. Whether you actually pay is a matter of luck or who you meet.

SUDAN

Even if you weren't expecting Las Vegas on stilts, **Wadi Halfa** is still no oasis. The original settlement is submerged beneath Lake Nasser, but there's everything here including a bank and any number of permit-issuing government offices – including the mandatory Alien Registration Office (do it here or in Khartoum) all helping to turn dollars into documents. Keep a stash for the **black market**, you'll get around a fifty percent better rate, otherwise Sudan can get pricey; **ATMs won't work** for you. Get insurance (you can't get the Comesa yellow card extension until Addis (see p257).

From Wadi Halfa two routes lead south, each tracking one side of the 1000-kilometre tall 'S' bend of the Nile between the border and the capital, Khartoum. The more-commonly driven western route is now **sealed**. It meets the east bank of the Nile about a third of the way to Dongola. Here you can take the west bank and join a sealed road all the way to Khartoum, or stick to the east bank and head south-east through the desert to the Meröe ferry in the middle of the 'S' bend.

The more isolated **eastern route** from Wadi follows the **railway** and telegraph line across the Nubian Desert to Abu Hamed on the Nile and subsequently Atbara at the Port Sudan junction, for Khartoum. If it's the cool season and your bike is up to it, on the initial stages of this route you can wander into the desert away from the sandy rail-side track. Depending on the duration of your visa, make the most of it; you'll miss the open desert later on. Just don't expect much help from the train up here, it runs about once a week and only a couple of the stops are manned.

Southbound travellers should have done it at Wadi Halfa, but if **coming from Ethiopia** you need to park your spaceship and **register as an Alien** within three days of entering Sudan. In **Khartoum** the Alien Registration Office is at the airport (less busy) or in a city market at N15° 36.0' E32° 31.1'. You'll need photocopies of your passport and Sudanese visa and possibly a letter from your lodgings. You may also need a Permit to Travel to get up to Wadi Halfa from the ministry about a mile southeast at N15° 35.4′ E32° 31.82′. Plus a photography permit from the Ministry of Tourism, though you can dodge this as long as you're not caught shooting a controversial, feature-length documentary about a telegraph pole. If you stay at the *German Guesthouse* near the airport (N15° 34.1′ E32° 33.8′) they'll help you get the first two permits. And it's said that the once-popular *Blue Nile Sailing Club* by the main bridge (N15° 36.7′ E32° 32.1′) is getting a long overdue makeover.

If you need a **visa for Egypt** in Khartoum (consulate: N15° 36.2′ E32° 31.4′), it costs SDG160 and can be valid for a month from the day of issue and is issued the same day. Heading south, get an **Ethiopian visa** often on the same day for $20 by applying in the morning at: Plot No. 04, Block 384BC, just west of the Farouq cemetery (N15° 34.9′ E32° 32.06′), or consider getting it in your home country. In London a six-month multiple entry tourist visa costs £54.

With the exception of Meröe, a couple of hours north of Khartoum on the Atbara road, Sudan doesn't match the ancient historical grandeur of Egypt or Ethiopia. However, despite the tedious bureaucracy many travellers report it's all done with a wily smile, much less *baksheesh* than Egypt and the people are among the most hospitable on this route. It's something not everyone proclaims about Ethiopia.

South Sudan looks no more accessible than before that country was formed in 2011, and the old route across **Chad** through Darfur doesn't look too promising either.

ETHIOPIA

From Khartoum most head straight down the sealed road to Gedaret and Doka and the border at Gallabat for **Metema** in northwest Ethiopia. On a good day Ethiopian immigration and customs formalities are said to be among the quickest in Africa, with **insurance** down the road in Gonder. They're happy to stamp your **carnet**, but Ethiopia isn't in the carnet zone (it ought to be excluded from the list on the back of the document), but so many travellers have their carnets blithely stamped here that getting a TIP can take some persuasion. Note that **ATMs** are only found in larger towns and cities.

A 30-day tourist **visa** obtained in Cairo is valid for three months, giving you plenty of time to get here, even if Lake Nasser freezes over and zombie pharaohs stalk the land. Or you can get it in Khartoum or your home country. Coming up from the south, you'll be very lucky to get an **Ethiopian visa** in Nairobi, or a Sudanese visa in Addis. For Ethiopia try **Harare** back down in Zimbabwe or call in DHL. A Sudanese visa can take three days in Nairobi. As always, your nationality will have much to do with it.

After the barren sands of Sudan, **Ethiopia** is an exceptional looking country. Particularly in the north the greenery and vistas as you climb into the highlands can be a real tonic. The classic northern tour into the Simian Mountains for Axum, past Debre Damos monastery and the climb up to the carved rock churches of Lalibela is not to be missed, even if the roads can hammer the stuffing out of you. With bad roads and steep mountain tracks, picking the right **season** in Ethiopia is important. The months building up to June get very hot in the lowlands of the south and east, while from then to September the rains can disrupt travel anywhere. You'll also be riding as high as 3350m (11,000′), so around January expect to be cold.

Unfortunately the welcome from the locals isn't always much warmer and the language barrier doesn't help. You may get worn down by the petty aggression and incessant yells of 'You, you, you!'. It's clear from the tone that they're not cheerfully reciting Alvin Stardust's chart-topping 1974 hit. Showers of sticks and stones can also make you wonder what you're doing here, although it seems some travellers draw more flack than others. Strategies range from waving in appeasement to riding straight at them, but at least the police aren't too demanding.

This primary axis through Ethiopia is relatively stable but the far west, the Danakil and more especially the Somali borders remain places to avoid. As African capitals go, **Addis Ababa** isn't what you've ridden thousands of miles to see but is the first place to buy your **COMESA Yellow Card** from the Ethiopian Insurance Corp. for the ride south. To meet up with the gang, stay at *Wim's Holland House* (N09° 00.6' E38° 45.3').

INTO KENYA VIA MARSABIT

Once regularly shortlisted for Africa's 'Most Corrugated Road' Award with the added thrill of being shot at or turned over by *shifta* bandits, this once notorious track is now sealed and another legendary African suspension wrecker is tamed. All the more reason to try the Omo valley route (see below). There are no more border **visas for Kenya**; it's now done online at 🖳 www.ecitizen.go.ke with 90 days validity and duration for $51.

From Moyale the 500km run down through Kenya goes via Marsabit to Isiolo. Halfway down the road, **Marsabit** doesn't offer much in the way of first class accommodation, but many overlanders choose to stay at the renowned *Henry's Camp* (ask for 'Henry the Swiss') on the west side of town (N02° 20.75' E37° 58.0'). The final 250km from Marsabit ends at **Isiolo** where you can legitimately beat your chest and make Tarzan noises: you've arrived in East Africa.

(right margin) AFRICA – ROUTE OUTLINES

TO KENYA VIA LAKE TURKANA

To string out your adventure head down to the **Omo Valley**, among other things the home of Mursi tribeswomen famed for their wooden lip plates, as well as the odd, trigger happy herdsman. This hyper-arid corner of Kenya around Lake Turkana is a hot, stony stage and actually barely borders the lake.

From the Rastafarian enclave of Shashemene, 220km south of Addis, head for Jinka or Abra Minch and Konso. Here it's another 190km to Turmi (last fuel, if they have any) where you pass the turn-off for the Kenyan border before **Omorate** (aka: Kelem) where you stamp out your carnet. Back at the

turn-off, cross into Kenya and at **Ileret** sign in with the police. You'll need to complete your immigration in Nairobi.

Head inland through the Sibiloi National Park coughing up a $20/day fee as you pass by. Loyangalani, about 222km from Ileret, may have the first expensive fuel. Continue another 230km to Maralal (ATM, fuel, shops) and on to Baragoi for Archers Post on the main road to Nairobi.

Now back on the highway, after a thousand kilometres there's the small matter of crossing the equator and remembering to ride on the **left**.

East and Southern Africa

Coming from the north, or less likely, the west, most trans-African riders customarily take a breather and get repairs done in **Kenya**, sub-Saharan Africa's most visited and touristy country after South Africa.

Along with a dramatic improvement in the road and tourist infrastructure, you also start **riding on the left** from here all the way down to the Cape, **English** is spoken and, depending on your nationality, the worst of the itinerary-restricting **visa hassles** should be over.

But the human psyche being what it is, it can all become a bit of a parade or extended *safari* (the Swahili word for 'journey') as you hop from one divine waterside lodge to the next, while dodging rowdy backpacker haunts or overland truck groups. Suddenly, it's like Southeast Asia with endless choices and a cold beer always in the fridge. After too much of this, some profess a nostalgia for the rough travelling in Ethiopia and Sudan, places which may have been rushed through early in your African experience.

In East Africa most riders **carry on camping** from around $10 per person as, along with national park entry fees (where accessible), fuel prices and tempting supermarkets, things can get **expensive**. A few lodging recommendations are given in the text, but **online** is clearly the place to see what's new – including LP's Thorn Tree or TripAdvisor.

INTO KENYA

Coming up with a South African registered bike, Kenya is the first country that may be a headache, requiring vehicles from outside the East African Community (EAC) to have a **carnet** as well as a licence disc for a 'Foreign Private Vehicle' (FPV) costing $40 a month at the border, or $100 for three months from the immigration office at Nyayo House in Nairobi (S01° 17.2' E36° 49.1'). From the north and heading for Uganda and Rwanda, ask about a **visa** to cover all three countries for $100.

Wherever you're coming from, armed with your FPV, a carnet, your Yellow Card (or local insurance) and some Swahili jokes, you'll be set to face down any bribe-extorting policeman. The **COMESA Yellow Card** programme (🖳 http://programmes.comesa.int) is similar to the Green Card issued in the EU and provides **extension** to your already obtained third party motor insurance in supposedly every country on the east side up to Sudan. Like a Green Card it isn't valid in the issuing country and coming from the south, Zambia is the first place to buy it; expect about $100 for six months all the way up to Sudan.

Police road blocks in Kenya concentrate around major towns and usually wave foreign bikes through, though not if you're caught speeding. Reflective patches on jackets aim to reduce the local moto death rate, though it's not clear if this gets enforced or applies to foreign bikers; if you meet the wrong cop, it could be because, as elsewhere in sub-Saharan Africa, you'll find the occasional officer stationed at a roadblock looking for an ATM to come rolling by.

Main overland routes across East and Southern Africa

Get into the habit of having all your paperwork handy and always ask for a receipt for all on the spot 'fines' because that'll usually put off anyone who's up to no good or reduce an official fine. Another good counter-scam is to claim your embassy insists you photograph and report all fine/receipt incidents immediately, to counter any possibility of corruption which has been known to occur in these parts.

Towards Nairobi

From **Isiolo** you'll no doubt want to pull up at **Nanyuki**, made famous in a thousand snaps because it straddles the **equator**. In town you'll also find guys demonstrating the water-down-a-plughole trick, a big supermarket, pharmacy and a few banks. Watching the GPS count down and arriving at the equator will be an event you're unlikely to have to yourself, though it's a good excuse to get off and stretch your legs before you reach Mount Kenya. The road to Nairobi passes west of the mountain with another excellent campsite at *Naro Moro River Lodge*, one of the base camps for those who want to have a crack at reaching the 5199-metre summit of the mountain. From here it's a straight 200km run to Nairobi.

WEST TO UGANDA AND THE RWENZORI MOUNTAINS

Depending on the season, the lush highlands and cool lakes of Uganda can be a tonic after Sudan and Ethiopia. Many travellers are startled by this verdant upland region because there's no shortage of arid savannah and desert further north or south.

As yet many find that Uganda lacks Kenya's commercialism and the prices found further south. Gorilla spotting in the rainforests is an exception, but there's rafting on the Nile at Jinja or you could just chill by a lake. With the relatively inexpensive fuel, many overlanders see Uganda as an East African favourite. **Visas** at the border for Brits and western Europeans are no hassle ($50 or $100 for one that covers Kenya and Rwanda too), but make sure you have your carnet and the Yellow Card, or buy it at the border. You'll also pay a vehicle tax adding up to about $20.

The road out of Nairobi passes through the **Rift Valley** with inexpensive camping at *Fisherman's Camp* on the south side of Lake Naivasha at a cool 1890m, and *Kembu Cottages* 25km west of Lake Nakuru. Crossing the **equator**, there are more lakes before reaching **Eldoret** and *Naiberi River Campsite*, 16km southeast of Eldoret.

In **Uganda**, the main road takes a turn towards Lake Victoria and Jinja, a popular place for white water rafting which may well have the same colouring effect on your hair.

If you decide to raft with them, *Nile River Explorers* at Bujagali Falls are recommended as well as offering inexpensive camping.

If coming up from the south, not least Kenya, travellers find **Kampala** a relaxed and inexpensive capital. The established *Red Chilli Hideaway* is 5km east of the city centre (N00° 19.21', E32° 37.8'); the Red Chilli folk also have a rest house at Murchison's Falls, 250km north of Kampala; a good base for visiting Murchison Falls National Park.

Along with the vast **Lake Victoria**, Uganda shares several smaller lakes with its neighbours, including Lake Albert and Lake Edward. Along the south shore of Lake Albert visit the Kibale Forest National Park and the Kibale Forest Primate Reserve. Here the *Lake Nkuruba Community Campsite* offers camping right next to the best of the crater lakes on a manicured lawn.

West of Kibale is Lake Bunyonyi between Kisoro and Kabale, and close to the Rwandan border. East of town you'll find the camping *Lake Bunyonyi Overland Resort* to be another idyllic place.

The road from Kibale to Kisoro looks due for asphalting, and as you progress southwest you're now heading towards the **Rwenzori Mountains**, Bwindi National Park, the Virunga Mountains, Rwanda's Parc des Volcans and of course, Dian Fossey's famous troop of silverback gorillas.

Nairobi

As you near Nairobi the road deteriorates, as does the quality of the driving. Hey ho, it's another crazy African capital. Passing Thika you'll be entering the city from the northeast so be prepared for several large, chaotic, roundabouts. If you brought your 'Ben Hur' wheel spikes, now's the time to fit them. One roundabout is where the A2 road filters down to Forrest Road; another is at the junction of Forrest and Ngara Roads. Try to avoid the rush hours, especially on the Uhuru and Mombasa Roads.

Dealing with Nairobi

The risk of crime in 'Nai-robbery' is overrated, especially if you're riding a battered bike (can it be anything else by now?). But as with any big city, keep your wits about you and have a destination in mind long before you get there.

If you're entering Nairobi from the north-east and heading towards the western side of the city where many **overlanders hang out**, when you hit the Museum Hill roundabout, get on the Waiyaki Highway (an extension of Uhuru to Mombasa Road) and head back out of town. Just after the ABC Plaza turn left and take a short cut along James Gicheru Road. This will take you to either the famous *Jungle Junction* (S01° 17.3' E36° 45.6') or *Upper Hill Campsite* (S01° 17.2' E36° 46.4'), a couple of kilometres east of the junction. For a **bike shop** try www.motoadvkenya.com on the southeast edge of the city.

East to the coast

By the time most southbound overlanders reach Kenya, the idea of laying up on an **Indian Ocean beach** while a local mechanic tends lovingly to your bike is an irresistible fantasy. Mombasa, Lamu or any of the other small resorts up and down the Indian Ocean coast are perfect places to recuperate before heading south to Tanzania. If you head to **Mombasa**, first make sure you survive the ride. Crashes with matatus are prevalent on this road.

AFRICA – ROUTE OUTLINES

RWANDA AND BURUNDI

Entering from Uganda near the Parc des Volcans, **Rwanda** doesn't require visas for UK citizens, they'll just stamp your passport. This is a beautiful country too, but some travellers find it quite 'hard' by regional standards as the locals aren't really interested in travellers or tourism; they have their hands full serving aid workers and the UN.

Camping doesn't exist as elsewhere in East Africa, so Presbyterian missions are your best bet. Add **fuel** that's up to 25 percent more than Kenya or Uganda, as well as national parks fees and it all becomes an expensive proposition. Furthermore, currently Rwandan **ATMs** only accept local bank cards so arrive with plenty of dollars to exchange, though some banks will advance cash on Visa cards.

To the south, **Burundi** may no longer issue **visas** at the border so pick them up on Boulevard de l'Umuganda, Kigali west (S01° 56.5' E30° 05.2'). With that you can take a loop via Makebuko to Bujumbura, then down the east shore of Lake Tanganyika to Mabanda to cross into Tanzania for Kigoma.

If you don't want to visit Burundi you can leave Rwanda via the border post either side of the bridge at Kagera River, however the route south alongside Lake Tanganyika is rough. Instead, you can head east to Mwanza at the southern end of Lake Victoria and on eastwards to the Serengeti, adjacent to Kenya's Masai Mara where the wildebeest are stamping their hooves and calling your name. Or, head south for Mbeya and so to Zambia via the Tunduma border post.

KENYA TO TANZANIA

As the travel hardships ease beyond Kenya, suitably refreshed and with your bike running like the Swiss watch it once was, you can now entertain all sorts of ways of complicating things again. Going south into **Tanzania**, world-class game parks and natural spectacles abound, including Kilimanjaro, the Ngorongoro Crater and the Serengeti, as well as Dar es Salaam and Zanzibar on the Indian Ocean. From Nairobi there are **two main ways** to get south: either the well trodden route through Namanga, Moshi, Same and Korogwe – or from Mombasa south along the coast through the Lunga Lunga–Hora Hora border post and all sealed road to Tanga in Tanzania.

Kenya-Tanzania border

Whichever you decide, at the Tanzanian **border** get a one-month tourist visa from $50-100 depending on nationality. A two-week transit visa costs from $30, though you'll need a full tourist visa to visit Zanzibar. The **Temporary Import Permit** (TIP) for your bike is another 50 bucks. The choice is yours as to whether you use your carnet or not, but a TIP requires using a customs agent to clear the bike. No bond is required, but it takes an extra hour and of course the agent charges for the service. There is also a fuel levy of $25.

Exiting Kenya via the Namanga border post, 170km south of Nairobi, is a relatively painless business: the only irritation may be the many Maasai women who throng around, pressing their colourful wares on you.

Kenya may well have caught up by now, but in Tanzania and in many countries south of here, watch out for radar gun slinging **speed traps** with the choice of an on-the-spot fine, reduced 'receipt-free' rates, or your day in court. Note they do the Russian trick of ending the '50kph' town speed limit zone miles down the road when your guard is down. Quite often they're just looking for a 'kitu kidogo' ('a little something'); always check their speed guns are working. You'll learn to love or loathe the Tanzanian Police department in their powder blue uniforms.

Kenya to Tanzania via Namanga

Once through the border you'll find Tanzania's main highways are well maintained, although they deteriorate quickly out bush (as does the use of English, Swahili's the lingua franca here more than in Kenya). Expect a band of unsigned and especially acute **speed bumps** at the beginning of any village.

Heading south to **Arusha**, Tanzania's safari hub, there are lots of places to stay, from 1970s-style hotels in town, to camping out of town at places like *Meserani Snake Park*, about 25km west of Arusha on the Dodoma Road. This is also the way to Lake Manyara, the Ngorongoro Crater and the Serengeti.

East leads to Moshi, the tourist hub for Kilimanjaro, and again full of places to stay, most geared up to accommodate tourists and overlanders with bars, food and secure parking. There are also **campsites** just out of town, such as *Maasai Camp* in Arusha (noisy at weekends) or the nicer and cheaper *Marungu Campsite* on the way to the 5900-metre mass of Kilimanjaro. If you're saddle weary and serious about climbing Kili, Trailblazer has the *Kilimanjaro* guidebook for you, or check out the author's informative website: ⌨ www.climbmountkilimanjaro.com.

The road to Dar es Salaam

Heading for Dar, if you fancy visiting historic Bagamoyo on the way – once the end of the trail for slaves heading to Arabia – then head south from Segera where, 37km north of Chalinze at Msata (S06° 20.0' E38° 23.4') there's a 60km long track running east to a former old trading post. From Bagamoyo to Dar is another 70 clicks down along the coast. Alternatively, if heading northward, 44km east at Chalinze on the road to Dar, at Mlandizi (S06° 43.0' E38° 44.3') you'll find a gravel track leading north to Bagamoyo.

Dar es Salaam is another one of those cities whose romance is these days more a sepia-tinted memory than reality, but it's a lot more agreeable than many African cities. Primarily it's the jumping off point for Zanzibar or the Pemba islands (no bikes allowed). Traditionally overlanders stay north of Dar at *Silversands*, however there are many more campsites on the coast to the southeast via a ferry over the harbour mouth. They include *Kipepeo Beach Village* which lives up to its name with chalets or camping plus secure parking while you visit the islands, or the nearby *Makadi Beach Resort*. The *YMCA* in town can also look after your bike for a small fee.

SOUTH OF TANZANIA

Whether you've taken the road to Arusha, past Kilimanjaro, or down the coast, both roads meet at Segera before continuing south to **Chalinze** where you can either turn east for Dar es Salaam or west on to Morogoro. For most overlanders it's a choice between keeping inland for Malawi and Zambia, or east for Mozambique and the coast. The latter can lead you directly to the eastern border with South Africa, from where Cape Town and the end of the road is less than 2000km away. As with many such crossroads, much will depend on the state of you, your wallet and your bike, as well as your capacity for more adventure and border games.

Tanzania to Zambia

If you skipped Dar and pushed on to **Morogoro** there's plenty of accommodation on the way, and the Mikumi National Park is one of the few you can ride through so there's a chance to see giraffe, zebras and elephants if you've not seen any yet, as well as warnings for hippos.

Coming down from Morogoro, the next major town is **Iringa** (*Iringa Farm* has great camping), with access to the Ruaha National Park. From Iringa, heading on south and west it's a long trek to Mbeya. The Tunduma border post with Zambia is now 100km down the road where again, all visas and other papers can be bought at the border.

Zambia

Like Uganda, Zambia delivers a surprisingly verdant country that's the home of the two Luangwa National Parks. Brits pay $50 for a visa at the border where you might also be asked to cough up for a carbon emissions tax, $30 road access fee plus motor insurance sold for one or three months ($20), if you don't have a Yellow Card (see p258). If heading south check that bikes don't require reflective stickers, as foreign cars do. **Climate**-wise, you're south of the equator with the cool dry season from May to August; the build-up sets in and the rains let loose from December until April when tracks become impassable.

Taking a short cut by **crossing DRC** via Sakania is said to be OK but it's another visa; the western border crossing with Angola is very rarely used by travellers. Elsewhere the main roads are in good condition; you can shoot across Zambia in three days if the pipes are calling, or you can spend time and a whole lot of money in the national parks; even waterfalls can cost you $15 for a quick look-see. As often in sub-Saharan Africa, the capital **Lusaka** is a place to be wary after dark with tourist resorts like **Livingstone** near Victoria Falls also attracting nocturnal thieves and muggers.

In Zambia

The road from Tanzania enters Zambia at the Tunduma–Nakonde border post which can be particularly overwhelming due to the sheer number of trucks, money changers and touts offering to expedite your paperwork for a fee. Park up outside immigration, roll your sleeves up and get stuck in. Once you've cleared customs, had your carnet stamped and paid all the rest, they open the barrier and let you loose.

This road is known as the 'TanZam Highway' and passes the North and South Luangwa National Parks to its south and Kapishya Hot Springs to the north. There are lots of places to stay in Lusaka itself, otherwise 50km before you enter the city, there's helpful *Fringilla Lodge*.

Your choice now is either to continue south-east and enter Zimbabwe through Chirundu, or head west to Kaufe National Park 200km west of Lusaka. Otherwise, head past Choma to Livingstone and the **Victoria Falls,** close to where Namibia, Botswana and Zimbabwe meet Zambia.

Tanzania to Malawi

Backing up a bit, the other main route from Tanzania runs south to **Malawi**. About 10km east of Mbeya at Uyole, turn south on the B345 and enter Malawi at the Songwe–Kasumulu border post alongside Lake Malawi. Show your yellow card or buy **insurance** and a TIP for 1200 Malawi kwatcha if you think your carnet needs a rest. Most Europeans don't need an advance visa.

The road starts close to the shore and passing Karonga, it then climbs towards Mzuzu and the Viphya Mountains on the way to the capital, **Lilongwe**. You can also take the lakeside road which passes through Nkhata Bay and Senga. Both this road and the main road from Lilongwe carry on to the south end of the lake where you'll find *Monkey Bay* on **Cape Maclear**, an overlanders' favourite.

There are other border posts in the south of Malawi, but most are now heading for South Luangwa National Park in Zambia and so need to retrace their steps back to Lilongwe, before heading 110km west for the Mchinji crossing to Chipata in Zambia.

In Malawi

Malawi can be a place to rest up, but it can also get **expensive**, with pricey fuel and 8% charged on Visa card transactions. Be aware too of the **national speed limit** of 80kph out of towns. For a place to camp in the capital, Lilongwe, the central *Sanctuary Lodge* on Youth Drive (S13° 58.1' E33° 47.2') has been recommended in preference to the better known *Golf Course* a couple of kilometres to the south.

ZAMBIA TO BOTSWANA

From Kazungula you can catch the ferry across the Zambezi to **Botswana**. As you approach the crossing, ride past the long line of trucks at the side of the road to the passenger vehicle queue.

Once there you need to pay around 20 pula for a Road Fund (about $2) which is valid till the end of the year, as well as a Road Permit of P50 for a single transit. There's no Yellow Card here, so insurance is about P50 for 90 days.

Considered a sub-Saharan success story, Botswana has taken the 'high quality, low impact' tourism route and if you're not yet 'gamed-out', a number of reserves and national parks fill nearly a fifth of the country, including Chobe close to the above border post, as well as Moremi Wildlife Reserve in the Okavango Delta, the Central Kalahari Game Reserve and the incredible Makgadikgadi Salt Pans. If you've chosen to string out the impending end of the road, the only entry into **Namibia** outside of the Caprivi Strip is at Mamuno, west of the Central Kalahari Game Reserve.

MOZAMBIQUE

One of Africa's oldest former colonies, **Mozambique** was never the jewel in Portugal's crown and ended up more exploited and less developed than most. As elsewhere, independence led to a ruinous civil war (stirred by neighbouring countries) from which Mozambique is still recovering.

On a bike the country's sole attraction is its comparatively undeveloped **coastline**. Along with a visit to Ilha de Mozambique, if you've not had your statutory week off by the Indian Ocean yet, then the resorts opposite the Bazaruto Islands near **Vilanculos** in the far south could be what you're after.

Inland you'll find not much more than a hot arid plain until you rise up into the mountains bordering the east side of Lake Nyasa (Lake Malawi). Few people venture here so it's bound to be an adventure.

Like much of the region, the **police** in Mozambique have a reputation for being a little overzealous, so observe the speed limits or pay the price. If pulled over they may want to see all the usual papers.

The infrastructure in Mozambique may not have got quite as trashed as Angola's, but both of these countries share the menace of **landmines**. It's why most overlanders still view Mozambique as a short transit rather than a place to explore.

If time, money or will are drying up, **cross into South Africa** at Ressano-Garcia (95km northwest of Maputo) for Lemombo (Kotmatipoort) south of the famous Kruger Park. Coming into Mozambique, visas are expensive; they're cheaper via Swaziland.

Some 250km upriver from the coast, between Mtambatswala village in Tanzania and Negomano in Mozambique, the **Unity Bridge** across the Rovuma River was inaugurated by the respective presidents. All-weather roads to the crossing may not be complete, but the fact that there's a bridge is half the battle won.

There's another route further inland towards Lake Malawi. Head south from Makambako to Songea, then another 100km south to cross the bridge over the Rovuma (S11° 34.7' E35° 25.7'). **Border formalities** can be rather informal on both sides, but you continue south to Lupilchi (aka: Segunda Congresso or Olivença) for Cobue on Lake Nyasa (Lake Malawi), Metangula and so Lichinga, back on the main road network. You can now strike out for Malawi at Mandimba by Lake Nyasa, or cross at Milange further south, for Zimbabwe via the once infamous Tete Corridor (the road from Zimbabwe to Malawi via the Zambezi bridge at Tete). Or head for the coast at Inhambane to meet the backpackers.

Moz' visa in Lilongwe, Malawi

You can get a 30-day visa at some non-Tanzanian land borders for $90 or in advance in Dar es Salaam or most easily in Lilongwe, Malawi (S13° 57.7' E33° 47.3'). Here bring two photos, one form, 5700MK (under $40). Issued same day.

For a great up-to-date source of information on overland travel in Mozambique, check out 💻 www.mozguide.com.

ZIMBABWE

The US dollar is now the *de facto* currency in Zimbabwe and unlike for white farmers and members of the MDC, **security** for visitors has never been a problem. However, there are a lot of poor people and beggars on the streets of Harare or Victoria Falls. They aren't dangerous, just the product of Mugabe's disastrous Land Reform Programme.

Police, riding and currency

The **police** in their khaki uniforms are usually educated, polite and speak English; the paramilitary police in dark blue outfits with ZRP flashes may not be as polite but despite what you might think, you won't be robbed blind by the authorities. **Roadblocks** are plentiful and you may occasionally be asked for a little food or drink, but the outright solicitation of bribes is rare.

Take care though, **speed traps** abound and Zimbabwe has instituted a system of road tolls – usually with a police-manned toll gate just outside most towns. As a biker you'll be waved through most of these.

Although the US dollar is now the currency, you can also use the South African rand or Botswanan pula, especially in the west and south. US dollars come from ATMs in all major cities. You'll need lots of **small denomination** notes for the toll roads you can't dodge – usually one dollar.

Zambia to Zimbabwe via Victoria Falls

Leaving Lusaka it's a 500km ride to **Livingstone** which has picked up on the 'adrenalin' activities offered over the border at the tourist resort of Victoria Falls. Accommodation for backpackers and overlanders can be found at places like *Fawlty Towers*, *Jollyboys Backpackers* behind the Livingstone Museum, or *Maramba River Lodge*, out of town, quiet and safe.

Victoria Falls can be an easy border. After checking out of Zambia you cross the bridge over the Zambezi from which tourists can be seen hurling themselves into the abyss below. Once on the Zimbabwean side, park up and enter the little office to get your visa. Be prepared to pay $55 for that; $55 for your TIP (carnets aren't valid but give it a go); more for insurance if you don't have a Yellow Card, a Road Access fee, possibly a Carbon Tax and whatever else they've dreamt up since.

Victoria Falls, Hwange and Bulawayo

Victoria Falls is the name of both the waterfall and the small Zimbabwean resort. Accommodation ranges from five-star hotels to basic camping at the municipal campsite (S17° 55.5′ E25° 50.2′) or national park lodges. There are a few fast food joints in town, but make sure you spend an evening at *The Boma* to get a taste of the wildlife you couldn't eat at home without getting raided by the RSPCA.

Food and fuel are plentiful at the Falls, although for spare parts or mechanics you'll need to get to Hwange, 100km south. Hwange lends its name to Zimbabwe's largest national park. They say there's only one place to stay in **Hwange** town and that's the *Baobab Hotel* (S18° 20.65′ E26° 30.2′) on top of the hill to the north of the main road to Bulawayo.

Carrying on east from Hwange leads to Lake Kariba and the small resort of Mlibizi, the lake's southwestern terminal for the ferry. Passing by Mlibizi is the road to Binga where you'll find another little piece of waterside paradise called *Masumu River Lodge* (S17° 35.4′ E27° 25.3′) right by the lake.

Bulawayo is a lovely quiet city with wide open streets and a relaxed, friendly atmosphere. There's a municipal **campsite** (S20° 09.5′ E28° 35.6′), but a better choice might be some of the small lodges in the southeastern suburbs, such as *Burkes' Paradise*. Having refreshed yourself in Bulawayo, you're ready for quite possibly your last African border crossing into South Africa.

SOUTHERN AFRICA ONLINE

What some grandly call overlanding is simply recreation to many South Africans. They also benefit from minimal carnet or visa issues across southern Africa right up to DRC and Kenya. As in Australia, a huge off-road scene exists with books, DVDs, tours, detailed GPS routes and of course forums.

Although aimed at 4x4s, the **South African Overland Forum** covers six country categories plus the South African former homelands, medical and GPS chat. 💻 www.overland.co.za.

SELLING BIKES IN OR FROM SOUTH AFRICA

Selling a foreign-registered bike in South Africa at the end of your ride will attract approximately 65% tax. This doesn't apply to SA residents returning home after more than a year with a bike in their name for that time, unless it was registered before 2000. There are also restrictions on selling it on again within two years. For the full story see 💻 www.sars.gov.za.

Coming the other way, selling a South African-registered bike in the UK for example, will be subject to VAT of 20% plus 10% import tax, along with a not-too-stringent test of roadworthiness.

FLYING A BIKE OUT OF SOUTH AFRICA

Flying my TTR home from Cape Town after riding down through Africa was just about as easy as sending a parcel home. On arrival I contacted Air Menzies (AMI) who'd been mentioned on the HUBB. They advised me to buy my ticket home, then drop the TTR to the AMI's depot (S33° 57.7′ E18° 35.6′) the day before.

Here I removed the front wheel, mudguard, screen and handlebars to make the package fit on a pallet with the wheel and luggage stowed around it (see right). The tank was half full, the tyres weren't deflated but the battery was disconnected. They then nailed the forks in place with wooden blocks and strapped everything down.

The bike and gear weighed in at 131kg for which I was charged 8500 rand (£670; they take cash only from private customers) and directed to the nearby customs office for carnet stamping. They also inspected the bike, then the Airway Bill and a Dangerous Goods certificate were issued and I got a lift back to my airport motel. Job done.

On the way home I recognised the BA flight number on the Air Way Bill was the same as my flight, but a few days later, so it was strange to be flying home thinking my bike could be in the hold.

The tracking page on BA's website confirmed my bike had landed in the UK, so I nipped off to BA Cargo in a van, where the staff assisted in the straightforward process of customs clearance (as personal effects, only the bike ownership papers were needed), and released the bike.

KEN THOMAS

Zambia to Zimbabwe via Chirundu

Chirundu border post is about 150km southeast of Lusaka and after passing the turn-off for Livingstone, you start your descent towards the Zambezi River and the border. Being the main trade route between Lusaka and Harare, it can be blocked for days by overturned or trapped lorries. If you look over the edge you'll see the wrecks of trucks that didn't make the bends.

Entering Zimbabwe at Chirundu finds you close to various safari and hunting areas that bound the western edge of Mana Pools National Park. This is a truly amazing wilderness area for walks or canoe safaris. The park charges at least $20 per person for campsites that really are in a wilderness, so the wildlife can be a concern, if they let you in at all. You'll need to pay in Marangora before heading back into the park along the 70km of dirt to Nyamepi Parks Office. From Makuti you can take a ride down to Kariba where a ferry may be waiting to take you all the way to the lake's southwestern end at Mlibizi (about $280 full board with bike; 22 hours; 🖥 www.kariba ferries.com). Otherwise, carry on towards Harare.

Harare is a bland city laid out in a grid fashion, rather like Bulawayo. The Rufaro Stadium is where Bob Marley and Paul Simon played during Zimbabwe's 1980 independence celebrations; there hasn't been a lot to celebrate since. From Harare you can ride south-east and enter Mozambique at Nyamapanda or go directly east to visit Mutare, Mount Nyangani and the beautiful Vumba mountains before crossing into Mozambique.

Zimbabwe to South Africa via Beitbridge

Both routes south from Harare and Bulawayo end at the hot, dusty town of **Beitbridge**, the major crossing between Zimbabwe and **South Africa**. It's well known for its crippling summer heat and the huge volume of traffic that passes through during the holiday seasons, so knowing this you may want to use a less busy border. For you the process is relatively simple but can take hours.

On the South African side show your carnet if you've come from Zimbabwe or Mozambique (no need to show it or get it stamped if you've come from Botswana or Namibia). Basic **third party insurance** is included in the price of fuel. If staying for a while comprehensive insurance is available.

TTR on the finishing line. © Ken Thomas

Once clear of Beitbridge or any other border with the adjacent countries, you'll be on some of the best roads in Africa and suddenly find yourself the slowest thing on the road whilst still being the target for every speed cop with a twitchy finger, but try as they might they can't touch you now. The journey is over and the end (or turning point) is in sight.

LATIN AMERICA ROUTE OUTLINES

6

Of the three continents covered in this book, the countries south of the US border offer the easiest destination in terms of language and documentation, along with about as much geographical diversity as the planet can handle. For North Americans in particular, Latin America also conjures up images of banditry and corrupt officials. Living standards and the state of security vary greatly from country to country or even regionally but, as usual, once you actually ride there the reality is far more benign.

Above all, compared to parts of Africa and Asia, the lack of a **carnet and most visas** in advance greatly simplifies border crossings, particularly in South America, though in Central America they still like to make a meal of a simple crossing. A **yellow fever certificate** may be required at some borders.

Right across the region a temporary vehicle import permit (TIP) is readily issued and usually lasts three months. Just remember to cancel your TIP before leaving a country; it's not always demanded but if you come back your bike will still be registered and you could have problems. The lack of an expensive carnet also makes **buying a bike** possible, either locally or more easily off another foreigner, enabling a fly-in trip which time or budget might otherwise forbid. Check the tips on the Horizons Unlimited South America forum, the best resource for riding down here.

The cost of living is not always so modest and compared to the US, in most places **fuel** will be more expensive. And whatever the season (see p283), there's a decent network of sealed roads so a dual sport bike isn't necessary (though there's as much off-road action as you can cram between the knobs of a TKC). Most will find the crazy local driving standards adventure enough, particularly in Peru.

No surprise that the **US dollar** is the most useful hard currency and is even the actual currency in El Salvador, Panama and Ecuador. For other local places, wait until you're in the country and then change just enough to get you to an ATM where you'll get the regular exchange rate, although the exception is Venezuela, where a currency black market thrives. Above all, outside Brazil and the Guianas, knowing or learning some **Spanish** will transform your ride and reduce 'gringo' taxes. Early on, consider parking up for a month and attending a school. It's an easy language to learn.

Mexico and Central America

Mexico has been going through a bad patch these last few years and although problems still exist, they're mainly in the north in places like Juarez, so plan to get clear of the border zone on day one. The crossing into Mexico is actually easy and efficient, and little notice will be taken of you on the US side if you're a US citizen.

South of the border

Mexico immigration issues a **tourist card** (FMT; *forma migratoria para tourista, transmigrante*; or FM3 for multiple entry) valid for 180 days. It can also be acquired in advance from Mexican consulates. Once in the country it's rare to show your FMT, and unlike elsewhere in the world, the police may be more interested in a driving licence (*licencia*) than a passport.

Unless making an excursion to Baja, around Sonora, or staying within the 'Free Zone' close to the border, you'll need to buy a **temporary import permit** sticker by showing proof of ownership (original US title), vehicle registration (not the same as title in the US), your passport, driver's licence and proof of Mexican vehicle insurance. The TIP (*Declaración de Ingreso de Vehiculo Automotivo*) costs around $50 with a $400 bond (less for pre-2007 bikes) deposited with the *Banjercito* bank (🖳 www.banjercito.com.mx) with a credit card. On leaving Mexico make sure you cancel the TIP and get a refund from the *Banjercito* (not present at smaller borders), otherwise you may run into trouble returning into Mexico which has computerised the TIP process.

Vehicle insurance (*seguro de vehiculo*) is required and unlike further south, needs to be taken seriously; you're looking at around $130 a month or not much more for six months. Following an accident everyone's considered guilty until proven innocent, and having insurance can be the difference between having your bike impounded, or moving on. Insurance from a Mexican provider is easily obtained at the border or over the web from places like 🖳 www.mexinsure.com, 🖳 www.mexpro.com or 🖳 mexadventure.com.

If you have an accident in Mexico, immediately contact your insurance provider who usually has a legal advisor who can help you in negotiations with the police. Don't sign anything before involving your insurance company, especially settlement agreements with other parties, as they could invalidate your insurance. These companies and many more in North America can sell residents **vehicle recovery insurance** valid throughout Central America. A relay of local providers will shuttle you back up to the border and though it won't be a seamless transit as in the States, you will be recovered. Without it you can of course organise an informal recovery, as you would elsewhere.

On the road in Mexico

Riding in Mexico is reasonably sane, though chaos can reign in urban areas plus the usual livestock and night riding hazards. Roads often have no hard shoulder and asphalt can stop suddenly. Truck drivers also have a habit of

AN AMERICAN IN MEXICO

I lived in Mexico for a year and found it to be safe. Yes petty theft occurs, and yes drug smugglers get killed in horrible ways, but the average tourist will feel safe and welcomed. You won't be shot at while riding your bike in Mexico. Has it ever happened? Sure; same can be said for the US.

Now the important stuff! Smiles, *holas*, *buenos dias*, *buenas tardes*, *buenas noches*, *por favors* and *gracias* go a long way. Get a **Mexican Spanish phrasebook** and practice the basics. If nothing else say *hola*, smile and look people in the eye. Mexico is a slower paced society too, so it's rude to rush or be too direct. Start a question with salutations or pleasantries then fire away, you'll get a better response.

If you're lost, asking for the next location is best. Mexicans think it rude to not have an answer, even if it's the wrong one, plus many haven't travelled more than a village or two away. In cities I ask for the next biggest city and often ask someone again just to verify (see p141 for more). For **GPS** I use routeable bicimaps (⌨ www.bicimapas.com.mx), plus the Guia Roji paper atlas already mentioned.

Mexico is a cash society. If businesses accept cards they're probably over-priced tourist joints. The easiest and safest way to get cash is from an ATM; let your bank know you'll be in Mexico. You might pay a transaction fee so get the maximum each time.

If you offer a gift to a Mexican they'll say no, then expect you to offer it again when they will accept. Works the same if receiving.

Almost anything can be haggled over except at stores, fuel and tolls. At a market it's expected. For a cheap hotel, ask for *habatacion mas barato* or *economico*.

Expect to pay for a public toilet and bring your own tissues or use a restaurant toilet when you can. Fuel station attendants are paid with tips; they'll let you pump but give them a few pesos or stop shy of a round figure and let them keep the change. Food store baggers also survive on tips and as in the US, 15% is normal at restaurants.

Accept that the boundaries of personal space are smaller than in the US, so when lines form be assertive or they'll pass you by.

Photocopy your important papers and show them to the cops if stopped. After that give a copy of your driving licence. By law they can't keep your passport so never even show it. If you've done nothing wrong wait it out; insist they write a ticket or let you go. They're waiting for a bribe. I resisted a transit cop in Puerto Vallarta for ten minutes, then he gave up and only transit cops tend to give tickets. On the road Mexican drivers are fast but alert and compared to the US traffic rules are less rigid which can be liberating once you get in the swing. And try as many types of **foods** as possible. The variety will blow you away. The best meals and prices come from street vendors.

BILL EAKINS ⌨ www.butlermaps.com

© THEDARIENPLAN.COM

LATIN AMERICA – ROUTE OUTLINES

signalling left to indicate that it's safe for you to pass – or do they plan to move out or turn left? Engage your telepathic sensors before you attempt to pass. Roads through towns have speed bumps (*topes*) that are often unmarked and can frighten the suspension if ridden over too fast.

In rural areas here and in Central America, delays occur when militant locals set up road blocks in response to some injustice or complaint; a frequent Latino way of expressing grudges with authorities. Handle it right and as a foreigner you might slip through, but don't count on it. Just because the protestors aren't state officials doesn't mean they're inconsequential.

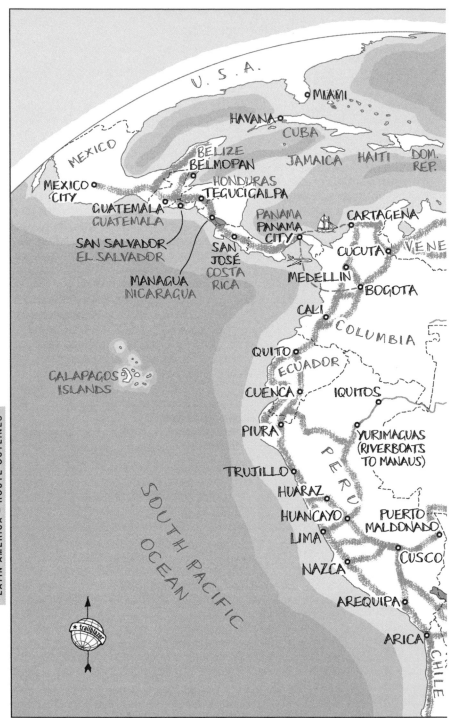

Main overland routes across Central and South America

You'll find **fuel** at the state-run Pemex stations. Nationwide, **ATMs** take most credit cards but it's also possible to pay in dollars and get change in pesos at the normal rate for most services, including fuel.

In Mexico **police checkpoints** are more of a problem than the military equivalent. Heading north towards the US, they're looking for drugs, so a sniffer dog may make the rounds. Police are less professional, especially around Mexico City. To avoid that area get the national road atlas, the **Guia Roji** (🖥 www.guiaroji.com.mx) at around $15. It gets updated annually.

Riding South

Baja can be regarded as a recreational extension of California that also happens to be an easy introduction to Mexico, with ferries from the southern tip to the mainland. Bush camping is easy and safe, beaches are easily accessible and remote deserts and mountains make for great adventures.

Crossing is easier at the smaller border posts like Tecate or Mexicali in the east, rather than busy Tijuana. Make sure you do the full tourist card/insurance/TIP deal here as detailed earlier; it's easier than at La Paz where ferries leave daily to the mainland from the Pichilingue terminal. One docks at Mazatlan after a 12-hour crossing; the other at Topolobampo (six hours). For route planning get the Baja Almanac (🖥 www.baja-almanac.com).

Mainland Mexico is not like Baja. While remote areas can certainly still be found, it's harder to locate discreet **bush camps** as towns and private fenced land becomes more common. Picturesque beaches can be found all the way down the mainland side of the Gulf of California which also allows exploring of the Sonoran Desert. On the Caribbean coast Mayan ruins in the south offer some of the finest archeological sites in North America. Palenque is considered one of the best, but travelling into the **Yucatán** you'll have no end of great choices.

Tolls and more checkpoints

On the way south another big mainland feature are the **toll roads**. Main highways have toll booths and can end up being pretty expensive. Again, watch your change from the toll attendants as you do at fuel stations.

There are **military checkpoints** all over mainland Mexico, but especially along the coast directly west of Mexico City and in the state of Chiapas on the Pacific border with Guatemala. Just as in Baja, the main reason for these posts is to limit drug and illegal immigrant traffic. The soldiers are often pleasant and may want to see your paperwork as well as to perform a cursory search but asking for *mordidas* (bribes) is extremely unusual. The police aren't quite the same.

MEXICO & CENTRAL AMERICA: RELATIVE FUEL PRICES

Outside of Mexico, the countries of Central America are small and distances modest, but everywhere except in Panama gasoline or petrol is more expensive than in the US.

In Mexico prices are about 20% more than the US, but Belize is double. El Salvador and Guatemala are 10% over the US, Nicaragua and Honduras 25% and Costa Rica 30% more.

In Colombia gasoline is about the same. Of course, one currency crash or a fuel crisis will mess up these figures, but it's a start.

BELIZE AND GUATEMALA 275

BELIZE

Crossing from Mexico to Belize you pass from a Latino to a Caribbean culture which itself has diverse origins and influences. As the former colony of British Honduras, **English** is the official language here which can make things easier except when you need to act dumb. There's great **diving** and kayaking on the coast, and inland the jungle offers more Mayan ruins.

Bringing a bike into Belize involves nothing more than showing proof of vehicle ownership along with passport and a driving licence. Your domestic licence will be accepted for visits under three months; for longer stays an IDP (see p22) is required, but on any big ride a 'disposable' IDP is handy anyway. They'll also require three copies of all your documents (title, registration, passport and licence) as well local **insurance** which costs about $50 for three months; you'll get an ICB insurance sticker. As with much of Latin America, the **temporary import permit** is valid for 90 days. On leaving the country you may be charged a departure tax, though this is more usual at airports.

Belize isn't heavily populated, with only 20,000 in the capital, **Belmopan**. Roads between the few cities aren't busy, but few are paved. **Driving standards** are consistent with developing countries and vehicles are often in bad shape – the two seem to go hand in hand. In the **rainy season** from June to November downpours transform the top layer into a tread-clogging greasy mire. For **fuel**, fill up in Mexico and before Guatemala and you'll save a bit.

Travel is easy until you close in on the Guatemalan border. **Police** tend to keep a low profile and in rural areas are virtually non-existent, although Belize City has a bad reputation.

Bush camping is difficult in Belize mainly due to the amount of private land or the density of the jungle. When on jungle tracks it can be hard to find enough space to camp, though traffic is sparse in many areas, so camping by the road itself may be possible.

GUATEMALA

Guatemala gets a bad rap and border experience can support this. Mexico and Belize are all very well, but in poorer Guatemala border officials can be surly and make heavy demands on your paperwork.

As elsewhere you'll need proof of vehicle ownership along with passport and driving licence. Three copies of each document are required and can be made at the main border posts. Things might start with a **fumigation** for a few quetzals, and if entering from Mexico you may be asked to show the receipt for cancelling your Mexican TIP. A passport stamp comes next and may cost a few pesos or quetzals, but no motor **insurance** is required. Show a US driving licence or an IDP and buy a tourist permit for some 40 quetzals.

Temporary vehicle importation permits are issued for another 40 quetzals and last for 90 days with extensions available. Since Guatemala is part of the Central America Four Border Control Agreement (CA4) with Honduras, El Salvador and Nicaragua, you should be covered for 90 days for all of these countries on immigration, but in practice there seems to be no reciprocity on vehicle imports, at least for foreigners, so you'll have to repeat the procedure in each country. Just like in Mexico you'll be issued a sticker which needs to be surrendered on export. All up the border experience comes to around $15.

LATIN AMERICA – ROUTE OUTLINES

On the road

The CA13 highway heading north to south is in good shape, and the Western Highway from Belize may be the same. **Guatemala City** is the largest city in Central America and the traffic is horrendous. To add to the torment, just as in Mexico, large and often unmarked **speed bumps** (*topes* or *tumulos*) are ready to catch the unwary. Guatemalan drivers in the capital are aggressive, but elsewhere driving is no worse than usual.

Once away from the border and Guatemala City, **police** tend to keep a low profile and checkpoints aren't too common. **Fuel** is easy to come by with branded stations from Shell and Texaco provide most of the service.

Attractions in Guatemala centre on the **Mayan ruins** and ancient sites, Tikal being best known. There's camping here in a non-fenced site with a night watchman. North of Tikal, Uaxactun can prove a challenge to reach, but offers entry into the Mayan Biosphere Reserve as well as the ruins of Petén. Finca Ixobel, just south of Poptún near the Belize border, offers nice camping, good food, wi-fi and tour services.

HONDURAS

Entry is the same story except they might want four copies of each of your documents, as well as four copies of each of the import permit documents issued at the border and the stamps in your passport. Facilities for money changing and copies are available at the borders, as are pushy fixers. No proof of **insurance** is required to leave the border and the 90-day vehicle *temporal* costs some 235 lempira.

Some riders report bribes being demanded at Honduran borders, especially El Florido east of Guatemala City where you may also pay a foreign licence plate fee of L435 and a few more to the customs. Membership of CA-4 makes little odds and the usual vehicle import hoops still have to be cleared with space-consuming stamps in your passport on entering and leaving the country. Total border costs are around $35 for vehicle import fees.

There'll often be a police checkpoint shortly after the border, watching for infractions and demanding a copy of your TIP. Making extra copies at the border can alleviate hassle here. Leaving the country, some travellers end up paying a couple of dollars for a passport stamp and a few dollars more to fill out a customs form, others pay nothing which you assume is the norm.

Honduras is very mountainous in the west where roads are narrow and the going slow, especially behind heavy trucks. Overland travel is more difficult in the lowlands to the east of the country as there are few roads.

Police checkpoints are frequent along the Pan-American highway approaching borders. Usually you'll just be asked for your papers, but some officers will go further or just be a pain. On the CA-3 highway from Choluteca to the Nicaraguan border at Guasaule some get stopped half-a-dozen times.

Because of these well known hassles in Honduras, some travellers cross from Guatemala into El Salvador and from there try to nip across Honduras to Nicaragua in a couple of hours. It's less than 200km but El Amatillo border is notorious and the Honduran police know your game; a lot of shakedowns occur on this section. Use any other border for Honduras.

In the pine forests in Honduras **bush camping** spots can easily be found, but near towns it gets difficult and security can be a concern.

EL SALVADOR

With well-paved roads for the main arteries, El Salvador can be crossed quickly and navigated easily. Along with many familiar US fast food franchises and the US dollar currency, **beaches** are the major draw here, with every beach running six-foot plus surf between March and October.

At the border it's the same story as before, but with only two copies of everything required. No one asks for **insurance**, but it is a good idea, as is an IDP. Entry permits last 90 days and extensions are possible. Fumigation costs a couple of bucks but only happens at some crossings. Otherwise, there's a $5 road use fee. Fixers or *tramitadores* inhabit all borders and can be helpful, especially if you don't speak Spanish. **Police** do set up checkpoints, but dodgy dealings are less common than neighbouring countries.

El Salvador is the most densely populated country in Central America so **bush camping** can be quite a challenge. Beach camping is possible in certain areas, but check with the locals. Since the beaches are the main tourist attraction, there are many hotels along the coast.

NICARAGUA

These days Nicaragua has good roads, especially in the west, and travel is easy. As in El Salvador and Panama, you'll find the familiar American fast food joints and a much more developed feel than in Honduras or Guatemala.

At the border it's another Xerox hoedown with three copies of everything. Buy **insurance** for around $12 a month and a 90-day TIP once you've shown your *boleta de revision turismo* or **tourist card** that's surrendered on exit. **Fuel** is at familiar fuel stations like Shell.

Police hassle is less common here and experiences vary greatly from polite hellos to full shakedowns. Nicaragua seems to be split down the middle; the west is mainly Spanish-speaking with a well maintained infrastructure and some charming colonial towns, while the English-speaking east is a wild and remote jungle, once the stronghold of the Sandinistas and with less intact infrastructure. With fewer ancient ruins in Nicaragua, the interesting historical sites are old cities like León and Grenada. Both are well worth exploring, with a wonderful colonial ambience as well as great restaurants and charming (if expensive) hotels. **Volcanoes** dominate the skyline especially between lakes Managua and Nicaragua.

There was a spate of so called 'express kidnappings' in Managua, where tourists were briefly abducted (usually from unauthorised taxis) and led to an ATM. On a bike you ought to be immune to that, but even on a good day Managua itself can be difficult to get around. Protests are frequent and roads get closed by the police.

COSTA RICA

By Central American standards Costa Rica is a mainstream tourist destination, and as such might offer a bit of a respite if you're still finding the going hard. North Americans and backpackers fly here to enjoy regular vacations; they wouldn't dream of taking in most of the neighbouring countries. There's lots to see here, but with the usual tourist-related issues which include the relatively greater cost of living. There are several biosphere reserves, zip line canopy tours, volcano hikes and fabulous sandy beaches.

To get in it's the usual procedure: they want vehicle ownership (original US title) and registration along with passport, driving licence and your mother-in-law's birth certificate; three copies of each. **Insurance** costs around $14 a month. Where it's required, fumigation costs $2 so if there were any bugs stowing away when you left Mexico, by now they're well and truly extinct. Borders teem with fixers and as elsewhere, before you hire anyone, agree on a price, set some conditions under which they won't be paid (if extra costs are incurred, for instance) and don't pay until the border dance is complete. Also don't hand over any of your documentation; often they'll try to get things going in a second line while you're waiting in the first. A little patience here can be invaluable and avoid situations where your documents are held to ransom. On leaving fill in a form to cancel your vehicle import permit.

DOING THE DARIEN: PANAMA TO SOUTH AMERICA

La Panamericana comes to a stop at Yaviza alongside the so-called **Darien Gap**. The next nearest town is Turbo in Colombia, 300km north of Medellín. It may seem absurd that over 27,000 kilometres of road are separated by less than 90 kilometres of jungle and swamp, when just up the road a canal nearly as long was built a century ago to link two oceans. Colombia being the world's biggest producer of cocaine may be why the world's biggest consumer of that narcotic – the US – is happy for any crossing to remain plugged.

In 2014 another RoRo ferry service started running between Colon and Turbo in Colombia. Initially it had great prices, but within a year it folded. The fact is it's a long crossing and the demand just wasn't sustainable. Commercial goods go by sea, people fly and cocaine finds its own way.

That leaves you with putting yourself and the bike on a sailing boat the 500km to or from **Cartagena**, or air freighting and flying out of Tucomen airport in Panama City. You can also ship your bike in a container, but for such a short stretch this is the worst of both worlds; use air freight or get on a boat.

Do your research with the **boat options**. It's a couple of days at sea and some smaller boats are overloaded, ill-equipped or may have issues with customs. In Panama the Mamallena hostel 🖳 www.mamallena.com acts as a broker for smaller boats, and for many years the *Stahlratte*, a 120-foot converted schooner, has generated few complaints from riders but doesn't run all year. It uses a jetty just east of **Carti** airstrip (N09° 27.38' W78° 58.75') 140km northeast of Panama City. Head along the Pan-Am past Chepo and after El Llano and three steel bridges, turn

north at the sign. It's all sealed but hilly and at one point you cough up $10 to enter the Kuna Indian reservation. At Carti airstrip head for a concrete pier a hundred metres left of the airstrip hut. If the ship's there and expecting you, it'll come in and winch your bike on deck. On all these boats your bike gets stowed on deck so get a cover and an oily spray.

It's about 30 hours sailing, plus stop offs on the San Blas islands. On the fourth day you berth at the Club Nautico de Manga marina in **Cartagena** (N10° 24.72' W75° 32.48') where the crew help sort out the immigration. The Stahlratte costs over $1000 which perhaps not coincidentally is the same as Girag air freight, but you save on your flight and the snorkelling comes free.

Air freighting with Girag can be organised in a few hours, no reservations required, nor even possible. Ride out to the cargo area of Tocumen airport, east of the city and at the gate the guard will know what you're after and direct you towards Girag's offices. Leave your bike there early in the morning without a full tank and it might be in Bogota next day, though two to three days seems more usual. At the cargo warehouse shrink wrap your luggage for security and make sure you take a photo of your bike; you'll read occasional complaints about damage as well as delays. The total price is at least $1000 whatever the bike's weight, a taxi back to town is $25 and a flight for yourself is another $500.

At Bogota's international cargo terminal allow half a day to get through customs. Flying north *from* Bogota it's said the staff are a bit more tuned in, while arriving in Panama the immigration is less so.

PANAMA

For much of the last century the US controlled the **Panama Canal**, and these days Panama feels like a state of the USA. The **US dollar** is the currency, highways abound, ex-pats roam the streets and there's a lot of construction.

Vehicle import, you know the drill by now: **insurance** is bought at the border for $15 a month, while temporary vehicle importation permits (TIP) are good for just 30 days, but can be extended at customs. If you're freighting out of Panama it's vital that this document is completed correctly and that they know the difference between your licence plate (registration number) and your VIN (chassis ID plate). As mentioned at the start of the book, it helps to highlight the long VIN on your vehicle ownership documents (or copies) with a marker pen so it's clearly distinguishable from your licence plate. Fumigation costs at least a dollar and individuals buy a $10 tourist card plus a $1 sticker for the passport. These stickers are sometimes offered by bystanders, probably looking for a tip.

Once on the way, checkpoints tend to be staged closer to the border with Costa Rica so watch your speed within the first few miles. It's possible to store bikes at Panama customs in both David and Panama City for around $1 a day, though some have had mixed results with the security in Panama City. The famous canal is the main attraction here, offering impressive views of huge ships gliding past (the Chinese are planning something similar in Nicaragua).

Panama City itself has modern high-rises with the feel of Dubai in some places, but in the old town squatters live in bombed-out buildings with no roofs while the Pan-American highway is in pretty good condition. Road signs aren't common though and finding your way can mean asking the locals. The ride from David north to Boquete is well worth the scenic views and visiting Parque Nacional Volcán Barú makes a great end to that ride.

NOT RIDING BUT DROWNING

Back in 2006 yachties were just getting into taking bikers over to Panama. With my visa about to expire, in haste I accepted a lift from a 60-year-old Italian, 'Alberto'. It's ironic that having spent three wonderful months in then 'dangerous' Colombia, I should have my most terrifying experience leaving.

I'd ignored warnings about Alberto's people-smuggling activities, incompetence and hostility, putting it down to rivalry. But shortly after we set sail, with my Enfield lashed to the foredeck, things started to worry me. The compass light and the autopilot didn't work and the anchor was inadequate, a faulty alternator disabled access to computerised sea charts and dirty diesel was clogging the injectors. These weren't my observations – what do I know? – but Alberto's! Then the weather turned, snorkelling was off and we spent two days sitting out a gale. Alberto started behaving like a caged animal, snarling abusively, and during a lull late one afternoon made a desperate break for Porvenir island, near Carti.

I still recall the terror of drowning that night as the storm intensified and the boat drifted towards a reef when the anchor wouldn't hold. When he wasn't either wailing with despair or rigid with panic, Alberto screamed abuse at me for getting him in this mess. Luckily, some islanders appeared on the jetty and waved torches to guide us in, but it took three hours to get safely ashore.

The next morning, still far from the agreed drop-off point, Alberto ordered me off his boat. I didn't hesitate. A deal was made with some fishermen and $30 later, I was dropped at a Kuna village on the Panamanian mainland from where I chugged up to Panama City, thrilled to be safely back on two wheels.

JACQUI FURNEAUX

South America

WITH MARK HARFENIST

Riding around Central America isn't so difficult if you're based in North America, and it's a great way of dipping your toe into the overland experience. In South America you're overlanding for real, if for no other reason than you can't nip home inexpensively. But when you add it all up, South America is among the best motorcycling destinations on the planet. An extreme range of environments await you, from barely-penetrable jungle, hyper-arid deserts, wildlife-rich wetlands and fern-clad mesas, the shimmering volcano-dotted altiplano and the snowbound passes across the Andes. Did I miss anything? Yes, a rich pre-Conquest heritage, nearly a single language, fewer tedious borders than Central America and visa issues only for los Americanos.

That leaves only **crazy drivers**, shaky infrastructure in the poorer Andean countries, and the **fear of crime** in some cities, all of which can either be avoided or taken on with your wits about you. **Costs** will average out at around $70/day, less in the Andean countries and more down south or in Brazil.

Routes in South America

There are thirteen countries in South America, but most overlanders are satisfied visiting about half. They follow the **Pan-American Highway** along the Andean-Pacific axis where Colombia leads to Ecuador, Peru and Bolivia where you criss-cross the Chile-Argentine border to Ushuaia and **Tierra del Fuego**. That done, many head for **Buenos Aires** and ship out.

In taking that ride of 10,000 miles or more, it's not impossible to rise 13,000 feet or four kilometres in a single day which can mess with rider and machine, but mile-for-mile this route delivers uninterrupted spectacle and if time, funds or will are limited, you'll certainly see the best of South America this way.

From the **inland borders** of Colombia, Ecuador and Peru no reliable roads lead into the Amazon basin. Linked by an hour's ride, Nauta and **Iquitos** are in the heart of this area in eastern Peru, but both are only accessible by boat or air. So in Colombia or Venezuela you must decide: PanAm, the Caribbean route via the Guianas, or straight down the middle through the Amazon.

LATIN AMERICA – ROUTE OUTLINES

SHIPPING FROM US TO SOUTH AMERICA DIRECT

Not everyone is inspired to tackle the multiple borders of Central America, only to pay a grand to continue to South America.

If you want to head straight to the main event, from the US **Miami** is the best port to organise shipping to Cartagena, Rio, Buenos Aires (BA) or even Santiago. No need to ride there, they can pick up your bike from anywhere in the US; budget on at least $1200 to get the job done and see what bike freighting specialist SamericaXplorer has to offer on the usual forums. Coming from Europe see p299.

On the way back see if Dakar Motos in BA (🖥 www.dakarmotos.com) can help or check out the HUBB's shipping database.

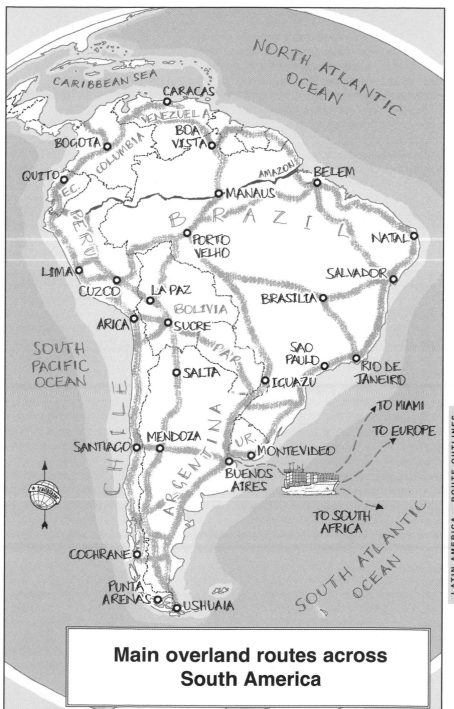

Main overland routes across South America

SOUTH AMERICA: RELATIVE FUEL PRICES

Taking US fuel prices as a benchmark with 95-octane gasoline at 70 cents a litre, as things stand now in South America you're paying less than a cent in Venezuela. In Ecuador it's about two-thirds of the US price and in Bolivia three quarters (where you're able to pay local rates, see p290). In Colombia it's about the same as the US or half as much again up north, same as in Guyana. In Brazil it's 20% more, in Chile 30% and Peru 50%. Gasoline is up to double or more in Surinam, Argentina and Uruguay and in French Guiana you pay around $2 a litre, about the same as western Europe.

In Ecuador, Bolivia and Peru gasoline at octanes above 90 can be hard to find in rural areas, and what you do get in the mid-80s can be hard on lean-burning, high-compression engines. But as long as the fuel is clean and unadulterated, when compared to carburettors, modern computerised electronic fuel injection can compensate for low octane fuel as well as very high altitude.

In Brazil most light vehicles run on E25 'gasohol', composed of 25% cane-based anhydrous ethanol; pure gasoline costs nearly as much as in Guiana. Fuel pumps in Brazil are marked: A for alcohol; D for diesel and G for gasoline. 'Gas' refers to CNG, also widely used. Running a bike on E25 ought not ruin it, but E100 (100% hydrated ethanol) costing around 60% of E25 won't go down so well at the spark plug.

As mentioned elsewhere, fuel prices in remote, roadless states like Amazonas (the far west) can be double those of heavily agricultural or urban states like Mato Grosso, Panara or Sao Paulo.

COLOMBIA

Despite its once notorious reputation, Colombia has become a hit with riders. The idyllic beaches, jagged mountains and verdant jungles were always an attraction and the people welcoming. Roads are sometimes superb, not least when twisting through the Andean sub-ranges, though on occasion riders find themselves tailing long lines of belching trucks crawling up winding grades. Main roads will be paved and may include tolls unless you go out of your way to look for gravel or dirt. There's also at least one bike-friendly hostel, a thriving local riding scene, relatively easy availability of parts and an upbeat air in a country emerging from a long civil war. Expect to spend longer and have more fun in Colombia than you may have expected.

Although most areas in Colombia are considered safe, there's an element of street crime in the cities, and it's still a good idea to ask locally before venturing off the main highways to some of the standard tourist destinations. In some cities the front line between safe and unsafe *barrios* may not be apparent to outsiders. Certain rural routes are still known for banditry which may or may not relate to FARC or other revolutionary activities – particularly in the south.

After Central America, Colombia is a big country but unless you're an amphibious tapir of some kind, you can write off the eastern Amazonian provinces. That leaves the two lofty eastern and western cordilleras which converge to the point of a 'V' at the Ecuadorian border. How you get there is up to you.

Insurance is mandatory in Colombia, and chances are you'll be checked at some point, so either buy a month's worth or be ready with a convincing 'self-generated' document of some sort. In theory this compulsory traffic accident insurance (*Seguro Obligatorio de Accidentes Tráfico* or just SOAT) can be bought in fuel stations, shopping malls and bike shops, but usually for a minimum of

SOUTH AMERICA: CLIMATE AND SEASONS

The immense size of the continent, along with its extreme variations in landforms and altitude tend to make generalisations difficult. The only certainty is that you'll experience a certain amount of uncomfortable weather. With this in mind, let's make a few generalisations.

During the **southern summer** (November to March) storms in southern Brazil, northern Argentina and the altiplano of Bolivia, Peru and Chile are largely thunderstorms rather than unbroken periods of rain. In places they may temporarily disrupt travel, but they're localised; you'll often spy black clouds stalking the altiplano without feeling a drop.

Summer temperatures in the **altiplano** often slip below freezing at night but during winter (May to September) it gets brutally cold, although this is also dry season, and the sun quickly warms the thin air. Take this into account if you camp or use budget lodgings.

At lower elevations throughout southern Brazil, Paraguay, Uruguay and northern Argentina summers tend to be hot and humid. This area can more comfortably be visited during March and April. During winter it gets surprisingly chilly and a damp 10°C/50°F is not uncommon.

Down in Patagonia moisture-laden air runs up along the Pacific slopes of the Andes from Tierra del Fuego through the ice fields and rain forests to the Lakes District of Chile and Argentina before petering out completely around the latitude of Santiago. If trying to pinpoint your own scheduling, this storm track shifts markedly between seasons, hovering between 45 and 55 degrees latitude in summer and 35 to 45 degrees in winter. This produces gorgeous weather in the Chilean Lakes District during summer, after which winter storms roll in. At the same time, areas on the western side of the range south of 45 degrees latitude tend to have damp, chilly summers until the storm track shifts northward. Shielded by the heights of the southern Andes, Patagonia is generally dry, if famously windy. Note the abrupt change as you transit from steppes to mountains just before reaching Ushuaia; the winds die, you're suddenly surrounded by forest, and almost instantly it begins to rain and snow, particularly during summer.

North of the equator, you'll find that there's no real dry season in the Amazon, although there are 'less wet' periods. December to March is generally rainiest; April to November slightly cooler, June to August a bit drier. In Colombia the dry season is most pronounced from January to March; in Andean regions of Ecuador it's June to September, while the rest of the year can be cloudy and cool, obscuring views of the volcanoes. In the Guianas and Venezuela, two rainy seasons prevail: one from October to February with a peak from December onwards, the other April to July. However, with August to October even hotter than the rest of the year, the best travel window is February and March.

These guidelines should be taken with a grain of salt and the influence of altitude; while Cartagena boils, Bogotá can be chilly. No one's managed to come up with an itinerary that visits everywhere in the best season. Crossing the Guianas might be ideal in March, but Angel Falls in neighbouring Venezuela are best in June when the falls are at full tilt. Similarly, no single trip can see the best conditions in Colombia, Ecuador and the Peruvian altiplano.

MARK HARFENIST

a year. But in Cartagena the Sura seguros office may still be doing three months insurance for around $50. It's located on the crossroads of Calle 25 and Carrera 17 or 17A (blue and white sign; aim for N10° 24.94' W75° 32.51'), a ten minute walk north of the Manga marina on the Calle 24 esplanade where you may have arrived from Panama. After Central America, it'll feel pleasantly reassuring to be insured again.

Most motorcycle brands are sold in Colombia and **parts** will be readily available in Bogotá, so if you've been nursing your rig, this is your best opportunity to service it. For routeable **GPS maps** for your satnav look up 🖳 www.mygisco.com or 🖳 www.colrut.com – or of course OSM.

Approaching Cartagena. © jamminglobal.com

Riding around Colombia

For many riders **Cartagena** is their first sight of South America which is a good start as it's said to be one of the continent's most beautiful colonial cities. Not so inspiring is the humid climate and relatively drab hinterland. Just up the road from Manga marina, past the Texaco and over the bridge, is the renovated old walled town of Getsamani where most of the lodgings, bars and cafés are to be found.

Air arrivals are 1000km down the road in the capital **Bogotá,** where the feeling in the safer, upscale barios is of a vibrant and energetic European city, but with a heavy police, military and security guard presence. Situated at around 2600m/8500′, the climate is comfortable after the torpor of Panama or Cartagena. Most riders establish themselves at a hotel before taxi-ing to the airport's cargo zone on the northwest edge of the city to collect the bike from Girag. There'll be some fees to pay and as usual, speaking some Spanish helps, before riding back down Calle 26 into the city. Heading up to Panama, expect arrangements to be as simple; give it half a day.

As is happening elsewhere in the world, to discourage moto-mounted assassins and robbers, local riders must wear **dayglo vests** and helmets bearing license plate numbers matching their bikes. It's said tourists are exempt, but expect to be stopped if not riding in full overland regalia.

Leaving Bogotá by road, all directions are enticing. Routes north toward Bucaramanga and northwest 450km to Medellín are fun, while the same distance over the mountains towards Cali is obvious but clogged with trucks. The less direct and even more scenic route southwest through the Neiva valley had a reputation for FARC activity so ask around first.

Formerly the home of drug cartels, **Medellín** is a common stopover when heading down from the Caribbean coast. The surrounding area is rugged, with ranches and coffee plantations scattered between small villages and colonial towns so the riding is rewarding no matter which way you go.

Cali is another stop for many riders. The well-known riders' hang-out, *Casablanca Hostel* (🖳 www.casablancahostel.com, N03° 28.14′ W76° 31.79′) manages to combine repair services, long-term parking, help with shipping, bike rentals, guided tours and even a micro-brewery into one well-run operation. The owner can also give reliable advice about local roads and routes.

South from Cali, most make a 140-km beeline to beautiful **Popoyán** from where rough roads loop through the mountains to San Agustín and Tierradentro. Enquire locally about safety, but in any case allow at least a couple of days to go exploring.

The day's ride south towards the Ecuadorian border is a cracker: huge, gorge-cut mountains on all sides, deep canyons carrying roiling rivers far below, and always the magical light in which the distant grassy hillsides glow unearthly green. A left off the Pan-Am just before the border at Ipiales takes you to Santuario Del Las Lajas, a short but worthwhile side trip.

LATIN AMERICA – ROUTE OUTLINES

ECUADOR, PERU AND BOLIVIA

Between them these three countries boast some of the most spectacular mountain riding and highest passes in the continent, unfortunately shared with the craziest drivers and treacherous conditions.

In between grand colonial cities like Quito and Sucre, Inca ruins and puffing volcanoes, you get a well-developed tourist infrastructure which adds up to easy travelling and a rich experience on the road through the cordilleras. Heading east for Venezuela and the Guianas? Fast forward to p299.

Colombia-Ecuador border

The main Colombia–Ecuador crossing at Ipiales–Tulcán is open daily from early till 9pm. It may be your first internal border in South America so compared to what went on in Central America, you'll be thrilled by the speed and efficiency. Only single copies of the usual documents are required: passport, vehicle ownership and driving licence. On leaving Colombia you need to cancel your vehicle TIP as you do in most countries here, and in Ecuador fill out a *Tarjeta Andina de Migraciones* (TAM) immigration card, making sure not to lose the half they return to re-present on leaving the country. You can stay for 90 days in any 12-month period, though you may get only a month on arrival. If they ask, say you want *noventa días, por favor*.

In Ecuador the **US dollar** is the currency which simplifies things. Getting some **insurance** is less so as from 2015 they don't do SOATs anymore. Some manage to cross the country without it while others won't get away from a border. You may not be asked to present it at checkpoints but if you have an accident you may well go to jail before it's sorted out.

Ecuador

For such a relatively small country Ecuador has a lot going on; beach and mangrove seacoasts, glaciated volcanoes, pristine island ecosystems, rainforest jungles and cities with yet more colonial splendour. Border formalities are relaxed, services are cheap, and as the American dollar is the currency you can stock up on cash for the weeks or months ahead at any ATM.

Coming from Colombia, the scenery in northern Ecuador resembles what you just left: looming volcanoes and pretty upland farms and villages. A 100km from the border, Ibarra and Otavalo (another 25km) have services and another 100 clicks down the Panamericana takes you over **the equator** just south of Cayambe to **Quito** (2800m/9300') where you can reasonably expect to get completely lost and – if you're very careless or unlucky – robbed too. Local streets are clogged with traffic, but there's a bypass through the hills to the west of town or, once you find it, exploring Quito's old town will have been worth the effort.

Having fought your way back out of Quito, the Parque Nacional Cotopaxi has a road which, though it deteriorates markedly as you follow it uphill, ends at a parking area at about 4800m/15,800'. From here try and stagger another kilometre to the refuge from where, on a clear day, the views over the ash- and snowscapes can be impressive indeed.

Often described as one of Ecuador's highlights, at Latacunga, some 30km south of the Cotopaxi turnoff you'll find the beginning of the famous **Quilatoa Loop** to the west, a day's dirt roading at around 4000m through small highland

Airey bridge in Ecuador © Ken Thomas

towns alongside a crater lake. The scenery is otherworldly and there are ample places to eat and sleep should you decide to spend more than a day up here. Be prepared for cold and the thin air (guidelines on p167).

That said, on a heavy road bike the scenery on the Pan-Am down to Cuenca won't exactly give you nightmares. A couple of hours south of Quito, a left turn in Ambato leads to **Baños** set in a deep canyon at the foot of the 5000m Tungurahua volcano which has lived up to its name – 'Throat of Fire' – since the turn of the century. The surrounding area is well worth exploring, despite the subsequent closure of some back roads, and the town itself is attractive, cheap and friendly.

An interesting alternative to returning to the Pan-Am for Cuenca heads downhill through the canyon and past waterfalls, then takes a right in Puyo onto the E45, a paved road to Macas and a little beyond. Even here in the lowlands you're at 600m, so it gets warm but not blindingly hot. From **Macas** a splendid road winds back up through the Sangay NP over to Guamote, where you rejoin the Pan-Am. Otherwise, continue south on the E45 for 100km to Limon and turn west through deep, jungle-clad valleys over a high pass to Cuenca. As long as it's not raining cats and dogs the route's not difficult.

Back north on the Pan-Am, most will stop in **Cuenca** to admire the picturesque cobblestone, whitewash and red tile Old Town before dropping down to **Loja** and deciding on meeting the Peru border at Macará (180km), up on the coast at Huaquillas (210km), or the less reported dirt route south-east to **San Ignatio** down in the jungle. The tar resumes at Jaen so in good weather allow a couple of days and enough fuel for that one.

Ecuador–Peru border

Depending on what time of day or the week you arrive, the coastal border crossing at Huaquillas/Aguas Verdes near **Tumbez**, Peru can be a little chaotic and intimidating, with the *aduana* done a few miles before at Chacras. Low-level smuggling goes on here and with the 'gringo' element, on a bad day there can be a fair amount of scammery going down with the local entrepreneurs as you make your way to the bridge over the frontier creek (S03° 28.88' W80° 14.59'). The **Peruvian formalities** are done a couple of kilometres down the road. Coming from Peru to Huaquillas, it's said a month's SOAT is obtainable. To buy it, less than 500m from the border, turn north into Santa Rosa past the park; the SOAT office is just after the Banco de Machala (around S03° 28.81' W80° 14.33').

Knowing all this and depending on your destination and the weather, you will find the inland border crossing at **Macara** more relaxed. It's said to be open round the clock and involves crossing the Puente International bridge at S04° 23.58' W79° 57.83', a couple of kilometres southwest of town. (Coming north from Peru, no one mentions insurance and there are no costs.) The first Peruvian town of Suyo is 16km on. In most cases you'll be given 90 days on entry to Peru and even if you don't visit the well known sites at Machu Picchu and Nazca, it's easy to spend a month exploring this country. Wherever you cross, fill out the usual forms and get a SUNAT (*Superintendencia Nacional de Administración Tributaria*) temporary import permit and a two-part form; hand your section back on leaving Peru. You'll need SOAT **insurance** in Peru from a Mapfre bureau (🖳 www.mapfreperu.com, or try 🖳 www.soat.com.pe). A month can cost you $30. Coming from Ecuador, La Positiva Seguros in Piura has been recommended – it's on Lima #544, east of the main cathedral and towards the river (aim for S05° 11.82' W80° 37.52'). Otherwise, you may want to avoid Trujillo where the cops have been known to take an earnest concern in correct paperwork. If starting out from Buenos Aires and looking for insurance to cover Argentina, Chile, Ecuador, Paraguay, Brazil, Bolivia and Peru, see p295.

Without a GPS-equipped bike the best **maps** are a set of three sold by the Touring y Automóvil Club del Peru (🖳 www.touringperu.com.pe). They have offices in major cities, including Piura on Ave. Sánchez Cerro #1237, the Pan-Am main road in the town centre. For your routeable satnavs 🖳 www.perut.org gets the nod.

Peru

Improbable though it seems, Peru has it all but in greater quantities: the deepest canyons; the tallest peaks; uncounted miles of desolate coastal deserts alongside a substantial chunk of Amazon jungle; fantastic biking roads and moderate prices.

It's over 1000km to Lima, and from the north initially at least, it's tempting to follow the arid Pan-Am across the coastal desert before cutting east over to Cusco by whichever route you fancy. Don't make the mistake of proceeding directly into northern Chile, unless you're on some record-breaking high-speed caper. Do the right thing and pay your respects to Machu Picchu before carrying on from Cusco into Bolivia, or over into southern Brazil (see p290). A glance at a map of Peru will show roads resembling so much over-boiled spaghetti thrown against a wall; it's why the folding footrest was invented.

Tyres and many other **parts** are cheap in Peru; postponing repairs until Bolivia may be tempting fate and Chile, Argentina or Brazil may cost you double. Lima has the best selection, but parts are also found in Cusco or even Ica, because avoiding Lima's notorious traffic is another one of Peru's must-dos.

Entering Peru from Ecuador, there's no apparent lodging along the Pan-Am for a couple of hours, so time things with that in mind. Having temporarily forsaken the scenic Andean plateau it's likely you'll be in a mild state of sensory under-stimulation, surfing arrow-straight highways over barren, trash-strewn scrub. Furthermore, the instant you cross into Peru **driving standards** collapse. Pedestrians don't stroll across the roads here; they get their heads down and sprint. Other hazards lie down this coast too: ferocious crosswinds and drifting sand that's more dangerous than it looks when hit at speed.

So stay alert or get off the Pan-Am; it's the Andes roads you want, from smooth *pavimento* to dirt tracks through boulder fields with stream crossings and gaping washouts. Just remember, passes reach well above 4500m or 15,000 feet so swift climbs from near sea level may give you a headache if rushed.

LATIN AMERICA – ROUTE OUTLINES

Perusing Peru

Assuming you've not set off for Tarapaco and the road's end at **Yurimaguas** for a river boat down the Amazon to **Iquitos** and western Brazil (in which case, *hasta la vista*, baby), from the north the first obvious side trip leads into the peaks of the Cordilleras Blanca and Huayhuash rising to over 6500m/21,500'. At only 3000m **Huaráz**, 430km north of Lima is a favourite base hereabouts. There are various approaches, including from Santa on the coast (just before Chimbote) into the **Cañon de Pato** for Carza on Ruta 3 north of Huaráz. The road follows a former rail grade through countless car-wide tunnels as well as a few airy bridges over the churning Rio Santa below. Another is the 14A leaving the Pan-Am at Casma, ascending more precipitous slopes before dropping directly into Huaráz. For more check out Trailblazer's route guide to this mind-blowing region at 💻 blancahuayhuash.com.

Cruising the cordillera to Cusco

The roads from Huaráz through the **cordillera** are world class and the possibilities numerous, including following Ruta 3 south then west onto 14 for a superbly-twisting descent to Paramonga on the coast. Or take any number of single lane dirt tracks up into the Cordillera Blanca for glaciers, lakes and ancient ruins. Careful study of maps, blogs and forums will reveal one- to three-day loops past remote villages, high passes and through deep canyons. By now you're understanding why you left the Panamericana to the crows, but inquire locally before venturing too far afield, as security can be a concern.

Heading inland, at Ruta 3 junction south of Huaráz continue down to Huánuco over the vast and infinitely variable altiplano ringed by spectacular mountain views and lined with hardscrabble Quechua villages. It can be a rough 330km so allow a full day, if not two. Pushing on from Huánuco, keep going to Huancayo. You can make no bad choices here: the two routes reaching south-east from Cerro de Pasco are equally stunning. Down in Huancayo more superb roads extend to Ayacucho where you can bail onto the paved Ruta 24 to the coast at Pisco.

Ayacucho is a splendid colonial-era town set deep in the Andes and well off the popular routes to Cusco, yet easily accessed by the paved highway from Pisco on the coast. This was a prime battleground during the *Sendero Luminoso* (Shining Path) years, and there's a moving museum and memorial to all victims of that struggle. The road over to Abancay is another knockout; allow a full day from Ayacucho, joining the main route from Nazca to Cuzco.

Back on the coast, **Lima** is one of the largest cities on the continent, but transiting on the main highway is actually surprisingly painless. With composure and a degree of blind faith you'll be through almost before you notice. To the south, the desert tightens its grip and brings you to Nazca, passing the huge dunes in Huacachina just out of **Ica**, where the backpacking throng is to be found, as well as moto-related parts and services.

Nazca itself is pleasant enough; the job here is to cough up for a flight over the enigmatic Nazca Lines. The shrewd overland rider will skip breakfast and be airborne over Nazca early in the day to avoid afternoon breezes and the risk of hurling over that backpacker they fancy, once jammed into the confines of the cabin. Aside from the lines themselves, Nazca has ruins, mummies, graveyards and Cerro Blanco: five hours up, two minutes down on a sandboard.

(Cont'd after Trip Reports section)

* * * * T R I P   R E P O R T * * * *

South America – KTM 990 Adventure

Name, Year of birth, Job Mathieu Bernage, 1987, engineer
Trip and date South America, 2014-16
Duration, distance, cost 18 months +; 50,000km, $800/month
Bike model and year KTM 990 Adventure, 2006
Modifications Water-pump seal and shaft, slave cylinder, usual protection, extra tank
Bike's strong points Fun! Powerful engine + great off-road ability
Bike problems Injectors, subframe and shock, starter
Biggest headache Met the right people when problems occurred
Biggest surprise It's a long story ...
Favourite places Iguazu, Torres del Paine, Atacama, Uyuni

Photo Atacama © Steph Jeavons

RTW – Honda CRF250

Name, Year of birth, Job Peter Scheltens, 1977, Engineer;
Leonie Sinnige, 1981, Lawyer

Trip and date RTW 2013-2016

Duration, distance, cost So far 2½ years, 100,000 km, $50 a day

Bike model and year Two Honda CRF250s, 2012

Modifications Many, most important: suspension + bigger tank

Bike's strong points Reliable, light, economical

Bike problems None

Biggest headache Not enough money to keep riding

Biggest surprise No flat tyres!

Favourite places We loved Africa

Next trip Mongolia and the 'Stans'

Photo Bolivia (Lagunas Route) © Peter Scheltens

RTW – Yamaha XT660Z Ténéré

Name, Year of birth, Job Jamie Duncan, 1975, travel journo
Trip and date RTW, 2012
Duration, distance, cost 18 months, 40,000 km, £15,000
Bike model and year Yamaha XT660Z Ténéré, 2007
Modifications Cup holder
Bike's strong points 500km range on stock tank
Bike problems Reg/rect failed three times, rear hub disintegrated
Biggest headache Refused Pakistan visa, had to fly
Biggest surprise Snow in the Middle East
Favourite places Valley of the Assassins, Iran;
   Carretera Austral, Chile; all of Argentina
Next trip Central Asia   **Photo** Salar de Uyuni © Jamie Duncan

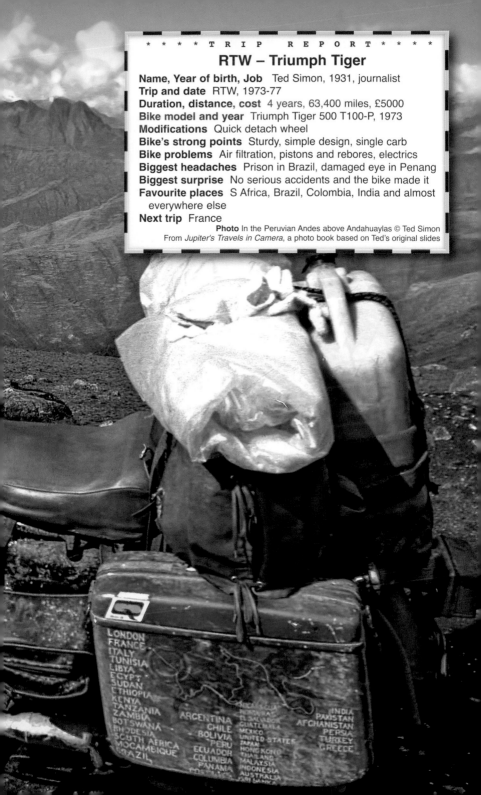

RTW – Triumph Tiger

Name, Year of birth, Job   Ted Simon, 1931, journalist

Trip and date   RTW, 1973-77

Duration, distance, cost   4 years, 63,400 miles, £5000

Bike model and year   Triumph Tiger 500 T100-P, 1973

Modifications   Quick detach wheel

Bike's strong points   Sturdy, simple design, single carb

Bike problems   Air filtration, pistons and rebores, electrics

Biggest headaches   Prison in Brazil, damaged eye in Penang

Biggest surprise   No serious accidents and the bike made it

Favourite places   S Africa, Brazil, Colombia, India and almost everywhere else

Next trip   France

Photo In the Peruvian Andes above Andahuaylas © Ted Simon
From *Jupiter's Travels in Camera*, a photo book based on Ted's original slides

* * * T R I P   R E P O R T * * *
RTW – Jawa 350/634

Name, Year of birth, Job Pavel Suchy, 1974, Journalist
Trip and date RTW, 2013-14
Duration, distance, cost 8 months, 49,000 km, $20,000
Bike model and year Jawa 350/634, 1978
Modifications 12v conversion, subframe, gearbox breather
Bike's strong points Simple, cheap, theft-proof, spares available in Asia and South America
Bike problems Rear suspension and spokes after Mongolia
Biggest headache Bureaucracy everywhere
Biggest surprise Jawa stamina, friendly Russians & S Americans
Favourite places Russia, Ecuador, Argentina
Next trip Australia and New Zealand

Photo Aboard the *Stahlratte*, Panama © Dave Ranson

Antarctica – Honda CRF250L

Name, Year of birth, Job Steph Jeavons, 1975, on the road
Trip and date Antarctica, 2015
Duration, distance, cost Three weeks, not far, £6000 for boat
Bike model and year Honda CRF250L, 2013
Modifications Front sprocket bars, racks, tank
Bike's strong points Light, economical, handles dirt, reliable
Bike problems Skinny subframe
Biggest headache How to get ashore
Biggest surprise Started first time after a week on deck
Favourite places Paradise Harbour (there was only one!)
Next trip South America to continue my RTW

Photo Paradise Harbour, Antarctica peninsula © Steph Jeavons

* * * T R I P   R E P O R T * * *

North to South America – Suzuki DR650SE

Name, Year of birth, Job Dave Ranson, 1963, Sales
Trip and date Alberta to Ushuaia, 2013-14
Duration, distance, cost Six months, 32,000 km, Can$13,000
Bike model and year Suzuki DR650SE, 2009
Modifications Suspension, big tank, re-jet, centre stand
Bike's strong point Ran from sea level to 5000m without re-jet
Bike problems Rear wheel bearings (had spares)
Biggest headache Central American borders
Biggest surprise No corrupt cops!
Favourite places Ecuador
Next trip Back to Alaska

Photo Ecuador © Dave Ranson

MENU
D/CASA
D/PAVO
D/CARNE
HORNO C/N
HUACATAY
SA D/POLLO
FRITA

THE WAY TO MACHU PICCHU

Machu Picchu can be done as a long daytrip from Cusco or by overnighting in Aguas Calientes (now aka: Machu Picchu Pueblo) below the ruins. But you're on a bike so can leave the herd and ride into the Sacred Valley to spend some time exploring the numerous ruins in the area.

Ollantaytambo makes a good base; you can catch the train to Machu Picchu from here – buy your train- and entry ticket in Cusco online.

The back way into Machu Picchu, which climbs on pavement to a high pass past Ollantaytambo, then turns to dirt and descends to river level, has become increasingly travelled since big floods washed out the railroad. It's still not possible to actually ride all the way to Aguas Calientes, but you

© BINGHAM THOMAS

might get to the town called Hydroelectrica, where you can park by the police station and walk along the seldom-used railroad tracks to Aguas. A small tip will ensure continued access for bikes.

However, if the latest landslide hasn't been cleared you may get only as far as Santa Theresa, 10km from Aguas. Walking is still an option, as is the train.

You'll find basic lodgings in Santa Theresa, which is also a base for exploring the tracks into the highland jungles beyond. It should go without saying that inquiries should be made locally before pinning your hopes on any of these roads; all are prone to landslides as recently as 2015.

MARK HARFENIST

Leaving Nazca, some riders strike out south-east to Arequipa before backtracking north to Cusco. **Arequipa** is a spectacular town in a spectacular setting, flanked by picture-perfect volcanoes and surrounded by wild high country cut by a canyon twice as deep as Arizona's famed example. Although it's possible to continue to Chile, most follow a winding road north to Cusco.

An alternative route to Cusco is the paved Ruta 26 from Nazca through Puquio to Abancay. You may be getting blasé about Peru but listen up; this is a stellar route with two highland sections teeming with comely vicuñas and split by a deep river valley awash in the shifting light and colours of the afternoon. Allow at least twelve hours, so start early or take a break in Abancay. Don't underestimate the distance; temperatures drop quicker than your keys over a drain and sudden summer storms will flush you back to the Pacific before you can say '*Qué bonitos ojos tienes, mi querida vicuñita*'.

Cusco

Cusco may be touristy and therefore pricey, but it was the former capital of the Incas empire so it's a destination in its own right, even without the nearby splendours of Machu Picchu. Off-street parking is not the norm with budget lodging so many riders park in the courtyard at the *Casa Grande* (S13° 31.01' W71° 58.58'), just east of the Plaza de Armas. Another option is the *Hostal Estrellita*, on Avenida Tullumayo 445 (S13° 31.12' W71° 58.44'). Once installed, unpacked and gelled up, two-wheel pilgrims set off to swap yarns at the famous *Norton Rats* tavern on the southeast corner of the Plaza. And once they've had their fill, like Cassidy and Sundance, the overland gang swings out the kickstarter and lights out towards Bolivia down Ruta 3, perhaps stopping after 400km in Puno on Lake Titicaca, before reaching the border crossings another 150km on for Copacabana or La Paz.

Others might choose to leave the Cusco–Puno highway before **Urcos** and ride over the passes and down to **Puerto Maldonado** (430km) and so to Brazil. Bearing the grand name of the Carretera Interoceanica, this road is being upgraded in the hope of living up to its name by linking Lima with Santos near Rio, over 5000km away on the Atlantic, although your stake in the Panama Canal is probably secure for a few years yet. If you're hardcore, it's also the way across the Amazon basin north towards Venezuela (more on p305). Cusco to Caracas, how hard can it be?

Over the border into Bolivia

Whichever way you get into Bolivia from the five bordering countries, Canadian and most EU nationals can enter without a **visa**, getting from 30 to 90 days. South Africans need a visa and US citizens can buy one at the border for a hefty $140 with a passport photo. On top of that you'll need to fill out a tourist card, possibly show an international **vaccination certificate** and get a TIP for the bike.

It's said foreigners don't need motor **insurance** (SOAT) for stays of less than a month, because like Peru you can only buy a policy for a year. Other overlanders just try and pass off their IDP or similar document, manage to buy an international policy covering Bolivia, or have a document which says as much. See p295 for an Argentinian policy which could get you out of a fix if involved in an accident.

At the moment **petrol** works out about 50 cents a litre but those on foreign plates must pay up to three times more. This isn't intended as a tourist-gouging measure, more a way of stopping those from neighbouring countries taking advantage. On major highways the stations sell at the high rate or aren't allowed to sell to foreigners. In smaller towns fuel goes for local price.

In Bolivia

Most sources list Bolivia as South America's poorest country and as having the highest percentage of indigenous inhabitants. To most riders it's one of the richest experiences on the continent, the least expensive and where the thin air gives the sky a deep cerulean hue matched by brightly dressed locals, impressive colonial-era cities and dense jungle lowlands. Oh, and don't forget those refreshing green leaves sold in local markets right across the land.

Roads in Bolivia are undergoing long-overdue upgrades which means being braced for gruelling sections of mud, gravel and sand before slithering onto steaming fresh asphalt. You might try and catch up with the state of play on the official **map** at 🖳 www.abc.gob.bo, while Geogroup (🖳 www.geogroup-online.com) produces a Garmin satnav-compatible routeable **GPS map**, as does 🖳 vwww.viajerosmapas.com which also covers Chile and Argentina. Don't forget that like Peru, rural Bolivians will mount roadblocks at a moment's notice in the name of political expression. As a consequence nowhere in South America are you more likely to be trapped by the resultant fuel and commodity shortages or complete shutdowns of major highways. However, these evaporate as fast as they arrive so park up and meet the locals.

At 3700m **La Paz** is by far the highest capital in the world with most of the main sights and lodgings in the central district within walking distance of the Plaza San Francisco. The main thoroughfare, which follows the canyon bottom, has various names but is generally referred to as The Prado. Streets in La Paz are steep, and with the altitude's effects you may gasp a bit. Motorcycle parts and repairs are available, though not in the quantity and quality found elsewhere, so don't pass up tyres and other necessary items when in Peru or Argentina. If arriving during the summer watch out for torrential afternoon storms which briefly turn the steep streets into white-knuckle kayak chutes.

The Road of Death and other fun days out

A popular day trip from La Paz is along the North Yungas Road or 'Road of Death' which over 70km takes a stomach-lifting 3500m drop to the pleasant lowland town of Coroico and Bolivia's steamy **Yungas** region where the anacondas grow thicker than a redwood pine. It's not just a nickname. Before they built the less dangerous bypass, the mist-shrouded Carretera de la Muerte annually saw off hundreds when it served as one of the main access roads to the capital. It now attracts thrill-seeking mountain bikers as well as a smattering of overland motorcyclists and even quad riders – some of whom continue to feed La Muerte's deadly appetite. As you have

© Steph Jeavons

brakes, hands and eyes, the Road of Death needn't be a fatal ride. The roadway is one lane of mostly dirt with some spectacular drop-offs.

As elsewhere in Bolivia, local custom dictates the driver's side of a vehicle hugs the **outside edge** along the abyss so they can better judge if space remains when squeezing past oncoming vehicles. This may mean they drive on the wrong side so be prepared in the unlikely event of an encounter, though the main hazard is more likely a panic-stricken mountain biker with smoking brakes. The best photos are near the top where the drop-offs are most impressive. And don't overlook the new highway to La Paz which is spectacular in itself, cresting at 4700m/15,400ft and featuring plenty of satisfyingly banked sweepers on both sides of the pass.

Elsewhere in Bolivia

How about leaving La Paz north for the 1000-km ride down through the misty Yungas and along corrugated lowland tracks via Rurrenabaque to the **Brazilian border** over the Rio Guapore (outboard canoe, $10) at **Guajara Mirim** for Porto Velho (p305) or the Pantanal (p306). Or cross the altiplano to Oruro then Potosi, before deciding whether to head for Uyuni or turn east towards Sucre, Santa Cruz and beyond. Another option is to access Sucre directly from Oruro via Ruta 6, which mixes pavement with gravel and dirt.

All routes in this area traverse the lonely altiplano, with towns and cities located at 3000–4000m (10,000–13,200ft) and separated by higher passes. In summer be prepared for storms which come on suddenly, then dissipate after clobbering you with cold rain, hail or snow.

LATIN AMERICA – ROUTE OUTLINES

Each of the cities in this part of Bolivia has its own character – Potosi with its gritty remnants of colonial wealth and jarring mine tours; **Sucre** more conventionally pretty, surrounded by indigenous towns and endless back road adventures; tropical Santa Cruz, staging point for tours into sweaty lowland jungles. From Sucre few riders continue to **Santa Cruz**, and fewer still continue all the way into the Brazilian Pantanal on the paved road via Quijarro to **Corumbá**. Most prefer to double back towards the mind-bending shapes and colours surrounding the fabulous **Salar de Uyuni**, pictured below and rightly regarded as the best dual sport touring locales around.

The Salar salt flat often floods during the winter rains by just a few inches. While this is undeniably photogenic, the corrosive spray will eat your bike's electrics quicker than a shoal of piranhas, possibly causing problems for months to come. During the dry season, it's easy enough to shoot straight across directly to Chile or as an excursion from town. Either way, riding the glaring pan is surreal and exhilarating.

Descent into Chile

Two routes head from Uyuni to Chile along the southern edge of the Salar. One can be completed in a long day on actual roads to the border at **Ollagüe**, then on to Calama, through valleys rimmed with psychedelic shades, perfectly formed volcanoes and smaller salars choked with flamingos on diamox.

The tougher route takes a series of roads and tracks, passing Laguna Colorado and Laguna Verde before intersecting the Paso de Jama road and dropping to San Pedro de Atacama. Riders manage with neither GPS or a guide, but most will prefer to obtain a GPS track online or hire a 4x4 guide.

In all cases it's easier to have **passports** stamped out of Bolivia at the *migración* in Uyuni, since remote border posts can be unmanned. Aduana offices remain at, or near border crossings. Bolivian fuel is cheaper than Chile so smuggling is rife and fuel is scarce. You'd want a range of 500km, otherwise ask in Ollagüe. Whatever your route, remember it gets chilly after sundown.

Other great roads in Bolivia include the spectacular ride from Oruro off the altiplano down to Arica in Chile; the mostly unsurfaced routes south from Uyuni to Tupiza, Oruro to Tarija and Sucre to Yacuiba for Argentina, as well as the routes east and north from Oruro or La Paz which descend to the Yungas jungles of the Amazon basin.

© STEPH JEAVONS

LATIN AMERICA – ROUTE OUTLINES

CHILE

Chile! Twenty times longer than it is wide, it slices through climates, seasons, expectations and landforms like lava through a glacier, and appropriately throws everything at you from temperate rainforests, tidewater glaciers, hyper-arid deserts and a chain of active volcanoes with some of the world's highest peaks looming over lakes and forests. Oil the chain and kick the tyres, the party's not over yet!

On the list are more eye-popping landscapes surrounding San Pedro de Atacama, the novelty of the modern, Europeanised cities of Santiago or Valparaiso, but above all it's the picturesque Lakes District around Puerto Montt, the relatively untravelled Carretera Austral south of there, and way down in the southern latitudes, the incomparable Torres del Paine. After weeks or months in the tropics, you're back in temperate lands where good roads and summer days last longer.

Infrastructure in Chile is of a high standard and for the most part a road on a map will correspond to a well-constructed and maintained highway. For a **map** it's Copec's Rutas de Chile and the atlases produced by Telefonica CTC Chile, or ⌨ viajerosmapas.com and ⌨ proyectomapear.com.ar for the satnav.

At the bordillera

You're unlikely to need a **visa** in advance or at the border. Instead, fill out an immigration form or *tarjeta* of which you keep a copy for you to get stamped when you leave the country and indeed to show to Argentinian immigration. Next you get your *temporal* for the bike and maybe fill out an SAG (Agriculture and Livestock Service) form declaring what foodstuffs you're bringing into the country. Chile has strict laws on this so declare everything and don't bring any fresh produce or meat into the country. They might then inspect your bike and once that's done, you pay the immigration fee of a few dollars and ride on. If you're planning on crossing the border with Argentina a few times you'll have to go through this all again each time. Unlike in Central America 'helpers' (*tramitadores*) are absent and blatant scams are rare. And as an overlander you're not required to pay the fees paid by international air arrivals – US$140 for Americans arriving in either country.

Insurance isn't asked for at the border and is said not to be required or available to non-residents. The driving is at least recognisably saner than up north, and with perseverance cover can be bought locally for a minimum of three months for around $50. They may also sell you a **regional policy** for all neighbouring countries for a few months but as elsewhere, this can take some effort; among others check out ⌨ www.svs.cl or ⌨ www.bciseguros.cl.

Hitting the road

San Pedro de Atacama is an easy jaunt from the copper mines at Calama and is worth a look if you missed out Uyuni in Bolivia. You could spend a day to a full week exploring the area. And where the Pan-Am ducks inland away from the coast there are alternative unpaved routes, mainly along the seaside through parks and small towns.

North of Santiago a dozen or so roads, mostly gravel, penetrate the Andes to Argentina via high, arid passes skirting brooding 6000m volcanoes. The easiest is certainly the southernmost, on the main route to Mendoza, which features high-speed switchbacks, heavy traffic, glimpses of Aconcagua (6962m, 22,841') and a notoriously busy border crossing. This route also features a gravel alternative which follows the original road far above the modern highway; see p296. In the far north, Paso de Jama is also paved but don't overlook exit formalities at the customs on the outskirts of San Pedro de Atacama or you'll be refused entry to Argentina, two or three hours down the road. Between these two stretches of pavement are a series of 4500-5000m passes transected by gravel roads. Even further north, a few passes lead into Bolivia: one paved road from Arica to Oruro, plus a couple of high, sand and washboard routes to Uyuni (see p292).

Southbound riders had better have a pretty good excuse to cross into Argentina at **Santiago** or sooner – most probably the icy onset of winter. From Santiago highways lead south through fertile valleys full of farms and vineyards. Then multiple routes diverge to the mountains or the coast and the terrain gets wilder as you enter the Lakes District – here, as in adjacent Argentina, a region of lakes, mountains and statuesque volcanoes. From Puerto Montt a right turn leads to pretty Chiloé island, while a left takes you onto the initial stretches of the **Carretera Austral** which ends at **Cochrane**.

The Carretera, Chile's Ruta 7, links formerly isolated towns, parks and wilderness areas over 1200km south from Puerto Montt. In good weather it makes for a fabulous ride, but in 2008 a volcano eruption buried the town of Chaitén and severed the Carretera near its northern terminus. There's no indication this section will be repaired anytime soon, so from the north you need to **ferry** to Chaitén from Puerto Montt or from Quellón on Chiloé.

With its ghost town ambience and half buried in muddy ash, Chaitén is definitely worth a visit. The volcano remains active but there are several houses renting rooms, as well as a hotel plus a few restaurants and bars. There's also beach camping north of the ferry terminal, and the road continues north to remoter spots near the airfield, before dwindling rapidly.

South of Chaitén, the Carretera consists of a mix of pavement and gravel – generally of a higher standard than the Argentine alternative, Ruta 40 and without the lashing gales. Services are available in Coyhoique and to a lesser extent in Cochrane. Small hotels and campgrounds are widely scattered and wild camping is possible. The route is spectacular in its own right, but there are even more impressive side roads to explore, including toward the coast at Puerto Aisén and Puerto Cisnes. The easiest exit to Argentina hereabouts is via Chile Chico after riding around Lago General Carrera (or ferrying across to shorten the journey).

Riders heading north will exit via Futaleufú or carry on to Chaiten and one of the ferries. From Quellón or Puerto Montt, you can explore Chile's Lake Country up to Santiago and Valparaiso, or cut back into Argentina near Bariloche and make the long trek across to Buenos Aires on the back roads. One more option bears a mention; Navimag (💻 www.navimag.com) runs cruises down the 'inside passage' from Puerto Montt to Punta Natales over three nights. Riders who catch good weather give glowing reports about the stunning scenery. Pay from a seasonal US$450 for yourself and bike.

The weather is most tolerable in summer; it begins to get stormy during the autumn and as you'd expect, the winters are brutal.

ARGENTINA

Like Brazil, Argentina can be a bit too big for its own good at times, but if you pick your spots you'll find still more eye-popping natural spectacle and riding adventures, plus cosmopolitan Buenos Aires and the best beef steaks or *asado* on the planet. Those interminable grass-covered Pampas do have their uses.

Argentina has among the highest per capita income in South America with **prices** now almost equivalent to Chile, and the remote south can be downright expensive. Motorcycles are well-supported too, with parts for most marques. No need for **visas** for up to 90-day stays for all westerners except North Americans and Australians who must pay a $100 reciprocity fee online. You may not get past a border without **insurance** either, particularly if coming from Bolivia. Insurance may be available at border towns and is certainly available from bike insurance spacialist ATM (🖳 www.atmseguros.com.ar) to cover Argentina, Bolivia, Brazil, Chile, Ecuador, Paraguay, Peru and Uruguay for around $20 a month. Another broker to try is 🖳 speiserseguros.com.ar.

Buenos Aires is a grand city sometimes compared to Paris for its expansive boulevards and café culture. It also features a lively and accessible motorcycle culture. **Dakar Motos** (🖳 www.dakarmotos.com; S34° 32.47' W58° 31.01') is a good address to know, combining repairs, storage, a basic hostel and assistance with air freight, shipping and insurance. The shop is also a contact point to buy or sell an overland-ready bike from other riders.

To those making the 5600km round trip to Ushuaia from Buenos Aires, Argentina will feel unnecessarily vast. Days will pass with little change in terrain which is pretty boring to begin with. Instead, head west for some Andean action along the Chilean border. In the north are volcanic peaks and desert; the central regions have vineyards, lakes and forests; further south, glaciers and ice fields are pierced by jagged peaks. You may find 🖳 www.ruta0.com useful; for the satnav it's 🖳 proyectomapear.com.ar.

North to Brazil

The falls at **Iguazú** on the Argentinian border are one of the continent's premier attractions, and worth admiring even if you think you've seen enough waterfalls elsewhere in the world. The most direct routes between BA and Iguazú follow Argentina's Rutas 14 or 12, but on these highways the famously corrupt **cops** have had a habit of flagging down foreign bikers and issuing tickets for offences real or imagined. Despite the officious-looking paperwork – which can even include documents purporting to enable customs to seize bikes or forbid their export – pay nothing if you weren't actually doing anything wrong. Just watch your speed and make sure your papers are in order.

Iguazú is a decision point: east leads to the Brazilian coast's sandy beaches, north goes to the vast inland wetlands of the Pantanal. Otherwise hop over into Paraguay on your way to north-western Argentina and the Andes, or take the Trans-Chaco highway north to Bolivia (p291).

Coming from the altiplano

Swooping over from Chile like a Condorman, you'll enter by one of the couple of dozen passes through the Andes. These vary greatly in character, scenery and difficulty: in the far north the Paso de Jama is paved all the way from **San Pedro de Atacama** to **Salta** and is the easiest Andes crossing north of

Mendoza. Just to the south of Jama is the more remote, unpaved Paso de Sico winding past multi-coloured lakes and soaring volcanoes. Between Jama and Ruta 7 near Mendoza, half a dozen roads cross less used passes of varying difficulty. Paso de San Francisco is a favourite, requiring a 500-km fuel range and frequent stops to record the epic landscapes. Others are harder still, and all top out around 4000 or 5000 metres (13,100-16,500'). Always enquire about food and fuel because for the most part there isn't much of either.

The 360km route between Santiago and **Mendoza** (Argentina Ruta 7/Chile Ruta 60) is fun too, and during the summer you can avoid the tunnel by taking the old unpaved 'Road of Curves' up and over the pass. Start looking for the signed turn-offs from the main highway on either side of the tunnel. Be aware that this Argentinian border station is renowned for lengthy queues, although these won't faze anyone recently caught in Turkmenistan on the president's birthday.

South of Mendoza another dozen roads cross lower passes, like the Osorno to Bariloche (240km); others include the crossing near Futaleufú and another outside Los Antiguos. Southbound riders also enter Argentina directly from Bolivia, usually via La Quiaca or Aguas Blancas. These border roads are scenic and fun, but forgo the distinct appeal of the arid Andean crossings from Chile.

Ruta 40 – the road south

Argentina's **Ruta 40** has long held iconic stature among adventure riders. Che Guevara came this way in the early 1950s and since then countless riders, both local and gringo, have followed in his Norton's wake. Other great rides in this area include the twisty 190km of Ruta 68 between Cafayate and **Salta**, the mix of *ripio* (see below) and tar on Ruta 33 from Cachi to Salta (160km), and Ruta 9 north from Salta. This is just the tip of the ripio iceberg.

Mendoza is a popular stopping place for those hankering after spares, repairs and winery tours. If heading south, this is the last place to feature whole blocks crammed with bike dealers and mechanics, so get ahead of the maintenance curve while you can. Lodgings can fill up here but they say *La Casa de Mhayl* (S32° 53.38' W68° 49.96') has secure parking and the Bolivian consulate is just down the road.

West of Mendoza, Ruta 7 crosses into Chile with stunning views of Aconcagua, the highest mountain in the Americas, on cloud-free days. Conversely, eastwards Ruta 7 traverses nothing much at all for the twelve hours or more to Buenos Aires. Knowing this, most discerning adventurists continue on Ruta 40 or parallel roads south toward the Lakes District. This section of 40 is paved and the riding not so thrilling; hugging the Andes on parallel routes is more like it if you don't mind long hours on gravel roads.

The Lakes District comes with snow-capped mountains framing pretty lakes, cosy cabins, forests and cute towns brimming with adventure tourism opportunities. Hereabouts your satnav is trying to show you the 200km Ruta de Siete Lagos following Ruta 234 from San Martín de los Andes to **Bariloche**.

During the summer season, streets in the major Lakes towns are full of brightly clothed tourists so lodging spaces can get lean, though most towns have campgrounds. Just don't expect privacy and quiet – as in Spain, camping for the Argentines is a gregarious affair.

After a day or two wandering south through the lakes and forests, subtle changes are noticed. Your bike labours more than it should and you meet northbound riders carrying a thousand-yard stare, cradling armfuls of broken plastic. Yes, it's **windy**; Patagonian windy. Somewhere south of El Bolsón the famed *ventarrón del diablo* manifests itself, usually blowing out of the south or off the peaks. Many riders fight gales at a steady 100kph/60mph with gusts up to 160kph, and once you're out in the steppes, a fallen bike and a crumpled Zega is your only shelter.

The round stones or *ripio* with which Patagonian roads are often surfaced doesn't help at all, and may well be named after the effect it has on plastic bodywork and jeans. Tracks often consist of half-metre wide ruts with 8-inch high berms to either side. When the roads get muddy more ripio is tipped on with only cursory attempts at compaction. Catch a front wheel in one of these berms while bracing against a 120kph gust and be ready for a ripio faceplant. This can happen many times daily for days on end.

A MIGHTY WIND

I found a hostel where the owners spoke English. That was enough for me and I gladly took the windowless cell on offer then parked Rhonda in an indoor car park two blocks away so she'd be safe from the wind. The next day the owners told me the wind was going to be really bad tomorrow and that I shouldn't attempt to ride on. It regularly took out cars and trucks in such conditions and on a 250 trail bike I'd have no chance.

Now you can say I was foolish to ignore local advice, but if I had followed it all so far, I'd still be on my first odometer.

Next day I made sure the luggage was lashed down and the helmet strap tight, but even before I left the shelter of town, I could sense this was all a bad idea. I wanted to make some distance so I checked the map and saw the next town was only 70km away. Surely I could crawl there then push on to San Julian the day after. This was my mistake: not listening to my gut instincts.

The buildings ended and I was now out in the open, battling to keep the front wheel pointing forward as the blast swept it sideways. I kept the speed down but this was not good; 70km might take all day. Oh well, not to worry. Knuckle down and think positive. But as I passed some cliffs and rounded a corner the real meaning of the warning I'd been given became evident. An almighty gust picked us up and hurled us into the path of an oncoming lorry which – thankfully – stopped in time with a hiss of brakes and a whiff of burned rubber.

As you do, I jumped to my feet and made sure the bike was OK, then looked around to see who was going to help me get her up. A car stopped and the driver ran over to help and with the lorry driver the three of us got Rhonda out of harm's way.

The car sped off but the lorry driver insisted on waiting until he saw I was able to get going again. The wind was coming in gusts so strong I could barely stand. I knew I had to get back behind those cliffs, but with the force of the wind I couldn't even get my leg over the bike, let alone hold her up. I lifted the side stand in an attempt to face her in the right direction but nearly got flattened to the ground. I clung on, braced against the gale, hand gripping the front brake lever. Seeing my predicament the truck driver came over to help and between us we got Rhonda facing in the right direction. He held her up as I got on, and after a few attempts I unsteadily retraced the couple of hundred yards back to the cliffs where I parked up and assessed the damage. Aside from broken gear and clutch levers all appeared fine and anyway, I had spares.

The trucker sailed passed with a wave and I was left sitting on the roadside. My neck and back hurt but I could ride. I didn't want to face the road back to town and there was no way I was going to poke my head out from behind the relative shelter of these cliffs again either. Not for the first time in my long travels I wondered: how am I going to get out of this one.

STEPH JEAVONS

Ferry at the end of the world © Steph Jeavons

Start early as the wind takes a while to get going, giving you a good six hours before things get scary. If you've had enough, the sealed Ruta 3 runs from BA to Tierra del Fuego with several connections to Ruta 40. The problem with dodging Ruta 40 is that much of Patagonia's epic scenery lies at its foot, notably El Chaltén and the Fitzroy range, El Calafate and the Perito Moreno glacier, plus Torres del Paine National Park. Stay on Ruta 3 and you'll miss it all, so unless you can cook up a believable excuse, soldier on before crossing to the Atlantic coast and Ruta 3 at Rio Gallegos.

You probably know this already but **Tierra del Fuego** is actually an island divided between Chile and Argentina. To get there you take one of the two **ferries** back in Chile: from either **Punta Arenas** ($20; 2.5 hours) or further east from **Punta Delgada** off the end of Ruta 3 (20 mins). Keep your receipt as you might get a discount on boat trips out of Ushuaia.

Once on the island, lodging options become increasingly scarce and pricey so unless equipped with a Whillans Box tent you may find yourself pushing onward into the austral twilight in search of a bed. There's a roadhouse in Paso San Sebastián, just before the crossing back into Argentina, and a hostel in the centre of Rio Grande, but both fill up during high season.

From either ferry it's still about 100km of gravel to the Argentine border with no fuel stations, so fill up in Punta or Rio Gallegos, or at Rio Grande 230km north of Ushuaia. In Argentina the road is sealed and it's about three hours over the mountains to Ushuaia. At this latitude expect snow and rain, even in high summer.

Ushuaia this way please.
© thedarienplan.com

Ushuaia is a surprisingly bustling place, with a lively pub scene and a surfeit of penguin-themed souvenirage. There are quite a few hostels, hotels and vast numbers of guest houses, but only the crowded hostels come cheap. The Campground Rio Pipio or the Rugby Club, on the western edge of town (S54° 49.90' W68° 21.56') are favoured among riders, the latter with a bar, internet and secure parking.

Your obligatory end-of-the-road shot by that famous wooden sign board is waiting for you another ten kilometres to the west, at the end of Ruta 3 and within the Parque Nacional Tierra del Fuego. You'll have to pay a park entrance fee to get there, but few begrudge that after all those hard won miles. Wherever you've come from, it's been a long old ride to get here and it's not over yet.

FREIGHT CRUISING THE ATLANTIC: EUROPE TO URUGUAY

With Grimaldi (🖳 www.grimaldi-freighter-cruises.com) you and your bike can get shipped between Antwerp or Hamburg and Montevideo in Uruguay. Expect about four weeks southbound, including days ashore in Dakar, Rio, and Santos, and three weeks northbound.

No crating required, you ride the bike on and off. Departure dates are fortnightly but can vary and sailing times are also estimates – one couple ended up on a six-week cruise when this service served Buenos Aires via additional West African ports.

On arrival in Uruguay a Grimaldi agent will help with formalities and there will be port fees to pay. The cost for a shared cabin is €1800 with full board; the bike's another €600. If you have the month to spare compare that with the £1250 MotoFreight were quoting in 2016 plus, of course, the cost of your flight.

FLYING A BIKE FROM UK TO BA

I'd read that Buenos Aires docks can get expensive so I got James Cargo to air freight my XTZ to BA for just under £1800.

I found the cheapest flights with Alitalia from Barcelona and on arrival in Argentina got a free 90-day tourist visa. There were some questions about the bike parts in my luggage, but in the end the nice chap was more interested in my plans.

To pick up the bike I needed a copy of my passport's visa stamp and Argentinean bike insurance, plus copies and originals of the bike's registration document, my IDP and passport. I was walked through the process by Sandra from Dakar Motos, so it was pretty easy.

At the airport south of town I paid about £85 at the freight office. They prepared my file, then we walked over to the customs building opposite. I showed my passport and the file and was given a security slip.

When the office opened around 10am we took a number from the machine and joined those already there. It was an hour's wait to be seen, but in the meantime they brought the Yamaha in its box to the entrance. My bike was here!

I must confess that I then got a little lost with the series of visits to various desks, but that included authorising the opening of the box so we could take the bike out – inside all was OK.

Then back to customs to check the bike. More stamps and £167 storage paid over a holiday weekend. More stamps, back to the customs chap, more paperwork, and I was finally handed a slip which enabled me to ride out of the compound. Thanks to Sandra's help we were back in Dakar Motos in time for lunch.

PAT McCARTHY
🖳 www.patonabike.blogspot.co.uk

VENEZUELA AND THE GUIANAS

Most riders stay west and keep to the high roads and cooler temperatures through the Andean countries, partly because eastward, Venezuela and the three countries known collectively as the **Guianas** have a reputation for high prices and an uninspiring coastline of mud flats. From Georgetown in Guyana to Macapa in Brazil you're stuck on a single transit route which still isn't entirely sealed and so prone to wet weather delays. Add the low elevation and it's always **hot and muggy**, year round.

Even with a dual sport, **inland exploration** in the Guianas takes some commitment, and there's no way into Brazil after Venezuela. So once you do get to Belem you'd better hope you're a fan of Brazil because you're about as far from anywhere else in South America as it gets.

Venezuela

You may get tired of reading this but to the roaming motard Venezuela has plenty to offer: great scenery, reasonable food and lodgings, and of course the world's cheapest gasoline. Fifty dollars of fuel in Brazil costs you a buck in

... wetlands teeming with bizarre wildlife which, if you've been in the jungle too long, may well include yourself.

Venezuela and even by South American standards you'll find unique landscapes among the tepui mesas, Caribbean beaches and islands, lowland jungles where cocoa evolved, serrated peaks draped with remnant glaciers, and inland wetlands teeming with bizarre wildlife which, if you've been in the jungle too long, may well include yourself.

Now for the small print. If you credit the US State Department warnings on Venezuela you'll be tempted to give the place a miss. After all, it's not like there's a shortage of great destinations in the region where you don't risk robbery, scams, kidnapping, carjacking and other forms of mayhem. As always, a generous helping of traveller's salt is in order as the advice has as much to do with politics as your journey.

There's no doubt that inflation in Venezuela is rampant. Disenchanted businessmen describe with great gusto the crisis that has befallen them. However, while this might not bode well for the country as a whole, it doesn't mean Venezuela is a bad country to ride in or that you'll have a rough time there. The few gringo motorcyclists who pass through each year report great riding, spectacular sights and friendly people who go out of their way to be helpful and kind, as is often the case in places with a bad rap. In fact, the main problem with Venezuela is that it tends to fall at the beginning or end of a big South American journey when riders are either fired up for the charge south or running low on funds and willpower.

There's no doubt your **security** requires attention here, as it does in parts of Colombia. **Caracas** in particular is famously corrupt and sometimes violent; most riders don't bother visiting because, like many big cities, the stress/relaxation ratio is against you. You need to know which barrios not to blunder into and at what time informal curfews start. Cops can fish for bribes too, but it's said they're not particularly persistent or intimidating about it. Shipping a bike into or out of Caracas isn't recommended; do it in Colombia.

On top of **fuel** that's virtually free, Venezuelan currency is subject to a robust **black market**. According to the government you're allotted six bolívars per US dollar. If you use a credit card, ATM, or change money at a bank, this is the rate you'll get at which point the country gets nearly as expensive as Argentina. Change your dollars informally and you'll triple your bolívars. You'll get about twice the official rate for Colombian pesos or Brazilian reais too, provided you change them near the relevant borders. There's obviously a furtive aspect to these exchanges and getting ripped off or plain mugged is a risk; guest houses and hotels owned by Europeans are your best bet. Rates will be better in border towns if not just across the border in Colombia or Brazil, since currency exchange is not illegal there. Obviously you don't want these bolívars declared or found on entering Venezuela.

At the borders

Americans now need a visa issued back home, but coming from Colombia exit procedures at **Maicao** are easy and the Venezuelan entry is also quickly processed, with vehicle paperwork completed a few kilometres on at Guarero. However, the main crossing point is at **Cucuta** for San Antonio del Tachira or

San Cristobal. The DIAN customs office is in Cucuta back at N07° 55.1' W72 30.1' where you need to check your bike out; the DAS immigration is at the border. On the Venezuelan side, Onidex (immigration N07° 48.85' W72° 26.65') is a kilometre from the bridge in the border town of **San Antonio del Tachira**. You'll also need to visit SENIAT (customs N07° 49.05' W72° 26.87') right opposite the border post for your TIP. At the first fuel stop expect to be shocked and if heading into Colombia expect long queues for petrol and that Colombian insurance may take some organising before applying for your TIP.

The country's main attractions lie in the Paramo cordillera around Mérida and many national parks, as well as an excursion to Angel Falls or Salto Angel. Good timing is required to ensure full flow over the Falls (June) while beating the onset of rains in the Amazon. Ciudad Bolívar is the starting point for flights to Angel Falls from where you travel up-river by motorised canoe to the base of the world's tallest waterfall, a real jungle adventure. You have to stash your bike for the few days you'll spend upcountry; it's easily done.

South of here is the Gran Sabana, a vast flatland on a plateau dotted with table-top mesas or *tepuis* emerging, Lost World-like, from the mists. You'll have some spectacular wild camps, refreshing waterfalls and rivers and all-round gorgeous scenery.

If coming up from Manaus it's an easy two day ride into southern Venezuela and the gradual rise in elevation is refreshing after the enervating tropics. From Guyana join the road from Manaus in Boa Vista, where ATMs are your last chance to stock up on Brazilian currency to change at the border.

It's best to arrive at **Santa Elena Uairén** during regular business hours on a weekday, failing which there's basic accommodation just short of the border in Brazil. From Santa Elena, trekking tours set off to the famous Roraima, but most riders are keen to start burning that cheap fuel on the road to Ciudad Bolivar. From Ciudad red-blooded motorcyclists head for the terminal peaks of the Andean range which even here still manage to scale 5000m/16,500' near **Merida**, an uninspiring long day's ride to the west. Merida is a centre for all sorts of adventure travel tours and activities.

THE GUIANAS

Like Belize, Guyana, Suriname and French Guiana – the Guianas – have a Caribbean rather than Latino culture, and like Belize, few riders make the diversion so for those that do there's a sense of pioneering rather than following the hordes. The route is obvious; in fact from one end to the other there's no choice. Once there, fly-in tourists may wonder how on earth you got here.

The colonial history of the Guianas saw the rice and sugar plantations helped along with immigration from the former British and Dutch territories in India and Indonesia as well as Hmong refugees from Laos and Maroons, descendants of African slaves. The less accessible and developed inland regions not suited to cattle ranching remains largely pristine, unlogged jungle populated by protected Amerindian tribes.

A few years ago, bandits were the scourge of roads in the Guianas, but like Colombia, the worst seems to have passed so now only the usual vigilance is required, especially in the cities. Rain and muddy roads will be much more significant impediments to travel. August to November is the main **dry season**, with a dry pause in February, although tropical deluges hit at any time.

Guyana

There's **no road link** between Venezuela and Guyana. Access from the west is via the sealed road from **Boa Vista** in Brazil, itself some 200km south of the Venezuelan border. Here head northwest 140km to **Lethem** (hotels) on the Guyanese border at the bridge on the Takutu River – a ride that's doable from Venezuela in a day. Coming from Guyana, Brazilian immigration can be slow.

As you cross the bridge start **riding on the left** and speaking **English**. An IDP may not be accepted, so along with **insurance** you may need to acquire a local driving permit if you're here as well as in Suriname for more than a month. Note that if coming from Suriname to Guyana at Moleson Creek (see below), you'll have to get insurance at Corriverton, 12km up the road.

Still known as 'The Trail', the once notorious dirt road 460km to **Georgetown** is OK even during the rainy season, with a few mudholes on the northern section. Note that **maps** of this route are inaccurate – not least Google. Realistically, it's a two-day ride so take a break halfway at somewhere like the *Iwokrama Lodge* just before the Essequibo ferry crossing (N05° 18.71′ W58° 54.11′). Full board is pricey but this area is famous for jaguar sightings so you may get lucky.

Guyana's government runs more red tape than the infant Khrushchev's birthday presents; as in India another legacy left by those Brits. In **Georgetown** ordinary folks are friendly, polite, helpful, though at night a cautious person might not stagger around drunk with pocketfuls of cash. Scotia Bank's offices have possibly the only international **ATM** in the land. Food, lodging and services are a notch or two below Suriname, but so are prices. The *Melbourne Hotel* on Sheriff Street is in a good neighbourhood and has secure parking. To get there aim for N06° 48.95′ W58° 8.15′.

Suriname

Suriname has an odd mixture of British and Dutch names befitting its colonial origins. Towns called Glasgow or Manchester are a few kilometres from Europlodder, while Bombay is just down the road and Hindu temples dot the countryside. It's also one of the few South American countries where you'll probably need a **visa in advance** (check 🖥 www.surinameembassy.org). They're available in Georgetown at 171 Peter St (near Rose & Crown St; N06° 48.76′ W58° 08.88′) same day for around $45. In Cayenne you may get it next day for a hefty €100, from the consulate on rue Madame Payee, just off rue Mole on the north side of the street, or from the nearby address more commonly given: 3 Avenue Leopold Helder (near N04° 56.39′, W52° 20.06′).

There's a daily **ferry** around 11am from **Moleson Creek** (N05° 46.75′ W57° 10.21′), some 12km south of Corriverton over the Corentyne River to South Drain (N05° 44.56′ W57° 08.18′). This brings you in 40km south of **Nieuw Nickerie** where you'll need to buy **insurance** (🖥 www.assuria.sr).

Riding is still **on the left** and it's a rough metalled road from Nieuw Nickerie 230km to **Paramaribo** which is said to be less edgy after dark than Georgetown or Cayenne. Suriname does have a few roads which penetrate the interior, offering glimpses of primeval forest without resorting to river or air travel. Try the Brownsberg Nature Reserve, 130km south of Paramaribo.

Freighting bikes by air or sea to the Netherlands used to be surprisingly cheap with quotes of €500 for shipping without crating. Track down N.V.

Global Expedition in Paramaribo just south of the bridge (aim for N05° 47.85′ W55° 10.45′; 🖳 www.nvglobalexpedition.com/en) for sea shipments or Surinam Air Cargo (🖳 www.surinamaircargo.nl) at the airport 50km south of town. From Paramaribo the road runs in good shape through uncut jungle some 140km to Albina on the Maroni River to St Laurent with several daily ferry runs to French Guiana.

French Guiana

French Guiana is a former penal colony that's still an overseas province or *département* of France, just like Hawaii is a US state. As such EU nationals can scoot right on in as if they were riding off a ferry at Calais; others have to do the usual trampolining between police and customs. Just as in France you **ride on the right**, the currency is the **euro**, the food ought to be to your liking, but the **prices** probably won't be. French is the dominant language, Portuguese may see you through but Spanish is rarely spoken. Customs will hint that you need to arrange **insurance** (insurance from the EU or a Green Card is valid), but coming from Brazil you can't buy it until **Cayenne** anyway; in Paramaribo buy from Assuria at a hefty €180 a month. Often enough, insurance papers aren't checked until you leave, but at that point they seem to be essential. **Fuel** is among the most expensive in South America, though at 450km border to border, you won't need much more than a tank's worth and some of this expense is reflected in roads which you could happily take home to meet the parents.

With 5.5 million square kilometres of jungle at your disposal in the Amazon basin, most take more notice of Guiana's man-made attractions, namely the **space centre** at Kourou, located here not because the labour's cheap, but because gravity is moderately less strong near the equator and, as with Cape Canaveral in Florida, an aborted launch can fall harmlessly into the Caribbean, not Dijon. The other attraction is the former prison at Devil's Island just off the coast and made famous in the book and film, *Papillon*.

On to northeast Brazil

The good road continues to the border with Brazil at Saint Georges. The suspension bridge here was ready years ago but is still not in use due to unexplained delays (or unpaid incentives) on the Brazilian side. Until that day, pay around $40 for the ferry to **Oiapoque** or less for an alarmingly tippy canoe.

Once over, get stamped at the police station, then get your TIP at the *aduana* (customs) at the north end of town (N03° 51.0′ W51° 49.9′). From here to Macapá is nearly 600km, but 60km out of town the tarmac deserts you again, leaving around 150km of dirt and possibly mud until Calcoene, 290km from Macapá. If it's been pouring and you're two-up on an FJ Twelve, wait a day or two, and whatever you're riding, fill up before you leave; fuel stations get stretched out in the middle.

Located on the 400km-wide Amazon estuary and strung across the equator, expect to perspire somewhat in **Macapá**. For a hotel with parking try the *America Novo Mundo* on Ave Coaracy Nunes 333 (N00° 01.94′ W51° 03.23′). To get the pontoon ferry to Belém, track down Sanave (🖳 www.gruposanave.com.br). They're based by the river in Porto Santana, west of Macapá (S00° 00.88′ W51° 12.17′). Expect a daily **barge** pulled by a tug and a bill of a couple of hundred dollars for the 36-hour trip.

BRAZIL

Spreading across nearly half the continent and accounting for over half its population, Brazil borders every other South American country except Ecuador and Chile. You'd think you can't avoid it, but as the Pan-Am slips down the west side, many riders skim this vast country or don't bother, citing language and visa issues, vast distances and the fact that, mile for mile, Brazil is scenically less diverse than some of its smaller but more spectacular neighbours. In the south, sugar cane plantations stretch for hours and days and arrow-straight highways are clogged with trucks. The northern interior is a semi-arid scrub broken by occasional mesas where again the hours turn to days without appreciable changes in scenery. The vast Amazon basin is fascinating to see up close, but rideable roadways are few and surrounding jungles have often been levelled for timber then farming.

Having said that, there are a few worthwhile destinations: for wildlife there's the famous Pantanal in the south; Rio de Janeiro for all the well-known reasons; the pretty colonial towns of Minas Gerais 500km northeast of Rio; the Afro-Brazilian vibe in Salvador and the adjacent beaches of Bahia; the epic Foz do Iguaçu waterfalls (see p306) and of course the Amazon Basin. If only they were more geographically condensed.

There are mountains too – notably around Curitiba in the south, between Sao Paulo and Rio along the coast, throughout Minas Gerais province and in the Chapada Diamantina further north. These highlands are full of winding roads, ranging from tiny dirt tracks to smooth ribbons of *asfalto*. There are also stately colonial towns and Brazil features thousands of miles of stunning coastline lapped by perfectly formed waves from the southern border to the Amazon delta. Riding Brazilian back roads can be confusing, but you're never far from somewhere and most small towns will have some form of lodging, food and mechanical services.

Most fortunate of all, wherever you go Brazilians are friendly and welcoming. This spirit is the country's core appeal and because overland riders are less common here, every gas or food stop will attract interest and invitations, and it'll be difficult to spend any length of time here without making local friends. There are also riding clubs throughout the country, and emailed invitations from local riders are frequent if you have an internet presence.

Not only is Brazil huge but it's comparatively expensive. Tyres, for example, are more expensive than elsewhere, despite the fact that most are manufactured in Brazil where rubber was invented. Expect to pay more for lodging and **fuel**, at about $0.90 a litre.

EU nationals get **visas** on arrival for up to 90 days; Americans need a $150 visa in advance; for Australians it's $35. The consulate in Puerto Iguazú (Argentina) is said to do a next day service. You might be asked for a handwritten promise to export your bike, but motor **insurance** isn't asked for.

Unlike elsewhere down here, they speak **Portuguese** and English speakers are few. Most Brazilians see no reason to speak even Spanish (not as similar to Portuguese as you might think) so learning a few words will greatly enhance any trip. Of course it's possible to eat, drink, take a leak and book a hotel (usually in that order) without speaking too much Portuguese, but where's the fun in that?

TRANS AMAZON NORTH TO SOUTH

The Andes offer spectacular and lively mountain roads, but the Amazon basin is the other definitive South American habitat; a humid, partially-depleted rainforest that spreads across at least half a dozen countries creating an untameable obstacle to overland travel. New roads are boldly carved to snatch resources, but one good 'Wet' (which in some places *is* the climate) and a few overloaded trucks will churn up a mire that gets reclaimed by the jungle as soon as you turn your back.

Unless you're a hyacinth macaw, up or down the Amazon, the smartest way to travel (and west of Manaus, the only way) is on river boats. There are some fast ferries but it's more of a freight barge scene, especially over longer distances; see where Sanave (🖥 www.gruposanave.com.br) are operating.

Top down though, you can ride across Amazonia. Start at **Santa Elena de Uairen** on the Venezuela–Brazil border. It depends on your nationality, but most bar Americans get into Brazil without a visa in advance, though you may need to show an international vaccination certificate. From there to Manaus is just over 1000km all sealed, via Boa Vista and the turn off to Guyana (see p302).

In **Manaus** the Amazon is already three kilometres wide. Locals take the boat up the Rio Madeira to **Humaita** but with a bike they'll try and stiff you for up to 1500 reais when it's worth a third of that.

© dwq.com.br

As it is, improvements have been undertaken on the once notorious **BR319**, with the more dilapidated of the 200-plus bridges repaired. Like on the Russian BAM, bikes can cross what cars dare not. Overnight, crawl behind the fenced-off telecom mast stations to avoid the marauding pumas.

Once ferried to the south side of the Amazon the first couple of hundred kilometres are paved and include three short ferry crossings. Thereafter, it's broken tarmac with short stretches of mud and wooden bridges which may be reaching their cross-by date. The next two days will be tough if it's been

raining and you're on the wrong tyres, but after that the track is interspersed with stretches of tarmac again, and some 650km from the Amazon you get to a point 30km north of Humaita where Brazil's network of sealed roads resumes. I now pronounce the ordeal suspended, you may stop and kiss the tar. Just remember this isn't a tourist area but an isolated beef and logging region with drugs smuggled in from Peru and Bolivia, so in places like **Porto Velho**, 215km down the road, be alert and check your exits.

From Porto Velho you can stay in Brazil and fight it out with the truck traffic southeast towards the Mato Grosso, the Pantanal wetlands, eastern Bolivia and Iguazu Falls on the Argentina-Paraguay border, some 1400km from Buenos Aires (see p306).

Or in the dry season from April to November head for Peru via **Rio Branco**, 540km from Porto Velho with a one-hour time change on the way. Another 220km gets you to Brasileia (check out with the police) and a final 100km or so to Assis Brazil opposite the Peruvian **border** at a corner with Bolivia. A bridge here crosses the river to Inapari; left after the bridge is immigration and customs.

It's said to be sealed from here at least halfway to **Puerto Maldonado**, 240km to the south. At a lowly 200m or 650 feet, once you ferry over the Rio Madre de Dios you're in the hot humid epicentre of Peru's Amazonian tourism scene with plenty of places to stay, eat, rest and get healed at the hands of shamen with their mind-expanding potions.

With that done, straighten your tie and brush down your hair; it's 430km along nothing less than the **Interoceanic highway** to **Cusco** up in the Andes at a cool 3500m (11,600'), with the 4950m (16,000') Hualla Hualla pass on the way and Machu Picchu nearby (see p289). They're working on making the road live up to its name, but until that happy day, expect the ride to take a couple of days to Cusco. Once in Cusco grab a cold one at the *Norton Rats* tavern – you've earned it.

Routes

Coming from Buenos Aires, riders usually enter along the coastal route from Uruguay where roads are good but riding and scenery uninspired until mountains appear near **Florianópolis**. At 1800m they offer some relief from the heat as well as good roads and colonial-era towns in various states of decay. Parque Nacional de Aparados da Serra and Canela are recommended points of interest and riders often gather at the well-known *Residencial Holandês* (▣ www.pousadadoholandes.com; S27° 08.08′ W48° 30.97′) in Bombas, 60km north of Florianopolis. There is a small workshop here, and one of the owners is a former mechanic.

Continuing along the coast the mountains get more rugged, the colonial towns more beautiful and the beaches more sandy between São Paulo and Rio and onwards into Espirito Santo and Minas Gerais. Note that neither Rio or São Paulo are relaxed biking destinations (you may have heard of the nasty, kite-wire bikejackings). Better to locate secure parking then explore by other means. Smaller cities like Petrópolis, Buzios and Paraty are more amenable.

Rio aside, the biggest tourist draw in southern Brazil is **Foz do Iguaçu** at the borders of Paraguay and Argentina. Quite a few riders make their way here from Buenos Aires along Ruta 14 for the ease with which Brazilian visas are issued in Puerto Iguazú. Although this inland route misses some nice beaches and winding roads through the hills, you'll get your fill further north.

A solid day's ride north from Iguaçu is the **Pantanal**, the world's largest savannah wetland. Reports differ on the best season for visits; some say rainy season floods concentrate the animals on high ground; others that the dry concentrates animals at the shrinking water sources and you don't need a boat to get around. It's easy to ride the dirt roads into the Pantanal, stopping at whatever lodge looks interesting and negotiating the services you want, otherwise you might depart wondering what all the fuss was about. Contrary to what some maps show, the Trans-Pantanal highway doesn't connect the northern and southern sections and probably never will.

From the Pantanal, one paved route stretches northwest. At Ariquemes turn west for **Guajará-Mirim** (310km) and a crossing to Bolivia (see p291). Otherwise carry on for **Porto Velho**, with a sealed road to Humaitá from where river boats head down the Rio Madeira to **Manaus**. Expect to pay a couple of hundred dollars for about three days. Or from Humaitá you can set off along the once infamous BR319 track – more on p305 – as well as the route to Peru or Bolivia. From Manaus you can reach Iquitos in Peru by riverboat, or spend days on the choking red dirt of the BR230 Trans-Amazonian Highway all the way back west. Riding in this area, often your view will be over the acres of deforestation you've been hearing about all these years.

Another option from Iguaçu is to cut east across the country, via the flawed modernist capital of **Brasilia** to Minas Gerais province, where you'll find more great riding and pretty sights than the rest of Brazil put together. Head for Ouro Prêto or Tiradentes among the crags. Virtually any route will divulge cosy villages and entertaining roads or tracks, a huge relief from the interminable truck-clogged highways further west and south.

North of Rio, beaches stretch for thousands of kilometres and larger cities like **Recife** (Olinda), **Salvador da Bahia**, São Luís and **Belém** all throb with

WHAT ABOUT URUGUAY AND PARAGUAY?

Although both are undoubtably great places to live, most travellers' closest contact with Uruguay is gazing across the River Plate estuary from BA – and with Paraguay from Iguazú Falls. You could say these two countries are the opposite of the equally obscure Guianas (see p301) which are harder to get to but, by and large, reward the effort.

Paraguay's Ciudad del Este lies just across the bridge from Foz do Iguaçu (Brazil), a decrepit border town with corrupt officials surviving off contraband. Americans cough up $140 for a visa.

Paraguay's long been a smugglers' haven and a wide variety of grey- or black-market goods, including bike parts, can be found in Ciudad del Este or Asunción, 330km to the west. A foreigner can easily buy a bike here too. It's not legal, but then neither is smuggling so ask around.

The remainder of Paraguay is not entirely without interest. Asunción has attractive colonial barrios, more shopping plus bike dealers and parts. Elsewhere there are the remains of Jesuit monasteries and prosperous Mennonite towns adrift in the Chaco which fills the barely populated north.

Across this prairie stretches Ruta 9, El Transchaco, running 1400km from Asunción to Sucre in Bolivia on rapidly deteriorating pavement. Get here in late September and you have a chance of being run over by the Transchaco Rally.

If that makes Uruguay sound all the more tempting then a ferry (🖳 www.buque bus.com) crosses the estuary to Colonia, 160km west of Montevideo, costing from $100 and taking about two hours. You can freight-cruise to Europe from Montevideo, too: see p299.

---

energy, while Itacaré, Porto Seguro, Arraial d'Adjuda, Jericoacoara and others offer smaller-scale charms and all the relaxation you can handle. Throughout Bahia the ethnic and cultural connections originating from the West African slave trade are very pronounced.

Although everyone owes themselves at least a quick look at Salvador and the Bahia coast, inland roads from Rio are the quicker way to Belém. A half-day's ride west of Salvador, the Chapada Diamantina offers a bit of highland relief and tracks diverge from Lençóis out to mesas, waterfalls and swimming holes. These and other inland parks offer relief in the midst of thousands of square miles of dreary, semi-arid *sertão* (but don't tell BMW that).

Belém is a hustling waterfront city with a picturesque old town, but like many big South American cities, has a reputation for skullduggery. Ferry yourself over the huge Amazon delta to Macapá for the Guianas (see p303), or boat upstream to Manaus (3 to 5 days and from $250-500 depending on your negotiating skills). Head to the marine terminal; brokers will find you and offer to secure whatever tickets you need. Prices are negotiable; you'll pay separately for bike and rider, with a reasonable surcharge if you want a cabin.

All these trips are on riverboats or even more basic barges, not lavish ferries equipped with casinos and cinemas, so come prepared for crowds, noise, unsanitary conditions and limited food. Loading, unloading and stowage are subject to the tides and the whims of baggage handlers who'll demand tips. The precarious loading process involves narrow, wooden ramps and a couple of sweaty guys in flip-flops, so carry baggage separately.

Manaus is a city of a million inhabitants in the midst of the jungle, and teems with decaying grandeur from its 19th-century rubber boom. Or you may just find it grimy, sweaty and depressing. The city is the focal point for tours into the Amazon hinterland, but scammers are on the prowl so exercise caution. For your next step see the box on p305.

LATIN AMERICA – ROUTE OUTLINES

7

TALES FROM THE SADDLE

A Line in the Salt

Now Bike *magazine's roving reporter,* **Jamie Duncan** *cuts up a line of salt on the Bolivian high plains with his 660 Ténéré.*

For a while it looks like we might get away with it, as the weathered Policia Frontera seems more interested in our bikes than our passports. As usual, my Yamaha XTZ might as well not be there, as sidekick Nigel's 650 Dakar garners the admiring coos, because although the Ténéré might get nodding respect from those in the bike know, it's the blue and white allure of the BMW badge that bewitches the casual observer like no other marque.

Sadly the distraction doesn't last, and before long the uniformed obstacle wants to know where our Chilean exit stamps are. I mumble a confused *no hablo español*, but quick as a flash he retorts an *obvio amigo* and my involuntary snigger blows our cover before we're even under it. Undeterred, I point to an old exit stamp smudged indecipherable just before arriving at this deep-space desolate hut that is the immigration point for Bolivia. He's having none of it and points back down the road towards San Pedro de Atacama, where the Chilean side of immigration is, fifty clicks below us.

San Pedro is a postcard-perfect tourist trap of a town, a jumping off point for package tours to the Atacama Desert and the Bolivian Altiplano. All the way up Chile we've been chatting horsepower and top speed over cold beers and ceviche at truckstops tucked between the Panamericana and the Pacific, but now we've turned inland and suddenly it's all cocktails and sushi with Taking-Some-Time-Out-Tarquin and Finding-Herself-Felicity. Our two shabby, road-weary bikes look as out of place as, well, two shabby, road-weary bikers. I've never been to a middle class desert before. Trouble is, when we finally shrugged off

> **... now we've turned inland and suddenly it's all cocktails and sushi with Taking-Some-Time-Out-Tarquin and Finding-Herself-Felicity**

the Mojito malaise and pointed the bikes towards Bolivia, we were rewarded with an endless orderly queue of tourists fiddling with their designer walking sticks and tutting at my popping exhaust. Arse. No locals, of course; they don't bother with such formalities. So neither did we, because you're supposed to make like the locals when on the road and far from home, right? And because I sure don't ride a motorcycle to queue up behind a bunch of bus-jockey back-packers blogging on their iPhones.

Luckily, the border-plod rubs thumb and forefinger together – the international symbol for problem solving. Friendly negotiation over his coffee and my smokes leaves us twenty bucks lighter, a hundred click round trip to the good, and on the right side of the Bolivian border. Bargain.

Named after El Libertador himself, scene of Che's last stand, Butch and Sundance's fatal shootout, and civil disobedience at the drop of a bowler hat, there can be few countries that fellate the soul of the on-the-roader in quite the same way as Bolivia. We're heading for the Salar de Uyuni, the world's largest salt flat and thousand mile playground for overlanders to do donuts, ride with their eyes wide shut, and generally dick about.

... there can be few countries that fellate the soul of the on-the-roader in quite the same way as Bolivia

Between us and it is the Altiplano, a desolate wasteland of asphalt-free high plains and even higher peaks, and that's got me all anxious because this is proper dirt for proper dirty girls and boys, but I'm certainly no Crusty Demon. The big Yam's taken me around the world, and although it's failed me a few times (a clutch, two rectifiers, a selection of lights and a rear-wheel hub, since you're asking), it's fair to say I've failed it more than it's failed me, and my failures are always on the loose stuff. Truth is, I know the Tonka-toy tough Ténéré is built for this shit, but am I?

But I've forgotten all of that right now because this road, through this dreamscape landscape is more wet-dream than dirty nightmare. It arrows purposefully across the high sandy plains towards a three-sixty horizon defined by a savage collection of snow-covered peaks, and Nigel is already disappearing fast towards it on the chubby, planted Beemer, in his familiar head down, arse up, dusty cloud of speedy angst.

The centre of the trail is full-attack hard-pack, so I do just that, and for once I'm right there with him. This is where the big Yam feels right at home, the top-heavy bulk caused by oversized tank, bag and rider dissipating with speed. But who ever wanted to be middle of the road? So I drift to the edge of the track and sure enough the sand sets me squirrely for an authentic off-road scare, the unstable lankiness instantly returning. Rising altitude and speed combining to both scare and excite, I force myself to stand, relax and look far ahead, as the thirty-thousand mile suspension finds enough life to mop up the ruts and the knobbly TKC80s bite hard. Would you believe it, the ungainly old XT is floating like flotsam, along with my spirits.

I relax into the groove that this dusty track is playing and take time to gawp at the gobsmacking vista. Boy this place is weird. The lake on my left is gleaming bright white, while another on my left glows as green as a treehugger's snot. I blame the surreal saturation on the altitude, which by now is climbing faster than my unauthorised overdraft. When an enormous pink flamingo flaps lazily by, I start to doubt whether I'm really seeing what I'm seeing or having some sort of altitude-induced Andean acid trip. Either way, it sure is awful fun.

But the doors of perception are slammed firmly shut by that cruellest of comedowns: bureaucracy. There's a sign pointing up a track to tell us Aduana is that way. And that way is definitely up, as the muddy track climbs straight to a ramshackle building clinging to the distant snow-line far above. I've no idea how high we are now, but it just took me twenty minutes to smoke a cigarette, and boy does that building look small from down here. Who the hell puts customs at the top of a mountain?

On the slippery scramble up, the toxic altitude infects me and I just manage to paddle the bike to the shack before I'm engulfed by nausea and my balance deserts me. I've never been this high, at least not without chemical assistance. The clouds are so close, but I've no time for gazing. I need to get down from here fast, before this trip turns bad.

A snail-slow search through the deserted building reveals a solitary customs stamper, who sorts out the bikes as fast as the thin air will allow. He tells us we're at sixteen thousand feet and should get back get down to the main track as soon as, but I'm pissed on elevation and as green as the lake I just passed. Somehow the Ténéré slides its way down the muddy track as I slump and cling on, but the effect of the thicker air is as immediate as anti-venom and the relief is overwhelming as the bad trip becomes past-tense.

Feeling brand new and flying on the plains again, I've got time on my mind. The trip to customs in the clouds has robbed us of another precious hour, and now the sun is setting fast. Back in San Ped some of the local lads told us we might find a bed for the night on Lake Colorada. You can't miss it, they said, it's the purple one. Err, right.

... we swap five bucks worth of Bolivianos for warm beds, bowls of stew and a moon-rise so ethereal I start to doubt my own atheism

Sure enough they are right, and I can't miss the ever expanding purple-patch sliding slowly from the horizon towards me. A frantic sandy blast around the lakeshore brings us to a couple of tumbledowns, where we swap five bucks worth of Bolivianos for warm beds, bowls of stew and a moon-rise so ethereal I start to doubt my own atheism.

We're up with the sun for breakfast with the family, whose welcome is warmer than the crackling fire we're all sitting around. I could lazy chat all day, but we're only half way to the Salar, so it's back out onto the lakeshore and straight into deeper sand. It's horribly hard to muscle the weighty XT through, but nothing ignites a lethargic mind like a couple of big sandy slides on a quarter-ton of enduro bike – except coca tea for breakfast, maybe.

We climb away from the lake and leave the sandy plains behind. The trails are easier to see than yesterday's were, but strewn with rocks designed for shredding tyres. My progress has to slow to increase my chances of remaining in one piece.

But the faster sections are fantastic, even for a rookie like me. The trail clings to the edge of yet another lake, this time a boiling cauldron of stinking sulphur. Not so much a lake as a chemistry experiment, although by now the extraordinary is becoming ordinary. As the sulphurous stink fades, so does the trail, and we find ourselves picking our way across barely-there grass strewn with newly formed streams running parallel with the river we need to cross.

I get soaked to my waist and instantly frozen as I give it some gas and hope for the best, but the chilly wet is the least of my worries as my clumsy throttle control lacks the deft required for the slippery far bank.

> ... the bike and I end up sprawled in the undergrowth, glowering at one another

The rear spins up fast and I exit the bike over the handlebars. No harm done, as my pride takes the brunt of the impact, and the bike and I end up sprawled in the undergrowth, glowering at one another. A few satisfying stamps on the brake lever returns the resilient XT to road-worthy condition, at least as road worthy as it was before. I wish my confidence was as easy to fix. Sorry Big Tén, I let you down again.

My contrition is cut short by a truck thundering past from where we're, err, lost. So that'll be the road then, and a main one at that. Not sealed of course, but as fast, hard and wide as a heavyweight boxer. With the riding one-handed easy and triple-digit fast, the final sixty into Uyuni is dispatched in under an hour. I've barely enough time to be disgruntled about almost-but not-quite making it across the Altiplano without crashing. And be pretty damn gruntled for exactly the same reason.

The horizon starts to glow luminescent as the diamond-white vastness of the Salar turns down the contrast on the surrounding terrain

The horizon starts to glow luminescent as the diamond-white vastness of the Salar turns down the contrast on the surrounding terrain. They say it can be seen from space and I'm not surprised, as it glows like a giant halogen headlight.

Up close the salt is spectacular, shimmering a heat haze as it reflects the cotton-wool clouds like a mirror. Who knew that salt reflects sky like the calmest of water? Nigel shoots me the sort of look he usually reserves for vegetarians, and helpfully explains that it is, in fact, covered in water. Ah, yup, right. Turns out it does that for a couple of months a year and our timing is as off as the Yam's.

But I really couldn't care, because I've just had two of the biking days of my life and proved to myself that you don't need a plan to tackle the Altiplano. The plan, as it always seems to, takes care of itself. Truth is, I'm not bothered at all, because what I've got here is a sopping wet reason to come back down this way again someday, and what could be better than that?

Living and Loving on the Road

After over a dozen years on the road with Simon, **Lisa Thomas** *shares her insights on sticking together.*

Of course there are times when I want to ram a skewer into his fat head! And I know for sure there've been times when he has wanted to strangle me, bury me in a shallow grave and sell my 650 for scrap. Our relationship is more intense than most, but Simon and I have been together for over twenty-three years. Twenty years married with thirteen of those bashing out hundreds of thousands of kilometres all over the planet, side by side, 24/7. We're all too aware of the dangers of taking each other for granted so over the years we came up with the seven Cs:

> **Care** – Make sure you do.
> **Chill** – Make sure you do this; chill together and alone.
> **Compromise** – Make sure you do it.
> **Communicate** – Make sure you listen.
> **Cash** – Make sure you don't argue about it.
> **Cruel** – Make sure you aren't.
> **Climax** – Make sure you make time to!

CARE
If we calculate the time and experiences we've shared in the last two decades, I'd say we've packed the equivalent of sixty years of married life.

It's included intense periods without family or friends on hand to help release the pressures, and when we've the other to take the full brunt of our frustration, stresses, hopes and fears.

Why do we work? We care what the other thinks and we care what the other wants. We take care, most days to tell each other we love each other. It may sound daft but out there, on the road, it's just too easy to overlook this simple stuff. Relationships can be tough at the best of times, be it between family, friends, girlfriends, boyfriends or the person wearing the ring you gave them to symbolize 'forever'. Throw in some heat, exhaustion, bike gremlins, illness and any other combination of first-time experiences and things can go from explosive to full-on meltdown in the time in takes you to flick down a sidestand and reach for your skewer.

Do we have the perfect relationship? Not a chance but we have what works for us. The key here is 'work'. OK, it's not mining for coal or yammering at a keyboard with three calls on hold – it's about being aware of each others moods, our situation and then thoughtfully choosing to side-step certain responses that we know would send the other over the top when stressed.

Travelling with anyone full-time can be a risky business. Even the most closely matched are going to have moments of meltdown when the relationship gets temporarily obliterated by the fallout.

Even the most closely matched are going to have moments of meltdown when the relationship gets temporarily obliterated by the fallout

When you're on the road, out of your depth culturally or physically, caring has little to do with that warm fuzzy crap they spout on the Disney Channel. Caring about your partner comes down to caring enough to bite your tongue and staying quiet when all you want to do is let loose a rant with both barrels.

CHILL

Time and again Simon and I have watched riders and friends set off on their long-planned big trip, only to be amazed as they blitzed through countries or regions like a tornado, and spending as much time blogging, writing, reporting and photographing the journey as they've actually spent riding it. Slow down! You're only coming this way once so stop the dash. The rush was part of your old life, this is your new life, irrespective of how long or short your planned journey. Start it as you mean to go on and enjoy the ride. Take time to chill-out with your partner and enjoy the new places you visit.

Over the years we've also learned that giving each other space is essential. A few scattered moments to yourself can be a great way to regain perspective. Simon and I have redefined 'personal space'. It doesn't mean we're on our own geographically or separated. When on the road it can just mean being left alone to be quiet. So walk together, photograph together, blog, update or even work on the bikes

Slow down! You're only coming this way once so stop the dash. The rush was part of your old life, this is your new life ...

together, but be aware that chat and conversation aren't always required.

As a traveller it's easy to become intoxicated by the cultural cocktail being poured down your throat, and overwhelmed by the non-stop stimulus of moving forward to the next adventure. We've learnt that a few hours of quiet is all you need to calm your head space and make sense of all the emotion and adrenalin that real adventure motorcycling generates. So, if you have communication systems, give them a rest once in a while. Watch a movie on the laptop, pore over the maps, just do it separately and above all, leave each other alone when you are doing it. Trust me you'll appreciate the mutual detox when it's time to get back together.

> ... a few hours of quiet is all you need to calm your head space and make sense of all the emotion and adrenalin that real adventure motorcycling generates

It's all too easy to want to cram in as many experiences as possible, to want to impress your friends and riding mates back home. But if you're worn out, take a break. Now and again we indulge in a bit of luxury and book into a hotel to enjoy a hot shower and privacy of a real bedroom. A break like this can be rejuvenating and in a hot, humid country a night of air-conditioning makes all the difference to being able to be near your partner without growling that it's too hot. A good night's sleep and feeling clean always brings a smile back to our faces.

COMPROMISE

Compromise is one of the biggest elements of sustaining a healthy relationship. It's not a word that's big in our vocabulary as we're both assertive and, at times, over-bearing but compromise is something that we've learned to practice. Contrary to popular belief, compromise isn't a show of weakness, it's a show of respect. Being aware of each other's differences and differing expectations can actually open a range of possibilities that neither would have considered alone. But perhaps Simon and I are just lucky. Invariably we usually do want to do the same thing which is probably why we've been able to stay on the road together for so long.

COMMUNICATE

Listen up, guys! The strong silent types aren't all that strong – they're bloody annoying! Long-term travel is work: a different kind of work for sure, but the trip doesn't organize itself. This is not the time to stay quiet, if either of you has doubts, or concerns, share them. Just make sure you balance this with telling each other your positive thoughts.

Rifts on the road can be caused by the most innocuous of unintended slights. Simon and I have learnt the hard way that any negativity, irritation or argument needs to be dealt with immediately. On the road, there's not much down time to sorting whatever issue has come up between you. It's a cliché, sure, but get issues out in the open and deal with them.

> Listen up, guys! The strong silent types aren't all that strong – they're bloody annoying!

And ladies, hard though it can be at times, resist sticking your man in the head with that skewer. It'll just make picking up your bike that much harder next time. Bottom line: Have a shout. Stomp off (not too far if you're in out in the wilds or a strange city) and take some time out. Be ready to apologise and then forget it.

Communicate also to sort out who's doing what. We share the workload with our own jobs using our own strengths. So, decide what yours are and stick to them.

> **Have a shout.
> Stomp off ... and take
> some time out.
> Be ready to apologise
> and then forget it**

Here's a tip: work on not undermining each other: never re-do a job that the other has completed, unless the first attempt results in life threatening risk. If something needs to be re-done, tell each other what needed changing and why.

CASH

This is something we've never enough of and the lack of it has caused many an argument. This is also where compromise and communication comes into play, as we're continually compromising on our desires of where to go and what to do due to lack of funds.

Our lack of funds is a surprise to many. 'How on earth do you afford to stay on the road for so long?' is a regularly asked question. The cash we got from selling our house and contents in the UK has long gone. For Simon and me, our biggest yelling matches arise from the amount of time required to spend yammering on those laptops, writing articles, sharing via our own website, or generating the photography we've become known for. The rows we have are ignited out of frustration at being forced to knuckle down and ignore the beauty of our surroundings.

It's hard on both sides: for the one having to sit and crank out the work and for the other dealing with feelings of resentment. There's no clever answer, we all need cash. For us it's not an extended holiday, it's a lifestyle that needs to be supported so we just have to buckle down and weather the storm. Let's face it, we've got a way more exotic office than most.

CRUEL

It's very easy to be cruel: a cutting word, a careless attitude, a mean utterance. I'm sure you all know the old adage, 'If you can't say something nice, don't say anything at all'. It's true and especially when you're on the road. My problem is I have a very sharp tongue and without thinking, I carelessly use this on Simon at times. When it's just the two of you on the road you really can't afford to take out bad feelings on each other. It'll end badly.

CLIMAX

OK, a part of me just wanted to make sure there was at least a hint of something sexual in here. Here are my words of wisdom. 'If you are having bad sex, or no sex, on your journey, then sex becomes 99% of the relationship. If you are having good sex then it is 1%.' Lack of opportunity and mostly circumstance can affect the intimate side of a relationship on the road. Living in a tent, dirty and tired doesn't always lead to a good sex life. However, it's important to keep a good sex life going! You need to make sure that you're not only good friends and riding buddies but also lovers. Ladies, make sure you're riding your man and not just your bike!

Ladies, make sure you're riding your man and not just your bike!

Remember, at the end of the day the privilege of travel isn't just born from the experiences and the moving forward, but more importantly from being able to share it with your mate, lover and best friend. This is what makes the whole thing real.

Into Africa

Travel addict **Sam Manicom** *planned a year to ride the length of Africa, but arrived home eight years, 200,000 miles and six continents later.*

I'd learned pretty quickly to hit the road in the early hours of the day. It's a lot more fun to ride a piki piki in the cool. By midday in many parts of Africa the asphalt is almost at melting point. The heat hammers up at you off the black surface and I'd learned that my concentration wasn't at its best when I was slowly cooking in my bike gear. On the road by seven would give at least three hours of cooler temperatures to ride in. The low, softer morning light was better for taking pictures and there was a much greater chance of seeing wildlife that also takes advantage of the cool to feed and move.

The first checkpoint of the day was just a few kilometres down the road. A long line of traffic waited. Two matatus, overloaded as usual, with their drivers' fingers tapping at the delay, formed the tail of the queue. Matatu drivers are a traditional target for palm grease so I suspected that the finger tapping might have a tinge of frustration to it. The policemen indicated to the first driver to pull over, and an argument started.

> **By midday in many parts of Africa the asphalt is almost at melting point. ... I'd learned that my concentration wasn't at its best when I was slowly cooking in my bike gear**

Suddenly, one of the officers walked round to the back of the mini bus and using his rifle butt he smashed the taillights on one side. Back at the cab, money changed hands – the driver was now 'legal' in this policeman's eyes and free to go. At least that is, until the next checkpoint where the broken taillights would cause more problems.

Then it was my turn. Another policeman directed me out of the line of traffic. I stopped the bike, pulled off my gloves and helmet and sat waiting. The extremely smart officer strode arrogantly over and stared at me from above the razor-edged creases in his trousers. He had a semi-automatic rifle slung over his shoulder and he didn't say a word, just watched me from below the patent rim of his hat. Not being able to see his eyes in the rim's shadow made him look really menacing. He strutted around the bike.

After moments that felt like ages he demanded abruptly, 'Where are you coming from?' 'Eldoret', I told him, wanting to keep things simple. 'No, before that!' he snapped. I began to wonder if there was some sort of sting in the question. Was my paperwork from the border not in order? I'd no choice but to tell him, 'Uganda.' 'I know', he stated in reply. But now he was stroking the bike with what I thought looked like boyish admiration. He then looked up and said, 'What is this?'

'What is this?' 'Um, a BMW motorcycle', I replied not quite knowing what else to say. 'No', he said. 'This is a car on two wheels!' and burst out laughing. 'Ha, ha, fooled you didn't I?' He'd just stopped me for a chat!

It turned out that he had been on the checkpoint between the border and Eldoret the day before and had seen me ride through. Normally in Kenya I'd just been waved on through the checks, so hadn't thought twice about it. As I breathed a sigh of relief my new 'friend' started walking round the bike muttering things like: 'What a machine!', 'A super bike', and 'Oh yes, indeed, a car on two wheels'. He chortled with laughter and pushed his rather forbidding hat back from his eyes, which shone. Here was a uniformed bike enthusiast!

'Would you like a ride?' I asked. 'Me, on this?' 'Sure', I said, and within seconds his hat and rifle were in the surprised hands of one of his mates, and he was on the bike. We set off down the road with him yelling 'Faster!' So I did. After a few kilometres I turned around to deposit him swaggering with glee back at the roadblock.

Was that a bribe? No, too much fun to be a bribe!

☆☆☆

I'd decided to return to Nairobi but this time to take the back roads through the Cherangani Hills. The hills run for roughly sixty or seventy kilometres, forming the western side of the Elgeyo Escarpment. The roads are mostly dirt which meant that many of them didn't show up on my map at all. In the middle of the day I sat in the cool shade of an acacia tree. It was a well-earned rest and the perfect spot to enjoy the view. Sweat had cling-filmed my shirt to my body and my leather jacket was ringed with salt stains again. The foam around my goggles had a salty metallic scent to them and dust had gathered in muddy smears along the lower rims where perspiration would always collect. My eyes were drawn out over the shimmering brown and yellow plain towards the cool greens of the distant mountains. The sense of phenomenal space was quite awesome and it was only after all these months in Africa that I was really beginning to feel inspired by them. In the first months I'd been too busy just coping with my immediate environment, and trying not to fall off my bike, to really take stock of just how big the land is. I felt that I was in a place where I could yell at the top of my voice for as long as I wanted-ed, and not a soul would hear.

Suddenly, a voice right behind me made me jump. 'Where are you coming from?' it said. It seemed that everywhere in the world was someone's back yard. The man's questions were predictable so I could reel off the usual answers without thinking too hard. 'England.' '43 litres.' '800ccs.' 'Several months.' 'Uganda.' 'Nairobi.' And, 'Tonight? I'll stay somewhere in the hills.' But I didn't mind

that people asked me questions and several times I'd wondered if I would have the interest or even courage in my own country to go and ask a total stranger these sort of questions about their life. Here, the questions weren't considered nosy; they were from a combination of curiosity, the desire to learn and a sort of innocence.

☆☆☆

That night an elder gave me permission to put my tent up next to his village. After the initial crowd had collected, stared, dawdled, and eventually decided that there was nothing else new to see, I was left alone. It was the perfect opportunity to be a fly on the wall. Trying hard not to be caught staring, I watched the village scene. It seemed that as I hadn't minded them watching me, they didn't appear to mind me watching them.

Many of the men in the village carried small, carved wooden stools and they carried them as if they were extensions to their bodies rather than something to sit on. One of the elders had sociably come and sat near me on his stool, and he told me that I was right, there was much more to them than 'just' something to sit on. Each stool could be hundreds of years old and each was a family heirloom, passed down from generation to generation. As he talked, he smoked a cigarette which he had clasped between forefinger and thumb so that the smoke wisped up between his yellowed fingers. He told me that the stool is the shrine of the family's soul and that each is decorated with the family name and design. When the head of the family died, this symbol of authority would be passed to the next in line as an indication to all, the village and the tribe, that power and responsibility were in new hands. A sort of African coat of arms, I thought.

The old man's knowledgeable calm impressed me, as did his clothing. I'd watched him come out of the low doorway of his mud hut. He was immaculately clean with spotless dark trousers and a gleaming white creaseless shirt.

I asked him if the village had a witch doctor. He replied, 'Not this village, but the area certainly has a doctor, we must have one.' He told me that, besides knowing vast amounts about the herbs and medicines of the land, the doctor was for many a spiritual leader and advisor. I also knew that some were dangerous. They know which of the hundreds of Africa's plants are poisonous. Historically, if you wanted to bump someone off then, for a fee, the doctor would either arrange it or give you the poison to do it. The favourite method was to dip the little finger in the poison and then, whilst serving them a drink, dip the finger discreetly in the liquid – 'doctoring the drink!' This man's doctor was also the teller of tales. I read that in the days when few could read, word of mouth had been the way that traditions and history were passed on. The storytellers had almost photographic memories for these historical tales. Witch doctors were often seers, too.

If you wanted to bump someone off then, for a fee, the doctor would arrange it or give you the poison to do it

One such seer dreamt of strangers coming out of the great waters to the east like yellow frogs. He dreamt that they would ride beasts with wings like butterflies and they would have magic sticks that would send out fire. The seer prophesied that some time would pass and then these strangers would arrive in great snakes whose skins would repel spears and arrows. The strangers would destroy them all. This story had been told for three generations before the explorers, slave traders and colonialists started to arrive. The great snake part of the prophecy had come true with the building of the railway from the port of Mombasa.

I slept surrounded by the village noises until the heat of the early sun got me up. My deep green tent was perfect for hiding away in corners but its dark colour sure did attract the heat. It only had one entrance so I could never get a through draft and on wet days it was too low to sit up in. It wasn't ideal but it kept me dry and the mosquitoes out. Some nights the mozzies had been so enthusiastic they'd been pinging off the inner lining as if flying full tilt at the tent would enable them to power through the fabric to get at me. I'd have to layer on the repellent in the morning before getting out in case there were any patient, hungry and determined types still around. There usually were.

☆☆☆

On a whim, I headed north. Time wasn't a problem, the bike was behaving really well, my water bottles were still pretty full and the map showed a road marked as 'improved but liable to be impassable in bad weather'. The weather was good and the dirt roads I'd just been on were fun, but easy and this road sounded a bit more of a challenge. I was ready for that now. 'Improved' turned out to be wishful thinking. Rut after rut rattled my teeth; soft sand made the bike squirm, and the heat was intense. But the rolling bush land was beautiful and there was hardly a soul on the road. Once again I felt like I had the world to myself ...

Extracted and adapted from *Into Africa*

Riding Siberia's One-Ten

With the original BAM road now just too obvious, **Jussi Hyttinen** *and a mate throw themselves at a short but tough trail, east of Lake Baikal.*

Standing at the southern bank, the Barguzin River rushed by, a hundred metres wide with deep, fast flowing channels churning between wide rocky rapids. Our track plunged straight into the river right in front of our wheels and the ford was clearly visible. The way across was not. My riding buddy Juha waded in and was soon thigh deep in fast-flowing water. No way to cross here.

Upstream, in the middle of the river, was a small sandy island scattered with flood debris. We managed to reach it via a chain of gravel bars and fordable rapids, our tyres spinning on the smooth submerged rocks. From here we were faced with a deep, ferocious channel to reach the far bank. Attacking it directly from the island was also impossible, but further downstream the current mellowed a little: still a serious crossing, but shorter. On the far bank was the start of the 110, a 160-kilometre Soviet-era ice road or *zimnik,* built in the 1970s to speed up the construction of BAM railroad. The One-Ten was our objective and if we wanted to ride it we'd have to cross right here.

We decided to power walk the KTMs, starting with mine. I was on the upstream side operating the throttle with Juha opposite. Little by little we inched the 690 into the channel and, as the force of current built up I braced against the flow. The air box intake just managed to keep its chin above the water and, with a rush of relief we ascended the north bank. Once Juha's bike was over we felt exhilarated to have finally reached the *zimnik*'s trailhead. The game was on.

Sixty kilometres up the trail the Barguzin swung east and the 110 forded it a second time. If it rained before we got there, the river would rise and we'd be trapped between the two crossings. We had to move now before the weather broke. We made good progress and reached the Kovyli River when, rounding a bend, I noticed a strange hulking shape in front of me. Realising it was a bear, I hit the brakes just as it ran off, lurching clumsily from side to side while looking back to see if we'd give chase. Although we have them in Finland, I'd never seen a wild bear and the realisation that they actually existed here produced a bittersweet cocktail of gratitude and anxiety.

We had to move on now before the weather broke

Our route continued in a vaguely straight line along the wide Kovyli valley. The track was in good shape but the skies were growing darker by the hour and eventually released a light drizzle. It was a chilling reminder of why we had to keep moving. Arriving at the fast-flowing Kovyli River I felt under pressure and over-confident. I rode straight in, hit an unseen boulder and tipped over with a splash. Luckily the bike didn't suck water but my confidence was dented, and that's all it takes to lose your nerve.

When it came to the second Barguzin ford, Juha waded in to scout a line, then rode over with ease. I was tired and shaken up, so took the safe option and power walked it. The crossing was beautiful and knowing we'd now at least cracked the Barguzin, we took the luxury of a short break before heading into the mountains for the night. Riding up the pass, we passed another three bears, and as darkness fell were forced to camp just a kilometre from where we'd spotted them.

In the comfort of my fluffy down bag I wrote up my trail notes and hoped that the weather would improve by the morning. Even though we'd managed to cross the Barguzin, the most difficult terrain lay ahead, with plenty more water. That night I slept fitfully, tormented by visions of drowning bikes and bears ransacking our camp. I was woken around six by rain hammering on the tent and knew then the way back was shut. The only way out was forward, a sobering yet fortifying realisation that lies at the heart of real adventure biking.

... the way back was shut. The only way out was forward, a sobering yet fortifying realisation that lies at the heart of real adventure biking

The track over the Ruhlovskogo Pass wasn't too bad, but dropping towards the Akumtu River it deteriorated into a deeply rutted trail of rocks and scattered debris. The Akumtu was strangely low and we crossed it with ease. A couple of hours later it might not have been the same. As if to underline that point, a stranded bridge stood abandoned next to it, a huge useless steel skeleton rusting away in the rain. (The frames were flown in with Mil Mi-6 helis but were never installed). The next few fords all resembled the Akumtu, each with the adjacent hulk of a rotting bridge frame looming over the ford.

By afternoon the water levels were beginning to rise as streams turned into creeks. The trail became riddled with puddles spanning the width of the track, with water up to our tyre tops. The world grew ominously dark and as the thick rainclouds jettisoned their loads, the air seemed saturated with moisture. I felt as if I was in a bubble, travelling through the Siberian taiga, with only the steady thud of the 690 breaking the spell. We'd been granted passage across the Barguzin, only to risk getting trapped on the northern side, like flies lured towards a web while a spider watched closely, just out of sight. There'd be no conquering the 110, only enduring and surviving by the skin of our teeth just as long as we held it together.

We crossed another big river after which the long, wide valleys turned into a world of rock and stone. A technical trail unwound before us, scoured raw by water where the old road had been. A grey scar, it led us through the lush pine forests to the beautiful Namana River. We rode down to its torn-up bank, navigating rocky obstacles until the trail climbed back into the forest burrowing through green tunnels of dripping foliage.

Approaching the confluence with the Svetlaya River, the terrain started to get seriously gnarly. Small side streams had flushed away all traces of sand and dirt, leaving glacial boulders the size of small ovens. The KTMs ate it all up of course, while we hung on to the handlebars like wet sheets.

I knew that up ahead we'd be riding into the taiga's heart of darkness, the Sramnaya Valley. It was like nothing I'd ever seen. The walls rose 500 metres as the valley plunged almost as deep in roughly eight kilometres. Swollen by the rains, the river here was a wild torrent raging over a riverbed strewn with boulders. The first crossings had some sand and few boulders but further down they got deeper and rockier until, in the end, the river was the track.

... but further down they got deeper and rockier until, in the end, the river was the track

Scouting this section, I recce'd a line until I saw a way out on the same side as our bikes, but we'd have to zigzag across the river twice just to get there. As always, Juha attacked without hesitation. I admired his commitment and attitude. There was no need for discussion – this was our line and we had to take it. The traverse was treacherous: water pushed me downstream while the knobblies slithered and bounced over unseen boulders. As I started the second traverse I hit a rock, put my foot out for support and found nothing. I fell helplessly while by chance the bike found a boulder to break its fall – saved again from a potentially disastrous hydraulic lock-up. Juha waded over to help and we both made the final traverse, squeezing between a waterfall and a deep pool.

Up ahead the trail was no better and we followed the rock-strewn bank, focussed intently on the task at hand, inching forward slowly. I knew the river would end up in a lake further down so the river-trail couldn't go on forever. We came to a rapid without an obvious way through. Juha scouted ahead on foot then promptly set off to ride it. There was no way to see beneath the rushing water and sure enough, he went down. Wading in to help out, I fell in myself up to my chest in icy water. Juha commented dryly that he didn't recommend trying to ride this bit.

One final crossing and we were out of the Sramnaya. The trail continued down the rocky western bank and, little by little, dirt crept between the boulders to smooth out the ride. It was still tricky, low-gear riding but felt luxuriously fast after battling the river bed at less than walking pace.

All at once the rocky forest track spat us out on a wide muddy trail churned up by 6WD trucks, which we took as a promising sign. It eventually connected with a proper dirt road where we looked at each other in disbelief – had we taken a wrong turn? We were expecting the 110 to keep us working all the way to the BAM, but here, 65 kilometres sooner than expected, it was all over.

We'd made it through the 110. As far as I knew only two Russian parties had ridden this way in recent years, one building a log raft then resorting to a big inflatable dinghy to cross the Barguzin in spate. We were most likely the third crew to ever traverse the slowly disappearing 110. We continued down the gravel road and the township of Novi Uoyan and miraculously found a hotel room where we peeled off our sodden clothes and collapsed onto the beds. Next morning we got on the BAM highway and headed west, back to the outside world.

Early Adventures with Motorcycles

AMH may be celebrating a quarter of a century in print but **Lois Pryce** *delves further back into the archives of the first motorcycle explorers to discover that once the 'motor-bicycle' became established, brave individuals soon saw the appeal of continent-spanning adventures.*

With the recent arrival of adventure motorcycling into the mainstream, you might be forgiven for thinking that this two-wheeled globe-trotting is a 21st century phenomenon. Far from it. The irresistible combination of motorcycle plus wanderlust has been inspiring men and women to hit the road since the first machines appeared in the early 20th century. As far back as 1913 and certainly by the 1920s there are records of Europeans and Americans making long-distance, international journeys by 'motor-bicycle' or in sidecar combinations. But as is the nature of unrecorded adventures, many of these expeditions have slipped into obscurity, existing only as a faded newspaper clipping or a tattered sepia photo that crops up occasionally on the internet.

The savvier of these early motorcycle travellers had the good sense to record their adventures, usually in a book, but occasionally on grainy black-and-white film too. Luckily for us their stories live on and show us not only how different the experience was all those years ago, but often how similar, too.

Here's my selection of a few of the greatest adventure motorcycling pioneers, in whose tyre treads we follow...

Robert Fulton Junior – Around the world 1932-34

To motorcycle solo around the world aged twenty-three would be a major achievement for anyone today. But back in the 1930s, for American, Robert Fulton Jnr, his eighteen-month odyssey through twenty-two countries was merely the springboard for a remarkable life as an inventor, writer, photographer, painter and sculptor.

In 1932 Fulton was a young man fresh out of college and, like most chaps of his age, keen to make an impression with the ladies. Finding himself at a dinner party in London, when asked by an attractive female guest about his plans to sail back home to New York, he announced, somewhat rashly 'Oh no! I'm going around the world on a motorcycle!' This was probably not the first testosterone-fuelled declaration in the history of motorcycling and it certainly wasn't the last, and if it hadn't been overheard by a fellow dinner guest it may well have gone no further. Little did Fulton know that he was sharing the table with the head of Douglas Motor Works who interjected, 'I say old chap, that sounds grand! We can furnish you with a machine for your journey.' Fulton's fate was sealed there and then, for as any budding adventurer knows, once you've mouthed off to all your friends, you have to go.

It was thus that Fulton found himself setting off on his very own *One Man Caravan*, the title of his marvellously entertaining book about his 40,000-mile ride. His route took him through a pre-war Europe, a Middle East still firmly under British control, an India seemingly destined to be British forever, the (then) Dutch East Indies, into pre-communist China, and finally to Japan before taking a steamship back to his native USA.

> **... as any budding adventurer knows, once you've mouthed off to all your friends, you have to go'**

He makes it clear from the beginning that he wasn't entirely sure how he got swept up in the whole plan, but his bluff having been called, he had no choice but to go along with it. However, the spirit of adventure was obviously

smouldering in him somewhere, as he describes how the idea of this grand expedition began to gradually fire his imagination, 'the lure of travel; a different road ever day, a different fireside every evening, beneath a different star every night.'

His romantic visions will resonate with anyone who's pored over a map and dreamed of getting away from it all on their bike; these are the same urges that have inspired travellers through the ages and will continue to do so. Unfortunately for Robert Fulton, the same annoyances and obstructions were also just as prevalent then as they are today, most notably the finger-wagging pessimist who enjoys nothing more than to pour water on the sparks of a young buck's dreams.

'How does one go around the world from London, heading east?' enquired Fulton to a 'beefy-faced, hearty attaché' of the Royal Automobile Club in London.

'Too easy, my dear fellow' came the reply, 'One simply doesn't!'

Fulton's response illustrates the practical, can-do attitude that would serve him well on his adventure: 'But surely, wherever there is man, there must be some sort of route?' he countered.

It's this approach to his journey, and to his frequent crashes, arrests and various other scrapes along the way that make Fulton's story so engaging. His tribulations with both man and machine are treated with a warmth and wisdom and he's not afraid to admit to his own weaknesses and misgivings. The book captures perfectly the agonies and ecstasies of what we now call adventure motorcycling while transporting the reader to a bygone age of colonial-era travel – exotic Baghdad, wild Waziristan, steamy Sumatra and primitive China. But for all the ups and downs of overland travel, it's Fulton's intense curiosity, insightfulness and humane approach to his fellow man that makes *One Man Caravan* such a refreshing read and the accompanying film, *Twice Upon a Caravan*, such a joy to watch.

Theresa Wallach – London to Cape Town 1934-35

While Robert Fulton was making his way home to New York another ground-breaking expedition was preparing to depart from London. On the 11th December 1934 two adventurous motorcyclists were waved off by a cheering crowd, embarking on a venture that had never before been attempted – to ride a motorcycle the length of the African continent. It was a remarkable ambition in itself, but the fact that these motorcyclists were two young women in their twenties made it all the more incredible, and one can't help but wonder why Theresa Wallach and Florence Blenkiron aren't more famous. Their 14,000-mile journey to Cape Town, as told in Theresa Wallach's book *The Rugged Road*, took them almost eight months and saw the two women tackling gruelling conditions, incredible hardships and mechanical calamities that would defeat many of today's machines and riders!

Theresa and Blenk were no ordinary ladies, and not to be put off by a bunch of nay-saying men in suits

As keen trials riders and racers, Theresa and 'Blenk' were not averse to bucking trends, but when they tried to drum up sponsorship for the expedition no motorcycle manufacturer wanted to get involved in backing these two unlikely explorers.

'Preposterous, my dear!', 'You're going WHERE?', 'You'll never make it' declared their detractors. No company wanted to be associated with a project that was so obviously doomed. But as you'll no doubt have gathered by now, Theresa and Blenk were no ordinary ladies, and not to be put off by a bunch of nay-saying men in suits.

Eventually they managed to secure the sponsorship of a pioneering British motorcycle manufacturer of the day, Phelon & Moore, who produced the 600cc single-cylinder Panther. It was this bike, named The Venture, complete with sidecar and pulling a trailer, that would take the two women from London to Cape Town, although not without plenty of drama along the way.

Unsurprisingly, it was the crossing of the Sahara that proved to be the most demanding section of their trip. The sheer physical effort involved in motoring their five-wheeled rig across sand dunes, rocky plateaus and the steep tracks of the Hoggar mountains is exhausting just to read about. They became stuck on an alarmingly regular basis, resorting to hauling the trailer and sidecar out of endless sand drifts with a block and tackle, making progress of just fifteen feet at a time, and all of this in lead-lined pith helmets under a scorching 120°F sun! As their rig fell apart they routinely came up with ingenious fixes, raiding wrecked cars for parts as they worked through the night fuelled only by a bottle of smuggled Cognac. Emerging from the Sahara the drama continued with endless breakdowns, crashes and exciting forays into the central African jungle where they mingled with pygmy tribes and witch-doctors before finally rolling into Cape Town, weary but triumphant.

> **If you think you have ever done anything even slightly hardcore, read *The Rugged Road* and prepare to be humbled!**

Reading their story, it's obvious that modern-day adventure motorcyclists have the advantage when it comes to equipment and the machine itself. But from a cultural and logistical point of view, African travel actually seemed an easier business back in the colonial era of the 1930s. Their route through the European-controlled continent where safari-suited colonels saluted them at every border post, is a far cry from the interminable delays, intimidation and palm-greasing we know today. The fact they were two women travelling alone appears to be more a source of pleasant surprise to the people they encountered rather than a cause for concern, although they did have to argue long and hard with the French colonial authorities for permission to cross the Sahara. On the whole, their female novelty value barely gets a mention and Theresa's story is full of tales of assistance, kindness and generosity from colonialists and natives alike, something female travellers will still attest to today.

It really is a staggering tale of true grit, sheer bravery and lashings of British stiff upper lip. Theresa Wallach however, is remarkably self-effacing about the expedition. 'Our exploit was not intended to be a geographical expedition,' she states in the book, 'nor did we pretend to be geologists, photographers or journalists. Blenk and I, with a bit of true-life reality, were simply going to see Africa'. If you think you have ever done anything even slightly hardcore, read *The Rugged Road* and prepare to be humbled!

Danny Liska – Alaska to Tierra del Fuego 1959-61

While Robert Fulton Jnr. was born into a privileged family, Danny Liska's humble background was entirely the opposite. He is the everyman's motorcycle adventurer, son of a Czech immigrant, brought up on a farm and driven by a thirst for the unknown and the exotic. Liska's story is an inspiration for every small-town boy who's ever watched a motorcycle roar past his bedroom window and longed to take off for faraway lands. And indeed for any middle-aged man who longs to skip out on his wife and do the same.

In 1959, aged thirty, Danny Liska did just that. He left his wife and farm in Nebraska and set off on his BMW R60 to become the first person to ride a motorcycle the length of the Americas. In the style of the true purist, he went first to Arctic Circle City (then the most northerly town in Alaska) to begin his epic journey. Two years and 65,000 miles later he arrived in Ushuaia, at the tip of Argentina. But most significantly he eschewed the idea of skipping over the still unrideable Darien Gap between Panama and Colombia, and instead tackled this notorious jungle on foot and by canoe.

Liska's book about his journey *Two Wheels to Adventure* has become a classic of motorcycle literature

Liska's book about his journey *Two Wheels to Adventure* has become a classic of motorcycle literature. Written in the 1960s, it wasn't published until the '80s, and the original now sells for hundreds of dollars. It's a great, rip-roaring read accompanied by fabulous photos, illustrations and maps. A frankly written account, the book tells of his adventures along the Pan-American Highway which was still under construction in many of the countries he passed through, but the real highlight is the detailed account of his incredible trek through the jungles of the Darien. Along his journey he's attacked by Indian tribesmen, has his blood sucked by vampire bats, contracts malaria, and even ends up working as a stunt double for the actor Yul Brynner on the shoot of the little known Cossack revenge epic, *Taras Bulba*! Like all grand adventures, *Two Wheels to Adventure* has a cast of fantastically inglorious characters, a handful of loose women, some hard times, high jinks, a dash of desperation and a very complicated love-life!

Written in the 60s, Liska's tale verges on the comical in its lack of political correctness. He admits an excessive interest in the workings of Latin American brothels, visiting them for research purposes to provide detailed reports on the shape, size and quality of every pair of breasts he encounters and concludes that the finest prostitutes are to be found in El Salvador (you won't find that kind of travel tip in a Rough Guide). In keeping with the spirit of the age and his nationality, he's also openly disdainful of the Latinos, making scathing observations about their poor timekeeping, insincerity and deceitful nature. The spectre of Communism also runs through the book, a reminder of how in this era the Latin American countries were ripe for a leftwing revolution as had recently occurred in Cuba. The fear comes across as slightly hysterical now, but it's easy to forget how seriously the threat was considered at the time, and the parallels to the current 'War on Terror' are painfully obvious.

Although he can come over as the typical brash American, Danny Liska was no mindless oaf, more a product of his time. His human curiosity was

insatiable, his grasp of cultural and political situations intelligent and, like the best travel writers, he relished nothing more than to immerse himself in the heart of every culture he encountered. He was drawn to the mysterious, the exotic and the supernatural, and his nose for a good story outweighs any fear or discomfort that might have hampered a less brave or inquisitive traveller.

He admits an excessive interest in the workings of Latin American brothels, visiting them for research purposes ...

Ted Simon – Around the world 1973-77

Ted Simon will be well known to many readers of *AMH*. His 64,000 mile journey around the world in 1973 on a 500cc Triumph Tiger was impressive by any standards (see *Trip Reports*, pp288-9) but above all, he deserves a place in this pantheon for the fact that his four-year odyssey resulted in him writing *Jupiter's Travels*, the book that is responsible for bringing the notion of 'adventure motorcycling' to the wider public. It's become one of the classics of travel literature and more than any other motorcycle travel book, has inspired others to hit the road. As Ted states early on, 'It was going to be the journey of a lifetime, a journey that millions dream of and never make, and I wanted to do justice to all those dreams.'

In 1973 Ted was working in London as a journalist at *The Sunday Times* when he set off as a 42-year-old novice rider to explore the world. The resulting story is a beautifully written tale of what happens when a curious, enquiring mind meets a 1970s British motorcycle. It is full of humour and insights into the human condition as well as all the escapades one would expect from

Jupiter's Travels is the book that launched a thousand trips

such a grand adventure. *Jupiter's Travels* is a book that changes lives and the 400,000 copies it has sold is a testament to its lasting influence. In 2003 Ted Simon set off again to retrace his route, resulting in the book, *Dreaming of Jupiter*, a fascinating if sometimes melancholic view of how the world has changed in the thirty years since his original trip.

Although *Jupiter's Travels* is the book that launched a thousand trips, Ted is always keen to make the point: 'It's not about the motorcycle'. Robert Fulton had a similar sentiment regarding his choice of transport: 'The motorcycle wasn't the reason for taking the trip' he writes, 'rather the trip was the reason for the motorcycle.' Interestingly, this is a common theme among successful motorcycle travellers – they're often travellers first, motorcyclists second. As Ted would be the first to point out, it's all about the journey…

They Also Served …

There have been many other great pioneering motorcycle journeys, but they often remain unknown due to the fact that these adventurers hailed from outside the English-speaking world. Here are a few of the non-Anglo heroes…

Robert Sexe was a French reporter and photographer who rode around the world, including a brutal crossing of Siberia, on an obscure Belgian prototype motorcycle in the mid-1920s. He is reputed to be the inspiration for Hergé's character, Tintin.

The **Omidvar Brothers** were two Iranians who in 1957 acquired a pair of Matchless motorcycles and travelled the world for seven years, living with remote tribes and filming their adventures.

Adbab Husni Tello was a famous Syrian adventurer who rode the world in the 1950s on a BSA and reputedly visited 5000 cities and towns on four continents, and wrote eleven books about his travels. He makes an appearance in Danny Liska's book as a fellow traveller and successful lothario!

Zoltan Sulkowsky was a 25-year old Hungarian who set off with a friend on an eight-year ride around the world on a Harley Davidson outfit. His book, *Around the World on a Motorcycle: 1928 to 1936*, is now available in English.

APPENDIX

Fuel consumption conversion table

Miles per gallon (mpg)

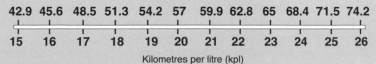

42.9	45.6	48.5	51.3	54.2	57	59.9	62.8	65	68.4	71.5	74.2
15	16	17	18	19	20	21	22	23	24	25	26

Kilometres per litre (kpl)

Miles per gallon (mpg)

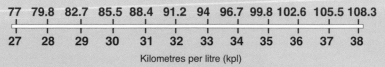

77	79.8	82.7	85.5	88.4	91.2	94	96.7	99.8	102.6	105.5	108.3
27	28	29	30	31	32	33	34	35	36	37	38

Kilometres per litre (kpl)

mpg x 0.35 = kpl   **100 divided by kpl = L/100km**

kpl x 2.85 = mpg   **100 divided by L/100km = kpl**

DECIMAL DEGREE CONVERTER

Long Lat co-ordinates can be given in different ways; the format given in this book is 'decimal minutes' shown as N00° 00.0' as opposed to the now seemingly obsolete N00° 00' 00". Sometimes you may receive a waypoint in seconds or even in decimal degrees (N00.0000°, the system preferred by scientists). These formats are sometimes known as DMM, DMS or DDD respectively. GPS units can display waypoints in any of the above formats (and more besides). If you're handy with multiples and divisions of 60 it's not too hard to work out the conversion in your head. Obviously N22.5000° in DDD equals N22° 30.0' in DMM but other fractions can be tricky so use the table below to reduce errors. And if you haven't got a clue what all this is about, don't worry, just keep your eyes on the road and your hands upon the handlebar.

1.	0.016	13.	0.216	25.	0.416	37.	0.616	49.	0.816
2.	0.033	14.	0.233	26.	0.433	38.	0.633	50.	0.833
3.	0.050	15.	0.250	27.	0.450	39.	0.650	51.	0.850
4.	0.066	16.	0.266	28.	0.466	40.	0.666	52.	0.866
5.	0.083	17.	0.283	29.	0.483	41.	0.683	53.	0.883
6.	0.10	18.	0.300	30.	0.500	42.	0.700	54.	0.900
7.	0.116	19.	0.316	31.	0.516	43.	0.716	55.	0.916
8.	0.133	20.	0.333	32.	0.533	44.	0.733	56.	0.933
9.	0.150	21.	0.350	33.	0.550	45.	0.750	57.	0.950
10.	0.166	22.	0.366	34.	0.566	46.	0.766	58.	0.966
11.	0.183	23.	0.383	35.	0.583	47.	0.783	59.	0.983
12.	0.200	24.	0.400	36.	0.600	48.	0.800	60.	1.00

AMH
CONTRIBUTORS

Brought up in Scotland and riding since he was fourteen years old, **Kelston Chorley** has biked around Europe, Scandinavia, Iceland, South America and India (particularly the high altitude northern areas). Prefers riding alone as he says you're more open to meeting people. Has plans to visit more of SA, Burma and Asia.

Jamie Duncan is a drifting waster with incessantly itchy feet. He's somehow managed to bumble his way through more than a hundred countries and is very much looking forward to another hundred. Only travels so he has an excuse not to go and see QPR on Saturday afternoons. Travel correspondent for *Bike* magazine.

Mark Harfenist lives in Bellingham Washington, dabbling in mountain biking, ski mountaineering, sea kayaking and world travel when not complaining loudly to anyone within earshot about the indignities of old age. Mark began motorcycling just recently,in a rare moment of clarity. He currently works as a family therapist.

Jussi Hyttinen is a Finnish marketing creative based in Berlin. His adventure alter ego is The Rolling Hobo, whose passion is adventure enduro on light KTMs. He constantly searches for the perfect line in the dark corners of the world. If he ever finds it, he'll share it on 💻 www.therollinghobo.com

Gaurav Jani films documentaries about remote places and indigenous people. Riding *Solo to the Top of the World* and *One Crazy Ride* have won awards at film festivals worldwide. Gaurav also founded the 60kph.com motorcycle travel club and is part of Ride of My Life which conducts motorcycle tours in India.

Steph Jeavons is currently on a solo RTW tour attempting to ride her CRF250L to all seven continents. Her recent mission to Antarctica was a success and she's now covered over 45,000 miles. Steph has published articles about her journey in several magazines and keeps her readers up to date with her blog: 💻 onestephbeyond.com

Originally from the USA, **Chris Lockwood** has been helping overland motorcyclists get in, out, and around his current home base of Japan since 2000. When not on the road, he's always willing to lend a hand to travellers in need in the Far East.

Pat McCarthy (aka Barcelona Pat), a Spanish based Welshman of Irish decent and lifelong motorcyclist has ridden in Europe extensively over many years. A new challenge for 2012 was a solo charity ride from Tierra del Fuego to Alaska. His story can be found at 💻 www.patonabike.blogspot.com

Travel addict **Sam Manicom** gave himself a year to ride the length of Africa, but arrived home eight years, 200,000 miles and six continents later. Aiming to share the fun and drama of the road, Sam is now the author of four acclaimed travel books. 💻 sam-manicom.com

James Morrison is a web developer from Luton, UK. With no adventure biking experience (or plan!) he set off for Southern Africa driving 29,000km in nine months through nine countries. He's currently working on a short video of his trip which will be available on 💻 whereisjames.com

Lois Pryce is a British travel writer who left the BBC to hit the road and never looked back. Her motorcycle journeys have been published around the world in several languages and have inspired many female (and male!) riders. She is also the co-founder and curator of the Adventure Travel Film Festival.
💻 www.loisontheloose.com

AMH
CONTRIBUTORS (cont'd)

With little experience, in May 2009 **David Radford** set off on his first big ride from Edmonton, Canada. Nearly 200,000km and ninety countries later he finds himself in Chiang Mai, Thailand, still on the road. 'I guess I might as well admit, I'm trying to go around the world'.
🖳 gsguy.wordpress.com

Dr Paul Rowe is a Cornishman who spends his time between biking and working as an anaesthetist in Western Australia. He and wife Jenni are taking a brief break from the longer trips until their three little bikers are old enough to get addicted too.

Ted Simon (🖳 jupitalia.com) has had many different interests in his 84 years but the one constant has been a passion for travel. He took up motorcycling at the age of 42 as a way of travelling around the world, and wrote *Jupiter's Travels*, still a steady favourite after 35 years. In 2001 he repeated the journey 'to see how things have changed' and produced another book, *Dreaming of Jupiter*.
  The Ted Simon Foundation (🖳 jupiterstravellers.org) offers to mentor other travellers 'with the aim of helping them transform the raw material of adventure into something stunning for the rest of the world to appreciate'.

David Smith set off on a DR650 to see his home country Australia in 2014, and although he had a ball, he found the trip didn't quite scratch the itch. One year later, he geared up again to ride from Sydney to London with girlfriend Ghighi in tow.

Ken Thomas started riding and racing in 1964. Thirty years later he rode a Ducati to Ukraine with daughter Caroline as pillion before backpacking around the world then cycling from Canada to Mexico along the Rockies. Recently he again rode with Caroline, this time to Cape Town. 🖳 www. horizonsunlimited.com/tstories/thomas

With more real-world experience than anyone else on the road today, **Lisa and Simon Thomas** have spent over twelve years exploring the planet on their BMW motorcycles. Now considered the world's leading motorcycle travellers, Lisa and Simon left their UK home in 2003 and have been inspiring adventure ever since. To date they've ridden over 400,000 miles through 78 countries on six continents and including 27 deserts. They've shared their experiences with over a hundred live audiences around the globe, authored articles for top travel and motorcycle publications and made over forty international TV appearances.
🖳 2ridetheworld.com

Austin Vince was in the Mondo Enduro team: the first Europeans to ride bikes across Siberia's Zilov Gap and make it to the far eastern prison town of Magadan (Aug 1995). Ewan McGregor is a big fan and Team Mondo were the lead Siberian advisors for *The Long Way Round*. He's also the co-founder and curator of the Adventure Travel Film Festival.
🖳 www.austinvince.com
🖳 www.adventuretravelfilmfestival.com

Growing up on Star Wars, Space Invaders, Punk, Judge Dredd and Mad Max in Cold War Britain, **Robin Webb** discovered long-distance, self-supported, lightweight, motorcycling to survive in the inevitable post-apocalyptic wastelands. After multiple Saharan trips, plus desert riding in Namibia, Australia, America and Iceland, he's still chasing the dream on his trusty TTR250.

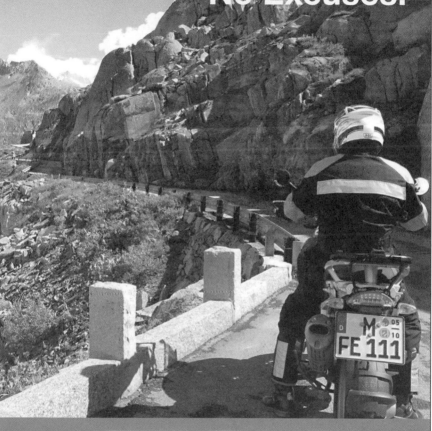

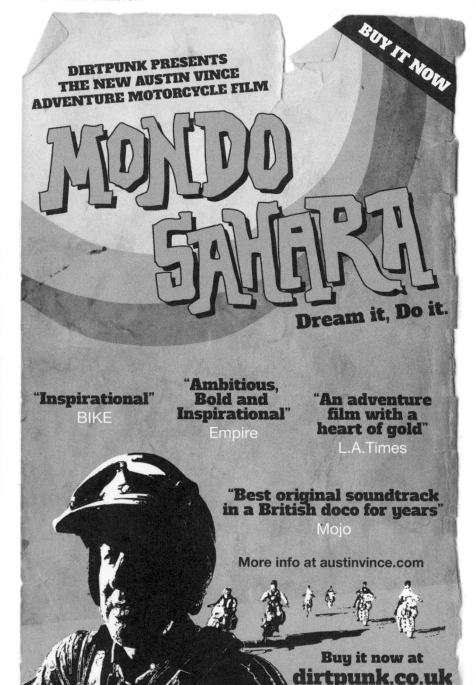

INDEX

TRAILBLAZER

Adventure Cycle-Touring Handbook
Adventure Motorcycling Handbook
Australia by Rail
Azerbaijan
Coast to Coast (British Walking Guide)
Cornwall Coast Path (British Walking Guide)
Corsica Trekking – GR20
Cotswold Way (British Walking Guide)
The Cyclist's Anthology
Dales Way (British Walking Guide) – due mid 2016
Dolomites Trekking – AV1 & AV2
Dorset & Sth Devon Coast Path (British Walking Gde)
Exmoor & Nth Devon Coast Path (British Walking Gde)
Hadrian's Wall Path (British Walking Guide)
Himalaya by Bike – a route and planning guide
Inca Trail, Cusco & Machu Picchu
Japan by Rail
Kilimanjaro – the trekking guide (includes Mt Meru)
Moroccan Atlas – The Trekking Guide
Morocco Overland (4WD/motorcycle/mountainbike)
Nepal Trekking & The Great Himalaya Trail
New Zealand – The Great Walks
Offa's Dyke Path (British Walking Guide)
Overlanders' Handbook – worldwide driving guide
Peddars Way & Norfolk Coast Path (British Walking Gde)
Pembrokeshire Coast Path (British Walking Guide)
Pennine Way (British Walking Guide)
Peru's Cordilleras Blanca & Huayhuash – Hiking/Biking
The Railway Anthology
The Ridgeway (British Walking Guide)
Sahara Overland – a route and planning guide
Scottish Highlands – The Hillwalking Guide
Siberian BAM Guide – rail, rivers & road
The Silk Roads – a route and planning guide
Sinai – the trekking guide
South Downs Way (British Walking Guide)
Thames Path (British Walking Guide)
Tour du Mont Blanc
Trans-Canada Rail Guide
Trans-Siberian Handbook
Trekking in the Everest Region
The Walker's Anthology
The Walker's Haute Route – Mont Blanc to Matterhorn
West Highland Way (British Walking Guide)

www.trailblazer-guides.com
ROUTE GUIDES FOR THE ADVENTUROUS TRAVELLER